The Providence of Wit

The
Providence of Wit

*Aspects of Form in
Augustan Literature and
the Arts*

MARTIN C. BATTESTIN

University Press of Virginia
Charlottesville

THE UNIVERSITY PRESS OF VIRGINIA
Copyright © 1989 by the Rector and Visitors
of the University of Virginia

This edition first published 1989

Originally published by Oxford University Press, 1974

Library of Congress Cataloging-in-Publication Data

Battestin, Martin C.
    The providence of wit : aspects of form in Augustan literature and
the arts / Martin C. Battestin.
        p. cm.
    Reprint. Originally published: Oxford : Clarendon Press, 1974.
    Includes index.
    ISBN 0-8139-1235-0
    1. English literature—18th century—History and criticism.
    2. Art and literature—Great Britain—History—18th century.
    3. Aesthetics, British—18th century. 4. Nature in literature.
    5. Form (Aesthetics) 6. Literary form. I. Title.
PR448.A77B38 1989
820'.9'005—dc19   89-5467
                                                                       CIP

Printed in the United States of America

To
D. W. Robertson, Jr.
and
the memory of
Earl R. Wasserman

Preface

THIS book, which grew in a desultory way over the past ten years, is an attempt to account for the special quality of certain works of Augustan literature and art that I have enjoyed. Put simply, that quality is their deliberate artificiality—our sense of the craftsman's pleasure in careful shapes and bold contrivances. Form is the glory of Augustan art, and many of us—though the drab or jarring monuments of our own less gracious times suggest that we are a diminishing fellowship—continue to find it congenial.

In the present study I hope to make this aspect of early eighteenth-century aesthetics more understandable as a historical phenomenon by showing its relationship to ontological assumptions which by the latter part of the century were rapidly losing currency. The poetry of Pope and Gay, the fiction of Fielding and Goldsmith, the music and buildings and gardens of the period—all, in various ways, attest to the faith of the age in Order, to the conviction that Art is the attribute of Reality. I will be suggesting, in other words, that some at least of the salient formal features of Augustan literature and the arts—balance and proportion and design, for example, whether conceived geometrically or as a movement through time toward some pre-determined ending—are best understood in terms of the ontological assumptions of the Christian humanist tradition, that great coherent tradition of Western thought which Newton at first seemed magnificently to have confirmed, but which soon disintegrated under pressure of a new subjectivism implicit in Locke's epistemology.

The essential question I have asked is this: Since Art was considered to be the imitation of Nature, what were the consequences for the Augustan artist of the conviction, most memorably stated by Pope, that Nature is already the supreme Artefact, that Chance is in fact Direction? The first chapter attempts to answer this question by exploring the theoretical relationship between ontology and aesthetics in the period, roughly, from 1660 to 1750. By focusing on the abstract arts of music, architecture, and gardening—modes in which the artist's aim was to render purely Nature's own aesthetic attributes of harmony, symmetry, and variety—we may discern the fundamental formal principles of the age, principles, furthermore, which at one level inform the subtle harmonies of Pope's couplets or, at another level, the complex design of Fielding's 'great Creation'.

Proceeding from an investigation of the meaning of music and the movement of time in the *Pastorals*, the chapters on Pope define the sense in which, to the greatest poet of the age, all art was an imitation of the divine creation. Just as Dryden, in the phrase I have taken for the title of this study, could find in a well-made poem 'the providence of wit', so for Pope the paradigm of Order in art as in life was the fiat of Genesis. Chapter IV considers the meaning of art and the function of artifice in Gay's poetry, and particularly in *Trivia*, in which, while the exquisite formalism of the verse itself chastens and transforms rude actuality, the poet's theme, the art of walking the streets of London, evokes the analogous ideas of prudence and the wayfaring of Everyman through life. The essays on *Tom Jones*, the work that in the present context may be taken as the consummate achievement of the Augustan mode, argue that in both form and matter Art is Fielding's subject: the 'Art of God', implicit in the novel's symmetrical design and in the surprising control of the intrusive, omniscient narrator; and the 'Art of Life', disclosed through the hero's awkward progress toward the acquisition of prudence and his marriage with the lovely girl who, in the world Fielding has created, stands as Wisdom's divine 'Idea'. Recurrent indeed throughout Augustan literature, a similar conception of the meaning of Providence and Prudence, the complementary 'arts' of macrocosm and microcosm, underlies *The Vicar of Wakefield*, Goldsmith's comic redaction of the Job story. In one way or another, the idea of Providence—of Chance as Direction, of Time as a movement from Genesis to Apocalypse comprehending every contingency under the eye of God—affects the formal organization of Pope's *Pastorals* and his *Dunciad*, of *Trivia*, *Tom Jones*, and *The Vicar of Wakefield*. In *Trivia*, *Tom Jones*, and *The Vicar of Wakefield*, furthermore, wisdom is defined as Prudence, the *ars vivendi* of the Christian humanist tradition and the virtue in the human sphere analogous to the rational, foreseeing Power that governs the world. Both in theme and in its deliberate artificiality, the Augustan mode is a tribute to the idea of Art itself; form here has an ontological, even an ethical, value.

The final chapter comprises, as it were, a negative demonstration of this argument, for in Swift's *Tale of a Tub* and in Sterne's *Tristram Shandy* the formal principles of Augustan aesthetics are self-consciously violated, in Swift's case to affirm the ideals of rationality and regularity by ironically enacting their contraries, in Sterne's to reject these ideals out of hand as stultifying and, ultimately, irrelevant. If states of mind may be said to have their own topographies, with Swift, however curious and disturbing the terrain, we are in a country that would have been, in most essential respects, familiar to his contemporaries; with Sterne, they were entering a new world, the antithesis of the old, whose lonely features we are still charting.

Earlier versions of the chapters on Pope's *Pastorals* and on Gay and Fielding appeared as articles in *Eighteenth-Century Studies*, the *Journal of English and Germanic Philology*, *ELH*, and in *The Augustan Milieu*, a Festschrift in honour of my friend and mentor Louis Landa published by the Clarendon Press, Oxford. I wish to thank the publishers for permission to reprint these essays.

I wish also to thank those institutions which, through the generous financial support they extended me, provided me with time enough to write this book. Summer grants from the American Council of Learned Societies (1967), from Rice University (1968), and from the University of Virginia (1966, 1972) enabled me to prepare the chapters on Pope's *Pastorals* and on Fielding and to write the concluding section on Swift and Sterne. In 1970–1 my appointments as Sesquicentennial Research Associate of the Center for Advanced Studies at the University of Virginia and as Senior Fellow of the Council of the Humanities at Princeton University made it possible for me to complete the Introduction and to write the chapter on Goldsmith. Chapter III was written in the spring of 1972, when I was a Fellow of the American Council of Learned Societies and an Associate of Clare Hall, Cambridge. Such in our times are the true patrons of learning and to them all I am deeply grateful.

For their skill and courtesy in assisting me with my research, I am grateful, too, to the staffs of the British Museum and the

Bodleian Library, and of the libraries of Princeton University, the University of Cambridge, and the University of Virginia.

Parts of this study were read in draft by friends and colleagues whose advice was always helpful and whose encouragement sustained me: in particular I wish to thank Ralph Cohen, James Colvert, Alistair Duckworth, John Marshall, Donald Siebert, and Lois Sklepowich. I am especially indebted to my friend Samuel Holt Monk, who read the entire typescript and spared my readers more gaucheries of style than I care to admit.

My debt to my wife, Ruthe Rootes Battestin, is greatest of all. In a sense, this book is owing to her inspiration, for it was through sharing her own pleasure in the art and architecture of the eighteenth century that I came to study them. But she is not likely to covet the reputation of being Muse to any work of scholarship, and her favours to this one were more substantial than those most Muses bestow. She assisted in the research, helped to choose the illustrations, and, though she never typed a line of the manuscript (even her charity has its limits!), she read it all with piercing eye.

Finally, I have dedicated this book to two scholars whose insights have deepened my understanding of the literature of the past and whose way of approaching that literature through the reconstruction of the historical moment that conditioned it has been a model for my own. One of these men was my teacher; the other was the author of *The Subtler Language*.

M. C. B.

Charlottesville, Virginia
January 1973

Contents

List of Illustrations

List of Abbreviations

ASch	American Scholar
BNYPL	Bulletin of the New York Public Library
CamJ	Cambridge Journal
CE	College English
ECS	Eighteenth-Century Studies
EIC	Essays in Criticism
ELH	Journal of English Literary History
EM	English Miscellany
ES	English Studies
JAAC	Journal of Aesthetics and Art Criticism
JEGP	Journal of English and Germanic Philology
JRIBA	Journal of the Royal Institute of British Architects
MLN	Modern Language Notes
MLR	Modern Language Review
MLQ	Modern Language Quarterly
MP	Modern Philology
PMLA	Publications of the Modern Language Association of America
PQ	Philological Quarterly
RES	Review of English Studies
SAQ	South Atlantic Quarterly
SEL	Studies in English Literature, 1500–1900
SP	Studies in Philology
SR	Sewanee Review
SRen	Studies in the Renaissance
SSF	Studies in Short Fiction (Newberry College, S.C.)
TE	Twickenham Edition of the Poems of Alexander Pope, ed. John Butt (London and New Haven, Conn., 1939–67)
TQ	Texas Quarterly (University of Texas)
UTQ	University of Toronto Quarterly
VQR	Virginia Quarterly Review
YULG	Yale University Library Gazette

I

The Idea of Order in Nature and the Arts, 1660–1750

As England's Augustan Age began, Dryden somewhat extravagantly congratulated his friend Sir Robert Howard on the formal perfection of his poetry, which, like the creation itself, was the product not of accident, but of art:

> . . . this is a piece too fair
> To be the child of Chance, and not of Care.
> No Atoms casually together hurl'd
> Could e'er produce so beautifull a world.
> Nor dare I such a doctrine here admit,
> As would destroy the providence of wit.[1]

As the age that Dryden inaugurated drew to a close, Henry Fielding applied the same bold metaphor to *Tom Jones*, declaring the coherence and integrity of his own 'great Creation', which he had carefully contrived and over which he presided, omniscient and unerring.[2]

By adapting the metaphysical 'argument from design' to the celebration of art, both Dryden and Fielding bring into focus one of the most distinctive and significant aspects of the Augustan mode: specifically, an assumption about the interdependence of theology and aesthetics which profoundly affected the neoclassical doctrine of imitation in the arts—not in literature only, where it helps to account for the characteristic formal features of Pope's and Gay's poetry and of Fielding's and Goldsmith's fiction, but in architecture and landscape gardening, music and painting as well. Echoing Aristotle in *An Essay on Criticism* (1711), Pope advised the poet to 'First follow NATURE' (l. 68); in *An Essay on Man* (1733–4), reducing the Christian humanist philosophy of order to an epigram, he defined that Nature which the Augustan artist believed he was imitating: 'All Nature is but Art, unknown to thee; / All Chance, Direction, which thou canst not see' (i. 289–90).[3] The implications of this paradox, already present in Dryden's praise of 'the providence of wit', will be the subject of this essay.

I. NATURE AS ART

One of the special pleasures of neo-classical art—and, for many in a time of howling anarchy, perhaps its chief consolation—is the sense conveyed of the triumph of form, of a dynamic variety of materials having been reduced to order by the shaping intelligence. Pope's couplets and his garden at Twickenham, Fielding's periods and the design of *Tom Jones*, the buildings of Burlington's Palladian brotherhood, the fugues and canons of Purcell or Handel, the balanced compositions of Poussin: in all these works opposing parts have been reconciled and organized into a whole; in all, despite differences in modes and kinds, there is consistency in the conviction that harmony and pattern have value.

Having made this observation, it is well to be aware of the absurdities into which critics have fallen by spinning out tenuous analogies between the arts. René Wellek has given due warning that discussions of Pope's *Moral Essays*, for example, or of Mallet's *Excursion*, in terms of architectural styles, are neither very illuminating nor logically very sound.[4] From William Mitford, who developed at length a comparison between Pope's 'epic' verse and the symmetry of classical architecture,[5] to Mario Praz, who believes the principles of Pope's gardening to be 'very close to the pattern of his heroic couplet',[6] students of the period have resorted to such analogizing in an attempt to characterize the formal features of Augustan poetry. The awkwardness of this method as a tool of criticism is evident from the contradictory conclusions to which it sometimes leads: in contrast to Praz, Mitford insisted that the concealed artificiality of the English landscape garden can be usefully compared only to prose, poetry being, like architecture, 'so decidedly regular as to be obviously artificial' (p. 84). One shares Professor Wellek's impatience with this sort of impressionism. Clearly, a poem is neither a garden nor a building, but something else altogether.

That the poets themselves would have found nothing preposterous in such analogies is nevertheless equally true. As Hildebrand Jacob observed of 'the Sister Arts', the resemblance between poetry, painting, and music was so great 'that it is difficult to discourse upon either of them, particularly the two First, without a mutual borrowing of *Images* and *Terms*; insomuch that one of these *Arts* cannot well be explain'd, without giving some Insight into the other at the same Time'.[7] For, however disparate, all the arts had as their common purpose the accurate imitation of Nature. The effects of this doctrine, as everyone knows, were various and pervasive. Since, for example, Nature was to be found in universals rather than in particulars, a character in *Joseph Andrews* or in *The Rake's Progress* will represent 'not an Individual, but a Species',[8] and Imlac, *ut pictura poesis*, must advise the poet to avoid numbering the streaks of the tulip.[9] The notorious rules themselves were only '*Nature Methodiz'd*'.[10]

These premisses of neo-classical aesthetics are familiar enough. What we have less well appreciated is the degree to which, during the latter half of the seventeenth century, the idea of pure form in the arts was conditioned by a renewed theological emphasis on design in Nature. If Nature, as Pope's generation believed, was the Art of God, the harmonious and symmetrical product of divine contrivance, then these principles of harmony, balance, and regularity must find expression in the productions of human wit.

Despite the astute counsel of Earl Wasserman, who more than a decade ago proposed the essential continuity of Renaissance and neo-classical assumptions—'cosmic syntaxes', as he called them[11]—most scholars continue to regard these two periods as separate and irreconcilable, provinces in the history of ideas forever divided by the gulf caused by the new science and the Civil Wars. To mention three of the fields particularly relevant to our immediate concerns, this has been the view of Wittkower in architecture, of Hollander and Finney in music, and of Tayler in literature,[12] who concur in the suspicion that the attitudes of Renaissance platonism were no longer meaningful in the Age of Reason. On the contrary, one purpose of the present chapter—and of the essays in literary analysis to follow—is to suggest that, far from relinquishing the assumptions and metaphors of the past, the divines and poets and aestheticians of the period from 1660 to 1750 made them very much their own, refining them, to be sure, so as to accommodate the Christian humanist tradition to the discoveries of the scientists and mathematicians, but using them none the less in profound and viable ways.

As Spitzer and Lovejoy, Wasserman and Mack, have shown,[13] the universe of *Windsor Forest* and the *Essay on Man* is still to be conceived in terms of the Pythagorean principle of *concordia discors* and the Platonic metaphor of the Great Chain of Being. It is a universe of exquisite harmonies and of nice correspondences between macrocosm and microcosm. Though troubled at first by the metaphysics of Copernicus and Kepler and indignant at the materialism of Hobbes, scientists and divines responded dutifully and, for one bright moment before the darkness buried all, co-operatively reaffirmed the old ideas of cosmic design and providential direction.

Their victory, if short-lived, was complete; for the order of things had been newly founded upon experimental proof and mathematical demonstration. By the time of the *Essay on Man,* the world which Donne had found in pieces, 'all coherence gone', had been restored to sturdy and seamless perfection.[14] The harmony of the heavens which Kepler once regretted having silenced, was, through his own efforts and those of Newton, heard once more—a different music, an intricate polyphony, but no less divine. The metaphysical notions which had nourished Renaissance aesthetics and given meaning to the metaphors of poetry were sophisticated, but they did not change fundamentally. That would happen later, when the implications of Locke's subjectivism were fully grasped, as they were by Sterne in *Tristram Shandy* (1759–67). But those works which we regard as typically 'Augustan' —Pope's *Pastorals* or his *Dunciad,* Gay's *Trivia,* Fielding's *Joseph Andrews* and *Tom Jones,* even in its singular way Swift's *Tale of a Tub*—continued to be informed by the intellectual assumptions of the Christian humanist tradition.

i. *Harmony*

To understand how this was possible in an age which not only had witnessed the disintegration of the Ptolemaic system, but whose God, as Pope complained, had been supplanted by Descartes's 'Mechanic Cause' or been bound in matter by Hobbes,[15] let us consider how it happened that one of the central doctrines of Renaissance platonism, the doctrine of world harmony, was preserved—indeed, in a sense perfected—for the poets and artists of the Augustan Age. Though the struggle against mechanistic materialism had been effectively begun by his mentors at Cambridge—More and Barrow and Cudworth—the victory (for so it seemed) was not assured until, in the *Principia* (1687), Newton demonstrated that Descartes's vortices could be safely dismissed as a pernicious fantasy. It was Newton, as James Thomson declared, 'who from the wild Domain / Of the *French Dreamer* rescu'd Heaven and Earth' and restored the 'silent Harmony' of the world.[16] To the theory of the ancient Epicureans, recently revived by Hobbes, Newton and the Cambridge divines gave the answer of Pythagoras, Plato, and the Stoics, that a world so artfully designed could not be the product of fate, matter, and motion.[17]

Already in 1619 Kepler provides a paradigm of the change from despair to the joyous affirmation of order effected through the co-operation of science and theology. In the *Harmonices Mundi* Kepler relates that his own corroboration of Copernicus had effectually silenced the music of the spheres, until at length he saw that the new astronomy could be made to confirm the Pythagorean doctrine. By comparing the motions of the same planet at its greatest and least distances from the sun, and of the several planets in their orbits, Kepler succeeded in correlating these numbers with the musical intervals. He heard with rapture an intellectual polyphony attesting to the wisdom and love of the Creator:

> Accordingly the movements of the heavens are nothing but a kind of everlasting polyphony (intelligible not audible) with dissonant tunings . . . it is no longer a surprise that man, the ape of his Creator, should finally have discovered the art of singing polyphonically (*per concentum*), which was unknown to the ancients, namely in order that he might play the everlastingness of all created time in some short part of an hour by means of an artistic concord of many voices and that he might to some extent taste the satisfaction of God the Workman with his own works, in that very sweet sense of delight elicited from this music which imitates God.[18]

Although the men of the Enlightenment might scoff at Kepler's mysticism, they were nevertheless aware that, duly sophisticated, notions of world harmony were perfectly compatible with Newtonian physics. Colin MacLaurin, one of Newton's chief expositors, could thus observe that Copernicus, Kepler, and Galileo had merely restored the Pythagorean universe:

> If therefore we should suppose musical chords extended from the sun to each planet, that all these chords might become unison, it would be requisite to increase or diminish their tensions in the same proportions

as would be sufficient to render the gravities of the planets equal. And from the similitude of those proportions, the celebrated doctrine of the harmony of the spheres is supposed to have been derived.[19]

During the first part of the eighteenth century one did not need to be a mystic or a poet to find such Pythagorean notions persuasive. As a result of his experiments with light, Newton himself proposed an analogy between visual beauty and music. In a famous passage in the *Opticks*, to which proponents of an 'objective' aesthetics would point with satisfaction, he noted that the colours of the spectrum, taken in order, are proportionately related to one another 'as the Cube Roots of the Squares of the eight lengths of a Chord, which sound the Notes in an eighth . . .'[20]

May not [he asked] the harmony and discord of Colours arise from the proportions of the Vibrations propagated through the Fibres of the optick Nerves into the Brain, as the harmony and discord of Sounds arise from the proportions of the Vibrations of the Air? For some Colours, if they be view'd together, are agreeable to one another, as those of Gold and Indigo, and others disagree.[21]

What is less well known—and may come as a surprise to architectural historians who have been reluctant to extend the assumptions of Renaissance platonism into the Enlightenment—Newton's correspondence with John Harington reveals that the greatest scientist of the Age of Reason saw nothing odd in the Pythagorean hypothesis that beauty and order are founded upon the divinely ordained harmony of things. Following Pythagoras, Harington had drawn a strict analogy between the harmonic ratios and the most pleasing proportions in architecture. In his reply (30 May 1698) Newton advised his friend to consult Kepler and Mersenne on the harmony of the world, and he concurred in the view 'that the idea of beauty in surveying objects arises from *their* respective approximations to the simple constructions, and that the pleasure is more or less, as the approaches are nearer to the harmonic ratios'.[22] 'In fine', he concluded, 'I am inclined to believe some general laws of the Creator prevailed with respect to the agreeable or unpleasing affections of all our *senses*; at least the supposition does not derogate from the wisdom or power of God, and seems highly consonant to the macrocosm in general.'[23]

The notion is wrong that has been advanced in one influential study touching on the idea of music in the neo-classical period.[24] The Augustan poet did not abandon the tradition of *musica speculativa*; with the aid of Newton and the physico-theologians, he simply understood it better. It continued to afford him metaphors for the order of things, and, as critics of Dryden's and Pope's musical odes have recently proposed,[25] it continued to provide a rationale for the organic relationship between content and form. Gradually during the eighteenth century, as the subjectivism of Locke and the scepticism of Hume disturbed men's confidence in providential order, the Pythagorean system was emptied of meaning. As Leo Spitzer insists, 'the great caesura in occidental history is precisely this period, not the Renaissance . . .'.[26] The idea of world harmony, of God's creation as a *concordia discors*, continued to be a central article of Augustan faith. Indeed, in their tireless efforts to discredit the neo-epicureanism of Hobbes, the scientists and divines of the period gave a new emphasis to the Christian humanist argument from design: the argument— proved 'abundantly from the excellent *Variety, Order, Beauty*, and *Wonderful Contrivance*, and *Fitness of all Things in the World, to their proper and respective Ends*'[27]—that the creation was orderly and harmonious, and that from primordial chaos it had been called into being by God's Word and was governed by his Providence. More than ever, it seemed reasonable and necessary to conceive of the universe as the song which the divine Musician had sung into being, as the dance performed in perfect measure to his tune.

As Professor Spitzer has exhaustively demonstrated, the Christian humanist tradition rendered the idea of cosmic order in terms of the Pythagorean musical metaphor of *concordia discors*, harmony resulting from the reconciliation of conflicting elements. Music in this sense, Thomas Mace observed, recalls the pattern 'in whole *Nature*' and has 'a near *Affinity* to *Divinity*'.[28] Derived from this tradition, conventional Renaissance analogies comparing the world to a poem, song, or dance are delightfully presented in Sir John Davies's *Orchestra* (1596). But in the *Davideis* (1656), Cowley, the 'God-like Poet' whose 'Heav'nly Voice' Pope recalls in *Windsor Forest* (ll. 271–80), renders these ideas more succinctly and in a manner more congenial to an Augustan audience:

> As first a various unform'd *Hint* we find
> Rise in some god-like *Poets* fertile *Mind*,
> Till all the parts and words their places take,
> And with just marches *verse* and *musick* make;

Such was *Gods Poem*, this *Worlds* new *Essay*;
So wild and rude in its first *draught* it lay;
Th'ungovern'd parts no *Correspondence* knew,
An artless *war* from thwarting *Motions* grew;
Till they to *Number* and fixt rules were brought
By the *æternal minds Poetick Thought.*
Water and *Air* he for the *Tenor* chose,
Earth made the *Base*, the *Treble Flame* arose,
To th'active *Moon* a quick brisk stroke he gave,
To *Saturns string* a touch more soft and grave.
The *motions Strait*, and *Round*, and *Swift*, and *Slow*,
And *Short* and *Long*, were mixt and woven so,
Did in such artful *Figures* smoothly fall,
As made this decent measur'ed *Dance* of *All.*
And this is *Musick*; *Sounds* that charm our ears,
Is but one *Dressing* that rich *Science* wears.[29]

As an expression of the Pythagorean idea of cosmic harmony, these lines are lovelier, no doubt, but they were no more grateful to an age seeking to preserve its faith in divine Order than this famous passage from the *Opticks*, in which Newton reflects upon the creation, the organized atoms of the physicist having replaced the poet's imagined concert of water, air, earth, and fire:

. . . all material Things [writes Newton] seem to have been composed of the hard and solid Particles above-mention'd, variously associated in the first Creation by the Counsel of an intelligent Agent. For it became him who created them to set them in order. And if he did so, it's unphilosophical to seek for any other Origin of the World, or to pretend that it might arise out of a Chaos by the mere Laws of Nature . . . For while Comets move in very excentrick Orbs in all manner of Positions, blind Fate could never make all the Planets move one and the same way in Orbs concentrick, some inconsiderable Irregularities excepted . . . Such a wonderful Uniformity in the Planetary System must be allowed the Effect of Choice.[30]

Behind Newton's prosaic exposition of divine Order, contemporary poets heard echoes of the old celestial music. In a footnote to *The Power of Harmony* (1745), John Gilbert Cooper, for one, directed his readers to this passage from the *Opticks* as he celebrated the measured dance of the planets—'How these in tuneful order thro' the void / Their diff'rent stations keep'—and he rejoiced in

. . . this fair Creation, where, impell'd
By that great Author, every atom tends
To Universal Harmony . . .[31]

Similarly, to Bezaleel Morrice the worlds of Newton's universe and of Pope's in *An Essay on Man* moved to the measures of divine music:

> Behold in what harmonious Order plac'd,
> They move! How They alternately advance!
> Behold how, with *eternal Measure* grac'd,
> They circ'ling *glide* in their cælestial Dance![32]

That the music of creation which Morrice and Cooper celebrate need not be regarded merely as a quaint conceit for poetry, outmoded in a scientific age and scorned by philosophers, is apparent from two quite technical treatises spanning the period from 1688 to 1721. The underlying assumption of Thomas Salmon's *Proposal to Perform Musick, in Perfect and Mathematical Proportions* (1688) is the Pythagorean idea that, owing to 'the infinite Wisdom of the great Creator', all harmony is founded upon 'Proportions, which the Soul is from Heaven inform'd to Judge of, and the Body in Union with it, must Submit to'. Since, Salmon declares, harmony is 'divine', it is both the duty and the happiness of men 'to consider how the whole System of the World is framed in Consort'.[33]

Much more valuable as an index of musical thought in the period is Alexander Malcolm's *A Treatise of Musick, Speculative, Practical, and Historical* (1721), an ambitious essay addressed to the Directors of the Royal Academy of Music. The ease with which Pythagorean ideas were accommodated within the Newtonian system is clearly illustrated here both in the commendatory 'Ode on the Power of Musick' by the author's friend 'Mr. Mitchell', and in the concluding chapter of the work, in which Malcolm compares ancient and modern music. The ode is a perfect compendium of familiar neo-platonist ideas, the creation of macrocosm and microcosm being represented as a musical act, a *concordia discors*, performed by God's 'tuneful' voice. The fourth strophe reads:

> *Musick*, the best of Arts divine,
> Maintains the Tune it first began,
> And makes ev'n Opposites combine
>   To be of Use to Man.
> Discords with tuneful Concords move
>   Thro' all the spacious Frame;
> *Below* is breath'd the Sound of Love,
> While mystick Dances shine *Above*,
> And *Musick*'s Power to nether Worlds proclaim.

What various Globes in proper Spheres,
Perform their great Creator's Will?
While never silent never still,
Melodiously they run,
Unhurt by Chance, or Length of Years,
Around the central Sun.

The bulk of Malcolm's treatise is a technical discussion of music, whose laws, like those of gravitation (the analogy is his own), are attributable to divine wisdom.[34] The long concluding chapter, however, is particularly interesting in the present context, for it reveals how a knowledgeable contemporary of Newton and Pope could find new meaning in the doctrine of *musica speculativa*. Malcolm rehearses the theory of Pythagoras and the 'Platonicks' that the creation is an expression of '*divine Musick . . .* that which exists in the *divine* Mind, viz. these archetypal Ideas of Order and Symmetry, according to which GOD formed all Things', and he proceeds to distinguish its various modes:

First, Elementary or the Harmony of the first Elements of Things; and these according to the Philosophers, are Fire, Air, Water, and Earth, which tho' seemingly contrary to one another, are, by the Wisdom of the Creator, united and compounded in all the beautiful and regular Forms of Things that fall under our Senses. 2*d. Celestial*, comprehending the Order and Proportions in the Magnitudes, Distances, and Motions of the heavenly Bodies, and the Harmony of the Sounds proceeding from these Motions . . . 3*d. Human*, which consists chiefly in the Harmony of the Faculties of the human Soul, and its various Passions; and is also considered in the Proportion and Temperament, mutual Dependence and Connection, of all the Parts of this wonderful Machine of our Bodies. (pp. 452–4)

For the Augustan musician these old-fashioned ideas could have a more than merely academic appeal. Properly glossed and refurbished by the new science and dressed in the idiom of Shaftesburian metaphysics, they seemed delightfully compatible with his faith, newly confirmed, in Order. Thus, in a later passage defending modern symphonies from the strictures of those who believed that the ancients better understood the art of moving the passions in vocal compositions which united the powers of music and poetry,[35] Malcolm reveals that the notion of musical imitation which Kepler derived from Pythagoras was still tenable in the early decades of the eighteenth century. Like Kepler, Pythagoras taught that 'all the Harmony of Sounds here below, is but an

Imitation, and that imperfect too', of celestial harmony (p. 454).
For Malcolm, the modern art of pure instrumental harmony was
the perfect realization of this idea, for in the symphonies of a
Corelli, Nature's *concordia discors* was made audible, and the mind,
which seeks instinctively for unity in diversity, is delighted by the
apprehension of an intricate order:

> . . . what an Improvement in the Knowledge of pure *Harmony* has been
> made [Malcolm remarks], since the Introduction of the modern *Symphonies* ?
> Here it is, that the Mind is ravished with the Agreement of Things seem-
> ingly contrary to one another. We have here a Kind of Imitation of the
> Works of Nature, where different Things are wonderfully joyned in one
> harmonious Unity: And as some Things appear at first View the farthest
> removed from Symmetry and Order, which from the Course of Things we
> learn to be absolutely necessary for the Perfection and Beauty of the Whole;
> so *Discords* being artfully mixed with *Concords*, make a more perfect Com-
> position, which surprises us with Delight. If the Mind is naturally pleased
> with perceiving of Order and Proportion, with comparing several Things
> together, and discerning in the midst of a seeming Confusion, the most
> perfect and exact Disposition and united Agreement, then the modern
> *Concerts* must undoubtedly be allowed to be Entertainments worthy of
> our Natures . . .   (pp. 597–8)

In modern music, he continues, there is 'an intellectual Beauty'
comparable to the sense of design and proportion, of the relationship of the parts to each other and to the whole, which is the source
of our pleasure in the contemplation of 'a noble Building, or
a curious Painting' (pp. 598–9).

In this respect, music, like the other arts, was an imitation of
the universe of Newton and the physico-theologians, of Dryden,
Pope, and Fielding. Since God made all things 'in *Number, Weight,*
and *Measure*', observed Jeremy Collier inaugurating Cavendish
Weedon's festival of sacred music in 1702, 'What can be more
reasonable and Becoming, than to Praise him in the most exalted
Strains, and joyn the *Musick* of the Place, with that of the *Creation ?*'[36]
Collier's suggestion of an analogous and complementary relationship between the two harmonies—the one audible and human,
the other inaudible and divine—should not be too hastily dismissed
as a mere rhetorical flourish. The same theoretical conviction
underlies many masterpieces of baroque music, the cantatas of
Bach, for example, or the operas and oratorios of Handel, in which,
among other abstract and extra-musical schema, a symmetrical
'key architecture' attests to the composer's conception of form as

symbolic of a cosmic and transcendental harmony.[37] Just how clearly, for the baroque composer, the musical forms could be made to echo the divine order of things is evident from Handel's setting (1739) of Dryden's *Song for St. Cecilia's Day, 1687,* wherein, as Professor Bronson has brilliantly demonstrated, ideas of 'heavenly Harmony' and of God's final untuning of the sky are realized musically.[38] But in asserting the theory and practice of expressive form in this period, we can hardly improve on Manfred Bukofzer's authoritative statement:

> The distinction of audible form and inaudible order did not exist in baroque music. Music reached out from the audible into the inaudible world, it extended without a break from the world of the senses into that of the mind and intellect . . . We must recognize the speculative approach to music as one of the fundamentals of baroque music and baroque art in general without either exaggerating or belittling its importance. If abstract thoughts could be enhanced through poetic form, as we see in the philosophical poetry of the baroque era, then by the same token concrete works of art could be enhanced through abstract thought. Audible form and inaudible order were not mutually exclusive or opposed concepts, as they are today, but complementary aspects of one and the same experience: the unity of sensual and intellectual understanding.[39]

For musicians and musicologists throughout the seventeenth century—for Praetorius, Kepler, Berardi, Werckmeister—music, Bukofzer continues, was in fact regarded 'as an imitation of the music of the spheres, a simile of heavenly music'.[40] As we have already glimpsed in Malcolm, this same idea, accommodated to the theories of Newton and Shaftesbury, continued to find its advocates among British musicologists of the following century.[41]

For the Augustan poet, as well as the baroque musician, nothing, to answer Collier's question, could be more reasonable, more becoming, than to praise God in song for the harmony of creation. In doing so, they invariably returned to the Pythagorean doctrines of *musica mundana* and *musica humana,* doctrines newly refined and sanctioned by contemporary scientists and divines. As critical analysis has shown,[42] Dryden in his *Song* and Pope in his *Ode for Musick* (1713) employ the metaphors and complex forms of Renaissance platonism with surprising ease. What we are now in a better position to understand is that they did so precisely because that tradition was still very much alive. One might document this contention from dozens of other musical odes composed during the period for such occasions as the annual Feast of St. Cecilia or the Weedon festivals, in which God's wisdom, power, and love in harmonizing the creation are piously commemorated. Consider, for example, the odes by Thomas Fletcher (1686), Thomas Shadwell (1690), Nicholas Brady (1692), Theophilus Parsons (1693), William Congreve (1701), John Hughes (1703), and John Lockman (*c.* 1730), which are conveniently collected in an Appendix to W. H. Husk's *Account of the Musical Celebrations on St. Cecilia's Day* (1857), or the comparable poem by Nahum Tate performed at Weedon's festival in 1701 before the assembled Houses of Lords and Commons. The opening strophes of Congreve's *Hymn to Harmony* (1701) are typical in their Newtonian rendering of Pythagorean ideas:

> . . . All hail to thee
>   All pow'rful Harmony!
> Wise Nature owns thy undisputed sway,
> Her wond'rous works resigning to thy care;
> The planetary orbs thy rule obey,
> And tuneful roll, unerring in their way,
> Thy voice informing each melodious sphere.
>
> Thy voice, O Harmony, with awful sound
>   Could penetrate th'abyss profound,
>   Explore the realms of ancient night,
> And search the living source of unborn light.
>   Confusion heard thy voice and fled,
> And Chaos deeper plung'd his vanquish'd head.
>
>   Then didst thou, Harmony, give birth
>   To this fair form of heav'n and earth;
>   Then all those shining worlds above
>   In mystic dance began to move
> Around the radiant sphere of central fire,
> A never ceasing, never silent choir.[43]

Or, as a final example, less well known, here is the third strophe of John Taylor's *Ode for Music*, performed as part of the commencement ceremonies at Cambridge in 1730:

> Who was it pois'd the well-tun'd Spheres,
> And led the Chorus of the circling Years,
>   When Chaos held distemper'd Sway,
>   And jarring Atoms, Cold and Heat,

> The Light, the Grave, the Dry, the Wet,
> In sullen Discord lay?
> 'Twas Harmony, 'twas Builder Harmony:
> 'Twas Harmony compos'd this Concert Frame,
> 'Twas Harmony which upwards flung the active Flame,
> Prescrib'd the Air in middle Space to flow,
> And bade the Wave and grosser Earth subside below.
> Then all yon tuneful restless Choir
> Began their radiant Journeys to advance
> And with unerring Symphony to roll the central Dance.[44]

Nearly fifty years after Taylor had penned these lines, the distinguished musicologist Sir John Hawkins could sympathetically observe that 'numbers, especially the poets', continued to subscribe to the Pythagorean doctrine, 'which seems to prevail even at this day'.[45] For Hawkins, who could scarcely conceal his delight at those passages from the *Opticks* and from Newton's correspondence with Harington that seemed conclusively to prove the point,[46] harmony was the essential characteristic of all creation, of which audible music was merely the symbolic manifestation. With Newton's experiments specifically in mind, Hawkins makes plain the grounds on which the Pythagorean hypothesis could be preserved as an article of the Augustan faith in Order:

> Among many tenets of the Pythagoreans, one was that there is a general and universal concent or harmony in the parts of the universe, and that the principles of music pervade the whole material world . . .
> At a time when philosophy had derived very little assistance from experiment, such general conclusions as these, and that the universe was founded on harmonic principles, had little to recommend them but the bare probability that they might be well grounded; but how great must have been the astonishment of a Pythagorean or a Platonist, could he have been a witness to those improvements which a more cultivated philosophy has produced! And how would he who exulted in the discovery that the consonances had a ratio of 12.9.8.6, have been pleased to hear the consonances at the same instant in a sonorous body; or been transported to find, by the help of a prism, a similar coincidence of proportions among colours, and that the principles of harmony pervaded as well the objects of sight as hearing?[47]

As Lawrence Lipking has rightly observed, by the second half of the century such an attempt to revive the tradition of *musica speculativa*, then very much on the wane, must have struck Hawkins's rival theorists as a trifle perverse.[48] The new musicologists, such as Avison and Burney, turned not to Newton but to Locke in the effort to explain the psychological bases of musical effects. But if Hawkins as an exponent of the *harmonia mundi* must be regarded as 'old-fashioned', it should now be clear that he is not quite the egregious anachronism we had supposed.

Before mid century, certainly, it was Newton, not Locke, who exerted the most profound influence upon contemporary thought, making empirically respectable the marriage between theology and aesthetics that had long obtained. Because in the *Principia* and the *Opticks* he had scientifically validated the ancient argument from design and revitalized the idea of world harmony, Newton may properly be regarded as the protagonist in the most compelling intellectual drama of the period: the concerted attempt by a host of Christian rationalists to redeem the providential order of creation from those latter-day emissaries of Antichrist, Descartes and Hobbes. It was Newton, as Hurlbutt has remarked, who assured the victory by demonstrating that the universe exemplified 'one gigantic mathematical harmony, moving to the music of the dynamical principles established by the terrestrial experiments and inductions of Galileo and himself'.⁴⁹ In this he may be said to have substantiated empirically a line of argument already taken by the Cambridge divines, Barrow, More, and Cudworth, and later extended by the physico-theologians, Ray and Derham, and by the Boyle lecturers, Bentley and Clarke.⁵⁰

The process of adapting Pythagoras and Plato for the Augustan Age was completed, with appropriate urbanity, by the Earl of Shaftesbury and his disciple, Francis Hutcheson. In a strain reminiscent of the Cambridge school, Shaftesbury reasoned that, as the creature of a beneficent Deity, man was by nature sympathetically attuned to those principles of harmony which underlie the order and beauty of the universe. Though avoiding the esotericism of a Ficino or a Kepler, as befits an English lord in an age of common sense, Shaftesbury's theism and his aesthetics may none the less be seen as variations on the neo-platonic themes of *musica mundana* and *musica humana*.⁵¹ Nature for him is still a *concordia discors*:

> For 'tis not then [observes Philocles in *The Moralists*] that Men complain of the World's Order, or abhor the Face of things, when they see various Interests mix'd and interfering; Natures subordinate, of different kinds, oppos'd one to another, and in their different Operations submitted, the

higher to the lower. 'Tis on the contrary, from this Order of inferior
and superior Things, that we admire the World's Beauty, founded thus
on *Contrarietys:* whilst from such various and disagreeing Principles,
a universal Concord is establish'd.[52]

When well tuned, the human soul is naturally responsive to every
manifestation of this universal law. Beauty in the arts, no less than
moral beauty, results from the felicitous imitation of the harmony,
proportion, and design inherent in Nature. In another passage
from *The Moralists* (II. iv) particularly admired by Shaftesbury's
followers—by Robert Morris, for example, who used it as the
epigraph to his *Essay on Harmony* (1739)—Theocles enunciates one
of the cardinal principles of Augustan aesthetics: that all beauty,
whether in nature or in art, is a function of order.

'NOTHING surely is more strongly imprinted on our Minds, or more
closely interwoven with our Souls, than the Idea or Sense of *Order* and
Proportion. Hence all the Force of *Numbers,* and those powerful *Arts*
founded on their Management and Use. What a difference there is between
Harmony and *Discord! Cadency* and *Convulsion!* What a difference between compos'd and orderly Motion, and that which is ungovern'd and
accidental! between the regular and uniform Pile of some noble Architect,
and a Heap of Sand or Stones! between an organiz'd Body, and a Mist or
Cloud driven by the Wind!

'Now as this Difference is immediately perceiv'd by a plain internal
Sensation, so there is withal in Reason this account of it; That whatever
Things have *Order,* the same have *Unity of Design,* and concur *in one,* are
Parts constituent of *one* WHOLE, or are, in themselves, *intire Systems.* Such
is a *Tree,* with all its Branches; an *Animal,* with all its Members; an *Edifice,*
with all its exterior and interior Ornaments. What else is even a *Tune* or
Symphony, or any excellent Piece of Musick, than a certain *System* of
proportion'd Sounds?' (II. 284–5)

In Part I of his *Inquiry into the Original of our Ideas of Beauty and
Virtue* (1725), Hutcheson developed these ideas more systematically. Beauty he finds to consist invariably in the apprehension of
'*Uniformity amidst Variety*'.[53] We shall return to Hutcheson later,
for on the whole, though it has been strangely neglected by students
of the period, his essay 'Concerning Beauty, Order, Harmony,
Design' is the most effective statement of the Augustan aesthetics
of order. In the present context, we need only glance at his conception of musical harmony as an aspect of 'original' or 'absolute'
beauty. Though he is reluctant to follow Kepler or Malcolm in
explicitly suggesting that music is a mimetic art, the audible and

earthly manifestation of universal *concordia*—'*Harmony*', he remarks parenthetically, 'is not usually conceiv'd as an Imitation of any thing else' (p. 27)—yet it is clear that as a species of absolute beauty, satisfying the ear by reconciling and unifying disparate sounds, music for Hutcheson participates in the '*harmonious Form*' of the creation itself (p. 70).

Just as earlier platonists had proposed a correlation between the careful tuning of the macrocosm and the tempering of the microcosm, Shaftesbury, Hutcheson, and their followers considered moral virtue to result from the harmonious ordering of the passions, bringing the soul into sympathetic correspondence with the natural fitness of things. As the 'internal sense' prompts the individual instinctively to delight in order and harmony and to be repelled by the experience of disorder and cacophony, so the 'moral sense' incites him to pursue virtue and to shun vice:

> For HARMONY [Shaftesbury declares] is Harmony *by Nature*, let Men judg ever so ridiculously of Musick. So is *Symmetry* and *Proportion* founded still *in Nature*, let Mens Fancy prove ever so barbarous, or their Fashions ever so *Gothick* in their Architecture, Sculpture, or whatever other designing Art. 'Tis the same case, where *Life* and MANNERS are concern'd. *Virtue* has the same fix'd Standard. The same *Numbers, Harmony,* and *Proportion* will have place in MORALS . . .[54]

Philosophy, therefore, is '*the Study of inward Numbers and Proportions*'.[55]

One consequence of this fashionable reduction of the neoplatonist tradition, correlating ontology, morality, and aesthetics—the True, the Good, and the Beautiful—was the extreme importance attached to every manifestation of order in the arts. A good poem, through its decorum, design, and music, was the expression of these same qualities in Nature, as it was of the health of the author's soul. It was in a certain sense inevitable that the world of Pope's *Dunciad* is chaos and that the dunces themselves are irrational and depraved. To Shaftesbury, at least, '*the Love of Numbers, Decency and Proportion*' was characteristic of the true poet, whose measured verse is attuned to the music of creation and echoes an inner spiritual harmony: 'For this is the Effect, and this the Beauty of their Art; "in vocal Measures of Syllables, and Sounds, to express the Harmony and Numbers of an inward kind; and represent the Beautys of a human Soul, by proper Foils and Contrarietys, which serve as Graces in this Limning, and render this Musick of the Passions more powerful and enchanting".'[56] To Hutcheson, though the imitation of imperfect characters makes an epic poem or a tragedy an example of 'relative' beauty, yet the music of the poem, its '*Measures* and *Cadence*', reminds us of an ideal order: as 'instances of *Harmony*', the numbers of poetry 'come under the head of *absolute Beauty*' (p. 42).

The idea of world harmony, then, did not simply furnish neo-classical poets with an intellectually viable metaphor for Order, as in the musical odes of Dryden, Congreve, Pope, Mitchell, Taylor, and many others. It served as well, in more fundamental ways, to transform the theory and practice of Augustan prosody, resulting in the dominance of strict syllabic regularity during the period from 1660 to 1740.[57] To Cowley in the *Davideis*, the harmony of numbers was an imitation of the cosmic principle of order, for which reason he declared, 'Though no man hear't, though no man it reherse, / Yet will there still be *musick* in my Verse' (p. 13). A similar notion, implying a metaphysical basis for prosody, was set forth some time later by Joseph Trapp, who, in lectures delivered before the schools of natural philosophy at Oxford, traced the original of poetry to the 'Love implanted in Mankind of *Imitation* and *Harmony*':

> His Passion for Harmony is no Wonder; because whatever we call beautiful arises from a just Proportion, and proper Arrangement of its Parts. It is this composes the whole Frame of the Universe; and the more perfect every Individual of it is, the greater Share of Harmony it possesses.[58]

To imitate this pure harmony and regularity of the creation in heroic verse, the Augustan poet—though careful to insure at least a measure of variety by shifting the position of the caesura and substituting an occasional trochee—strove to establish a pattern of strict iambic pentameter. In *The Rambler*, No. 86 (12 January 1751), Johnson is quite explicit on this point:

> The heroic Measure of the English Language may be properly considered as pure or mixed. It is pure when the Accent rests upon every second Syllable through the whole Line . . . The Repetition of this Sound or Percussion at equal Times is the most complete Harmony of which a single Verse is capable, and should therefore be exactly preserved in Distichs . . .[59]

Resuming the subject in *The Rambler*, No. 88 (19 January 1751), Johnson is just as emphatic in declaring that it is only from the exact observation of such metrical regularity that the powers of verse may be fully realized: 'from the proper Disposition of single Sounds results that Harmony that adds Force to Reason, and gives Grace to Sublimity; that shackles Attention, and governs Passion.'[60] For readers who shared Johnson's prosodic expectations, Pope was the most musical of poets, whereas Milton sounded harsh. These two great poets became, indeed, the focus of a quarrel that grew more strident as the century advanced—the quarrel between 'regularists', such as Edward Manwaring, and those, such as Samuel Say, who preferred a more 'organic' method of versification.[61]

As Fussell observes, the conservative prosody of Pope and Johnson adds a further dimension to Augustan platonism, since the poet may be said to begin 'with a "pure" and unalterable aesthetic form which is always the same, and to lay this ideal form over the poetic matter, which must then adapt itself to the archetypal form. The process', he continues, 'is one of idealizing the real, of "improving" and "regularizing" phonetic materials which are by nature unimproved and devoid of the element of art.'[62] Just how congenial the theories of platonism could be to one of the keenest admirers of Pope's versification is evident from Manwaring's treatise, *Stichology* (1737). To Manwaring, 'all Poetry partakes of the Elements of Geometry and Musick . . .' (p. 74). And he recounts with approval the Pythagorean notion that, since the soul is 'a Composition of musical Harmonics', it is susceptible of being affected by the harmonic proportions, which, therefore, as the ancients understood, must serve as the basis for the rhythms and cadences of verse (pp. 20–1).

In the light of such theoretical attempts to supply a metaphysical basis for Augustan prosody, Wasserman's well-known analysis of Pope's verse form in *Windsor Forest* as an imitation of *concordia discors* gains a certain cogency.[63] For one as familiar as Pope with the aesthetics of Christian humanism, the idea could not have seemed far-fetched that the forms of art should embody and express those principles of order and coherency which inform Nature, the Art of God. This assumption—essentially the notion of expressive form—was fundamental to both classical and Christian art, as Leo Spitzer has shown. It may be more than merely coincidental that Pope should have fixed upon a structure for the heroic couplet which, in the syntactical and sonic achievement of balance, regularity, and unity, formally approximates the world he believed he inhabited. That world, Newton no less than Pythagoras had shown to be a *concordia discors* in which opposing forces were harmoniously reconciled. Imaginatively at least, from the myth of universal harmony Pope knew in Eustathius—

Jupiter, says he, who is the Lord of Nature, is well pleased with the War of the Gods, that is of Earth, Sea, and Air, *&c.* because the Harmony of all Beings arises from that Discord: Thus Earth is opposite to Water, Air to Earth, and Water to them all; and yet from this Opposition arises that discordant Concord by which all Nature subsists.[64]

—it is not very far to the conception of cosmic order which Pope and his contemporaries encountered in Newton:

> Great God, what Pow'r, and Prudence to the Full
> Are Scatter'd thro' the Expanded Whole!
> Stupendous Bulk and Symmetrie,
> Cross Motion and clear Harmonie,
> Close Union and Antipathie,
> Projectile Force, and Gravitie,
> In such well pois'd Proportions Fall,
> As strike this Artfull, Mathematic Dance of All.[65]

With the classical and Newtonian models of universal order in mind, it is curiously appropriate that Pope's couplet form, considered in paradigm, should be an enclosed, exquisitely unified system in which elemental pairs of opposing ideas or images are at once forced into dynamic equilibrium by means of syntactical symmetries, balancing hemistich against hemistich, line against line, and reconciled by means of harmonic devices, such as assonance, alliteration, and, most especially, rhyme. As a formal system, Pope's couplet closely corresponds both to the idea of *concordia discors* and to that other Pythagorean and Platonic model of cosmic order, the 'divine *tetraktys*', the principle by which the Demiurge of the *Timaeus* created the world, achieving unity through the proportionate blending of the four elements.[66] To a poetry which assumes the validity of these notions of world harmony, furthermore, the use of rhyme is particularly apposite, since, like the mysterious principle of *concordia discors*, rhyme serves to force disparate words, the literary 'elements' of a poem, into harmonic association. Consider, for example, Spitzer's astute observation, which explains St. Augustine's introduction of rhyme into modern poetry in precisely these terms:

. . . the 'musicalization' of poetry by the rhyme would be only another feature of the conception of art as musical art. The polyphony in which the manifoldness of the universe is brought into unity is echoed within the poem by a device which holds together words that strive apart. Both polyphony and rhyme are Christian developments, patterned on world harmony; in the ambiguity of the word *consonantia* in the Middle Ages ('chord' or 'rhyme') we may grasp the fundamental kinship of the two meanings. Rhyme is now redeemed from intellectualism, it is an acoustic and emotional phenomenon responding to the harmony of the world.[67]

Professor Spitzer's hypothesis may serve as well to explain Pope's unwavering loyalty to a device which some of the most influential critics of his time contemptuously decried as 'that monstrous Ornament which we call *Rhyme*'.[68]

Though centuries separate the age of Augustine from that of Augustan England, yet, as we have seen, the Christian humanist tradition of world harmony was continuous. Thanks to Newton, Shaftesbury, and the Cambridge divines, it was still possible to imagine the creation, and to render it in poetry, according to the theories and analogies of Pythagoras and Plato. For Pope, early and late, *concordia discors* remained the controlling metaphor for Order, most succinctly and clearly expressed in the well-known description of Windsor Forest:

> Here Hills and Vales, the Woodland and the Plain,
> Here Earth and Water seem to strive again,
> Not *Chaos*-like together crush'd and bruis'd,
> But as the World, harmoniously confus'd:
> Where Order in Variety we see,
> And where, tho' all things differ, all agree.   (ll. 11–16)

The influence of this doctrine upon Pope's verse form is already familiar from Professor Wasserman's analysis of such a line as this from the same poem—'Here in full Light the russet Plains extend; / There wrapt in Clouds the blueish Hills ascend' (ll. 23–4)—in which, by means of syntactical parallelism and rhyme, the poet reconciles antithetical images and harmonizes ideas as diametrically opposed as those of horizontal and vertical.[69] Innumerable other examples might be adduced to illustrate this unifying function of rhyme and syntactical symmetry in Pope's poetry. Together these devices serve to create a form perfectly consonant with the Christian humanist conception of the whole of life as a unity of opposing elements—of man as a paradox ('With too much knowledge for the Sceptic side, / With too much weakness for the Stoic's pride'), of woman as at best a contradiction still ('Now deep in Taylor and the Book of Martyrs, / Now drinking citron with his Grace and Chartres'), of the universe itself as unity in diversity ('As full, as perfect, in vile Man that mourns, / As the rapt Seraph that adores and burns').[70] Here perhaps, in Pope's mastery of the couplet's expressive form, may be found the true significance for Augustan aesthetics of the doctrine of world harmony.

ii. *Symmetry*

In Augustan England, as in Renaissance Italy, the idea of harmony was closely related to another aspect of pure form: that of symmetry and proportion in the visual arts. 'Harmony', indeed, as Edward Manwaring asserted, 'is a Species of the Cause, which produces Symmetry.'[71] Or, as the poet William Thompson put it, beauty is 'silent Harmony'; music, 'fine-proportion'd sounds'.[72] We have seen that the discoveries of Newton and the moralizing of Shaftesbury had lent a new cogency to the doctrine of Pythagoras and the Platonists 'that Nature is sure to act consistently, and with a constant Analogy in all her Operations'.[73] Newton, we recall, had found nothing objectionable in the hypothesis that visual beauty is dependent upon the musical proportions, because such a view 'tends to exemplify the simplicity in all the works of the Creator . . .'.[74]

The most dramatic evidence of the survival of the Renaissance aesthetic in the neo-classical period comes from theorists on both sides of the Channel who persisted in the Pythagorean notion that beauty is essentially, and quite literally, a visual harmony: that the forms of architecture, sculpture, and painting are more pleasing to the eye the more closely they approximate the mathematical proportions that produce the musical concords—a principle testifying to the harmonic and mathematical structure of all creation. In his brilliant study, *Architectural Principles in the Age of Humanism*, Rudolf Wittkower has conclusively demonstrated that this belief was fundamental to such Renaissance architectural theorists as Leon Battista Alberti and Daniele Barbaro, and that it governed Palladio's practice.[75] Though he finds the same principles informing the architecture of Inigo Jones[76]—who, after the master himself, served as the chief model for Burlington's Palladian brotherhood —and though he is aware of later advocates of the musical analogy such as François Blondel, Robert Morris, and Charles Étienne Briseux,[77] Wittkower yet hesitates to affirm that this rather arcane doctrine had any significant influence in the Age of Reason; and more recent historians have been disposed to reject the possibility altogether.[78]

It is doubtless true that neo-classical theorists no longer sensed the same mysterious symbolism in the Pythagorean ratios that had fascinated Alberti and Palladio, but it is no less evident that they continued to believe that beauty was objectively founded in a principle of Nature as firmly fixed as the law of gravity: namely, the principle of symmetry and proportion—often, indeed, musical proportion. Within the context of the design argument, the assertion of these laws was crucial, for a world founded upon the rational principles of geometry and harmony declared the wisdom and goodness of the Creator in all its parts. Recalling Wittkower's suspicion that a sixteenth-century Platonist such as Daniele Barbaro could experience 'under a Renaissance dome . . . a faint echo of the inaudible music of the spheres',[79] Maynard Mack asks whether Pope at Twickenham might have sensed a similar consonance between the order of art and that of Nature: 'Could an eighteenth-century poet and Palladian experience, or imagine that he experienced, in the great salon at Marble Hill, or possibly in the interior of his own dwelling, if not so metaphysical an echo, at least an exhilarating access of confidence that all things are One?'[80] It is likely, as we shall see, that he could.

The Pythagorean musical analogy continued to be seriously advanced by aestheticians throughout—indeed, well beyond—the period with which we are concerned, though the fact that the idea is generally presented with an air of discovery suggests that it was no longer quite the commonplace matter it had been for Alberti and Palladio. In France, for example, the distinguished musicologist René Ouvrard published in 1679 a treatise entitled, *L'Architecture harmonique: ou, l'application de la doctrine des proportions de la musique à l'architecture*, in which he expressed the hope that, by adopting the musical proportions (which God Himself had decreed for the Temple of Solomon), modern architecture would soon rival the Greek. In 1683 the theory was assured the widest possible currency by François Blondel, Director of the Académie Royale d'Architecture, who made it the capstone of his *Cours d'architecture*, the published version of a series of lectures he had presented to the Academy. From the study of ancient and modern architecture—Vitruvius, Alberti, Palladio, Scamozzi—Blondel arrived independently at Ouvrard's conclusions.[81] The soul, he declares, craves order, '*ce Concert Harmonique* que l'on appelle *la Beauté*' (v. xix);[82] and the source of all beauty, all harmony, is proportion, of which the fixed and invariable laws are founded in Nature. On this point Blondel was challenged by Claude Perrault in his *Ordonnance des cinq espèces de colonnes* (1683). Though Perrault never abandoned the indispensable standard of symmetry, he plainly saw that the proportions that please in architecture are not absolute, like those of music, but relative, depending on such subjective considerations as the viewer's angle of vision or his taste. Those who first determined the proportions of a column, he remarks, had 'scarce any other Rule than their Fancy, according as that has chang'd, new Proportions have been introduc'd, which likewise pleas'd in their turn'.[83] In effect, Perrault denied the basic premiss of the strict proportionists: that beauty, by a law of Nature which is ever the same, was the product of certain real qualities (chiefly, proportion and symmetry) belonging to external objects, as the musical concords are invariably dependent on certain fixed mathematical ratios. Inevitably, Perrault was denounced by Blondel,[84] but his views prevailed when he succeeded his rival as Director of the Academy. In the opinion of Charles Étienne Briseux, the consequences for French architecture of this triumph of subjectivism and arbitrary taste were disastrous. In his *Traité du beau essentiel dans les arts* (1752), Briseux, citing Solomon's Temple and Newton's *Opticks* in his behalf,[85] made it a fundamental law of Nature that visual beauty, no less than harmony, was a function of the musical proportions:

Il est donc certain, que les proportions et les progressions qui font l'harmonie, sont dans la nature dont elles tirent leur éxistence, et qu'elle ne les abandonne jamais, autant qu'il lui est possible. Aprés les avoir employées avec autant d'exactitude que de succès dans la construction du corps humain, vraisemblablement elle les observe également dans toutes les qualitez sensibles de ses productions, Cette Mere universelle agissant toujours avec la même sagesse et d'une maniere uniforme, l'on a droit de conclure, que le plaisir de l'Ouïe et de la vuë consiste dans la perception des raports harmoniques comme étant analogues à notre constitution et que ce principe a lieu nonseulement dans la Musique, mais encore dans toutes les productions des Arts: une même cause ne pouvant avoir deux effets differents.   (i. 44–5)

In France, Briseux was probably the last and certainly the most explicit exponent of the Pythagorean analogy in the eighteenth century. More pertinent to our immediate purpose, however, were the similar speculations of the Dutch philomath, Lambert Hermanson Ten Kate, whose discourse *Sur le Beau Idéal* (1728) was well known in England, where it contributed to the situation in aesthetics of which Hogarth complained in *The Analysis of Beauty* (1753), remarking that '*notions*' of musical proportion in the arts of design 'have so far prevail'd by time, that the words, *harmony of parts*, seem as applicable to form, as to music'.[86] To Ten Kate, who believed that ideal beauty in the human form was founded on the musical proportions, all Nature was a hymn of praise to the Creator, whose essential principle was harmony:

> Voilà comment tout le Fondement de la Musique, & tout ce qu'elle a de merveilleux, s'accorde admirablement avec ces Convenances & ces Proportions du *Beau Idéal*. O! quelle admirable Harmonie, quels Airs charmans chante sans cesse toute la Belle Nature, à la Louange de son Divin Auteur![87]

Though Hogarth scoffed at Ten Kate's claim to have discovered the secret that produced the masterpieces of antiquity,[88] the discourse was more cordially received by Robert Morris, Pope's neighbour at Twickenham and the principal theorist of the English Palladians.[89] In the Preface to his *Lectures on Architecture*, Part I (1734), Morris freely acknowledged his debt to the Dutch aesthetician, '*that Ingenious Gentleman*', from whom he had '*the first Hint . . . of the Harmonick Proportions*' which became the basis for his own theories.[90]

That Morris was not earlier acquainted with the Pythagorean analogy is surprising. Not only had the analogy figured prominently in the treatises of Ouvrard and Blondel, but in two works by theorists associated with Palladio and Inigo Jones, it had been either explicitly recommended or noticed with approbation: in Book IX of his *Architecture* (Englished by Giacomo Leoni in 1726), Alberti declared his faith in the system; and it was well known to Sir Henry Wotton, for whom Alberti had reduced '*Symmetrie* to *Symphonie*, and the *harmonie* of *Sounde*, to a kinde of *harmonie* in *Sight*'.[91] As for those '*vulgar Artizans*' who find such speculations too subtle and sublime, Wotton reminds them that even such a master as Vitruvius determined many things 'by *Musicall* grounds, and much commendeth in an *Architect*, a *Philosophical*

Spirit; that is, he would haue him . . . to be no superficiall, and floating *Artificer*; but a *Diuer* into *Causes*, and into the *Mysteries* of *Proportion* . . .' (pp. 54–5). Indeed, by the time Morris began to sound these depths for himself, the musical analogy was familiar enough to the master-builders of England to be casually applied by Batty Langley, no very abstruse philosopher, in explaining the splendid achievements of the ancient architects: 'the *Beauty* and the *Pleasure* their Works gave, were only the Effects of a *well-chosen Symmetry*, connected together according to the *harmonick Laws of Proportion*, which of necessity naturally produce that Effect upon the Mind thro' the Eye, as the Cords or Discords of Musick, please or displease the Soul thro' the Ear.'[92]

It is quite unlikely, then, that the principle of harmonic proportion which guided Palladio and Inigo Jones would have been unknown to the Burlington coterie, who took these men as models in attempting to reform architectural taste in England. At least one building, Lady Henrietta Howard's elegant mansion at Marble Hill, was designed by Lord Pembroke and Roger Morris in exact accordance to the musical proportions.[93] Yet only in Robert Morris, the architect's kinsman, is there any clear evidence that these ideas influenced contemporary theory, and even here the debt is as much to the physico-theologians, and to Shaftesbury and Pope, as it is to the continental disciples of Alberti and Barbaro. In his early work, *An Essay in Defence of Ancient Architecture* (1728), Morris takes as his motto the familiar lines from *An Essay on Criticism*: 'Learn hence for Ancient *Rules* a just Esteem; / To copy *Nature* is to copy *Them*' (ll. 139–40). Indeed, the parallel that Wittkower invites us to draw between the theoretical assumptions of the Palladian architects and those of the Augustan poets seems, in this instance, particularly apt.[94] Like Pope, Morris believed that Nature, the work of the divine Architect, was harmonious; that the rules of this harmony could be determined by analysis; and that the greatest geniuses of the past—Homer or Virgil, Vitruvius or Palladio—had discovered these principles and realized them in their art.

That Morris conceived the harmony of Nature in a quite literal sense is evident from the series of lectures on architecture which he delivered from 1730 to 1735 as President of the Society for the Improvement of Knowledge in Arts and Sciences. The universe, he declares, from Newton's whirling planets down to 'the Vegetative

Tribe', manifests proportion and order in all its parts.[95] Beauty, therefore, is founded on the laws of proportion in Nature, and specifically on those proportions that produce the musical concords. In Lecture V (21 January 1733/4), Morris writes:

NATURE has taught Mankind in *Musick* certain Rules for Proportion of Sounds, so Architecture has its Rules dependant on those Proportions, or at least such Proportions which are Arithmetical Harmony; and those I take to be dependant on Nature. The Square in *Geometry*, the Unison or Circle in *Musick*, and the Cube in *Building*, have all an inseparable Proportion; the Parts being equal, and the Sides, and Angles, &c. give the Eye and Ear an agreeable Pleasure; from hence may likewise be deduc'd the Cube and half, the Double Cube; the Diapason, and Diapenté, being founded on the same Principles in *Musick*.   (p. 74)

The idea is further developed in Lecture VI (undated):

As I consider [Morris continues] the Affinity between *Architecture* and *Musick*, so I have produc'd those Proportions from the same Rules: In *Musick* are only seven distinct Notes, in *Architecture* likewise are only seven distinct Proportions, which produce all the different Buildings in the Universe, *viz.*

THE Cube,—the Cube and half,—the Double Cube,—the Duplicates of 3, 2, and 1,—of 4, 3, and 2,—of 5, 4, and 3,—and of 6, 4, and 3, produce all the Harmonick Proportions of Rooms.   (p. 94)

Clearly, the Pythagorean mysteries seemed far from preposterous to at least one son of the Enlightenment. But Morris's revival of the Greek analogy is, as we shall see, only the most striking development of the assumption, widely held by neoclassical aestheticians, that form in the arts should be the expression of those sacred laws of harmony and symmetry on which the order of creation is founded. The doctrine of harmonic proportion reappeared from time to time: Sir John Hawkins regarded it as a proven fact in 1776,[96] and as late as 1815 Francis Webb was using Newton to authenticate his own version of the Pythagorean hypothesis.[97] But, as Wittkower and Scholfield have shown,[98] the intellectual currents of the latter half of the eighteenth century moved, in the direction marked out by Perrault, toward a new aesthetic relativism. The notion that the fundamental laws of music and the designing arts were congruent was ridiculed by Hogarth (1753) and logically refuted by Lord Kames (1762). It could obtain only so long as men subscribed to what Wittkower calls 'the basic axiom of all classical art-theory, according to which beauty is inherent in the object provided the latter is in tune with universal harmony'.[99] As it happened, the foundations of what may be called the objective theory of artistic imitation were swept away by empiricists such as Hume and Burke and Alison, who, developing the subjectivist implications of Locke's *Essay*, concluded that beauty, like reality itself, was a function of sensation and the individual consciousness.

But that philosophic cataclysm, which put an end to a continuous, homogeneous tradition of Western thought, had not yet occurred. To an English Palladian such as Robert Morris, beauty was by no means a relative thing; it sprang 'from the same unerring Law in Nature'—the law of proportion and symmetry— to which the soul, 'by some sympathizing Secret', was well attuned.[100] In architecture the maxim that art must imitate Nature had been variously interpreted from Vitruvius, who found that the proportions of the human figure were most natural,[101] to Marc-Antoine Laugier, who thought that the only 'natural' buildings were austere variations on the huts of primitive men.[102] What remained consistent, however—whether in Plato or Augustine, Newton or Shaftesbury—was the notion that harmony and symmetry were fundamental laws of the creation to be embodied in the forms of art. Like Edward Manwaring's poet,[103] God was both a Musician and a Geometrician. For Newton, the symmetry evident in the bodies of animals, like the order of the planetary system, was proof of a rational Creator.[104] For Shaftesbury, 'HARMONY is Harmony *by Nature*. . . . So is *Symmetry* and *Proportion* founded still *in Nature*.'

As Marjorie Nicolson has shown,[105] these assumptions so thoroughly conditioned men's expectations of the beautiful that they inhibited a taste for the natural sublime, for mountains and wild prospects, until the dawning of the Romantic period. To the Augustan mind, as we are here defining it, beauty, an emanation of the divine nature, was a rational principle characterized by harmony, regularity, symmetry; form and lucid order were the reassuring signs that the world had been redeemed from Chaos and dark Night. Part of Henry More's strategy in *An Antidote against Atheisme* (1653) is to plead to that innate craving for order and rationality which separated his readers from the brute creation: 'Besides I appeal to any man that is not sunk into so forlorne a pitch of Degeneracy, that he is as stupid to these things as the basest of Beasts, whether for Example a rightly cut *Tetraedrum*,

Cube or *Icosaedrum* have no more pulchritude in them, then any rude *broken stone* lying in the field or high wayes . . .' The geometrical figures, he continues,

gratifie our sight, as having a neerer cognation with the Soul of man, that is rationall and intellectuall; and therefore is well pleased when it meets with any outward object that fits and agrees with those congenit Ideas her own nature is furnished with. For *Symmetry, Equality,* and *Correspondency of parts* is the discernment of *Reason,* not the object of Sense . . . (pp. 62–3)

A similar faith in the efficacy of balance and regularity determined the aesthetic principles of the architect of St. Paul's Cathedral, for whom 'natural' beauty consists in geometric form:

Geometrical Figures are naturally more beautiful than other irregular; in this all consent as to a Law of Nature. Of geometrical Figures, the Square and the Circle are most beautiful, next, the Parallelogram & the Oval. Strait Lines are more beautiful than curve; next to strait Lines, equal & geometrical Flexures; an Object elevated in the Middle is more beautiful than depressed.

Position is necessary for perfecting Beauty. There are only two beautiful Positions of strait Lines, perpendicular & horizontal: this is from Nature, and consequently Necessity, no other than upright being firm. Oblique Positions are Discord to the Eye, unless answered in Parts, as in the Sides of an equicrural Triangle; therefore Gothick Buttresses are ill-favoured, and were avoided by the Ancients . . .[106]

Neither Hogarth nor Frank Lloyd Wright would agree that 'natural' beauty consists in straight lines and strict symmetry, but to aestheticians of the early eighteenth century the point was axiomatic. Art imitated Nature by reducing her materials, however various and abundant, to order, by comprehending them within a regular and uniform design. The Swiss theologian and mathematician, Jean Pierre de Crousaz, observed that the geometrical configurations of gardens and buildings gratified man's innate yearning for regularity, order, and proportion—'trois choses qui plaisent necessairement à l'Esprit humain, & qui effectivement meritent qu'on les aime': 'La varieté temperée par l'uniformité, la regularité, l'ordre, & la proportion', he insists, 'ne sont pas assurément des chimeres; elles ne sont pas du ressort de la fantaisie, ce n'est pas le caprice qui en décide.'[107]

Two other works by French aestheticians enforce these same principles. With Plato and Augustine as his guides, Yves Marie de L'Isle André finds that symmetry and order comprise 'le Beau essentiel', itself a manifestation of that divine Unity, 'originale, souveraine, & éternelle, parfaite', in which all things are comprehended.[108] Of this beauty, the laws are invariable, as in architecture, where the regular arrangement of columns, the parallelism of floors, the symmetry of the members are 'ordonnées par la nature indépendamment du choix de l'Architecte' (p. 47). Each man, by reason of 'la Géométrie naturelle', is born with 'un compas dans les yeux, pour juger de l'élégance d'une figure, ou de la perfection d'un ouvrage' (p. 14).

Similarly, Charles Batteux explains the maxim that the artist must imitate 'la belle Nature', the order of ideal Nature. In art, as in Nature, the soul delights in a plentiful variety, but without a principle of coherence to unite the parts into a whole, it is soon oppressed by the sense of multiplicity and confusion. The indispensable principles by which divers materials may be reduced to unity are symmetry and proportion—

deux qualités qui supposent la distinction & la différence des parties, & en même-tems un certain rapport de conformité entr'elles. La symmétrie partage, pour ainsi dire, l'objet en deux, place au milieu les parties uniques, & à côté celles qui sont répétées: ce qui forme une sorte de balance & d'équilibre qui donne de l'ordre, de la liberté, de la grace à l'objet. La Proportion va plus loin, elle entre dans le détail des parties qu'elle compare entr'elles & avec le tout, & présente sous un même point de vue l'unité, la variété, & le concert agréable de ces deux qualités entr'elles. Telle est l'étendue de la loi du Goût par rapport au choix & à l'arrangement des parties des objets.[109]

Batteux's ideals are those of poise and balance and relationship, of the creative intelligence imposing order on a rich variety of materials. The passage points both to the condition of 'la belle Nature', where symmetry and proportion prevail, and to the motives of form in neo-classical art.

In the treatises of these (today) little-read continental aestheticians, the grounds of the neo-classical faith in order are plainly delineated. But the unusual importance attached to formal regularity in English art of the period—whether in the prosody of Pope or Johnson, the buildings of Burlington or Gibbs, or the narrative architecture of Fielding—may best be understood if we turn to Francis Hutcheson, whose inquiry 'Concerning Beauty, Order, Harmony, Design' comprises the most substantial and carefully reasoned statement of aesthetic principles before Hume and Burke.

In Hutcheson, the neo-platonic premisses already operative in More and Wren and Shaftesbury are expounded systematically. Nature, the exquisitely wrought creation of 'the *Great* ARCHITECT' (p. 105), is represented as a perpetual demonstration of 'the Absurdity of the *Cartesian* or *Epicurean Hypothesis*' (p. 63): in the regular motions of the planets, in the uniformity of the several species, in the symmetrical shapes of the animal and vegetable creation, an invariable impulse for order attests to the designing hand of God. The great principle of the creation is '*Uniformity amidst Variety*', and the human soul, fashioned in the image of the Creator, is moved by an 'internal Sense' to find beauty in all objects, natural or artificial, which embody this law: 'what we call Beautiful in Objects, to speak in the Mathematical Style, seems to be in a compound *Ratio* of *Uniformity* and *Variety*: so that where the *Uniformity* of Bodys is equal, the Beauty is as the *Variety*; and where the *Variety* is equal, the Beauty is as the *Uniformity*' (p. 17). An equilateral triangle is less beautiful, therefore, than a square, a square less beautiful than a pentagon. Like Pope's Windsor Forest, the earth is '*beautifully* . . . diversify'd with various Degrees of *Light* and *Shade*, according to the different Situations of the Parts of its Surface, in *Mountains*, *Valleys*, *Hills*, and open *Plains*, which are variously inclin'd toward the great LUMINARY'; yet at the same time, Hutcheson exclaims, 'what vast *Uniformity* and Regularity of Figure is found in each particular *Plant*, *Leaf*, or *Flower!*' (p. 22).

In the productions of art, this instinctive desire for order is especially pronounced, our sense of beauty depending on the apprehension of uniformity, the effect of a controlling intelligence. However disparate the artefacts of different cultures may seem, the principle, Hutcheson insists, holds universally:

As to the Works of ART, were we to run thro the various artificial Contrivances or Structures, we should constantly find the Foundation of the *Beauty* which appears in them, to be some kind of *Uniformity*, or *Unity* of Proportion among the Parts, and of each Part to the Whole. As there is a vast Diversity of Proportions possible, and different Kinds of *Uniformity*, so there is room enough for that Diversity of Fancys observable in *Architecture*, *Gardening*, and such like Arts in different *Nations*; they all may have *Uniformity*, tho the Parts in one may differ from those in another. The *Chinese* or *Persian* Buildings are not like the *Grecian* and *Roman*, and yet the former has its *Uniformity* of the various Parts to each other, and to the Whole, as well as the latter. In that kind of Architecture which the

EUROPEANS call *Regular*, the *Uniformity* of Parts is very obvious, the several
Parts are *regular Figures*, and either *equal* or *similar* at least in the same
Range; the Pedestals are *Parallelopipedons* or square *Prisms*; the Pillars,
Cylinders nearly; the Arches *Circular*, and all those in the same Row *equal*;
there is the same Proportion every where observ'd in the same Range
between the *Diameters* of Pillars and their *Heights*, their *Capitals*, the
Diameters of *Arches*, the *Heights* of the *Pedestals*, the *Projections* of the
Cornice, and all the Ornaments in each of our *five Orders*. And tho other
Countrys do not follow the *Grecian* or *Roman* Proportions; yet there is even
among them a Proportion retain'd, a *Uniformity*, and Resemblance of
corresponding Figures; and every Deviation in one part from that Proportion which is observ'd in the rest of the Building, is displeasing to every
Eye, and destroys or diminishes at least the *Beauty* of the Whole. (pp. 38–9)

The same instinctive urge for uniformity and order is what causes
us, furthermore, to delight in those intellectual forms—the
theorems of Euclid or the laws of Newton—by which a multiplicity of particular ideas is subsumed under a general truth
(pp. 31–2).

Hutcheson's *Inquiry* comprises a useful anatomy of the
Augustan ideal. Order is presented both as the characteristic of
external nature and as the essential predisposition of the human
soul. In the familiar terms of the Christian humanist tradition, the
achievement of order in the macrocosm is the Art of God; in the
microcosm, the Art of Life. In aesthetics, as a consequence of these
metaphysical and moral assumptions, Form—the rational organization of divers materials into a coherent whole according to the
natural (indeed, sacred) principles of harmony, symmetry, and
proportion—became an indispensable requisite for the imitative
arts. It acquired, in fact, both an ethical and an ontological significance, for a work of art well ordered implied the health and
efficacy of the creative intelligence behind it and reflected that
higher reality of '*la belle Nature*' of which it was an imitation.

Form, therefore, in a certain sense *is* meaning. It was not, however, Hutcheson or his mentor Shaftesbury who assured the currency of this basic premiss of Augustan aesthetics. In urging the
argument from design against the threat of epicurean materialism
newly revived by Hobbes, the divines of the Church of England
had already raised the ideals of Order and Form to a theological
principle. This is the burden of countless poems, essays, homilies
which either celebrate the beauty of the creation in terms of the
analogy of art, or, conversely, formulate a system of aesthetics by

1. Inigo Jones: Banqueting House, Whitehall, showing the double cube room

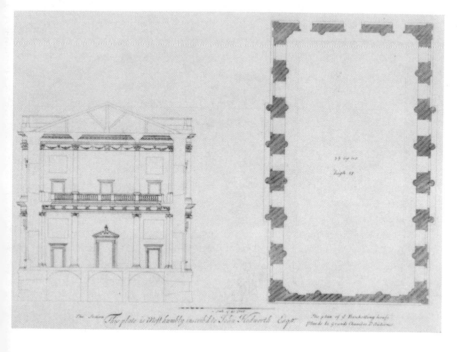

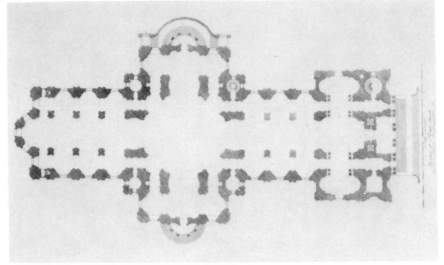

2 Sir Christopher Wren: St. Paul's Cathedral

3. Pope's House, Twickenham

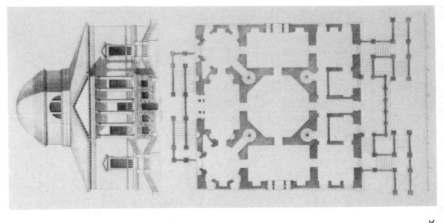

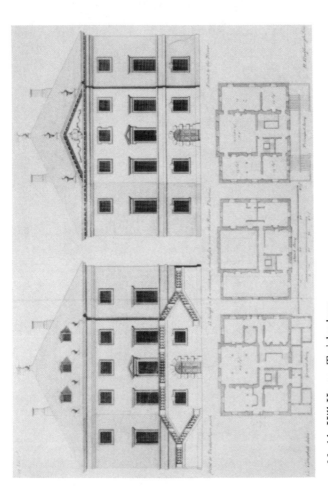

4. Marble Hill House, Twickenham

5. Burlington's Villa, Chiswick

reference to the inherent order of the creation. The two terms of the analogy were inextricably connected in Augustan thought: order in art and in the world—the one implied the other. For John Tillotson, for example, 'this vast curious engine of the world' argues for the existence of 'the great artificer' behind it, just as the human artefact—the poem, picture, or building—implies the poet, painter, or architect:[110]

> As any curious work, or rare engine doth argue the wit of the artificer; so the variety, and order, and regularity, and fitness of the works of GOD, argue the infinite wisdom of him who made them; a work so beautiful and magnificent, such a stately pile as heaven and earth is, so curious in the several pieces of it, so harmonious in all its parts, every part so fitted to the service of the whole, and each part for the service of another; is not this a plain argument that there was infinite wisdom in the contrivance of this frame?[111]

The point, indeed, was a commonplace among the divines of the seventeenth and eighteenth centuries—with John Ray, Isaac Barrow, Robert South, Samuel Clarke, and many others who celebrated the 'correspondence and symmetry',[112] the 'fulness and regularity',[113] the 'admirable Artifice and exact Proportion and Contrivance'[114] of the creation. For Barrow, 'Chance never writ a legible book; Chance never built a fair house; Chance never drew a neat picture'; and the world was a much more splendid work of art.[115] For Clarke, the Deity was '*That* Power, which in the frame and construction of the *natural* World, had adjusted all things by Weight and Measure: *That* Power, which with exquisite artifice has made every thing in the exactest harmony and pro-portion, to conspire regularly and uniformly towards accomplish-ing the best and wisest Ends, in compleating the beautiful Order and Fabrick of the *Material* Universe'.[116] For Blackmore, pious physician and poet of *Creation* (1712), the order and nice design of the world's fabric rivalled the productions of the master builder of the Renaissance:

> See, what bright Strokes of Architecture shine
> Thro' the whole Frame, what Beauty, what Design! . . .
> Does not this Skill ev'n vye with Reason's Reach?
> Can *Euclid* more, can more *Palladio* teach?[117]

To an age which cherished order and the rational virtues—an age, as we shall see, to which Providence and Prudence were analogous terms[118]—the pure forms of classical architecture served as a peculiarly appropriate metaphor for both macrocosm and microcosm alike; they are, as it were, the objective correlative of the Augustan ethos. To a man like John Evelyn, the architectural confusion of London in 1664 was a sign not merely of bad taste, but, more disturbingly, of the moral disorder of the age: he complained to John Denham, then Superintendent of the King's Works, '*It is from the* Asymmetry *of our* Buildings, *want of* Decorum *and* Proportion *in our* Houses, *that the* Irregularity *of our* Humours *and* Affections *may be shrewdly discerned* . . .'[119] For Pope, too, as Maynard Mack has shown,[120] the practice of good architecture was a moral act. Others seeking to define the rational or the civilized man found it a natural analogy. The deist Matthew Tindal speaks of 'the Rule of right Reason' as being alone capable of producing 'true Symmetry in [our] intellectual Buildings'.[121] And James Forrester describes his 'polite philosopher' in terms of one of the masterpieces of English Palladianism:

> That true Politeness we can only call,
> Which looks like *Jones*'s Fabrick at *Whitehall*:
> Where just Proportion we, with Pleasure, see,
> Tho' built by *Rule*, yet from all *Stiffness* free.
> Tho' grand, yet plain, magnificent, not fine,
> The Ornaments adorning the Design.
> It fills our Minds with rational Delight,
> And pleases on Reflection, as at Sight.[122]

Whether he addressed himself to the great world of Nature or the little world of man, the Augustan philosopher was likely to imagine his subject as an architectural—or as a musical—composition; for in these, the most abstract of the forms of art, Nature's ideals of proportion, decorum, and design might be rendered intelligible to the senses. In a building by Palladio or Jones, in a symphony by Corelli or Purcell, it was possible to understand that the Beautiful, the True, and the Good are One.

iii. *Variety*

The apparent exception to the Augustan rule of regularity and symmetry, the formal characteristics of ideal Nature, is of course the development in England during the eighteenth century of the 'natural' landscape garden—what Christopher Hussey has called

'England's greatest contribution, perhaps, to the visual arts of the world'.[123] The men who believed that Nature was well imitated in the exquisite proportions of Marble Hill or of Burlington's villa at Chiswick, or in the balance and measure of the heroic couplet, were exactly those who condemned the fashion for geometrical regularity in gardening, which on the Continent continued to be regarded as a mode of abstract art.[124] Though Pope was the most eloquent advocate of the new style, in virtually every other respect he subscribed to the aesthetic and philosophic principles which we have been considering. In his own house at Twickenham as in his poetry, Pope prized balance and proportion and delimitation, a delicate harmony and nice symmetry effected by means of the most painstaking artifice. These, too, were qualities he cherished both in the world at large, where *concordia discors* was the principle of order, and in the moral life, which, as Professor Mack observes, Pope like Horace saw as 'a poem to be "formed"':[125]

> To Rules of Poetry no more confin'd,
> I learn to smooth and harmonize my Mind,
> Teach ev'ry Thought within its bounds to roll,
> And keep the equal Measure of the Soul.[126]

The gardens of such a man might be expected to resemble those of Le Nôtre or the Dutch, where strict geometrical designs forced Nature into conformity with what Père André would call 'le beau essentiel'. In England, as on the Continent, this was indeed the prevalent conception of gardening until well into the eighteenth century.[127] To Waller in 1661, St. James's Park, laid out in the French manner at the King's command, was a second Eden, Nature restored to her original perfection.[128] In a well-known passage from his essay 'Upon the Gardens of Epicurus', Sir William Temple, contrasting European and Chinese styles of garden design, makes clear that in 1685 geometrical regularity was the standard on both sides of the Channel:

> Among us, the Beauty of Building and Planting is placed chiefly in some certain Proportions, Symmetries, or Uniformities; our Walks and our Trees ranged so, as to answer one another, and at exact Distances. The *Chineses* scorn this way of Planting, and say a Boy that can tell an Hundred, may plant Walks of Trees in strait Lines, and over-against one another, and to what Length and Extent he pleases.[129]

But in this period the most dramatic (and delightful) proof of the firm ideological association of ideal Nature with the pure geometrical forms may be found in Thomas Burnet's celebrated work, *The Sacred Theory of the Earth* (1681). Burnet's whole system, in fact, may be said to stand on this basic premiss; for he was led to his curious conception of a smooth antediluvian earth by his reluctance to believe that the world as we know it, its beauty marred by mountains and by the rough channels of the sea, could possibly represent the original creation of God, the divine Geometrician. For Burnet, Paradise, the whole earth before the Fall, is a sort of regular, symmetrical garden, whose smooth and fertile surface is intersected by canal-like rivers flowing from the poles and is encircled by an equitorial zone resembling a magnificent gravel walk.[130] The world now, owing to Adam's sin, is 'deformed and irregular':

> And there appearing nothing of order or any regular design in its parts, it seems reasonable to believe that it was not the work of Nature, according to her first intention, or according to the first model that was drawn in measure and proportion, by the Line and by the Plummet, but a secondary work, and the best that could be made of broken materials. . . . If the Sea had been drawn round the Earth in regular figures and borders, it might have been a great beauty to our Globe, and we should reasonably have concluded it a work of the first Creation, or of Nature's first production; but finding on the contrary all the marks of disorder and disproportion in it, we may as reasonably conclude, that it did not belong to the first order of things, but was something succedaneous, when the degeneracy of Mankind, and the judgments of God had destroy'd the first World, and subjected the Creation to some kind of Vanity.[131]

That these bizarre speculations seemed plausible to many readers of the period—to Gilbert Burnet, Newton, and James Thomson, for instance—is amply demonstrated in Marjorie Nicolson's account of the controversy Burnet's work stimulated.[132] To an age which saw the universe as the creation of a Being supremely rational and benign—a Being whom Richard Bentley, following Plato, represents as 'that eternal Fountain of Wisdom, the Creator of Heaven and Earth, who *always acts Geometrically*, by just and adequate numbers and weights and measures'[133]—nothing could have been more 'natural' than harmony, symmetry, proportion.

Burnet's theory was clearly troublesome to those scientists and divines who shared his aesthetic assumptions, yet who sought to deduce the divine attributes from the obviously irregular frame of the world. Bentley serves admirably to illustrate the dilemma.

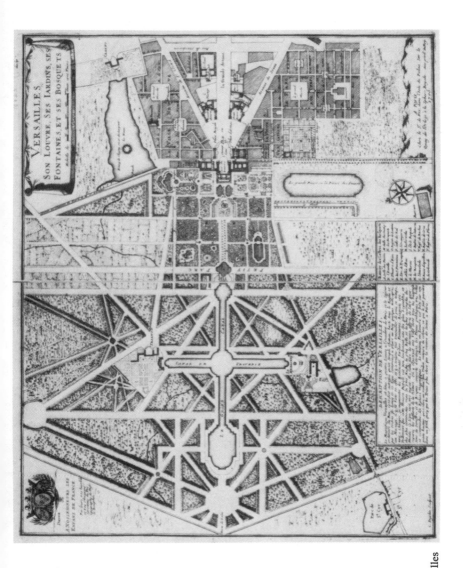

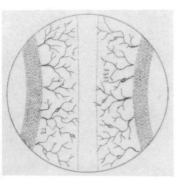

6. Burnet's Plan of Paradise

7. Le Nôtre's Gardens, Versailles

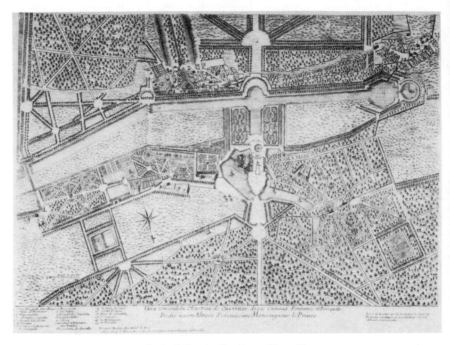

8. Le Nôtre's Gardens, Chantilly

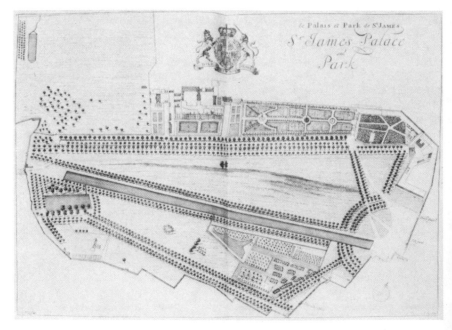

9. St. James's Park, as improved by Charles II

In the same Boyle lecture in which he praised God for working always according to geometrical laws, he mocks Burnet for inferring from the same premisses that the earth is fallen and deformed:

> But some men are out of Love with the features and meen of our Earth; they do not like this rugged and irregular Surface, these Precipices and Valleys and the gaping Channel of the Ocean. This with them is Deformity, and rather carries the face of a Ruin or a rude and undigested Lump of Atoms that casually convened so, than a Work of Divine Artifice. They would have the vast Body of a Planet to be as elegant and round as a factitious Globe represents it; to be every where smooth and equable, and as plain as the *Elysian Fields.* (p. 32)

In order to maintain the beauty and goodness of the creation—to answer, in effect, the charge that God was a less skilful gardener than Le Nôtre—Bentley is constrained to shift the grounds of the argument altogether; he became the first advocate in the period of an aesthetic subjectivism which looks forward to the theories of Burke and Alison. Bentley denies that beauty has any absolute basis in symmetry and regularity; it resides not in the shape of the object, but in the mind of the beholder. Of those who share Burnet's views, he says:

> Let them also consider, that this objected Deformity is in our Imaginations only, and not really in the Things themselves. There is no Universal Reason (I mean such as is not confined to Human Fancy, but will reach through the whole Intellectual Universe) that a Figure by us called Regular, which hath equal Sides and Angles, is absolutely more beautifull than any irregular one. All Pulchritude is relative; and all Bodies are truly and physically beautifull under all possible Shapes and Proportions; that are good in their Kind, that are fit for their proper uses and ends of their Natures. We ought not then to believe, that the Banks of the Ocean are really deformed, because they have not the form of a regular Bulwark; nor that the Mountains are mishapen, because they are not exact Pyramids or Cones; nor that the Starrs are unskilfully placed, because they are not all situated at uniform distances. These are not Natural Irregularities, but with respect to our Fancies only . . . (pp. 36–7)

Burnet might be perverse enough to find 'ravishing Charms in a dull unvaried Flat' (p. 39), but Bentley's notion of Eden is more Miltonic—more, we might add, like Pope's earthly paradise of Windsor Forest. It is '*a land of Hills and Valleys* with an infinite Variety of Scenes and Prospects' (p. 40).

Other causes doubtless contributed to effect what has been called 'the Great Gardening Revolution' in eighteenth-century

England, 'a reversal of taste without precedent in the history of gardening and hardly to be equalled in that of any other art'.[134] This signal departure from the aesthetics of regularity has been variously attributed to simple boredom with the dreary sameness of geometrical designs and to the rise of Whiggism, the English garden being, in Nikolaus Pevsner's phrase, 'the garden of liberalism'.[135] But it is difficult to believe that Frenchmen, not to mention the Italians and Dutch, were any less capable of being bored than their English counterparts, and Pope, like Bathurst, his friend and fellow gardener, was a Tory. To explain this peculiarly English phenomenon, we must look instead to ideas and circumstances which transcended political differences and which, as the seventeenth century turned, seemed of moment to Englishmen in particular. By promoting a radical reassessment of assumptions concerning the good and the beautiful in nature, Burnet's *Sacred Theory* led, as Miss Nicolson has shown, to a change in men's attitude toward the landscape and prepared the way for 'the aesthetics of the infinite'. In this respect, the different emphases in England and France during the period are perhaps comparable to what occurred in criticism; though in England the neo-classical rules of form continued to influence dramatic theory and practice, they were considerably liberalized. As the example of Shakespeare, let us say, required a greater latitude in estimating the importance of the unities, so in the appreciation of natural scenery, Burnet made it necessary for his countrymen to defend God's world from the charge of disorder and deformity. Well before Addison's papers on 'the Pleasures of the Imagination', pious divines such as Bentley and Erasmus Warren and John Ray had preferred, in Dryden's terms, the 'lively' to the 'just' in beholding the world's theatre; they declared their deeper satisfaction with the rich variety of nature as she was—with the pleasing spectacle of hills and valleys, woodlands and plains, and meandering rivers—than with Burnet's conception of a Paradise flat and geometrically arranged. Le Nôtre's gardens at Versailles may have been truer to the neo-classical theory that 'la belle Nature' was regular in all her ways, but the Burnet controversy made it possible—and not only possible, but in a sense theologically necessary—for men like Pope and William Kent to delight in the subtler harmonies of the English countryside.

At Timon's villa, Pope could despise as unnatural the very

manifestations of regularity, symmetry, and delimitation which he otherwise (as in the form of his verse, for instance) approved:

> His Gardens next your admiration call,
> On ev'ry side you look, behold the Wall!
> No pleasing Intricacies intervene,
> No artful wildness to perplex the scene;
> Grove nods at grove, each Alley has a brother,
> And half the platform just reflects the other.
> The suff'ring eye inverted Nature sees,
> Trees cut to Statues, Statues thick as trees . . .[136]

It was necessary instead to 'Consult the Genius of the Place in all' (l. 57), and to suggest in miniature Nature's diversity and her abhorrence of constraint: 'He gains all points, who pleasingly confounds, / Surprizes, varies, and conccals the Bounds' (ll. 55–6).

To be a gardener in this way was to make of one's estate a sort of paradigm of universal Nature, to emulate the subtle and beneficent designing of the Deity. If Timon is a standing example of how not to follow Nature in estate planning, the paragons in this respect are Bathurst and Burlington, 'earls of creation' as James Lees-Milne has called them, whose plantations and buildings express Nature's own principles of usefulness and delight. To be a proper gardener in Pope's view required every humane virtue: taste and sense and skill and benevolence. As the product of intelligence and sensibility subduing the living materials of earth so as to provide a setting to nourish both the spirit and the body of man, a garden may be seen to imply the benign Order of the world, the garden of God's own creation, and it may stand as a symbol of a sustaining reciprocal relationship between man and Nature. In this sense it functions in Pope's poetry as an index of health and order at every level of life, from the individual to the community to the nation at large. This, as Maynard Mack suggests,[137] would seem to be among the private meanings of the garden Pope created at Twickenham. Within the context of the Tory agrarian ideal, furthermore, Bathurst's fruitful, gracious estates at Cirencester and Riskins comprise an emblem of social order and social love:

> His Father's Acres who enjoys in peace,
> Or makes his Neighbours glad, if he encrease;
> Whose chearful Tenants bless their yearly toil,
> Yet to their Lord owe more than to the soil;

> Whose ample Lawns are not asham'd to feed
> The milky heifer and deserving steed;
> Whose rising Forests, not for pride or show,
> But future Buildings, future Navies grow:
> Let his plantations stretch from down to down,
> First shade a Country, and then raise a Town.   (ll. 181–90)

Such men may serve, therefore, as a pattern for the 'Imperial Works' of the King himself, keeper of that vast garden which is England. 'You too proceed,' Pope exhorts Burlington,

> Till Kings call forth th'Ideas of your mind,
> Proud to accomplish what such hands design'd,
> Bid Harbors open, public Ways extend,
> Bid Temples, worthier of the God, ascend;
> Bid the broad Arch the dang'rous Flood contain,
> The Mole projected break the roaring Main;
> Back to his bounds their subject Sea command,
> And roll obedient Rivers thro' the Land . . .   (ll. 195–202)

The allusions in these lines to the first chapter of Genesis complete the ever-widening circle of correspondences extending from the local and particular to the larger spheres of communal and national life to encompass at last the idea of creation itself.[138] This, ultimately, is the metaphysical meaning of the act of gardening for Pope—the ideal that informs his theory of the 'natural' garden and that colours most instances of the garden as an image in his works. For in their labours to set the land in order, princes and noble lords and poets emulate the divine Gardener, whose universe, various, full yet coherent, Pope in the *Essay on Man* had compared to a grand country estate which he and Bolingbroke would explore together:

> A mighty maze! but not without a plan;
> A Wild, where weeds and flow'rs promiscuous shoot,
> Or Garden, tempting with forbidden fruit.
> Together let us beat this ample field,
> Try what the open, what the covert yield;
> The latent tracts, the giddy heights explore
> Of all who blindly creep, or sightless soar;
> Eye Nature's walks, shoot Folly as it flies,
> And catch the Manners living as they rise . . .   (i. 6–14)

The emphasis upon an 'artful wildness' among British theorists of the 'natural' garden may be better understood once we sense the necessity, after Burnet and Newton, for scientists and divines alike to adopt a less simplistic view of the order of things, a view that would make Nature's rudeness and variety and limitless extent fundamental elements in a more intricate, though by no means less real, harmony of creation. Thus Kepler had found even the apparent irregularities of the planets the source of a more exquisite heavenly music. And Newton's God, no less than Pope's ideal gardener, gained all points by making a pleasing intricacy and the concealment of bounds essential to His great Design. Indeed, to Pope and his contemporaries the world of Newton and the physico-theologians in its artful complexity seemed aptly figured as a kind of magnificent estate. Henry Pemberton, for example, the popular expositor of Newton's theories, assured the polite reader that with the aid of his book he would 'form a comprehensive View of the stupendous Frame of Nature, and the Structure of the Universe, with the same Ease he now acquires a Taste of the Magnificence of a Plan of Architecture, or the Elegance of a beautiful Plantation; without engaging in the minute and tedious Calculations necessary to their Production'.[139] To William Derham the analogy seemed equally appropriate, prompting him to figure the Deity as the supreme building earl of creation, a Bathurst or Cobham of universal Nature:

A Man that should meet with a Palace, beset with pleasant Gardens, adorned with stately Avenues, furnished with well-contrived Aquaeducts, Cascades, and all other Appendages, conducing to convenience or Pleasure, would easily imagine, that proportionable Architecture, and Magnificence were within: But we should conclude the Man was out of his Wits, that should assert and plead that all was the Work of Chance, or other than of some wise and skilful Hand. And so when we survey the bare Out-works of this our Globe . . .; when we see nothing wanting, nothing redundant, or frivolous, nothing botching, or ill-made, but exactly answereth all its Ends, and Occasions: What else can be concluded, but that all was made with manifest Design, and that the whole Structure is the Work of some intelligent Being; some Artist, of Power and Skill equivalent to such a Work?[140]

The principle that especially guided the English gardening theorists of this period is one that Derham admired in the order of the universe: 'in greater Variety, the greater Art is seen' (p. 55).

The dependence of gardening theory upon the new physico-theology is, however, nowhere more clearly revealed than in the series of annual lectures delivered at the church of St. Leonard,

Shoreditch, commencing in 1730. Emulating that better-known naturalist, Robert Boyle, the founder of this series was one Thomas Fairchild of Hoxton (1666–1729), a horticulturist of some skill and piety, who left a small benefaction providing for a sermon every Whitsun Tuesday on the '*Wonderful Works of God in the Creation*', specifically in the vegetable creation.[141] In his treatise *The City Gardener* (1722) Fairchild reveals his own preference for the 'natural' as opposed to the geometrical garden, and, in a brief passage, anticipates the theme of those who later preached on his foundation: 'whoever understands, and loves a Garden, may have Content if he will, because he has Opportunity every Day of contemplating the Works of the Creation, and of admiring the Power and Wisdom of the Creator; which I think is the greatest Happiness' (p. 9). In the inaugural sermon of the series, John Denne echoed this sentiment after drawing freely on Derham, Ray, and the Boyle lecturers: 'Methinks every field and garden must be looked upon by wise and good men, as a place consecrated to religious worship, and dispose them to continual exercises of devotion.'[142] Three years later, Denne's sermon on the same occasion is notable for making clear the religious grounds which nourished the new movement in gardening. Since the beauty of the countryside is of God's own designing, Denne applauds Addison's preference of Nature to 'all the works of art', and he notes with satisfaction that the English aristocracy are at last achieving a genuine classicism in their gardens by 'following *Nature*', as Homer had represented in the gardens of Alcinous and as Virgil had advised in the *Georgics*. Denne, too, supplies the rationale for those such as William Kent who advocated the remodelling of entire estates into landscapes resembling the compositions of Claude and Poussin and Salvator Rosa. The rich, Denne observes,

. . . are now imitating the *Antients* in their taste, or rather following *Nature*, by making their gardens to resemble fields and orchards, and throwing down all inclosures, that they may see with every common eye the natural beauties of their whole estate, and the blessings of its increase, when cultivated and improved by the painful labours of the honest husbandman; that they may see the *valleys standing thick with corn*, the *hills* enrich'd with timber, the *orchards* in their bloom, or full of *fair* and *goodly fruit*, their *pastures clothed* with grass, and *arrayed* in all the *glory* of flowers, and their *fields* agreeably divided by trees and hedges; which all together do compose the finest Vista's, Prospects and Landschapes; such as the most skilful *Painter* faintly copies, or invents for the furniture of

Palaces. And to speak the truth, there are as many *Beauties*, and as great *Curiosities* growing wild in common fields, (were they but as rare) as can be collected at great expence in the best of gardens. The Country without much art opens into an inexpressible variety of scenes, which diversify the face of the earth, and fill the mind with a perpetual succession of pleasing images, so that 'one can hardly ever be weary of rambling from one labyrinth of *delight* to another': or if one is, we may [*vide Spectator*, No. 477] *sit down* with like *delight under the shadow* of Vegetables.[143]

Though Denne and his fellow lecturers on the Fairchild foundation have been neglected by students of the period, they help to make clear that one important basis for the change in attitude leading to the development of the 'natural' English garden was Christian, the marriage between science and religion that Newton and the physico-theologians had effected. Citing Ezekiel 36 : 35 and Ecclesiastes 2 : 5, Denne could find comfort in the knowledge that, if the world was fallen, the English aristocracy had succeeded in creating a new Eden through a better understanding of the 'Arts of Agriculture and Gardening':

And it is one *good* sign in these *bad* days to see [those arts] flourishing and improving; to see *natural Philosophy* in high repute; to see our *Princes*, our *Nobles*, and the *Rich* among us, conversant therein, and employing their thoughts and wealth in designing and *making gardens and orchards*, in *planting* them with *all kinds of fruit*, in laying out *Walks*, cutting *Avenues*, and opening *Vistas*, and *fertilizing* their Lands, till the *Country* around them, that was *barren* and *desolate*, becomes like the *Garden* of *Eden*, yielding whatever is *pleasant to the sight*, and *good for food*.   (p. 26)

Denne's exalted conception of the new mode is close to what we have observed in Pope—close, too, to that of Addison, for whom a proper garden, recalling 'the Habitation of our First Parents before the Fall', gave 'great Insight into the Contrivance and Wisdom of Providence . . .'.[144] The process they intend was not a capitulation to nature in her rude and random condition, but a realization, through the subtlest art, of her inherent potential for harmony and fruitfulness. By thus enhancing the English countryside, the Cobhams, Bathursts, and Burlingtons of this period were attempting to bring the terrain a little closer to the order in variety that once ideally obtained in Paradise—a Paradise quite unlike the geometrical garden of Burnet's imagination, but no less artfully contrived. As William Stukeley, another of the Fairchild lecturers, remarked thirty years after Denne: in creating the world,

'GOD almighty was not only a skilful, but an *orderly* workman; to teach us, to use order, and method, and regularity, in all our works [;] for we may say with great propriety, he plan'd it, and adorn'd; he laid it out, like a beautiful *garden*, and then planted it'.[145]

Denne's enthusiasm for natural beauty and Stukeley's insistence upon method and regularity throw into sharp relief a contradiction apparent (to a twentieth-century reader) in most gardening theorists of the period. Based on firm theological assumptions about the sacred attributes of ideal Nature, the aesthetics of regularity were not discarded at a stroke. By attending merely to what is *said* concerning the importance of 'natural' features in a garden, one might well be misled into the belief that English theorists had never applied the standards of pure form to gardening, in which, in a way obviously unlike that of any other art, Nature herself supplied the materials for imitation. This certainly appears to be Sir Henry Wotton's view as early as 1624, who noted 'a certaine contrarietie betweene *building* and *gardening*: For as Fabriques should bee *regular*, so Gardens should be *irregular*, or at least cast into a very wilde *Regularitie*'.[146] But the persistence of the strictly formal garden throughout the seventeenth century and well into the eighteenth century suggests that we probably misunderstand the assumptions and real intention behind such a caveat.

Once we arrive at the period of Pope, the problem of grasping what is meant by the imitation of Nature in a 'natural' garden is no less difficult. Introducing his translation of the Gardens of Alcinous in *The Guardian*, No. 173 (29 September 1713), Pope, a leader of the new movement, could praise Homer's description as 'the most beautiful Plan of this sort that can be imagined'; yet we find that the gardens themselves are as trim and artfully organized as they are various and useful: they are 'Fenc'd with a green enclosure all around', their 'order'd vines in equal ranks appear', with beds of herbs arranged 'In beauteous order'. To a modern reader, Addison and Shaftesbury, both often cited as champions of irregularity and wildness, seem just as inconsistent. Though Addison in certain moods could admire 'the rough careless Strokes of Nature', whose 'infinite Variety of Images' was a source of more lasting pleasure than the 'Beauties of the most stately Garden' could afford, he yet insists that 'we find the Works of Nature still more pleasant, the more they resemble those of Art'.[147] In *The Moralists*, Shaftesbury scorned 'the formal Mockery of princely Gardens', favouring instead 'Things of a *natural* kind; where neither *Art*, nor the *Conceit* or *Caprice* of Man has spoil'd their *genuine Order*, by breaking in upon that *primitive State*';[148] yet, as we have seen, he emphasized at the same time that the love of order and proportion was natural to man. Robert Morris sounds unequivocal enough as an advocate of naturalism: 'I would have no Garden laid out by Art, but such only as Nature it self produc'd . . .'; yet, as a staunch disciple of Shaftesbury, he could conceive of nothing beautiful unless formed according to the strictest rules of proportion, because, of course, proportion was 'natural':

. . . without it nothing can be perform'd to give Pleasure to the EYE. And I must at the same time observe, that all Proportions are founded upon *Rules*, and all *Rules* are dependent on *Nature*; and if in Nature there happen some Deviation, some *Luxuriancy* or *Want*, even those PHÆNOMENA may be mostly accounted for. The wanton *Vine* may be directed by Art not to shoot into superfluous Branches, and the more sturdy *Oak* may, by *Rules*, be *directed* in its Growth. Both flow from Causes in Nature, and both are to be guided by the skilful Hand of the Artist.[149]

Faced with contradictions this fundamental, we would do well to follow the most authoritative students of the English garden who resolve the paradox by defining Nature in terms that Pope and Addison, Shaftesbury and Morris, would have found congenial: not, in a nineteenth- or twentieth-century sense, as 'the sum of visible phenomena not made by artifice', but as 'the "ideal" form, theoretically achievable'. Shaftesbury, Christopher Hussey continues, 'used the concepts "wilderness" and nature's "primitive state" equally as symbols of the universal divine order: that scientific order revealed to the 17th century by Newton, Hooke and Wren through microscope and telescope . . .'.[150]

As the Augustan Age faded into the Age of Sensibility, a new breed of gardeners—practical men such as Launcelot Brown, Uvedale Price, and Humphry Repton—saw the task of imitating Nature in a more literal way, transforming the English country-side into a sort of panoramic landscape painting. Earlier, that same task was regarded as the process of bringing Nature closer to an ideal form more or less abstractly conceived. In France, as Wolfgang Herrmann points out, a man like Laugier, applying the identical criterion of 'truth to Nature', could summarily condemn the gardens at Versailles while at the same time praising Le Nôtre's (to us) equally geometrical design at Chantilly.[151] In England a variety of causes, of which the Burnet controversy was perhaps the most compelling, led to a more liberal conception of how Nature should be imitated in a garden; but even in England theorists were by no means yet prepared to abandon the aesthetics of regularity altogether. It was not wildness itself that Addison admired in a garden, but the *illusion* of it—what he called an 'artificial Rudeness': we take most pleasure, he declared, in 'such a Variety or Regularity as may seem the Effect of Design, in what we call the Works of Chance'.[152] To neo-classical aestheticians a high degree of artificiality was perfectly consistent with the doctrine of mimesis. By glancing at John Searle's diagram of Pope's grounds at Twickenham[153] and pondering the description published in *The Newcastle General Magazine* (January 1748),[154] one may better comprehend the extent to which Pope's conception of what is 'natural' in a garden can accommodate the Augustan faith in artifice and geometrical form. As Professor Mack remarks: 'The "naturalness" here is of course naturalness in an Augustan not a nineteenth-century sense: not oppressively trammeled or corseted by man, yet always conspicuously responding, as Ruskin would eventually point out of all classically arranged landscapes, to human pleasure and human need.'[155]

For a modern reader, the discrepancy between the theoretical statements and the actual productions of the English school is indeed marked enough to reinforce the point we have been making: the principles of formal regularity and deliberate artifice were so inextricably a part of Augustan thinking about the ways in which Art imitated Nature that, though they might be modified or disguised, they could not be wholly abandoned. Paradoxically, beauty in a 'natural' garden was still, and quite obviously, the effect of the orderly contrivances of Art.

Of this, graphic proof is available in two little-known works of the period, Stephen Switzer's *Ichnographia Rustica* (1718) and Robert Castell's *The Villas of the Ancients Illustrated* (1728). Switzer's voluminous treatise setting forth the rules for laying out a country estate is one of the earliest formulations of the new style. Like Pope, he recommends that the aspiring gardener conceal the bounds and 'cashiere that Mathematical Stiffness in our Gardens,

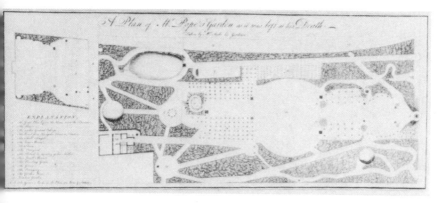

10. Pope's Gardens, Twickenham

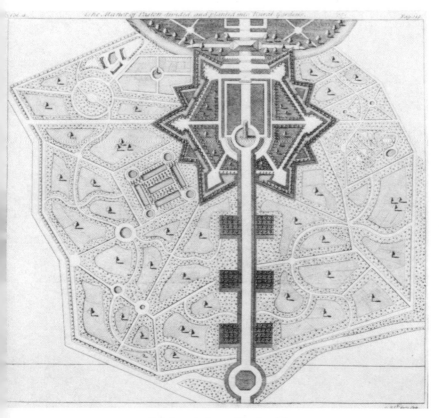

11. Stephen Switzer: Garden Plans

12. Robert Castell: Pliny's Estate, Tuscum

and imitate Nature more';[156] yet the designs he includes to exemplify these principles are, to a modern eye, extremely regular. From Castell we may gain a still clearer understanding of the ideals of the Burlington circle with regard to estate planning. A handsome folio volume appropriately dedicated to Burlington, *The Villas of the Ancients* is an attempt to reconstruct, through commentary and diagram, the Roman villas referred to by Pliny, Varro, and other historians. In Part III, Castell describes Pliny's estate at Tuscum as an ingenious combination of the two sorts of gardens, 'the Natural, *or those that are seemingly so*, and the Artificial or Regular'.[157] The charm of the place was owing to the deft arrangement of surprises and contrasts, an 'artful wildness', as Pope would say, serving to set off the predominant formality: 'through its winding Paths One as it were accidentally fell upon those Pieces of a rougher Taste, that seem to have been made with a Design to surprize those that arrived at them, through such a Scene of Regularities which (in the Opinion of some) might appear more beautiful by being near those plain Imitations of Nature, as Lights in Painting are heightened by Shades' (p. 117). That even the 'wildest' grounds were to be artfully contrived is clear from Castell's description of the Chinese garden, which, for him as for Sir William Temple, was the standard of extreme informality: its beauty consists 'in a close Imitation of Nature; where, tho' the Parts are disposed with the greatest Art, the Irregularity is still preserved; so that their Manner may not improperly be said to be an artful Confusion, where there is no Appearance of that Skill which is made use of, their *Rocks*, *Cascades*, and *Trees*, bearing their natural Forms' (pp. 116–17). As here we may recall Pope's ideal gardener, who 'pleasingly confounds', so in the following passage we may be reminded of Timon, whose 'Trees cut to Statues' afflict the 'suff'ring eye' with images of 'inverted Nature'. What Castell chiefly objects to in the formal garden is topiary work, whereby trees are 'cut into unwarrantable Forms, if the Ornaments of Gardens are allow'd to be only Imitations of Nature's Productions; for it cannot be supposed that Nature ever did or ever will produce Trees in the Form of Beasts, or Letters, or any Resemblance of Embroidery, which Imitations rather belong to the Statuary, and Workers with the Needle than the Architect; and tho' pleasing in those Arts, appear monstrous in this' (pp. 117–18). Both Castell and Pope insist that the gardener follow Nature, but, just as

C

Searle's plan is a better guide to the real significance of Pope's theories than any abstract statement, so Castell's design of Tuscum will serve to caution us against equating Augustan and twentieth-century notions of what is 'natural'. There is no suggestion that artifice is to be repudiated altogether, or even *entirely* concealed. Obvious distortions of natural shapes are rejected as displeasing, but the gardener, like any neo-classical artist, controls and organizes his materials. In general, the ideal is that Nature must be brought into harmony with Art.

Augustan aestheticians were not, of course, blind to the very real distinction between pure form in art or geometry and our actual experience of nature or life. The source of our pleasure in the abstract arts, such as music and architecture, was seen to be essentially different from the source of our pleasure in the imitative arts, such as painting or poetry—or gardening. No one in the period understood this better than Francis Hutcheson, who, as we have seen, defined 'absolute' or 'original' beauty by reference to our instinctive delight in harmony and design, but who also recognized that our pleasure in the imitative arts chiefly derives from a 'relative' or 'comparative' beauty: that is, in comparing the work with the original, we are gratified by the *justness* of the artist's representation of his subject, even though the subject in itself may be unlovely or terrifying. The painter's deft depiction of 'the *Deformitys* of old Age' or of 'the *rudest Rocks* or *Mountains* in a *Landskip*' (p. 41) may please in a way similar to the dramatist's rendering of the tragic circumstances of life. What is true of poetry or painting, he observes, is no less true of gardening, the greatest pleasure in these instances stemming from the artist's skilful mingling of the two kinds of beauty, the beauty of truth and the beauty of pure form. In tragedy, for example, meter and unity of design supply our instinctive desire for harmony and order, whereas the faithful representation of an Oedipus or a Tamerlane satisfies our desire for truth. Artists, Hutcheson explains, do not always

form their Works so as to attain the highest Perfection of *original Beauty* separately consider'd; because a Composition of this *relative Beauty*, along with some degree of the *original* Kind, may give more Pleasure, than a more *perfect original Beauty* separately. Thus we see, that strict *Regularity* in laying out of Gardens in *Parterres*, *Vista's*, *parallel Walks*, is often neglected, to obtain an Imitation of *Nature* even in some of its *Wildnesses*.

And we are more pleas'd with this *Imitation*, especially when the Scene is large and spacious, than with the more confin'd Exactness of *regular Works*. (p. 44)

Though Pope's garden at Twickenham was, like its maker, diminutive, not 'large and spacious', it otherwise serves admirably to exemplify these remarks: in its hillocks and rockeries, wildernesses and serpentine walks, the rough variety of Nature was closely imitated; in contrast, its alleys and vistas, serried groves and quincunces and plots of tidy lawn, offer pleasures of a different kind—the pleasures of Art, of pattern, design, and geometrical form.

A nice mixture of beauties, in Hutcheson's terms, both 'relative' and 'absolute', the English 'natural' garden of this period developed from the assumption that the proper function of Art is not to remake Nature in man's image (as Burnet had done in reconstructing Paradise by plumb-line and compass, or as Le Nôtre had done at Versailles), but to enhance and humanize her—bringing the terrain which is the immediate setting for a man's life appreciably closer to Nature's own benign ideals of discipline and profusion, of uniformity amidst diversity. At Twickenham, Pope fashioned a paradigm of the world's subtle harmony: 'Where Order in Variety we see, / And where, tho' all things differ, all agree.'[158] He did so knowing that this harmony could be heard only by the rational soul and that Art alone, reason's handmaid, could help to make it audible.

II. ART AS THE IMITATION OF NATURE

Part at least of what Pope's contemporaries understood by the paradox, 'All Nature is but Art', should now be clear. The delight in form and artifice that we have long associated with this period was a function of the Augustan faith in a world orderly in all its parts, from Newton's universe to the microcosm man: delight in form is the sympathetic response of rational men to those principles of harmony, symmetry, and proportion which they believed to be inherent in the creation. In redeeming the world from the threat of Chaos which Donne had feared in the disintegration of the Ptolemaic cosmology, and which others apprehended in the mechanism of Descartes and the materialism of Hobbes, the philosophers and divines of the late seventeenth and early eighteenth centuries had effectually re-established the Pythagorean and neo-platonic systems. Renaissance metaphors and modes of perceiving the world were not discredited by the new philosophy in any essential way; sophisticated, purged of mystery and superstition, they seemed more pertinent than ever in the pages of Newton, Shaftesbury, and the Cambridge theologians.

Another, equally important element in the Augustan world picture was the notion that, if Nature was Art, Chance, as Pope put it, was Direction. Both ideas ultimately derive from the Christian humanist tradition; both are fundamental premisses of the 'argument from design', newly revived in the period; and both, as we shall see, profoundly influenced the Augustan theory of imitation in the arts. As the work of the divine Artificer evincing harmony and proportion in all its parts, the world was aptly figured as an exquisite piece of music or architecture, or perhaps as an English garden; but as an event unfolding in time and involving human agents, it was properly seen as a play or poem with its own beginning, middle, and end—a drama whose every episode, from the fall of a sparrow to the bursting of a star, takes place within the providential scheme of history leading from Genesis to Apocalypse. History, for Henry More, was 'that large voluminous Period of Providence, which, beginning with the first *Fiat Lux* in *Genesis*, ends not till the last *Thunder-clap* intimated in the *Revelation*'.[159] Later, we shall consider how this idea influenced the formal organization of some of the masterpieces of Augustan literature, affecting the conception of chronological structure in Pope's *Pastorals* and *Dunciad* and Gay's *Trivia*, and of plot in Fielding's *Tom Jones* and Goldsmith's *Vicar of Wakefield*. It is time now to establish on firmer ground what we have so far been implying about the relation of the theory of Nature to the theory of Art in the period.

Another of the commonplace assumptions which the neo-classical poet or painter or sculptor inherited from the Renaissance was the idea of two levels of Nature: one, that perfect, orderly system of harmony and ideal beauty which God called into being at the beginning of time; the other, that imperfect, sublunary estate of flux and jarring multiplicity which is our wretched legacy from Adam. It was through the imitation of ideal Nature—in Batteux's phrase, '*la belle Nature*'—that Art improves upon actuality, restoring us, as it were, to Eden. In the latter sense above, Nature's world is 'brasen, the Poets only deliver a golden'.[160] Sidney's platonism in this regard is no more marked than that of the critics and aestheticians of the neo-classical period, whether in England or on the Continent. In his 'Parallel of Poetry and Painting' (1695), for example, Dryden quotes at length from Giovanni Bellori's *Vite de pittori, scultori, ed architetti moderni* (1672), a work that influenced the theory and practice of the visual arts for nearly a century:

'God Almighty [declares Bellori in Dryden's translation], in the fabric of the Universe, first contemplated himself, and reflected on his own excellencies; from which he drew and constituted those first forms which are called ideas. So that every species which was afterwards expressed was produced from that first idea, forming that wonderful contexture of all created beings. But the celestial bodies above the moon being incorruptible, and not subject to change, remained for ever fair, and in perpetual order; on the contrary, all things which are sublunary are subject to change, to deformity, and to decay. And though Nature always intends a consummate beauty in her productions, yet through the inequality of the matter the forms are altered; and in particular, human beauty suffers alteration for the worse, as we see to our mortification, in the deformities and disproportions which are in us. For which reason, the artful painter and the sculptor, imitating the Divine Maker, form to themselves, as well as they are able, a model of the superior beauties; and reflecting on them, endeavour to correct and amend the common nature, and to represent it as it was at first created, without fault, either in colour, or in lineament.'[161]

Accordingly, as Jonathan Richardson would have it, 'the painting-room must be like Eden before the fall, like Arcadia'.[162] As in painting, so in poetry, which John Dennis saw as 'a noble Attempt of Nature, by which it endeavours to exalt itself to its happy primitive State; and he who is entertain'd with an accomplish'd Poem, is, for a Time, at least, restored to Paradise'.[163] To Charles Gildon, who borrowed liberally from both Sidney and Dennis, the discrepancy between the poet's ideal world and the actual conditions of life was 'no small Argument to the incredulous of that first accursed Fall of *Adam*, since our Wit thus rais'd up by *Poetry*, makes us know what *Perfection* is, and yet our *Will*'s affected by that Fall, keep us from reaching up to the Practice of it'.[164]

In so far as he kept his eye on ideal Nature, the Augustan painter or poet could thus be regarded as a kind of redeemer, offering us bright images of Paradise, tuning our thoughts to the music of creation. Since the characteristics of Nature were Order and Design, harmony and symmetry and proportion, these would also be the formal qualities of Art. Ralph Cudworth may be allowed to summarize this relationship between the two artists, human and divine, the one creating Nature, the other imitating and reflecting that creation. Nature, like the written word, is the visible sign of its Author's mind, the 'living stamp or signature of the divine wisdom';[165] as 'the *orderly, regular and artificial frame* of things in the universe',[166] she is 'the stamp or impress of that infallibly omniscient art, of the divine understanding, which is the very law and rule of what is simply the best in every thing'.[167] As Cudworth and others glossed Aristotle for a later, Christian age, the function of the poet was thus to imitate the perfect art of Nature: 'When art is said to imitate nature, the meaning thereof is, that imperfect human art imitates that perfect art of nature, which is really no other than the divine art itself; as before *Aristotle, Plato* had declared in his Sophist, in these words . . . *Those things, which are said to be done by nature, are indeed done by divine art.*'[168]

Since, then, an artful design was the formal characteristic of Nature, the plastic expression of a wise and benevolent Creator, the business of the human artist was to reflect this fact in the symmetry and order of his own form, implying, as a consequence, the larger harmonies of the universe. The theories of the aestheticians and the critics were founded on the assumptions of the philosophers and divines. Shaftesbury, we remember, decried '*Gothick*' monstrosities in the designing arts, 'For HARMONY is Harmony *by Nature* . . . So is *Symmetry* and *Proportion* founded still *in Nature*.' For Dennis, since Nature 'is nothing but that Rule and Order, and Harmony, which we find in the visible Creation', so 'Poetry, which is an Imitation of Nature', must formally express these same qualities.[169] Similarly, when Gildon insists upon the strict observance of the dramatic unities, he does so by invoking Nature, 'that great plastic power that form'd all things, and rais'd this wonderful poem of the universe out of *chaos* and confusion into order, harmony, and number'.[170]

One of the clearest statements of this principle—which is in fine the principle of expressive form—is a little-known poem by Isaac Hawkins Browne, entitled *An Essay on Design and Beauty* (1739).[171] For Browne (or his anonymous collaborator), Design is the essential requisite for all art—'DESIGN, that Particle of heavenly Flame, / Soul of all BEAUTY' (p. 1). The poem is a useful compendium of terms and assumptions common in neo-classical aesthetics: the conception of art as artifice, the carefully fashioned and finished product of the human mind. The ultimate goal of the artist is seen as the achievement of 'lucid Order' (p. 7) and 'perfect Unity' (p. 8), wherein a 'Grateful Variety' (p. 7) is complemented and controlled by 'the Pow'rs of Symmetry . . . / Bright Emanation of Intelligence' (p. 10), and wherein part relates to part, harmoniously and proportionately, each 'directed to one common End' until 'the Relation centers in a Whole' (pp. 2–3). The rationale for this exaltation of design and artifice is essentially the same as that proposed by Cudworth, Dennis, Shaftesbury, Hutcheson, and many others—the notion that human art must emulate Nature, the perfect art of God:

> THE Love of Order, sure, from NATURE springs,
> A Taste adapted to the State of Things.
> NATURE the Power of Harmony displays,
> And Truth and Order shine thro' all her Ways.
> WHO that this ample Theatre beholds,
> Where fair Proportion all her Charms unfolds;
> The Sun, the glorious Orbs that roll above,
> Measuring alternate Seasons as they move;
> Who but admires a Fabrick so complete?
> And from admiring, aims to imitate?
> HENCE various Arts proceed; for human Wit
> But copies out the Plan by Nature writ.
> Truth of Design, which Nature's Works impart,
> Alike extends to every Work of Art;
> Where different Parts harmoniously agree,
> Together link'd in close Dependency;
> Supporting, and supported, in one Frame,
> Each has its several Use, and all the same.
> However various Ways they seem to tend,
> All are directed to one common End.
> Tho' wide dispers'd, yet in Proportion fall,
> Till the Relation centers in a Whole.   (pp. 2–3)

In this period a recurrent theme of all discussions of form in art is that, however imperfect she may appear to the clouded vision of men, Nature is the supreme Artefact, fashioned, according to John Gilbert Cooper, on the first day, when God's 'plastic word' dispelled 'dark Chaos . . . / And elemental Discord', bringing all creation into 'one harmonious plan'.[172] In *The Power of Harmony* (1745), a verse essay on the relation of beauty in Nature, morality, and art, Cooper asserts that the function of art is to comfort men, who are lost in this fallen, sublunary world, 'this vale of error' (p. 12), by reminding them of 'the plan / Of Nature' (p. 15), the

'UNIVERSAL HARMONY' (p. 48), which the Deity created and sustains. This is

> th' effect divine
> Of emulative Art, where human skill
> Steals with a Promethéan hand the fire
> Of Heav'n, to imitate cœlestial pow'r.   (p. 20)

To the Augustan artist, therefore, form had an ontological significance, implying the harmony and order of creation. It is not surprising that through Burlington's influence and example the early years of the eighteenth century saw the revival of interest in the pure geometrical forms of Palladian architecture, whose buildings embody those harmonic proportions and that symmetrical balance which were thought to inhere in the great frame of Nature. In the fourth book of his *Architecture*, Palladio himself had espoused the doctrine of design and expressive form which underlies Augustan art:

IF Labour and Industry are to be laid out upon any Fabrick, to the end that in all its parts it should have the exactest symmetry and proportion, this, without the least doubt, is to be practis'd in those Temples, wherein the most gracious and all-powerful God, the Creator and Giver of all things, ought to be ador'd by us . . . [God] being the chiefest good and perfection, it is highly agreeable, that all things dedicated to him should be brought to the greatest perfection we are capable to give them. And indeed, when we consider this beautiful Machine of the World, with how many marvellous Ornaments it is replenish'd, how the Heavens by their continual rounds change the Seasons according to the necessities of Men, and preserve themselves by the sweetest harmony and temperament of their motion; we cannot doubt, but that as these little Temples we raise, ought to bear a resemblance to that immense one of his infinite goodness, which by his bare word was perfectly compleated; so we are bound to beautify them with all the ornaments we possibly can, and to build them in such a manner and with such proportions, that all the parts together may fill the eyes of the beholders with the most pleasing harmony, and that each of them separately may conveniently answer the use for which it was design'd.[173]

This same analogy between 'natural' and 'artificial' architecture may well have been in Pope's mind when he satirized the *gaucheries* of a Timon and praised his friend Burlington, the building earl, for restoring 'Jones and Palladio to themselves'.[174]

Men like Burlington and Pope and Shaftesbury rejoiced in

Nature's fecund energy, her fulness and rich variety, but it was her other attribute, the principle of Order, on which their faith was founded. 'Method', Swift wrote to Stella, 'is good in all things. Order governs the world. The Devil is the author of confusion.'[175] And the synonymous term for Order is Art, the effect of the rational mind that shapes and organizes and directs. The universe of Newton and the physico-theologians is such a work of Art; so, too, is the little world of man, in so far as he has mastered what Cicero had called the *ars vivendi*.[176] As God's Providence orders and governs the world, so does the prudence of the moral man order and govern the passions. To the neo-classical critic or aesthetician, the implications of this belief were clear: since Order is the distinguishing characteristic of all creation—or of that part of it, at least, which did not fall with Adam—this fact must be expressed in the forms of Art, whether in architecture or music, painting or poetry or gardening. To fail in this obligation was not merely *gauche* and inelegant, an offence against the canons of good taste; much more to the point, it was to belie the proper character of Nature and of her divine Author.

No more explicit and comprehensive statement of this doctrine could be adduced than the following from John Dennis, who declares the necessity for rules and regularity in poetry by reminding his readers that Art, a rational Order, is the sacred principle both of Nature and of human life. The passage is long, but since it so admirably supplies the metaphysical rationale for the Augustan faith in Order, it deserves to be given in full:

Again [Dennis writes], if the End of Poetry be to instruct and reform the World, that is, to bring Mankind from Irregularity, Extravagance, and Confusion, to Rule and Order, how this should be done by a thing that is in it self irregular and extravagant, is difficult to be conceiv'd. Besides, the Work of every reasonable Creature must derive its Beauty from Regularity; for Reason is Rule and Order, and nothing can be irregular either in our Conceptions or our Actions, any further than it swerves from Rule, that is, from Reason. As Man is the more perfect, the more he resembles his Creator; the Works of Man must needs be more perfect, the more they resemble his Maker's. Now the Works of God, tho infinitely various, are extremely regular.

The Universe is regular in all its Parts, and it is to that exact Regularity that it owes its admirable Beauty. The Microcosm owes the Beauty and Health both of its Body and Soul to Order, and the Deformity and Distempers of both to nothing but the want of Order. Man was created, like the rest of the Creatures, regular, and as long as he remain'd so, he continu'd happy; but as soon as he fell from his Primitive State, by transgressing Order, Weakness and Misery was the immediate Consequence of that universal Disorder that immediately follow'd in his Conceptions, in his Passions and Actions.

The great Design of Arts is to restore the Decays that happen'd to human Nature by the Fall, by restoring Order: The Design of Logick is to bring back Order, and Rule, and Method to our Conceptions, the want of which causes most of our Ignorance, and all our Errors. The Design of moral Philosophy is to cure the Disorder that is found in our Passions, from which proceeds all our Unhappiness, and all our Vice; as from the due Order that is seen in them, comes all our Virtue and all our Pleasure. But how should these Arts re-establish Order, unless they themselves were regular? Those Arts that make the Senses instrumental to the Pleasure of the Mind, as Painting and Musick, do it by a great deal of Rule and Order: Since therefore Poetry comprehends the Force of all these Arts of Logick, of Ethicks, of Eloquence, of Painting, of Musick; can any thing be more ridiculous than to imagine, that Poetry it self should be without Rule and Order?[177]

For Dennis and his contemporaries, if not for the disciples of Ginsberg and Cage and Warhol in our own century, it was not through capitulation to accident or passion, but through the refining powers of form and reason that men could attune themselves to Nature's music and attain a liberating glimpse of Eden. In the chapters to follow, we shall consider the consequences of this assumption for the poetry of Pope and Gay and the fiction of Fielding and Goldsmith.

It should now be clear that the neo-classical poet, painter, or architect was no very servile imitator of ancient models, no merely passive reflector of Nature—a mirror, in Professor Abrams's figure, rather than a lamp. As John Gilbert Cooper understood, the Augustan artist regarded himself as emulating the 'cœlestial pow'r'. By submitting the energies of thought and passion to the control of form and artifice, he could be seen as recapitulating in paradigm the creative activity of the Logos, whose fiat first brought Order out of Chaos, Light out of Darkness. The true poet, Shaftesbury declared, is 'a real Master, or Architect in the kind, can describe both *Men* and *Manners*, and give to an *Action* its just Body and Proportions'; he is indeed 'a second *Maker*; a just PROMETHEUS, under JOVE. Like that Sovereign Artist or universal Plastick Nature, he forms *a Whole*, coherent and proportion'd in it-self, with due Subjection and Subordinacy of constituent Parts.'[178] In speaking the Word

that called the Book of Nature into being, the Deity, according to
Joseph Trapp, performed the archetypal poetic act: 'Poetry is co-
eval with the World itself, and . . . the Creator may be said in working up and finishing his beautiful Poem of the Universe, to have
performed the Part of a Poet, no less than of a Geometrician.'[179]
Accordingly, he continues, Virgil's *Æneid*, the most perfect production of human wit, has its model in Nature, the Art of God, in which
matter and abundant life are harmonized to form a coherent whole:

> To nothing this Work can with Justice be compar'd, unless to that,
> whose Duration will have the same Period, the great Machine of the Uni-
> verse. For where shall we find, in any human Composition, so exact a Har-
> mony between the several Parts, and so much Beauty in each of them; such
> an infinite Fecundity of Matter, without the least Exuberance of Style, or
> Crowding of Incidents? . . . in short, the most consummate Art, by which
> all these Things are brought into one uniform Piece?   (pp. 11–12)

Eventually, Hume would destroy the cogency of the argument
from design on which the assumptions of Augustan theology
and aesthetics mutually depended. In time, too, the subjectivist
implications of Locke's anatomy of the human mind would
deprive poets of any objective basis for the aesthetics of order and
artifice, by which harmony, symmetry, proportion had become
the indispensable formal attributes of the Augustan mode, the
symbolic expression of ideal Nature. For the present, however, the
analogy held between Nature and Art, between the divine Artificer
and what Dryden had called 'the providence of wit'. To Cowley
and to Pope, the skilful poet was 'God-like', the creator of harmonies
which once had echoed through the 'Groves of *Eden*'. To Fielding,
the intricate, regular design of *Tom Jones*, that 'great Creation',
reflected the providential order of things—the drama of life itself,
presided over by a genial, omniscient Author directing his actors
toward a just and joyous catastrophe. In a symphony by Corelli,
Alexander Malcolm could hear the music of creation. In the buildings of Palladio or Inigo Jones or his kinsman Roger Morris, Robert
Morris discerned that same harmony silently expressed through
proportion and symmetry. The victory of Chaos and old Night which
Pope envisioned in *The Dunciad* would soon be real enough; but
for one bright moment before the darkness fell, Newton and
the divines had restored the world to Order, giving new force to
the values and metaphors of the Christian humanist tradition. The
consequence for Augustan art was the triumph of Form.

II

Pope: Art and Time in the *Pastorals*

POPE'S poetic career began, as it ended, with the idea of the Golden Age—not with the myth only, but with its profoundest implications for the poet and the man, inheritor of the classicism that governed his conception of art and of the great Christian humanist tradition that conditioned his view of life. The butt of one of history's happier ironies, Pope found himself a Romanist Virgil in no very Augustan time. Like Virgil he began hopefully enough by celebrating the Golden Age in pastoral, recreating a lost ideal through the magical efficacy of artifice and the harmony of his numbers; but the promise of a second *Aeneid* which this beginning implied—an epic to immortalize the England of George Augustus—could be fulfilled in parody only, in satire proclaiming the grotesque apocalypse of 'Saturnian days of Lead and Gold'.[1] The distance between the green world of the *Pastorals* (1709) and the dark estate of *The Dunciad* (1728–43) is, to be sure, as immense as Pope's sad spiritual journey from the relative optimism of his youth (he began his eclogues when he was sixteen) to the utter disenchantment of his last years. But controlling and, in surprising ways, connecting both poems is the idea of the Golden Age—an idea comprehending both the Christian's conception of Time and History and, within this context, the poet's conception of the relationship of Art to Nature.

Pope's Virgilian poems make clear a fundamental assumption of his art and theology: this is the belief—as much moral and metaphysical as aesthetic—that Order, Form, Harmony are the sacred attributes of the highest reality, whether in the universe at large, or in the microcosm man, or in the artefact. Hence his continuing fascination with the creative act itself. Perhaps the simplest manifestation of this impulse in his poetry is the frequency with which he echoes and recalls the *fiat lux* of Genesis.[2] When Pope wishes to celebrate the institution of order in the body politic or in the physical sciences, or, conversely, when he wishes to deplore the subversion of order in morality or in literature, his language returns us to that moment when God's Word brought Light out of Darkness, Order out of Chaos:

> At length great *ANNA* said—Let Discord cease!
> She said, the World obey'd, and all was *Peace!*
>
> Nature, and Nature's Laws lay hid in Night.
> God said, *Let Newton be!* and All was *Light.*
>
> The skilful Nymph reviews her Force with Care;
> *Let Spades be Trumps!* she said, and Trumps they were.
>
> Lo! thy dread Empire, CHAOS! is restor'd;
> Light dies before thy uncreating word:
> Thy hand, great Anarch! lets the curtain fall;
> And Universal Darkness buries All.

The awful close of *The Dunciad* thus signals the triumph of Dulness, the death in a benighted world of the sacred values the poet has cherished. The forces of venality and barbarism, working their own perverse alchemy, have transformed the symbol of a golden age into the counterfeit of itself, where lead is substance and gilt the only value prized. But in *The Dunciad*, as in a negative image, one may discern the true shape of Pope's universe, the nature of his Christian vision of time, and the significance of those symbols and conceptual ideals that inform his work from first to last. Though the action of that poem, in a sardonic parody of Christian teleology, presents the apocalyptic victory of Chaos and Old Night, the *form* of the poem—Pope's nice control of language and his system of allusion—is the supreme assertion both of intellectual light, and of an order in history and in art that not even the prodigious incompetencies of a Cibber or the grasping machinations of a Walpole can abolish. The positive statement of these ideals had been given earlier in those complementary works, the *Essay on Criticism* (1711) and the *Essay on Man* (1733–4), wherein the neo-classical conception of Nature and of the poetic imitation of her is set forth discursively in couplets as finely wrought and balanced as the poet's universe itself. In the *Essay on Man* Pope had advised his reader that 'All Nature is but Art, unknown to thee; / All Chance, Direction, which thou canst not see'. Nature—according to Aristotle the subject of the poet's imitation—is, in

other words, the perfect artefact; and history, even more surely
than any play of Sophocles, has its own beginning, middle, and
end. To Pope, as to countless philosophers and divines of the
Christian humanist tradition,[3] the poet of the creation, of history,
is the Deity himself, the Word who brought Form and Order out
of Chaos, beginning propitiously enough what man has made
a tragic drama, and who at the final catastrophe will speak again,
dissolving time and the world into eternity. Of this creative function
of the Logos, the imitator and surrogate in the fallen, sublunary
realm of flux and decay is—or should be—the poet himself, whose
words and numbers have the transforming power to restore to us
a measure at least of grace and harmony, the power, as it were,
to remind us of the identity of Art and Nature that once obtained
in Eden, in the Golden Age.[4]

As Frank Kermode and Edward Tayler have demonstrated,[5]
the articulation of this theoretical relationship between Nature
and Art was long the special province of serious pastoral poetry
in the Christian era. In Virgil, whom Pope made his model, the
essential paradox of the pastoral mode is already clear; the most
sophisticated literary craftsmanship has become the means of
presenting, and therefore of recommending, an image of perfect
naturalness and simplicity. In Arcadia the Golden Age is restored,
Nature appears in her original unfallen condition, and the artificial manners and contrivances of civilization are scorned. Yet it
is only through the idealizing powers of imagination and the
refining powers of a mannered artifice that this return to Nature
has been effected. Pastoral is the product of the court, of an urbane,
sophisticated society very much aware that the loss of innocence
and simplicity is irremediable and that in this decadent Iron Age,
Art is the sole means of redeeming Eden. As in the myth of the
Golden Age recounted in the *Georgics*, Art may thus be seen as
man's compensation for the Fall. In his 'Discourse on Pastoral
Poetry' (1717), Pope insists on this redemptive function of artifice,
asserting that the Nature imitated by the pastoral poet is not that
discernible in the ordinary physical world of actuality, but is
rather that ideal realm available to us only through the imagination and expressible only in the images and harmonies of poetry:[6]
'If we would copy Nature,' he declares, 'it may be useful to take this
Idea along with us, that pastoral is an image of what they call
the Golden age. So that we are not to describe our shepherds as

shepherds at this day really are, but as they may be conceiv'd then to have been . . .'. The world of pastoral, he continues, is realized only through 'illusion' and by means of the most exquisite verbal harmonies, by numbers 'the smoothest, the most easy and flowing imaginable'.[7]

The essence of pastoral, as Pope understood, is the recognition of the Fall and of our desire to repudiate the wretched legacy of Adam. In this life, in the final stages of Nature's decay and of man's moral decadence, the Golden Age of innocence and perfect harmony between man and Nature is recoverable only through Art in the formal world of the eclogue itself. At the end of history, the true Golden Age will in fact be restored to men through the redeeming efficacy of Christ, the Logos and Messiah: this, as Christians from St. Augustine and Dante to Pope himself believed, was the esoteric import of that greatest and most curious of all pastoral poems of antiquity—Virgil's *Fourth Eclogue*. An awareness of these profounder implications of the mode will serve to clarify Pope's decision in 1717 to include his own sacred eclogue, 'Messiah', as the culminating poem in his series of Pastorals—a decision most critics regard as ill considered, but which was in fact necessary to the completion of a coherent and quite remarkable design. Taken together, Pope's poems on the seasons and his 'Messiah' comprise a unified, carefully developed paradigm of the relationship between Art and Nature in the context of Christian time. Though much useful scholarship has been published on the subject of the pastoral in the eighteenth century,[8] in our understanding of the poems themselves we have not yet progressed very far beyond Dr. Johnson's opinion that the form is 'easy, vulgar, and therefore disgusting'[9]—a mode suitable perhaps for juvenile versifiers to cut their teeth on, but not, after all, very substantial fare. To Johnson, the noblest prospect in Arcadia was the high road leading to something better; and to Pope himself, looking back as satirist upon the decorous productions of his youth, the *Pastorals* seemed little more than a holiday excursion in Fancy's maze.[10] Satire, after all, as the French critics had decided, was a nobler and more demanding genre than eclogue or georgic. However that may be, these five poems deserve a more careful reading than they have been given, for in them Pope realized, in some rather splendid verse, the latent aesthetic and philosophical implications of the pastoral mode.

If from Virgil Pope learned the function of high artifice in pastoral, it was in Spenser that he found a structure for the major theme of his work—the theme of Time. In his 'Discourse' Pope explained his admiration for Spenser's device of the calendar:

> The addition he has made of a Calendar to his Eclogues is very beautiful: since by this, besides the general moral of innocence and simplicity, which is common to other authors of pastoral, he has one peculiar to himself; he compares human Life to the several Seasons, and at once exposes to his readers a view of the great and little worlds, in their various changes and aspects.[11]

In adapting this structure to his own purposes, Pope fully elaborated the comparison between 'the great and little worlds', between the universe at large and the microcosm man, viewing both worlds from the perspective of Time implicit in the idea of the calendar itself.[12] The dominant tension in these poems is that between permanence and mutability, between the Great Year of Christian theology and the annual revolution of the seasons taken as a metaphor of human life and human history. In this way we are to understand Pope's assurance that he had improved upon Spenser's design by relating the seasons to 'the several ages of man, and the different passions proper to each age'.[13] In the movement of the year from spring to winter is implicit not only the idea of mortality, the troubled descent of man from youth to the grave, but also the mythic pattern of history, tracing mankind's sad decline from the Golden to the Iron Age, from Eden to the present moment. In this context of mortality and degeneration, Pope no less than Keats or Yeats believed the artist to be the sole agent of permanence and ideal beauty; for only in the Grecian urn or in the golden nightingales of Byzantium or in the formal world of pastoral is Time defeated, the fallen world perfected.

'Spring' depicts the Golden Age, the state of innocence before the Fall when art and life mirrored the perfection of Nature. The situation is a singing contest between the shepherds Daphnis and Strephon, who, after staking a bowl and a lamb as prizes and piously invoking Love and the Muse, proceed in counterpoint to celebrate the virtues of their sweethearts. Damon, the arbiter, determines that the contest is a draw, because, we may suppose, in this world judges are wise, poets equally skilful, and lovers equally fair and true: 'Blest Swains, whose Nymphs in ev'ry Grace excell; / Blest Nymphs, whose Swains those Graces sing so well!' (ll. 95–6). Although the poem develops according to a system of antitheses—Daphnis vs. Strephon, Sylvia vs. Delia, Venus (goddess of Love and Beauty) vs. Phoebus (god of poetry), the bowl vs. the lamb, Art vs. Nature—these tensions imply not conflict, but harmony. Like the genial debate of the shepherds proceeding in counterpoint to a perfect resolution—indeed, like the balanced form and musical repetitions of Pope's couplets—the opposing elements of the poem are happily reconciled; at the conclusion they are poised in a state at once of absolute autonomy and of mutual co-operation. In this Arcadian world the agent of harmony, who echoes the divine command of Genesis, is Damon, the judge and mediator: 'Cease to contend, for (*Daphnis*) I decree. / The Bowl to *Strephon*, and the Lamb to thee' (ll. 93–4). *Concordia discors*—the great principle of universal Order which Pope expounds in *Windsor Forest* and the *Essay on Man*—is in 'Spring' the condition of life.

This, then, is the image of the world the poem presents, the dramatic and formal expression of the idea of the Golden Age. The explicit moral of the poem is the one conventionally associated with this idea: the recommendation of innocence, of the naturalness and simplicity of the country as opposed to the affectation and worldly ambition of the court. Addressing Sir William Trumbull in the second paragraph, Pope dutifully declares his theme:

> *You*, that too Wise for Pride, too Good for Pow'r,
> Enjoy the Glory to be Great no more,
> And carrying with you all the World can boast,
> To all the World Illustriously are lost!   (ll. 7–10)

As Pope's footnote suggests, Trumbull—who 'was born in *Windsor*-Forest, to which he retreated after he had resign'd the post of Secretary of State to King *William* III'—is himself a living parable of this softly didactic theme of pastoral, which addresses a courtly and urbane audience to recommend a return to original innocence in the state of nature.

But all this is perfunctory. The intellectual impetus behind these poems is not so much ethical as aesthetic. What interests the poet is not so much the folly of the English court (*that* would come later!), nor, even at his tender age, any sanguine expectation that he may effect the wholesale translation of St. James to the Forest of Arden. Appropriately enough on this, the occasion of his first essay as a poet, what interests Pope is the making of poetry and the meaning of his art. This is the theme announced in the exordium and rendered in the emblem of Daphnis' bowl. The subject of the *Pastorals* is the nature, the mystery, the efficacy of Art itself, viewed in relation to those correlative concepts with which the artist is most nearly concerned: the meaning of Time and Nature in a fallen world.

> First in these Fields I try the Sylvan Strains,
> Nor blush to sport on *Windsor*'s blissful Plains:
> Fair *Thames* flow gently from thy sacred Spring,
> While on thy Banks *Sicilian* Muses sing;
> Let Vernal Airs thro' trembling Osiers play,
> And *Albion*'s Cliffs resound the Rural Lay.

Ostentatiously mellifluous and thick with allusions to the poets whose example he meant to imitate—to Theocritus and Virgil, Spenser and Milton—the opening of the *Pastorals* declares Pope's acceptance of the challenge of his art and, further, it implicitly asserts the power of the poet's song to transform '*Windsor*'s blissful Plains' into Arcadia, into Eden. In part, this transformation is effected through allusion, to Virgil and Milton in particular, with whom the literary ideas of Arcadia and Eden are chiefly associated: the 'Vernal Airs' and 'trembling Osiers' that play along the Thames in Windsor are echoes of Milton's description of Paradise and of the sacred river Jordan.[14] But the ideal of harmony and perfect order that Eden signifies—and which it will be the purpose of these eclogues to keep constantly before the reader—can be *realized* in the poem only through the music of Pope's numbers and his control of form. Hence the display of sonic devices such as alliteration and assonance and of mannered rhetorical symmetries; and hence, too, that elaborate fugal development of the principle of *concordia discors* which, as we have seen, is the formal expression of the idea of the Golden Age.

There is good reason, therefore, that Pope should have laboured to make these poems 'the most correct in the versification, and musical in the numbers, of all his works'.[15] In this design he succeeded so well that, in the opinion of his eighteenth-century critics, he effected a revolution in English prosody: Joseph Warton, for instance, found the *Pastorals* 'musical, to a degree of which rhyme could hardly be thought capable . . . the first specimen of that harmony in English verse, which is now become indispensably necessary';[16] and Dr. Johnson, who saw little else to approve in them, admired Pope's 'series of versification, which had in English poetry no precedent, nor has since had an imitation'.[17] What we have not appreciated is the *meaning* of the music. To a degree unparalleled in any of Pope's later works, music is the distinctive formal quality of the *Pastorals* because music, defined traditionally as a *concordia discors*, is here the poet's symbol for the Ideal, for order and perfection in Art and in the world. Though, as Warton and Dr. Johnson remarked, the harmony Pope achieved in these poems had no precedent in English verse, there was nothing novel about its symbolism. Thus, in his illuminating analysis of Dryden's and Pope's musical odes, Earl Wasserman observes that in the Christian humanist tradition music was a conventional metaphor for ideal creation: like the poet, God Himself is a 'Musician, and the universe is the song He sang into existence'.[18] In the *Pastorals*, no less than in the *Ode for Musick* (1713), formal harmony acquires an ontological significance: it is the expression and embodiment of the poet's theme, the recreation of an ideal order once, according to the myths of Eden and the Golden Age, known to men on earth but now attainable only through Art.

Pope's belief in this redemptive potency of poetry is clearly implicit in *Windsor Forest*: 'The Groves of *Eden*, vanish'd now so long, / Live in Description, and look green in Song' (ll. 7–8). Because they possessed this deific power, Denham and Cowley in the same poem are 'God-like' (l. 270) and—though one could wish Pope's choice of example were happier—Granville can effect a new creation, through song achieving, as it were, a second Nature[19] more perfect and durable than the world of actuality:

> But hark! the Groves rejoice, the Forest rings!
> Are these reviv'd or is it *Granville* sings?
>   'Tis yours, my Lord, to bless our soft Retreats,
> And call the Muses to their ancient Seats;
> To paint anew the flow'ry Sylvan Scenes,
> To crown the Forests with Immortal Greens,
> Make *Windsor* Hills in lofty Numbers rise,
> And lift her Turrets nearer to the Skies . . .   (ll. 281–8)

Like Diana, who metamorphosed the ravished Lodona into the chaste stream whose waters mirror an idealized landscape, the poet has the power to provide compensation for outrage, by a certain nobler alchemy transforming the Iron into the Golden Age.

In 'Spring' the relationship between Art and Nature is rendered by a different metaphor, not by an allegory of transformation, but by an object of art. The Bowl of Daphnis is here Pope's emblem for the *Pastorals* themselves. In the round perfection of its form and in the symbolic devices wrought upon it, the bowl embodies the meaning of the poet's work, which, as I have suggested, is the attempt by exquisite artifice and harmony to imitate ideal Nature, to recreate Eden. Though Pope has been more than once accused of slavishly following his predecessors in the pastoral tradition, the Bowl of Daphnis is no mere transcription of similar devices in Theocritus, Virgil, and Spenser;[20] in the economy of its representation and in its rich symbolic significance, it is quite unique— one of many instances in these eclogues in which Pope discloses new possibilities and new dimensions within the conventions of the genre. Here is the passage as Daphnis stakes his prize against Strephon's lamb:

> And I this Bowl, where wanton Ivy twines,
> And swelling Clusters bend the curling Vines:
> Four Figures rising from the Work appear,
> The various Seasons of the rowling Year;
> And what is That, which binds the Radiant Sky,
> Where twelve fair Signs in beauteous Order lye?   (ll. 35–40)

The several emblems engraved on the bowl symbolize the relationship between the poem and its subject, between Art and ideal Nature. As is clear from 'Summer', for instance, where Pope specifically identifies his work with 'this Wreath of Ivy' (l. 10), the circlet of evergreen ivy is one symbol of the poem, of the artefact itself; in contrast to this stand the 'swelling Clusters' of grapes that suggest both Nature's rich fruitfulness and her powers of inspiration. In the next line, the 'Four Figures rising from the Work' are immediately identified as an allegory of the seasons, and hence with the subject and the form of the *Pastorals* themselves. Moreover, the thought of the poem's relationship to the seasons and consequently to the theme of Time ('the rowling Year') leads to a final image—the 'beauteous Order' of the Zodiac, of the eternal heavens, the realm not of seasonal change and mutability, but of permanence and ideal reality. The answer to Daphnis' question— 'And what is That, which binds the Radiant Sky . . .?'—is clearly, then, the power of the Deity, the supreme Artificer of creation. As the bowl and its symbolism imply, the Art of God, binding the constellations in 'beauteous Order', is in an essential sense analogous to the craft of the poet, who fashions the 'Wreath of Ivy' that binds the materials of his art—Nature and the seasons— within the ordered and lovely fabric of the poem. In this context, the circle, traditional symbol of perfection, becomes Pope's metaphor for the power of art to unify, order, and contain: this is the import not only of the bowl itself, but of those images of roundness and encirclement it depicts—entwining ivy, swelling clusters, curling vines, the rolling year, and God's binding of the sky. The bowl of Daphnis is Pope's emblem for those other rounded artefacts, the *Pastorals* themselves and the sphere of the great creation. In it is implied the relation of Art to Nature which is the poet's chief concern in these poems.

As we have seen, the theme of 'Spring' is the celebration of *concordia*—the condition of the perfect harmony of life and art and nature in Eden. In contrast, the following three eclogues are elegiac in mood, depicting ever-worsening stages in man's estrangement from Eden. In 'Summer' the mourning song of Alexis for an unattainable mistress begins the theme of Time's victory, of deprivation and mortality, which culminates in 'Winter'. The poem is dedicated to the physician, Dr. Samuel Garth, because the world it describes is dis-eased. The sense of change and loss is immediate: spring has passed into summer, dawn into the heat of noon, youth into dissatisfied maturity, the Golden into the Silver Age. Love is here no longer a kindly god, but rather the cause of torment and distress: it is 'the sole Disease' the skilful physician cannot cure (l. 12), the only 'Serpent' in Eden (l. 68).

That this eclogue may be read as something more than a conventional love complaint is clear from the identity of the singer and the nature of his passion: Alexis is the figure of the Poet— indeed, of Alexander Pope, author of these pastorals[21]—and the object of his unrequited desire is nameless, that is, an abstraction. Through the efficacy of the shepherds' songs and the symbol of Daphnis' bowl, 'Spring' presented the triumph of Art, the mirror of ideal Nature; in the imperfect world of 'Summer' this happy condition no longer obtains. The opening lines echo Spenser's 'Januarye', Colin Clout's lament for the elusive Rosalind, and remind us that here, as in *The Shepheardes Calender*, the speaker is to be taken as a projection of the author himself.[22] But the despair

of Alexis is caused by the discrepancy between what he aspires to
achieve as a poet and what in fact is attainable. His ambition is
not to excel in the business of life, but to sing true songs, songs that
will gain him his mistress and secure his reputation:

> Let other Swains attend the Rural Care,
> Feed fairer Flocks, or richer Fleeces share;
> But nigh yon' Mountain let me tune my Lays,
> Embrace my Love, and bind my Brows with Bays.   (ll. 35–8)

Yet, though he has inherited the flute of Colin Clout, the master
poet of English pastoral, Alexis is sadly conscious of his own
inferior powers:

> That Flute is mine which *Colin's* tuneful Breath
> Inspir'd when living, and bequeath'd in Death;
> He said; *Alexis*, take this Pipe, the same
> That taught the Groves my *Rosalinda's* Name—
> But now the Reeds shall hang on yonder Tree,
> For ever silent, since despis'd by thee.   (ll. 39–44)

Seeking a cure for his disease, the burning after a hopeless love
that torments him, he has turned to poetry and found himself
inadequate. The Muses have deserted him, gracing the groves of
Academe where Cam and Isis flow, while he sits Narcissus-like,
disconsolately scrutinizing his face reflected in the crystal spring
(ll. 23–8). His art is good enough only to 'please the rural Throng'
(l. 49); for any higher purpose—to heal his heart (l. 34), to win
the object of his passion—it is unavailing.

Such doubts concerning his powers are perhaps understandable
and seemly enough in a 'Shepherd's Boy' of sixteen, but properly
to diagnose the poet's malaise, one must define the nameless
mistress he longs for. In 'Winter' we will find that she is to be
identified with Daphne—the principle of ideal Beauty and therefore of true poetic inspiration and power; according to the
Socratic view, she is the object of the higher *eros*. In 'Summer' she
is defined only through her attributes. Thus it is she alone who
deserves the poet's 'Wreath', for in her 'all Beauties are com-
priz'd in One' (l. 58). She is the source of all that is benign and
lovely in Nature:

> Where-e'er you walk, cool Gales shall fan the Glade,
> Trees, where you sit, shall crowd into a Shade,
> Where-e'er you tread, the blushing Flow'rs shall rise
> And all things flourish where you turn your Eyes.   (ll. 73–6)

And, most essentially in this context, the ideal harmony she expresses, like the song of Orpheus, is the means of an absolute power over Nature:

> But wou'd you sing, and rival *Orpheus*' Strain,
> The wondring Forests soon shou'd dance again,
> The moving Mountains hear the pow'rful Call,
> And headlong Streams hang list'ning in their Fall!   (ll. 81–4)

Alexis longs in vain to live with this ideal, to achieve the condition of perfect harmony enjoyed by the shepherd poets of 'Spring'. But in 'Summer' the Golden Age has passed; ideal Beauty has 'forsaken' (l. 71) the green world, where now 'the Serpent Love abides'—Love unsatisfied and insatiable. The poet cannot possess, though he can woo, the Ideal—in his words and numbers evoking her imperfect image, always and painfully aware of what he can never quite attain: 'On me Love's fiercer Flames for ever prey, / By Night he scorches, as he burns by Day' (ll. 91–2). The emblem for 'Summer' may be found in the image of Alexis viewing himself in the crystal spring, while 'Fresh rising Blushes paint the watry Glass' (ll. 27–8). For this poem is the parable of Alexander Pope's own self-scrutiny, the expression of the young poet's hopes and frustrations, aware of both the ideals and the limits of Art.

'Autumn', the next eclogue in the series, was the last in order of composition, and we may add that it is least successful in execution, least interesting in content. One feels that in 'Spring', 'Summer', and 'Winter' Pope had completed his intellectual design for the *Pastorals* and was now, for the sake of symmetry and wholeness, merely rounding out his Arcadian year. To be sure, there is an occasional felicitous couplet—'Here where the *Mountains* less'ning as they rise, / Lose the low Vales, and steal into the Skies' (ll. 59–60)—but for the most part the verse is, for Pope, undistinguished and the ideas are of a sort to justify Dr. Johnson's opinion that pastorals, 'not professing to imitate real life, require no experience, and, exhibiting only the simple operation of unmingled passions, admit no subtle reasoning or deep inquiry'.[23]

Still, the poem does carry forward Pope's parallelism between the gradual decline of the seasons toward the death of the year and the worsening condition of human life. In tracing the stages of man's estrangement from Saturnian felicity, we have in 'Autumn' reached the Age of Brass, when folly first entered the world and men became their own tormentors. Since Pope's theme is for the

first time moral, the usual topic of satire, the poem is appropriately dedicated to Wycherley, 'Whose Sense instructs us, and
whose Humour charms' (l. 9)—a comic writer, indeed, 'of infinite
spirit, satire, and wit'.[24] Hylas and Ægon are the speakers, love-
sick swains whose tribulations spring from different causes—'This
mourn'd a faithless, that an absent Love' (l. 3)—and whose folly
manifests itself in the different ways of suicidal despair and
euphoric self-delusion. For Hylas—as for Nature bereft of the warm-
ing sun—Delia's absence is death itself (ll. 27–30). But his 'melodious
Moan' makes '*Mountains* groan' (ll. 15–16), and the echoes of her
name he has started at last induce the happy fantasy that she has
returned to him:

> Go gentle Gales, and bear my Sighs away!
> Come, *Delia*, come; ah why this long Delay?
> Thro' Rocks and Caves the Name of *Delia* sounds,
> *Delia*, each Cave and ecchoing Rock rebounds.
> Ye Pow'rs, what pleasing Frensie sooths my Mind!
> Do Lovers dream, or is my *Delia* kind?
> She comes, my *Delia* comes!—Now cease my Lay,
> And cease ye Gales to bear my Sighs away!   (ll. 47–54)

Ægon, Hylas' fellow perpetrator of the 'mournful Strain',
laments a severer plight, the treachery of 'perjur'd *Doris*', who
has—one feels, understandably—abandoned him for another. In a
tuneful paroxysm of grief and self-pity, Ægon questions heaven's
justice (l. 76) and leaves his flock a prey: 'Ah! what avails it me,
the Flocks to keep, / Who lost my Heart while I preserv'd my
Sheep' (ll. 79–80). Though the shepherds reprove him for his
negligence and though Pan himself grows anxious at his ravings,
believing him bewitched, Ægon hugs his grief the closer, threatening to 'Forsake Mankind, and all the World—but Love!' (l. 88).
Suicide, he promises, will be his revenge on the world: 'One Leap
from yonder Cliff shall end my Pains. / No more ye Hills, no more
resound my Strains!' (ll. 95–6). Not Timon in affliction or Gloucester on the brink at Dover presents a more moving spectacle, it
would appear. But Pope's wry, hyperbolic language keeps us
aware of the absurdity of all this—of Ægon's ranting despair and
of Hylas' sanguine confidence in the efficacy of his sighs. When
the poet's voice is heard again at the conclusion, it is to assure
us that Delia's return was, indeed, the soothing effect of Hylas'
frenzy, and that Ægon, despite his threats of self-destruction, is

still alive and moaning in Arcady: 'Thus sung the Shepherds till th'Approach of Night . . .'.

Earlier I described the mood of 'Autumn' as elegiac, but it is so only with regard to the complaints of the shepherds themselves and to the sense, always a little distressing, of human folly which the poet means to convey. Pope's own attitude to the situation is rather one of dispassionate amusement, a stance vaguely reminiscent of Wycherley's, let us say, or that of the narrator of the *Rape of the Lock*. In a sense, 'Autumn', though an eclogue, is Pope's first essay in the satiric mode. Yet, though its tone is lighter than the plaintive music of 'Summer', 'Autumn' continues to deepen the impression of man's separation from Eden which is the dominant theme of the *Pastorals*. In these poems Love is Pope's metaphor of life, of the way one fares in the world; it is also the means of defining the relation of the singers to ideal innocence. In 'Spring' Love was perfectly reciprocal and benign; in 'Summer', though the source of spiritual dis-ease, it appeared as the higher *eros*—an irresistible yearning after ideal Beauty, forever elusive yet the source of all delight. In 'Autumn', where Pope first sounds his moral theme, Love is a baser god whose nature is seen in the faithlessness of Doris and in the passion, either self-deluding or self-consuming, of the shepherds. Though he is powerless to resist him, Ægon knows his enemy:

> I know thee Love! on foreign Mountains bred,
> Wolves gave thee suck, and savage Tygers fed.
> Thou wert from *Ætna's* burning Entrails torn,
> Got by fierce Whirlwinds, and in Thunder born!   (ll. 89–92)

This is the destructive principle within man, the source of all that is most inimical to his true happiness and fulfilment. Pope's theme in 'Autumn' is the folly of men, is *human* nature, and the poetic imitation of this is the proper subject of the satiric mode. 'Oh, skill'd in Nature!' the poet exclaims to Wycherley, 'see the Hearts of Swains, / Their artless Passions, and their tender Pains' (ll. 11–12). Doubtless Pope's design for the *Pastorals*, both formal and thematic, demanded such a poem; but the delicate frame of the eclogue strains under weighty matter it was never really meant to bear.

'Winter'—before 'Messiah' Pope's own favourite and certainly the richest poem of the four—completes the design. From the green, golden world of 'Spring' we have been plunged now into

darkest night and stormy weather, the situation for mankind in
the Iron Age. In this fallen world, death is the condition of life,
and death is Pope's subject: the death of the day and of the year,
the death of Nature, and most especially the death of Daphne.
Although the conceptual identity of Daphne is evident within the
eclogue itself—as Thyrsis reveals, she is the one who inspired
'sweet *Alexis*' Strain' (l. 11)—Pope's models for the poem make his
meaning still clearer. Among classical sources, she recalls the
Daphnis of Theocritus' *Idyll I* and of Virgil's *Eclogue V*: in Theocritus, Daphnis is the legendary inventor of pastoral song whose
death all Nature mourns; in Virgil, whose subject is Daphnis' death
and apotheosis, he represents some principle of cosmic Order
which has disappeared from the world but which still rules in
Elysium. Among the pastoral elegies of Pope's contemporaries,
Walsh's *Eclogue V* in memory of Mrs. Tempest provides a further
analogue in the death of Delia, the figure of ideal Love and Beauty,
whose demise has disastrous consequences in the sublunary world:
'Ev'n Nature's self in dire convulsions lies!' (l. 26). It was at Walsh's
suggestion, we recall, that Pope dedicated his own poem to Mrs.
Tempest—an apt decision, certainly, since in her name and in the
circumstances of her death (she died the night of the great storm
of November 1703),[25] this unfortunate woman perfectly exemplified Pope's theme of mortality and his symbolism of winter weather,
the climate of life in this fallen world.

In these poems Delia and Daphnis represent some beneficent
avatar of the Ideal whose death leaves the world diminished and
forlorn. Daphne is Pope's own expression of this concept. Ideal
Beauty, that unattainable abstraction which demanded Alexis' love
and inspired his song in 'Summer', has here been given a name.
And, befitting the wretchedness of our condition in the Iron Age,
at this withered end of history, she is no longer merely elusive, she
is dead; our estrangement from Eden is complete. As the changes
of Thyrsis' sad refrain declare, with Daphne every positive value
has vanished from the world: Love, Beauty, Pleasure, Sweetness,
Music—once 'our Glory' in Eden—are 'now no more'. In 'Spring',
the recreation of the Golden Age, all these values were enjoyed by
men; perfect justice and love and song were the conditions of life,
and Nature and Art were one. In 'Winter' this ideal relationship no
longer obtains: 'No more the Birds shall imitate her Lays' (l. 55).
Within the world of these pastorals, Daphne is the equivalent of

Astræa, goddess of Justice and Order, who fled the earth at the
deposition of Saturn by Jove, when the Iron Age succeeded the Age
of Gold. Like Astræa, Daphne has been translated from this sublunary realm of disorder and decay to the region of timeless beauty
beyond the stars. There—in the region of '*Amaranthine* Bow'rs'
familiar, since the Fall, only to the angels[26]—the original perfection of the divine creation remains unaltered, and Nature and
Art are one, as they were in Eden:

> But see! where *Daphne* wondring mounts on high,
> Above the Clouds, above the Starry Sky.
> Eternal Beauties grace the shining Scene,
> Fields ever fresh, and Groves for ever green!
> There, while You rest in *Amaranthine* Bow'rs,
> Or from those Meads select unfading Flow'rs,
> Behold us kindly who your Name implore,
> *Daphne*, our Goddess, and our Grief no more!   (ll. 69–76)

Daphne's death and the winter weather are Pope's metaphors
for Actuality, for the harsh conditions of life in this fallen, mortal
world. Thyrsis' valediction presents this world as it is, desolate and
decaying, inimical to man:

> But see, *Orion* sheds unwholesome Dews,
> Arise, the Pines a noxious Shade diffuse;
> Sharp *Boreas* blows, and Nature feels Decay,
> Time conquers All, and We must Time obey.   (ll. 85–8)

This last line, a significant variation upon the famous conclusion
of Virgil's *Eclogues* ('*Omnia vincit Amor: et nos cedamus Amori*'),
points to the dominant theme of Pope's *Pastorals* and to the spiritual
distance, at least, that separates him from the Roman poet. Pope's
eclogues record the triumph not of Love, which has died with
Daphne, but of Time. In terms of the carefully elaborated parallelisms
of the *Pastorals*, Time has carried us from spring to winter, from
dawn to midnight, from youth to the grave, from Eden to the
present moment. It is the inexorable process of degeneration and
decay leading to death.

Playing against this theme—indeed, at once containing and in
a sense transcending it—are the poems themselves, the music not
of time but of eternity, whose harmonies recall that ideal relationship between Art and Nature that once obtained. Daphne's dying
request implies this antagonism between mutability and permanence, between the ugliness of life and the loveliness of art:

'"Ye Shepherds, sing around my Grave!"' (l. 18). In Thyrsis' elegy Daphne is honoured and immortalized, his song so moving that all Nature listens in silence—'Such Silence' as 'waits on *Philomela*'s Strains' (l. 78). The analogy recalls that mythical power which changed the ravished girl into the nightingale, giving music in compensation for outrage. The poet's art, as Pope implies and demonstrates in these poems, has this same transforming power to restore imperfect Nature and redeem the fallen world. 'The Groves of *Eden*, vanish'd now so long, / Live in Description, and look green in Song.'

Though recent criticism has brilliantly illuminated the assumptions and techniques of Pope's other major poetry, the *Pastorals* continue to be regarded generally as little more than trivial exercises in versification and decorum with which Pope amused himself while learning his craft as a poet. Even those who admire his eclogues take refuge in uneasy analogizing, preferring to deal with them not as poems, but as expressions of Pope's 'choreographic sense' or as verbal paintings after the manner of Poussin or Zuccarelli.[27] The *Pastorals* deserve a better fate. In them Pope came to terms with the essential intellectual implications of the mode itself—the peculiarly generic relationship it bears to the ideas of Art and Nature, Permanence and Mutability—and, discerning the significance of Virgil's artificiality and Spenser's calendar, he devised a form and a structure that enabled him to develop, indeed to embody, these themes coherently in poetry. In this respect—in their nice adjustment of meaning and form—the *Pastorals* deserve not our condescension, but our warmest admiration. Far from constituting a deviation from the more serious philosophical concerns of Renaissance pastoral, as has been supposed,[28] they are rather the consummation of that tradition.

Even though the four poems published in Tonson's now famous *Poetical Miscellanies* of 1709 have a coherent shape and meaning of their own, they did not complete Pope's larger design for his Pastorals. As we have seen, these poems, in tracing the seasons from spring to winter, developed an analogy between 'the great and little worlds', between the decay of Nature and the regrettable progress of human life and human history. The loss of Eden and the triumph of Time had there been Pope's theme. But implicit in this idea and in the calendar structure of the *Pastorals* is the expectation of renewal —of a new dawn, a new spring, restoring the Golden Age. In the context of Christian teleology, the world's Great Year leads to the apocalypse, not to Time's victory but to its ultimate defeat. Published in *The Spectator* for 14 May 1712, Pope's 'Messiah' is thus the logical sequel to the poems on the seasons, as he himself indicated when, for the edition of his collected works five years later, he made room for his 'Sacred Eclogue' under the heading of 'Pastorals', giving it the climactic position in the series. To come from 'Winter' immediately to the 'Messiah', as readers of this volume would have done, is to sense at once the relationship of the two poems:

> Ye Nymphs of *Solyma!* begin the Song:
> To heav'nly Themes sublimer Strains belong.
> The Mossie Fountains and the Sylvan Shades,
> The Dreams of *Pindus* and th'*Aonian* Maids,
> Delight no more—O Thou my Voice inspire
> Who touch'd *Isaiah*'s hallow'd Lips with Fire!
> Rapt into future Times, the Bard begun;
> A *Virgin* shall conceive, a *Virgin* bear a Son!

Whereas Pope's secular eclogues had focused on the meaning of life and art in this world, his 'Messiah'—like its model, Virgil's 'Pollio', which was construed by Christian interpreters as a prophecy of the coming of Christ—turns to 'heav'nly Themes'. Whereas the earlier pastorals had carried us from the past to the present, from the Golden to the Iron Age, 'Messiah' will translate us 'into future Times'. Whereas 'Winter' left us with the image of death, this sacred eclogue heralds the birth of the Saviour. Deliberately, the themes and symbols which had earlier defined the temporal and spiritual condition of fallen man are now recalled in order to be contradicted. The heat and disease of 'Summer', the tempests of 'Winter', the moral disorders of 'Autumn'—all are remembered and their curse dispelled:

> The Sick and Weak the healing Plant shall aid;
> From Storms a Shelter, and from Heat a Shade.
> All Crimes shall cease, and ancient Fraud shall fail. (ll. 15–17)

Astræa, whose benign influence was manifest in 'Spring' in Damon's wise decision, had with every other virtue departed the earth when Daphne died in 'Winter'; now 'Returning Justice lift[s] aloft her Scale' (l. 18). And Death himself is bound 'In adamantine Chains' (l. 47).

It is the desolate, fallen world of 'Winter' which the imagery of the 'Messiah' joyously transforms. With the coming of Christ, 'the good Shepherd' (l. 49), a new and metaphysical spring revives the barren landscape, and Daphne's flower, the 'od'rous Myrtle', replaces 'the noisome Weed' (l. 76):

> The Swain in barren Desarts with surprize
> See Lillies spring, and sudden Verdure rise;
> And Starts, amidst the thirsty Wilds, to hear
> New Falls of Water murm'ring in his Ear:
> On rifted Rocks, the Dragon's late Abodes,
> The green Reed trembles, and the Bulrush nods.
> Waste sandy Vallies, once perplex'd with Thorn,
> The spiry Firr and shapely Box adorn;
> To leaf-less Shrubs the flow'ring Palms succeed,
> And od'rous Myrtle to the noisome Weed.   (ll. 67–76)

After winter's midnight, a new dawn bathes the world in 'a Flood of Day' (l. 98); but this day is 'eternal' (l. 104), the spiritual glory of 'The LIGHT HIMSELF' (l. 103). At the apocalypse we—or rather 'Imperial *Salem*' (l. 85), the true Church—shall be released from the tyranny of Time, from the perpetual revolution of the seasons and the succession of nights and days:

> No more the rising *Sun* shall gild the Morn,
> Nor evening *Cynthia* fill her silver Horn,
> But lost, dissolv'd in thy superior Rays;
> One Tyde of Glory, one unclouded Blaze,
> O'erflow thy Courts: The LIGHT HIMSELF shall shine
> Reveal'd; and *God's* eternal Day be thine!   (ll. 99–104)

As 'Winter' had closed with Thyrsis' complaint of Nature's decay and the triumph of Time, the final lines of 'Messiah' envision the dissolution of the world into eternity:

> The Seas shall waste; the Skies in Smoke decay;
> Rocks fall to Dust, and Mountains melt away;
> But fix'd *His* Word, *His* saving Pow'r remains:
> Thy *Realm* for ever lasts! thy own *Messiah* reigns!

In the *Pastorals* the ability to transform Nature had rested, though imperfectly, with the poet himself—imitator of the divine creative power and lover of ideal harmonies. It is the poet whose music and mastery of artifice recreate the Golden Age in 'Spring' and in 'Winter' recall the higher reality of Elysium, where Daphne dwells among 'unfading Flow'rs'. Yet, as Pope reminds us in his 'Discourse', we are finally aware that the green world of Arcadia is only a pleasant illusion. Figured in the complaint of Alexis and in the death of Daphne, the effect of the Fall has been the irrevocable separation of Art from ideal Beauty, and the passing of Order from the earth. In 'Messiah' the original Edenic harmony between Art and Nature is restored in transcendent perfection, the power of Art and the ideal of Order being united eternally in Christ. Pope's sacred eclogue is the celebration of the true transforming power, the Logos, the divine Artificer who made the world and who will at last redeem it from imperfection. In terms of the conventions of pastoral and the metaphors of the Christian tradition, Christ is the shepherd poet whose Word will make the Golden Age a reality.

Viewed in this way, 'Messiah' may be seen as the completion of Pope's intellectual design for the Pastorals— hence his decision in 1717 to include the poem under that heading. Despite his tender years, Pope at the very start of his career had not only achieved that mastery of technique which, as Joseph Warton and Dr. Johnson remarked, effected a revolution in English prosody; he had also formulated a coherent philosophy of art which in a sense demanded nothing less than technical excellence. For the function of art was to order the chaos of actuality—not to deny the chaos, which was always real enough for him, but to oppose it with music and form, which alone can put us in touch with a higher reality. Lytton Strachey sensed this when he observed that Pope's 'poetic criticism of life was, simply and solely, the heroic couplet'.[29] The eclogue provided him with a likely vehicle for the expression of this aesthetic philosophy. In the *Pastorals* Pope took as his subject the relation of Art to Nature (and to man!) within the context of Christian time. And significantly, the ideas he here first expressed continued to inform his work. In the *Essay on Man* ideal Nature is still the 'Art' of God, and the harmony of the Golden Age, from which man has fallen, is yet remembered:

> Nor think, in NATURE'S STATE they blindly trod;
> The state of Nature was the reign of God:
> Self-love and Social at her birth began,
> Union the bond of all things, and of Man.   (iii. 147–50)

In *The Dunciad*, to be sure, Arcadia survives only as a bitter joke, as 'the fresh vomit run[s] for ever green' (*A*, ii. 148). The ideas of

Eden and the Golden Age are mocked in the fantasies of the dunces, who cherish instead 'the Fool's paradise' and the miser's 'golden Dream' (*A*, iii. 9–10). There, the language of Virgil's *Fourth Eclogue* heralds the coming of a new Messiah bringing 'Saturnian times', Dulness's promised 'age of *Lead*' (*A*, iii. 317–18 and n.): 'Proceed great days! . . . Signs following signs lead on the Mighty Year' (*A*, iii. 329, 335). Where once Damon's fiat had declared the harmony of life and art at the beginning of the world's 'Mighty Year', now, in a darker season, Dulness presides over the noise-making contest, acknowledging with pleasure a universal caco-phony: 'Hold (cry'd the Queen) A Catcall each shall win, / Equal your merits! equal is your din!' (*A*, ii. 233–4).

But even in *The Dunciad*, which sardonically records the triumph of Chaos, Pope's skilful couplets and his control of form implicitly affirm the victory of Art, the power of form and music to redeem the time. In this sense, at least, the meaning of the *Pastorals* still obtains. In *The Dunciad*, of course, one hears a different music— still regular, still precise, still opposing harmony to discord and disorder, but, as befits Pope's theme, no longer merely lovely: an effect rather like that of Stravinsky imitating Mozart. Yet Pope's vision of life in 'Autumn' and 'Winter' is at least theoretically the same as the vision that darkens the major satires—the difference being that in the later poems he has *felt* the destructive conse-quences of folly and the painful effects of mortality, and has found that no retreat into Fancy's maze can make them tolerable. The progress of history, of the world's Great Year, has in *The Dunciad* led out of Arcadia to the spiritual midnight and winter weather of Georgian England, to a world of dunces for whom the Messiah is the 'uncreating word'. The same ideals of Art and Order, the same philosophy of Christian time, connect the *Pastorals* and the poems of Pope's last years. What separates them may be felt in the terrible metamorphosis that has transformed the Golden Age of 'Spring' and the 'Messiah' into that of *The Dunciad*.

III

Pope: The Idea of Creation

THE melody and movement of the *Pastorals* may serve, then, as
a kind of overture to the profounder harmonies of Pope's later
career. In sounding the theme of the Golden Age, Pope there
gave expression to aesthetic and philosophic assumptions which—
sometimes directly, as in *Windsor Forest*, sometimes obliquely, as
in the satires and *The Dunciad*—affected his serious work from first
to last. But Pope, though once it would have seemed odd to say so,
was a Christian poet. Beyond its quaint allure and its usefulness in
linking his own poetry with the classical tradition, the myth of
the Golden Age had meaning for him chiefly as a metaphor agreeable to the faith of his age in Order, the fundamental attribute of
creation, and to the Christian humanist conviction that Art alone,
the effect of the creative intelligence bringing Form out of Chaos,
is the human means of approximating that sacred ideal.

i. *The Paradigm of Order*

For a poet in this tradition, the paradigmatic act of history, to
be emulated both in the work of art and in the moral life, is the
fiat of Genesis, the potent command by which the idea of Order in
the mind of God was bodied forth in Nature: 'Let there be light:
and there was light.' The appeal of this text for poets of the period
is, of course, partly owing to the authority of Longinus, for whom
it exemplified the true sublime, representing 'the divine nature in
its true attributes, pure, majestic, and unique', expressing with the
most compelling simplicity 'a worthy conception of divine power'.[1]
More important, as fact and as paradigm, the ordering efficacy of
the divine Word supplied the premiss for the Augustan ethos; in
Newton and the divines, in Milton and Dennis and the aestheticians, it remained the ultimate authority for assertions about the
nature of reality. For by God's fiat, anarchy was dispelled, the

D

jarring elements harmonized, due bounds prescribed, and all things given form.

Appropriately enough considering his reputation as pre-eminently the Poet of Order, Pope's fascination with this, the supreme poetic act, was intense and constant. Like the myth of the Golden Age, or the emblematic contrast between Garden and City so well examined by Maynard Mack, the divine fiat may be seen, indeed, as one of the controlling motifs of Pope's poetry, implying the sacred grounds of both universal Order and artistic Form. In 'Spring' we already heard an echo of the divine command in Damon's injunction, 'Cease to contend': as God reconciled the warring elements at the beginning of Time, so Damon speaks the words that resolve the singing contest, achieving in fact that *concordia discors* which is the symbolic condition of the Golden Age. Applied in various moods to suit various purposes—to celebrate the institution of Order, or ironically to deplore its subversion, in society, morality, art—the fiat of Genesis serves as the paradigm of those rational and civilized values Pope cherished. As such it is the key to universal harmony in *Windsor Forest* and the *Essay on Man*, and the measure of discord in the satires and *The Dunciad*. To recall the hypothesis we earlier entertained,[2] it may even have helped to determine the very form and texture of his verse by supplying the theoretical grounds for his peculiar development of the heroic couplet: under Pope's hands the couplet becomes, curiously like the Pythagorean *tetraktys*, a model of *concordia discors*, comprehending within a single unified system those principles of balance, symmetry, and harmonic reconciliation which he and his contemporaries regarded as the characteristics of natural Order. Whether or not this effect was deliberate on Pope's part, his verse offers one of the happiest instances in literature of prosody recapitulating ontology.

The enumeration of images is among the least amusing of critical procedures (done in a bucolic setting, it has even enjoyed some currency as a soporific), but it can serve to indicate the bent of a poet's mind, and at present it will have the further virtue of providing a context for the explication both of an important episode in Pope's *Iliad* and of a major dimension of his masterpiece, *The Dunciad*. But before noticing how Pope applies the fiat motif in other contexts, we should have in mind his use of the concept in its essential form, as the Act which brought Order into being. We may begin in the period of his earliest juvenilia. Written in 1703, 'On Silence', Pope's playful imitation of Rochester's 'Upon Nothing', contains the first significant[3] occurrence of the idea:

> Thine was the Sway, e'er Heav'n was form'd or Earth,
> E'er fruitful *Thought* conceiv'd Creation's Birth,
> Or Midwife *Word* gave Aid, and spoke the Infant forth. (ll. 4–6)[4]

These verses, written in his fourteenth year, identify the elements of the paradigm and suggest the sort of importance it will later have for Pope as the epitome of creation and the creative process: what '*Thought*' conceives, the mysterious efficacy of the '*Word*' reifies, giving form and substance to the imagined ideal. For Pope in this early period, the larger implications of this act are most succinctly expressed in the paraphrase of Boethius, where the 'all-creating' God of Genesis, at whose bidding the drama of Christian Time began, is addressed as 'Eternal Reason', and praised not only for forming the universe, but for sustaining and governing it in His Providence:

> O Thou, whose all-creating hands sustain
> The radiant Heav'ns, and Earth, and ambient main!
> Eternal Reason! whose presiding soul
> Informs great nature and directs the whole!
> Who wert, e're time his rapid race begun,
> And bad'st the years in long procession run:
> Who fix't thy self amidst the rowling frame,
> Gav'st all things to be chang'd, yet art the same![5]

The Deity for Pope, early and late, is not only the 'First Great Cause'[6] of all things, but also 'that Directing Pow'r'[7] which controls and supervises the course of Nature. As Warburton put it in asserting the orthodoxy of the *Essay on Man* against the incredulous, Pope's purpose, made explicit in 'The Universal Prayer', was to show 'That the first cause was as well the Lord and Governor of the Universe as the Creator of it . . .'.[8]

Pope's contemporaries believed that the world called into being by the divine fiat was a work of art befitting the rationality of its creator—a work infinitely various, but formally ordered according to the principles of harmony and proportion, symmetry and balance. These are also the formal properties of the universe as Pope conceived of it, wherein Nature is Art, Chance is Direction. The importance of the idea of Harmony to this conception—of the world imagined as a *concordia discors* of reconciled extremes—has been ably expounded by Spitzer, Mack, and Wasserman[9] and is well known to every student of *Windsor Forest* and the *Essay on Man*. The elements of Pope's world exist in dynamic equilibrium,

> Not *Chaos*-like together crush'd and bruis'd,
> But as the World harmoniously confus'd:
> Where Order in Variety we see,
> And where, tho' all things differ, all agree.[10]

It is a world wherein 'ALL subsists by elemental strife', wherein apparent 'Discord' is in fact 'Harmony, not understood'.[11] 'Such', as Denham knew, 'was the discord, which did first disperse / Form, order, beauty through the Universe.'[12]

Implicit in this musical metaphor for Order are the correlative ideas of balance and symmetry, of a vital equilibrium achieved in the conflict of opposing elements. In the reconciliation of centripetal and centrifugal forces, Newton's universe sustains itself; similarly, the life of Pope's couplet form resides in the dynamic tension of antitheses, hemistich against hemistich, line against line. The principle is clearly articulated in the *Epistle to Bathurst* (1733), expressed in verse that is itself the formal embodiment of the idea of balance:

> 'Extremes in Nature equal good produce,
> 'Extremes in Man concur to gen'ral use.'
> Ask we what makes one keep, and one bestow?
> That Pow'r who bids the Ocean ebb and flow,
> Bids seed-time, harvest, equal course maintain,
> Thro' reconcil'd extremes of drought and rain,
> Builds Life on Death, on Change Duration founds,
> And gives th'eternal wheels to know their rounds.   (ll. 163–70)[13]

In the passage from *Bathurst* Pope's frame of reference is temporal: since he is treating the pattern of life itself, the idea of balance is rendered in terms of the cyclical ebb and flow of natural phenomena. More useful for our purpose—which is in a sense to discover Pope's conception of the abstract *form* of creation—is the familiar description of Windsor Forest (ll. 10–28) considered as an image of cosmic Order. More interesting, because less well known, is a comparable passage in *The Temple of Fame* (1715) in which Pope evokes the prospect of the 'whole Creation', recalling as he does Milton's vision of the world 'self-ballanc'd':[14]

> I stood, methought, betwixt Earth, Seas, and Skies;
> The whole Creation open to my Eyes:

> In Air self-ballanc'd hung the Globe below,
> Where Mountains rise, and circling Oceans flow;
> Here naked Rocks, and empty Wastes were seen,
> There Tow'ry Cities, and the Forests green:
> Here sailing Ships delight the wand'ring Eyes;
> There Trees, and intermingl'd Temples rise:
> Now a clear Sun the shining Scene displays,
> The transient Landscape now in Clouds decays. (ll. 11–20)

Here, as in the passage from *Windsor Forest* written at nearly the same time, Pope renders the creation in images suggesting symmetry and equilibrium. The placement of opposing images on either side of the caesura ('Mountains' vs. 'Oceans', 'naked Rocks' vs. 'empty Wastes', 'Tow'ry Cities' vs. 'Forests green'), or in separate lines of a couplet ('Ships' vs. 'Trees' and 'Temples', the 'Sun' vs. the 'Clouds'), has the effect of rendering the universal *concordia discors* in visual terms—an effect, one might add, almost viscerally reinforced through the rocking movement of the lines, which are *felt* as much as heard. The verse, like the world it presents, is 'self-ballanc'd'. It is the earth 'unbalanc'd', careening lawlessly through the void, that forms part of the nightmare vision of broken Order in the *Essay on Man* (i. 251), where, indeed, the harmony of the universal system as a whole—its fulness, coherence and nice gradations—is seen as a delicate equilibrium which the pride of man threatens to disturb.

Closely related to the idea of balance is another feature of the creation which Pope invariably associated with the fiat of Genesis, when God imposed Form on Chaos by an act of separation, dividing the light from the darkness, distinguishing the elements one from another:

> And God said, Let the waters under the heaven be gathered together unto one place, and let the dry *land* appear: and it was so.
> And God called the dry *land* Earth; and the gathering together of the waters called he Seas: and God saw that *it was* good. (Genesis 1: 9–10)

In Nature (and therefore, perhaps, in the couplet as Pope practised it)[15] form implies definition and restraint, the setting of bounds according to function. This, of course, is a cardinal assumption of Augustan aesthetics. As Pope has it in the *Essay on Criticism*, 'Nature to all things fix'd the Limits fit' (l. 52). Like liberty, a very different thing from anarchy, she is 'restrain'd / By the same Laws which first *herself* ordain'd' (ll. 90–1). To grasp and elucidate those

laws, established by God from the beginning of Time, was obviously
the business not only of the poet or critic, but of the natural
scientist as well. For this reason, when he came to devise an
epitaph for the greatest genius of the age, Pope appropriately
recalled the fiat of Genesis: 'NATURE, and Nature's Laws lay hid in
Night. / God said, *Let Newton be!* and All was *Light.*'[16]

Harmony, balance, delimitation—with Pope's view of the formal
characteristics of Nature clearly in mind, we may better appreciate
the larger implications of his persistent concern with the creative
act of divine Reason that called them into being. According to
the doctrine of correspondency that Pope and his contemporaries
inherited from the Christian humanist tradition, the natural Order,
divinely ordained and now reassuringly demonstrated by Newton,
supplied the paradigm for Order in society and in the microcosm:

> On their own Axis as the Planets run,
> Yet make at once their circle round the Sun:
> So two consistent motions act the Soul;
> And one regards Itself, and one the Whole.
>   Thus God and Nature link'd in the gen'ral frame,
> And bade Self-love and Social be the same.[17]

The notion of *concordia discors* applied as well to society, wherein, ideally speaking, the potentially conflicting interests of each
member at each station of the system are resolved through the
acknowledgement of mutual responsibilities and the awareness of
the interdependence of each on all:

> 'Till jarring int'rests of themselves create
> Th'according music of a well-mix'd State.
> Such is the World's great harmony, that springs
> From Order, Union, full Consent of things![18]

The correspondence between Order in the universe and Order
in society entailed the further analogy between God, the Governor
of Nature, and His earthly surrogates, the rulers of nations. The
king's authority and prudence in preserving the health of the body
politic reflected, though of course imperfectly, the benign Omnipotence and Providence of the Deity, who created and sustains the
harmony of the macrocosm. When, therefore, an Augustan poet
or divine celebrates the achievement of political union and concord by recalling the ordering fiat of Genesis, the allusion is something more than a fulsome compliment; it is a means of placing the

political event and its agent within the larger context of universal Order.[19] To Pope in *Windsor Forest*, for example, the accession of Anne to the throne, the last of the Stuart monarchs, marked the establishment of Order after the disturbances of the preceding century, when, in retribution for an unholy civil war and the martyrdom of the anointed king, England had been ravaged by pestilence and fire and oppressed by the consequences of an 'Inglorious' revolution. It was Anne, furthermore, whose Tory ministers had ended the debilitating war with France begun under William III. Both at home and abroad 'Peace and Plenty' told 'a STUART reigns' (l. 42). In quieting the strife and confusion of nearly three quarters of a century, Anne, once more God's own anointed on the throne, could appear (to a poet of Pope's political inclinations) as recapitulating the original, harmonizing act of Genesis:

> Make sacred *Charles*'s Tomb for ever known,
> (Obscure the Place, and uninscrib'd the Stone)
> Oh Fact accurst! What Tears has *Albion* shed,
> Heav'ns! what new Wounds, and how her old have bled?
> She saw her Sons with purple Deaths expire,
> Her sacred Domes involv'd in rolling Fire,
> A dreadful Series of Intestine Wars,
> Inglorious Triumphs, and dishonest Scars.
> At length great *ANNA* said—Let Discord cease!
> She said, the World obey'd, and all was *Peace*! (ll. 319–28)[20]

But Pope's dream of a Golden Age for England which Anne would usher in was soon dispelled. In 1715, by an act he regarded as sufficiently perverse, England gave itself to be governed by a line of venal and illiterate German kings. The reign of Dulness had begun and with it the depressing process of cultural stupefaction culminating, as revealed in the dark apocalypse of *The Dunciad*, in the obliteration of Order and intellectual light. 'Still', Pope wrote as George succeeded George, 'Dunce the second reigns like Dunce the first' (*A*, i. 6). Addressed to the presiding genius of England's own Augustan Age, Pope's *Epistle* (1737) to George Augustus archly recalls the traditional analogy between Creator and monarch in order to define the ways in which George is the negation of the Christian humanist ideal of kingship. The poem opens by echoing Boethius' praise of the Creator and Milton's image of the balanced world: 'While You, great Patron of Mankind, sustain / The balanc'd World, and open all the Main . . .'.[21] More explicit still is the conclusion of the epistle, where Pope, inviting comparison with his earlier praise of Queen Anne and anticipating the triumph of Dulness in *The Dunciad*, ironically likens the king's ruinous influence to the tranquillizing power of the *Logos*, Milton's 'Omnific Word':

> How barb'rous rage subsided at your word,
> And Nations wonder'd while they dropp'd the sword!
> How, when you nodded, o'er the land and deep,
> Peace stole her wing, and wrapt the world in sleep;
> Till Earth's extremes your mediation own,
> And Asia's Tyrants tremble at your Throne—   (ll. 398–403)

Far from creating and sustaining his 'Country's Peace' (l. 397) or the political order of Europe, the king's passive acquiescence in Walpole's pacific foreign policy had in fact upset the balance of power and left English ships vulnerable to marauding Spanish vessels. George's imitation of the divine fiat is a travesty of the traditional analogy: an inglorious peace, uneasy and merely nominal, achieved not through any positive act of government, but through refusing the responsible exercise of power. The allusion here serves to measure his distance from the ideal.

Complementing his role as the agent of political harmony, the ideal monarch, according to an analogy particularly congenial to the Tory ethos, was also regarded as the divinely appointed Lord of the Manor which is England. As ruler of the country he shared with any other landholder—with Pope's friends, for instance, the Earls of Bathurst and Burlington—the responsibility to improve his estate, to set his dominions physically in order. This, too, is a formal, creative act for which the specific paradigm is God's work on the Third Day, when the sea was divided from the land and the earth was made fruitful. Thus in 1664 John Evelyn found that by commanding new buildings to be erected and new plantations to be laid out, Charles II invited comparison with 'the *Divine Architect*'.[22] In his commentary on Genesis published some sixty years later, Matthew Henry explains the grounds of the analogy. On the Third Day, having kindled the light of heaven and established the firmament, God descended

... to this lower World, the Earth, which was designed *for the Children of Men*, design'd both for their *Habitation*, and for their *Maintenance*, and here we have an Account of the fitting of it for both; the Building of *their House*, and the spreading of *their Table*. Observe, 1. How the Earth was prepared to be a *Habitation* for Man, by the *gathering of the Waters together*, and the making of the *Dry Land* to *appear*. Thus instead of that Confusion which was *v.* 2. when Earth and Water were mixed in one great Mass; behold now there is *Order*, by such a Separation as render'd them both useful. God said, *Let it be so*, and *it was so*, no sooner said but done.

Since it is God 'that keeps the Sea with *Bars and Doors* in its *decreed Place*, and stays its proud Waves . . . We that to this Day enjoy the Benefit of the *Dry Land* . . . must own our selves Tenants to, and Dependants upon [Him] whose *Hands prepared the Dry Land*'. God, remarks Henry, is 'the rightful Owner and sovereign Disposer' of the earth; 'the Property still remains in him, and to his Service and Honour they must be us'd'.[23] God is to the world, as the king to the country, as the lord to the manor. In *Moral Essay IV* (1731) all three terms of the analogy are functional. Bathurst and Burlington—'earls of creation' as James Lees-Milne has called them —emulate the divine beneficence by making their estates beautiful and productive. But their fidelity to the Tory ideal contrasts implicitly with the king's dereliction, as churches sink on their foundations, the Thames overflows its banks, highways become impassable, and the building of Westminster Bridge is given as a job to an incompetent carpenter.[24] To make clear the nature and essential grounds of the king's obligation, Pope's language returns us to the Third Day of creation, when at God's bidding the lawless seas were controlled and the earth became habitable. Burlington's example, he hopes, will prevail:

> Till Kings call forth th'Idea's of your mind,
> Proud to accomplish what such hands design'd,
> Bid Harbors open, public Ways extend,
> Bid Temples, worthier of the God, ascend;
> Bid the broad Arch the dang'rous Flood contain,
> The Mole projected break the roaring Main;
> Back to his bounds their subject Sea command,
> And roll obedient Rivers thro' the Land;
> These Honours, Peace to happy Britain brings,
> These are Imperial Works, and worthy Kings.   (ll. 195–204)[25]

When Pope, applying the doctrine of correspondences, turned from the macrocosm or society at large to examine the nature of Order in the little world of man, the fiat of Genesis again provided the paradigm. Like the universe, the microcosm was comprised of warring elements, the passions, which, though essential to life, required a higher agency, the reason, to distinguish their proper functions and to direct them to suitable ends. As the dynamic materials of creation yield to the harmonizing Word of the Deity to form an ordered system under the wise disposition of Providence, so the moral health of the individual resides in the 'proper operation'[26] of the passions, reason, and the will. As Eloisa (1717) regretfully knows, Abelard's emasculation, though releasing him 'from pleasure and from pain', has rendered him passionless, inert like the primal matter before God spoke the energizing Word: 'Still as the sea, ere winds were taught to blow, / Or moving spirit bade the waters flow . . .' (ll. 249–54).[27] Lacking passion, Abelard exists in 'a long, dead calm of fix'd repose', and Stoics live on in 'lazy Apathy'.[28] For, as Pope declares in the Essay on Man, 'ALL subsists by elemental strife; / And Passions are the elements of Life' (i. 169–70). Though the vitality of both macrocosm and microcosm resides in 'elemental strife', yet Order in the one and Virtue in the other depend on rational control and restraint: 'Has Nature set no bounds to wild Desire?' Pope asks.[29] In the human soul, as in the great world, harmony is achieved through the artful process of tempering opposing claims and balancing antitheses:

> Passions, like Elements, tho' born to fight,
> Yet, mix'd and soften'd, in [God's] work unite . . .
> These mix'd with art, and to due bounds confin'd,
> Make and maintain the balance of the mind:
> The lights and shades, whose well accorded strife
> Gives all the strength and colour of our life.[30]

The shaping principle of the soul, distinguishing virtue from vice and turning 'the byass . . . to good from ill',[31] is Reason itself, whose function in the microcosm corresponds to that of the Logos, creating order out of chaos: 'This light and darkness in our chaos join'd, / What shall divide? The God within the mind.'[32]

Signifying the sacred ideal of Order in a metaphysical, social, or moral context, the multiple implications of Pope's use of fiat lux serve to illuminate the most delightful instance of the allusion in all his works—the divine Belinda's dread command at the Game of Ombre: 'Let Spades be Trumps! she said, and Trumps they were.'[33] Together with similar patterns of imagery and allusion—comparing her to the sun, for example (ii. 1–14), source of light and order in the universe and emblem of divinity itself—Belinda's travesty of the 'Omnific Word' recalls the signs and values of Christianity in order (as later and less playfully in The Dunciad) to make clear the essential absurdity of a vain and disproportioned world. Belinda is the cynosure and 'Goddess' (i. 132) of that world, a world as elegant and as superficial as the 'Velvet Plain' (iii. 44) over which she so skilfully presides. In the beginning her command defines her universe, where life is love, and love, the struggle for conquest between gentle belles and well-bred lords, is no more than an idle game governed by empty forms and enacted by pasteboard figures.

A final application of the *fiat lux* motif, especially prominent in Pope's early verse, will help to clarify his conception of the creative process itself. If Nature for Pope and his contemporaries was the supreme Artefact, spoken into being by God's ordering Word, the human artist who successfully imitated her rich variety and formal perfection was inevitably seen as re-enacting, however painfully, the miracle of Genesis. In this sense, as we have seen, the poet of the *Pastorals* redeems the time, through bright figures of the imagination and the harmony of his numbers recalling the Golden Age; and in *Windsor Forest* a vanished Eden lives again in description and looks green in song. In this sense, Milton, Denham, Cowley, Granville were for Pope 'God-like'; and in Robert Howard's careful verse, producing 'so beautifull a world', Dryden had discerned 'the providence of wit'. Often in his early verse Pope triumphantly celebrates this magical, deific power of the artist to give form and substance to ideal Beauty. It is Granville who can 'Make *Windsor* Hills in lofty Numbers rise, / And lift her Turrets nearer to the Skies', and who thus shares with the mythical poets of the past, with Orpheus and Amphion, the marvellous power to re-order the materials of Nature:

> Here *Orpheus* sings; Trees moving to the Sound
> Start from their Roots, and form a Shade around:
> *Amphion* there the loud creating Lyre
> Strikes, and behold a sudden *Thebes* aspire!
> *Cythæron*'s Ecchoes answer to his Call,
> And half the Mountain rolls into a Wall:
> There might you see the length'ning Spires ascend,
> The Domes swell up, the widening Arches bend,
> The growing Tow'rs like Exhalations rise,
> And the huge Columns heave into the Skies.[34]

Again, however, as in the *Essay on Criticism* (ll. 484–7), it is not classical myth but the Book of Genesis that supplies the ultimate paradigm for the creative act, for the power of Art to effect a new Creation:

> So when the faithful *Pencil* has design'd
> Some *bright Idea* of the Master's Mind,
> Where a *new World* leaps out at his command,
> And ready Nature waits upon his Hand . . .

Whether in painting or poetry or gardening—or even, for that matter, in needlework![35]—the contemplation of the aesthetic act seems inevitably to have started this association in Pope's mind. Writing, for example, to his friend the Earl of Oxford as the floods of winter began to subside, his thoughts turned naturally to the pleasures of spring, to the time of year when devoted gardeners, like God creating Eden, could see Nature respond to their designs:

> Now the face of the Earth is seen again, & now the Snows are gone away, and every Green thing appears above the waters, I'm pleased to think your Bowling-green is one of the first of those green things I envy you the pleasure of creating, when one month's time will give you all your Idæas in lively colours, responsive to your expectation. It is now a season of the Year, when to plant, is in a manner but to say, Let it be! and it is done.[36]

In Pope, however, the analogy between the two artists, human and divine, does not carry, as it may do in the Romantic Period, any very serious suggestion of the miraculous efficacy of the creative imagination. No one better knew that gardens and poems do not spring spontaneously into being. The work of art originates in the imagination, but it must be disciplined by the judgement and fashioned by patient dexterity. If Pope took pleasure in the correspondence between ideal Nature and the successful artefact, he was well aware of the arduous formal process by which the artist achieved that analogy. In his paraphrase of Ovid (*Metamorphoses*, xiv), Pomona is seen as taming intractable Nature. She teaches 'the Trees a nobler Race to bear' and improves 'the Vegetable Care':

> The Hook she bore, instead of *Cynthia*'s Spear,
> To lop the Growth of the luxuriant Year,
> To decent Form the lawless Shoots to bring,
> And teach th'obedient Branches where to spring.
> Now the cleft Rind inserted Graffs receives,
> And yields an Off-spring more than Nature gives . . .[37]

For Pope the poem, if it is to nourish and delight us, must be, like

Pomona's garden, the product of care and discipline and good taste.

> But how severely with themselves proceed
> The Men, who write such Verse as we can read?
> Their own strict Judges, not a word they spare
> That wants or Force, or Light, or Weight, or Care,
> Howe'er unwillingly it quits its place,
> Nay tho' at Court (perhaps) it may find grace:
> Such they'll degrade; and sometimes, in its stead,
> In downright Charity revive the dead;
> Mark where a bold expressive Phrase appears,
> Bright thro' the rubbish of some hundred years;
> Command old words that long have slept, to wake,
> Words, that wise *Bacon*, or brave *Raleigh* spake;
> Or bid the new be *English*, Ages hence,
> (For Use will father what's begot by Sense)
> Pour the full Tide of Eloquence along,
> Serenely pure, and yet divinely strong,
> Rich with the Treasures of each foreign Tongue;
> Prune the luxuriant, the uncouth refine,
> But show no mercy to an empty line;
> Then polish all, with so much life and ease,
> You think 'tis Nature, and a knack to please:
> 'But Ease in writing flows from Art, not Chance,
> 'As those move easiest who have learn'd to dance.[38]

It is the finished object—vital in its fidelity to life, yet ordered, harmonious, refined—that elicits comparison with the divine creation and earns for its maker the epithet 'God-like'.

ii. *The Parable of Art*

The doubts of at least one recent critic notwithstanding,[39] Pope could scarcely have failed to sense the relevance of this analogy to one of the splendid episodes of the most admired poem of antiquity: Homer's account of the making of Achilles' shield in the *Iliad*, Book XVIII. Well before he undertook to translate that poem, he had shown in the *Pastorals* his readiness to construe the conventions of classical poetry with a fresh eye, to draw out their profoundest implications and to make them shine anew within the system of his own aesthetic values. In 'Spring' the traditional bowl of pastoral has been newly wrought, transformed into an exquisite symbol of the relationship between Art and ideal Nature. We have seen, furthermore, how inevitably Pope thought of the productions

of human art in terms of the paradigm of Genesis. Even as he
instructed Lintot's engraver in designing a map of the ancient
world for the *Iliad*, he amused himself by recalling the Third Day
of creation. He wrote to his friend Edward Blount on 27 August
1714:

> I have been forced to write him [the engraver] in so high a style, that
> were my epistle intercepted, it would raise no small admiration in an
> ordinary man. There is scarce an order in it of less importance, than to
> remove such and such mountains, alter the course of such and such rivers,
> place a large city on such a coast, and raze another in another country.
> I have set bounds to the sea, and said to the land, *thus far shalt thou advance
> and no further.*[40]

To make Daphnis' Bowl the emblem of his aesthetic concerns in
the *Pastorals*, Pope had had to redesign a conventional device,
improving upon tradition; Achilles' Shield, more vividly than any
map, was already the image of art imitating universal Nature.

Moreover, as Pope well knew, the episode itself had long been
interpreted as a parable of creation. In Eustathius and Heraclides
Ponticus, Hephaistos' forging the shield was thus allegorically
construed; indeed, like the exegetes who christianized Virgil's
Fourth Eclogue, Clement of Alexandria had gone so far as to declare
Homer's debt to the first chapter of Genesis.[41] The traditional interpretation is summarized by George Chapman:

> . . . for what is here prefigurde by our miraculous Artist, but the
> universall world, which being so spatious and almost unmeasurable, one
> circlet of a Shield representes and imbraceth? In it heauen turnes, the
> starres shine, the earth is enflowred, the sea swelles and rageth, Citties are
> built: one in the happinesse and sweetnesse of peace, the other in open
> warre & the terrors of ambush &c. And all these so liuely proposde, as not
> without reason many in times past haue belieued, that all these thinges
> haue in them a kind of voluntarie motion: euen as those Tripods of *Vulcan*,
> and that *Dedalian Venus* . . . for so are all things here described, by our
> diuenest Poet, as if they consisted not of hard and solid mettals, but of
> a truely, liuing, and mouing soule: The ground of his inuention he shews
> out of *Eustathius*: intending by the Orbiguitie of the Shield, the roundnesse
> of the world: by the foure mettalles, the foure elementes: viz. by gold fire:
> by brasse earth for the hardnes: by Tinne water, for the softnes, and inclina-
> tion to fluxure: by siluer, Aire, for the grosnes & obscuritie of the mettal
> before it be refind.[42]

This is the exegetical tradition in which Pope read the episode and
which, duly purged of its more arcane and extravagant features,

he found confirmed by such reputable contemporary critics as the Daciers: Homer, writes Mme Dacier, deserves 'tres grandes loüanges d'avoir executé avec tant d'ordre, tant d'harmonie, & avec si peu de figures un aussi grand dessein que celuy de representer l'univers & tout ce qui fait l'occupation des hommes pendant la guerre & pendant la paix'.[43] In his own note to the passage, Pope makes certain that his readers will bear this context in mind. He rehearses the allegory at length, explaining its 'philosophical Mysteries' from Eustathius and Heraclides and glossing other details by reference to Heraclitus, for whom '*All things . . .* [*were*] *made by the Operation of Fire*', and to Empedocles, whose doctrine of *concordia discors*, 'that all Things had their Original from *Strife* and *Friendship*', is said to be adumbrated in Homer's '*two Allegorical Cities, one of Peace*, the other of *War*', engraved on the shield.[44]

Considering the trouble he takes to review the commentaries, what is one to make of his concluding protestation that they are, after all, silly? 'All these Refinements (not to call 'em absolute Whimsies) I leave just as I found 'em, to the Reader's Judgment or Mercy. They call it *Learning* to have read 'em, but I fear it is *Folly* to quote 'em.' Having firmly fixed the allegorical dimension in the reader's mind, Pope scoffs and coyly reassumes his Augustan urbanity. One suspects a certain disingenuousness (comparable, say, to Sterne's solemn denial that the word *nose* in *Tristram Shandy* carries any but a strictly literal signification!). That Pope was impatient with the pedantry and esotericism of Homer's commentators is, of course, plain enough from his complaints to friends, and he was sufficiently alert to the absurdity of making a heathen author 'talk too like a Christian'.[45] He pored over the critics, none the less, looking for clues to Homer's 'art or contrivance'. It is clear from his correspondence with Broome, who was digesting Eustathius for him, that he had no objection in principle to allegorical readings so long as they were 'obvious and ingenious' and not 'far-fetched'.[46] Introducing *The Temple of Fame*, in fact, he expressly defends allegory, an unfashionable mode, against critics of '*a pretended Refinement of Taste*': '*We find*', he protests, '*an uncommon Charm in Truth, when it is convey'd by this Side-way to our Understanding.*' What he chiefly objects to—especially in the epic, which should adhere to the rules of probability—is the *gaucherie* of pursuing an allegory in '*too nice and exact*' a manner, of 'insisting on it too closely, and carrying it too far'.[47] He may well have felt that the subtle scholiasts who allegorized Homer had exceeded these sensible bounds; but, like the Daciers, he seems also to have recognized that the passage invited this kind of reading. I shall argue, indeed, that Pope saw the episode of Achilles' Shield as a parable of Art—that for him with peculiar appropriateness, the figure of the crippled artificer forging the image of universal Nature stood as the consummate metaphor for the mystery (and consolation) of the poetic act.

From the 'Observations' he appended to Book XVIII it appears not only that Pope admired Homer's description of the shield extremely, but that it held a special significance for him. Homer, he declares, has here provided 'a complete *Idea* of *Painting*, and a Sketch for what one may call an *universal Picture*'.[48]

His Intention was no less, than to draw the Picture of the whole World in the Compass of this Shield. We see first the Universe in general; the Heavens are spread, the Stars are hung up, the Earth is stretched forth, the Seas are pour'd round: We next see the World in a nearer and more particular view; the Cities, delightful in Peace, or formidable in War; the Labours of the Country, and the Fruit of those Labours, in the Harvests and the Vintages; the Pastoral Life in its Pleasures and its Dangers: In a word, all the Occupations, all the Ambitions, and all the Diversions of Mankind.[49]

One inference about Pope's view of the episode should already be clear: if, as he believed, Art was the imitation of ideal Nature, Vulcan, in fashioning the shield, has produced what amounts to the quintessential artefact, a work that is literally the image of the world, the representation in epitome of the drama of human life enacted against the background of cosmic Order. But to grasp what further meaning the episode had for him, we must notice what Pope does with it; for, like his poem as a whole, Pope's version of Achilles' Shield is as much an interpretation as a translation of the original. By adding some details and omitting others, by altering Homer's emphases, by requiring that the poetry be read in the light of the notes and commentary, by making the verse echo the language and evoke the contexts of later poems, *Paradise Lost* in particular—by such strategies Pope makes Homer's epic very much his own.

Consider, for instance, the effect of Nicolas Vleughels's design of the shield, which, with slight modifications, was included in the

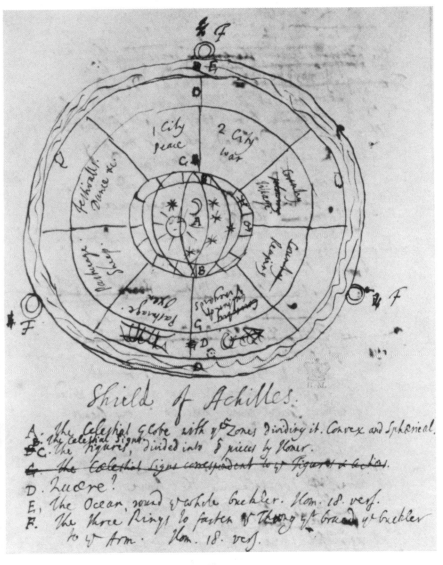

13. Pope's Sketch of Achilles' Shield

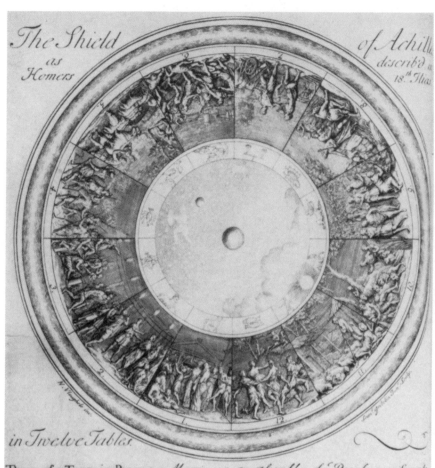

The Shield as Homers of Achilles described in 18.th Ilias

in Twelve Tables.

Three of a Town in Peace. *1. a Marriage 2 an Assembly of y. People. 3. a Senate.*
Three of a Town in War. *4. The Besieg'd making a Sally. 5. Shepherds*
their Flocks falling into an Ambuscade. 6. a Combat.
Three of Agriculture. *7. Tillage. 8. Harvest. 9. a Vintage.*
Three of a Pastoral Life. *10. Lions & Herds of Cattle. 11. Sheep.*
12. the Dance.

14. Vleughels' Design of Achilles' Shield

first edition.[50] Vleughels's design is a complete sophistication of the original description, an almost entirely fanciful elaboration of the merest hints in Homer. By reproducing it and by basing his own commentary upon it, Pope actually controls the way his readers will *see* the shield. Where Homer's account is vague and rather haphazard, Vleughels and Pope present a pattern of vividly delineated images formally organized as a system of balanced contrasts within a series of concentric circles. The first circle depicts the macrocosm, whose centre is the earth poised between night and day and whose circumference is the circle of the Zodiac; the next ring, divided into equal compartments under the twelve signs of the Zodiac, depicts twelve contrasting scenes of human life, representing the town in peace and war and the country in its various aspects; the final ring depicts the ocean, encompassing the whole. Pope's shield, like Daphnis' bowl, imitates the world in its roundness and circularity, and in the implicit contrast between cosmic Order and earthly mutability; in these respects it is faithful enough to Homer. But in the number of his scenes,[51] and especially in the controlling use of antitheses, Pope has no real authority in the text. Whereas Homer, for example, introducing the description of human life on the shield, simply begins, 'Therein fashioned he also two cities of mortal men exceeding fair',[52] Pope's couplet presents these towns in a neatly balanced antithesis: 'Two Cities radiant on the Shield appear, / The Image one of Peace, and one of War' (ll. 567–8). Throughout he is at pains to have Homer conform with his own thoroughly Augustan assumptions concerning life and art. He imagines that Homer saw the world, and therefore represented it on the shield, as a *concordia discors*, the great principle of Order in Nature and Form in the arts. 'Nothing is more wonderful', he remarks, than Homer's 'exact Observation of the *Contrast*, not only between Figure and Figure, but between Subject and Subject.'[53] He develops this point at length, noting how Homer has paired scenes of peace and scenes of strife, scenes in town and scenes in the country, scenes of gaiety and scenes of labour, the old and the young, men and women. Concluding this catalogue of contrasts, he remarks Homer's variation of the three dances engraved on the shield, which, for Pope appropriately enough, seem to stand as an emblematic allusion to the principle of harmonic reconciliation that governs the world: 'That at the Wedding is in a circular Figure, that of the Vineyard in a Row, that in the last Picture, a mingled one.'[54] As Pope later declares, Homer saw life as a *concordia discors*, believing that 'the Harmony of all Beings arises from . . . Discord', that from 'Opposition arises that discordant Concord by which all Nature subsists'.[55] To Pope, clearly, the art of the shield reflects and embodies this universal law. Indeed, he carries the Augustanizing of his subject to the point of insisting that Homer, in designing his scenes, anticipates the rules of neo-aristotelian criticism by scrupulously observing 'the *three Unities*' of '*Action*', '*Time*', and '*Point of View*'.[56] Like Vleughels, Pope has seen the shield in the light of his own aesthetic and philosophical assumptions, as a work depicting the Order of universal Nature in terms of its own balanced and harmonious form. He has, as it were, remade it.

By a similar process of transformation, Homer's Hephaistos, the grotesque artificer of Olympus, becomes Pope's Vulcan, the idealized figure of 'the Artist-God' (l. 531). Though Hephaistos appears in the *Iliad* as the supreme craftsman, the descriptive formula most often applied to him emphasizes his physical powers rather than his artistry: he is 'the famed god of the two strong arms'.[57] Vulcan is not so crude. Pope's epithets for him stress his skill and his crippled body: he is 'the Architect divine' (l. 179), 'the lame Architect' (l. 435); 'th' immortal Artist' (xix. 24), 'the lame Artist' (l. 479). We are meant to admire his 'matchless Art' (xix. 26) and to pity his 'aukward Form' (l. 464). Typical of the way in which Pope refines and idealizes his model is his rendering of the passage in which Hephaistos abandons the forge and prepares to welcome Thetis. Homer has him rising from the anvil, 'a huge, panting bulk', stumbling on his 'slender legs' as he gathers his tools into a chest.[58] In Pope the effect is utterly different:

> Then from his Anvil the lame Artist rose;
> Wide with distorted Legs, oblique he goes,
> And stills the Bellows, and (in order laid)
> Locks in their Chest his Instruments of Trade.   (ll. 479–82)

What was grotesque in the original has become graceful, the ugly image made almost lovely through the use of sonic devices such as alliteration and assonance, and the elegant latinisms of the second line; the notion of Vulcan's fastidiousness, his instruments 'in order laid', is entirely new. Besides softening the rough physical aspect of the god, Pope renders his skilfulness more vividly than Homer by showing the artificer in the act of creation—pouring 'the glowing Ore' into moulds (l. 446), turning 'the vex'd Metal round' (l. 549) as he hammers it into shape, miraculously causing 'god-like Labours' to rise on the surface of the shield (l. 556). In Pope's version, Vulcan has transcended his deformity, moving among the gods 'with awkward Grace' (i. 770); and his consummate artistry, the gift given in compensation for his affliction, has acquired a new importance.

Under Pope's hands, indeed, the myth of Vulcan's forging the shield takes on the aspect of parable: in a sense epitomizing those aesthetic concerns we have traced in the *Pastorals* and in the motif of *fiat lux*, it appears as the archetypal representation of the artist's relationship to ideal Nature, the divine Artefact. In seeing the episode this way, Pope may owe something to the exegetical tradition, but he was too much a man of his times to take very seriously the 'Refinements', as he called them, of those commentators who whimsically expounded the Pythagorean 'Mysteries' of creation that Homer was supposedly celebrating. Pope deepens the meaning of the episode not through the techniques of allegory, by relying on the reader's knowledge of an arcane symbolism; but rather through his favourite method of allusion, by allowing his language to echo other poems and to evoke other poetic contexts.[59] In this way, by recalling *Paradise Lost* in particular, he associates Vulcan's powers with those of the Logos, and he makes us see the world depicted on the shield as an image of Milton's universe. His point is surely not, as Homer's critics would have it, that Vulcan *is* the Demiurge of Genesis mystically prefigured, but that, in his role as archetypal artificer, the mythic pattern of the ideal Artist, Vulcan in some distant yet apposite sense recapitulates the creative act of Genesis. Vulcan is not a figure in an allegory, but the essential expression of an analogy, recurrent in Pope's works, between the Artist and the creating Word.

The association between Vulcan's powers and those of Milton's 'Omnific Word' is established at once, as Thetis finds 'the lame Architect' at 'no common Task', forging golden tripods that move marvellously on 'living Wheels', responding to his will:

> Full twenty Tripods for his Hall he fram'd,
> That plac'd on living Wheels of massy Gold,
> (Wond'rous to tell) instinct with Spirit roll'd
> From Place to Place, around the blest Abodes,
> Self-mov'd, obedient to the Beck of Gods . . .   (ll. 440–4)

Pope's phrasing, 'on living Wheels . . . instinct with Spirit', echoes
Paradise Lost (vi. 846, 752), where Milton describes the miraculous
wheels of 'The Chariot of Paternal Deitie', instrument of God's
Omnipotence, which the Son rides to subdue the rebellious angels
and, later (vii. 197 ff.), to create the new world. As Pope points
out in a footnote to the passage, giving the scriptural text in
full,[60] the similarity between Homer's living wheels and those
in Ezekiel (1: 20–1), from which Milton drew his account of
the divine chariot, had been remarked by Addison in his series
of critical papers on *Paradise Lost*.[61] Though the Miltonic context would have been sufficient for this purpose, Pope may also
have known the conventional interpretation of Ezekiel's wheels,
which were construed by the commentators as agents expressing God's Power and Providence.[62] In any case, by evoking the
idea of the Power that created the world, Pope's quotations of
Milton and Ezekiel heighten the reader's sense of Vulcan's
awesome artistry. He is, at a level Homer did not intend, master
of the creative element, 'the Father' and 'Sov'reign of the Fire'
(ll. 537, 487).

By similar techniques of allusion and magnification, and
by changes in emphasis, the image of the world Vulcan works
upon the shield is brought closer to the Miltonic conception of
the universe. Pope seems to have sensed an analogy between
the situations in Homer and in *Paradise Lost*, Book VII, as the
process of creation begins. Vulcan, having stilled the 'living
Wheels', begins to forge the shield by an act of definition, cir-
cumscribing its verge within 'a threefold Circle' (l. 533); so Milton's
'Omnific Word'

> Then staid the fervid Wheeles, and in his hand
> He took the golden Compasses, prepar'd
> In Gods Eternal store, to circumscribe
> This Universe, and all created things:
> One foot he center'd, and the other turn'd
> Round through the vast profunditie obscure,
> And said, thus farr extend, thus farr thy bounds,
> This be thy just Circumference, O World.
>
> (vii. 224–31)

Certainly Pope's next line, 'A silver Chain suspends the
massy Round' (l. 554), a curious embellishment of the original,[63]
seems calculated to recall Milton's description of the universe

('this great Round' (vii. 267)) and his vision of the 'pendant world':

> And fast by hanging in a golden Chain
> This pendant world, in bigness as a Starr
> Of smallest Magnitude . . .   (ii. 1051–3)[64]

Introducing the description of Vulcan's '*universal Picture*', Pope again alters his original in order to convey the impression of a world taking form seemingly at the will of its maker, a world which is the faithful embodiment of the artist's conceptualizing imagination: 'And god-like Labours on the Surface rose. / There shone the Image of the Master Mind' (ll. 556–7). The last line is entirely Pope's own interpolation—another instance of his favourite notion of the creative process for which the paradigm, as we have seen, was the fiat of Genesis. As he describes the static image on the shield, Pope, furthermore, uses several strategies to enforce its correspondence with the real world and to impart life and motion to the whole. In doing so, he follows Homer's lead, using the techniques of the original more systematically. Besides exaggerating the element of contrast, the aspect of the world as a *concordia discors*, he seizes every opportunity to stress 'the Idea of Roundness', by which, he remarks, Homer 'hints at the Figure of the World'.[65] (With the same purpose, we may recall, a similar pattern of imagery operates in the description of Daphnis' bowl.)[66] The circularity of the shield as a whole is emphasized at the beginning and at the conclusion of the passage:

> Its utmost Verge a threefold Circle bound;
> A silver Chain suspends the massy Round . . .   (ll. 553–4)

> Thus the broad Shield complete the Artist crown'd
> With his last Hand, and pour'd the Ocean round:
> In living Silver seem'd the Waves to roll,
> And beat the Buckler's Verge, and bound the whole.   (ll. 701–4)

The scenes themselves abound with words and images denoting roundness, circularity, rotation: the moon is 'compleatly round' (l. 559); the stars 'Heav'ns high Convex crown'd' (l. 560); the constellation of the Bear is seen 'around the Axle of the Sky . . . revolving' (ll. 563–4); dancers 'in a Circle bound' (l. 573); heralds 'form a Ring' (l. 584); besiegers 'embrace' the town (l. 593); squadrons in ambush rise 'round' the unsuspecting enemy (l. 611); ploughmen 'wheel around' to meet their master

'with his Goblet crown'd' (ll. 631–2); the earth 'in Ridges roll'd'
(l. 635); the farmer sees the harvested corn 'around him rise'
(l. 646); 'Clusters' of grapes hang 'curl'd' (ll. 653–4). And Pope
throughout brilliantly animates his figures. Duplicating an effect
for which Homer was famous, he charges the world fixed and
frozen on the shield with vibrant life and movement.

In the final, masterly scene all these devices function to clarify
the meaning of Vulcan's artistry. Here the ideas of harmony and
design—the formal principles of Nature and Art—are symbolically
enacted in the 'figur'd Dance' (l. 681) of youths and maidens.
Moving 'Hand in Hand' to music's measures, they celebrate the
joy of love and unity in a dance whose form and intricate harmony
imply the patterned concert of universal Nature. The particular
dance Pope believed he was describing,[67] was the perfect expression of *concordia discors*, combining by the power of '*Dœdalean* Art'
the antithetical principles of the line and the circle, high and low,
male and female, war and love.

> A figur'd Dance succeeds: Such once was seen
> In lofty *Gnossus*, for the *Cretan* Queen,
> Form'd by *Dœdalean* Art. A comely Band
> Of Youths and Maidens, bounding Hand in Hand:
> The Maids in soft Cymarrs of Linen drest;
> The Youths all graceful in the glossy Vest;
> Of those the Locks with flow'ry Wreaths inroll'd,
> Of these the Sides adorn'd with Swords of Gold,
> That glitt'ring gay, from silver Belts depend.
> Now all at once they rise, at once descend,
> With well-taught Feet: Now shape, in oblique ways,
> Confus'dly regular, the moving Maze:
> Now forth at once, too swift for sight, they spring,
> And undistinguish'd blend the flying Ring:
> So whirls a Wheel, in giddy Circle tost,
> And rapid as it runs, the single Spokes are lost.
> The gazing Multitudes admire around;
> Two active Tumblers in the Center bound;
> Now high, now low, their pliant Limbs they bend,
> And gen'ral Songs the sprightly Revel end.   (ll. 681–700)

Altering Homer's scene quite boldly, Pope's image of the dance
'Confus'dly regular' invites comparison with the world of *Windsor
Forest*, 'harmoniously confus'd', or with 'the regular confusion'
of the universe described in Addison's *Cato* (I. i. 48–53). But it

resembles most nearly the dance of Milton's angels, whose motions, intricate yet regular, imitate the pattern of cosmic Order:

> Mystical dance, which yonder starrie Spheare
> Of Planets and of fixt in all her Wheeles
> Resembles nearest, mazes intricate,
> Eccentric, intervolv'd, yet regular
> Then most, when most irregular they seem:
> And in thir motions harmonie Divine
> So smooths her charming tones, that Gods own ear
> Listens delighted. (v. 620–7)

In Art the human world may mirror universal Harmony.

In the loveliness of the 'figur'd Dance', as in the exquisite artifice of the shield as a whole, Vulcan's clumsiness is forgotten, his deformity transcended. Pope seems to encourage such an interpretation by applying to the graceful movements of the dancers phrases used to describe Vulcan's lameness or his headlong fall from heaven. The lines, 'the lame Artist rose, / Wide with distorted Legs, oblique he goes' (ll. 479–80), echo strangely in the description of the dancers:

> Now all at once they rise, at once descend,
> With well-taught Feet: Now shape, in oblique ways,
> Confus'dly regular, the moving Maze . . .

As the dancers spin round—'So whirls a Wheel, in giddy Circle tost, / And rapid as it runs, the single Spokes are lost'—we seem to hear again the tale of Vulcan's fall: 'Tost all the Day in rapid Circles round; /. . . Breathless I fell, in giddy Motion lost' (i. 762–4). Whatever Pope may have meant by this curious counterpoint, he must have thought it fitting that so awkward a god should be the author of a work so splendid and correct. It is the world of Art that matters to Vulcan, who knows that shields offer no protection against the cruelty of life. But if life is short, a work well made will last. To Thetis, 'the Artist-God' regrets that he is powerless to prevent Achilles' fate, in compensation offering only what he can —a work worthy of immortal fame:

> Thy Griefs resign,
> Secure, what *Vulcan* can, is ever thine.
> O could I hide him from the Fates as well,
> Or with these Hands the cruel Stroke repell,

As I shall forge most envy'd Arms, the Gaze
Of wond'ring Ages, and the World's Amaze!   (ll. 531–6)[68]

Might Pope have found—whose own 'Evil Forme' was a plain enough memorial of life's vexations,[69] and whose own careful art was the glory of its time—a particular poignancy in Homer's myth of the lame artificer? Perhaps so. There is little doubt, at least, that as a poet he made that myth peculiarly his own.

iii. *The Uncreating Word*

Like the bowl of Daphnis, though on a grander scale, Vulcan's shield may be seen as the objective embodiment of the ideal relationship in Pope's thought between Art and Nature, between the human artist and the divine. It stands as the emblem of the Augustan ideal of natural Order and aesthetic Form, just as the divine fiat of Genesis serves as the paradigm of that ideal and, ultimately, supplies its sanction. Together these two ideas help to clarify the positive standard against which Pope as a satirist measured the character of his age in morality and the arts. As Aubrey Williams has shown,[70] what troubled him about the hackney writers and free-thinkers who swarm in *The Dunciad* is precisely that, in their incompetency and pride, they threaten to undo the sacred work of creation, preferring anarchy to order, obfuscation to intellectual light, noise to harmony, the love of self to the love of God and their neighbour. Forgetting the divinely appointed order of things, they busily set about recreating the world in their own image, achieving a monstrous parody of the Christian system. Though this theme reaches its consummate expression in *The New Dunciad* (1743), it is present in Pope's work much earlier. In *An Essay on Criticism* the false critics who relish the affected manner of metaphysical verse share with the dunces a certain delight in disorder: 'Pleas'd with a Work where nothing's just or fit; / One *glaring Chaos* and *wild Heap* of *Wit*' (ll. 291–2). Similarly, the 'wild creation' of Dulness in *The Dunciad* (*A*, i. 53–82) differs only in degree from the wonders wrought by Ambrose Philips in his pastorals, who 'by a poetical Creation' improving upon God's own, 'hath raised up finer beds of Flowers than the most industrious Gardiner; his Roses, Endives, Lillies, Kingcups and Daffadils blow *all in the same season*'.[71] And Blackmore, by celebrating the order of Nature in bungled verse, 'Un-did *Creation* at a Jerk',[72] thereby epitomizing in Pope's view the destructive business of duncery everywhere—though in this Blackmore succeeds abruptly at what is usually the more insidious process of attrition, the gradual undermining of foundations.

Paradoxically, it is in *The Dunciad*, the epic of a world restored to Chaos and dark Night, that the theme of creation—alluding both to the original fiat of Genesis and to the 'new World' of Revelation—receives its fullest expression. By presenting Dulness and her minions engaged in a perverse parody of the acts which began and which will end the world's drama, Pope keeps before us, as in a negative image, those Christian ideals of rational order and benign purpose which the dunces have betrayed.[73] Dulness is the 'uncreating word' (*A*, iii. 340) uttering the *fiat nox* of annihilation:

> Let there be darkness! (the dread pow'r shall say)
> All shall be darkness, as it ne'er were Day;
> To their first Chaos Wit's vain works shall fall,
> And universal Dulness cover all.

These lines, with which the 1728 version closed, suggest that well before he came under Warburton's sobering influence, Pope had his 'deep Intent' (iv. 4) for the poem firmly in mind. However much he doubtless enjoyed embarrassing the likes of Theobald and Dennis, his larger purpose—though, as we shall see, more effectively realized in 1743—was from the start to define the nature and consequences of human folly and presumption, which here as in the *Essay on Man* he saw essentially as the inversion of 'the laws / Of ORDER', the cardinal sin 'against th'Eternal Cause'.[74] Dulness, he later noted to make the point clear, is a kind of insanity, the condition of the mind bereft of reason, confusing true and false, order and anarchy:

> . . . Dulness here is not to be taken contractedly for mere Stupidity, but in the enlarged sense of the word, for all Slowness of Apprehension, Shortness of Sight, or imperfect Sense of things. It includes . . . Labour, Industry, and some degree of Activity and Boldness: a ruling principle not inert, but turning topsy-turvy the Understanding, and inducing an Anarchy or confused State of Mind. (*B*, i. 15 n.)

The mirror of their minds, the world of the dunces is downside up. Since they have distorted the real nature of things—preferring chaos to order, darkness to light, illusion to truth—the world they inhabit is in its every detail an inverted reflection of the one called into being by the divine fiat: it has its own perverse 'Nature' created by Dulness in her image, its own 'sacred' history unfolded by its own prophets and leading to the advent of its own 'Messiah', who comes at last in triumph '*to substitute the* Kingdom of the Dull *upon earth*' (iv. Argument). Like the Bible itself, *The Dunciad* moves from Genesis to Revelation. The pattern of Christian Time which Pope, in a different mood, had celebrated in the *Pastorals* and *Messiah* now provides the ironic framework for his last and greatest poem.

Underlying the macabre projection in *The Dunciad* of a world benighted and deranged is the analogy between Art and ideal Nature that we have remarked as a distinguishing characteristic of Augustan aesthetic thought, found in Dryden's praise of 'the providence of wit', in Fielding's view of *Tom Jones* as an imitation of God's 'great Creation', in Pope's conception of the true poet as 'God-like', the re-creator, in description and song, of the 'Groves of *Eden*'. It is in this sense that Pope imagined the successful artist, whose archetype was Homer's Vulcan, as emulating 'th'Omnific Word'. If Nature is already Art, a universe evoked in love and wisdom according to the formal principles of harmony, proportion, regularity, then Art, the imitation of Nature, will reflect her rich variety and lucid order in its own productions, duly respectful of the 'decorum' of creation. In this way the true artist mimics the Deity. Conversely, the false artist—a Theobald or a Cibber, let us say—in presuming to emulate the Logos manages instead to resemble the arch-agent of 'un-creation'; he is 'the Antichrist of Wit' (*A*, ii. 12). Caught in the process of composition, he appears like Satan struggling to undo the order of things, floundering through Chaos, the proper element of a mind confused and the proper emblem of its works:

> Studious he sate, with all his books around,
> Sinking from thought to thought, a vast profound!
> Plung'd for his sense, but found no bottom there;
> Then writ, and flounder'd on, in mere despair.
> He roll'd his eyes that witness'd huge dismay . . .   (*A*, i. 111–15)

In *The Dunciad*, therefore, incompetence in the arts—most obviously in poetry, but also, as Pope's view of his subject broadened, in the intellectual arts of science, philosophy, theology—is seen essentially as the violation of Nature. In the mirror of art what the dunces project is 'a new world, to Nature's laws unknown' (*A*, iii. 237), yet a world resembling Nature in the way that sophistry resembles rhetoric, casuistry morality, a play by Theobald (or Cibber) poetry. Since the world the dunces inhabit is the counterfeit and parody of the true order of things, Pope's mocking allusions to scripture, to Virgil, to Milton, enforce the point by making it part of the very texture of the poem. As Nature and Nature's God supply the pattern for the true artist to follow, so Dulness—'Mighty Mother' of Dissonance and Discord—spawns the formless, phantasmagoric world which passes with her children for reality, the world imaged in their works. The result is a new orthodoxy, the shadow and negation of the old.

To make clear what has been lost and how, Pope presents Dulness in sublime travesty of the act on which the Augustan faith in Order was founded. Like the Spirit of God she hovers brooding over the abyss that is Georgian England, 'her mighty wings outspread, / To hatch a new Saturnian age of Lead' (*A*, i. 25–6).[75] As she proceeds in her 'wild creation', Pope enforces comparison with the Logos in a remarkable passage comprising an absurd abridgement of the Mosaic and Miltonic accounts of creation:

> Here she beholds the Chaos dark and deep,
> Where nameless somethings in their causes sleep,
> 'Till genial Jacob, or a warm Third-day
> Call forth each mass, a poem or a play.
> How Hints, like spawn, scarce quick in embryo lie,
> How new-born Nonsense first is taught to cry,
> Maggots half-form'd, in rhyme exactly meet,
> And learn to crawl upon poetic feet.
> Here one poor Word a hundred clenches makes,
> And ductile dulness new meanders takes;
> There motley Images her fancy strike,
> Figures ill-pair'd, and Similes unlike.
> She sees a Mob of Metaphors advance,
> Pleas'd with the Madness of the mazy dance:
> How Tragedy and Comedy embrace;
> How Farce and Epic get a jumbled race;
> How Time himself stands still at her command,
> Realms shift their place, and Ocean turns to land.
> Here gay Description Ægypt glads with showers;
> Or gives to Zembla fruits, to Barca flowers;
> Glitt'ring with ice here hoary hills are seen,
> There painted vallies of eternal green,

> On cold December fragrant chaplets blow,
> And heavy harvests nod beneath the snow.
> All these and more, the cloud-compelling Queen
> Beholds thro' fogs that magnify the scene:
> She, tinsel'd o'er in robes of varying hues,
> With self-applause her wild creation views,
> Sees momentary monsters rise and fall,
> And with her own fool's colours gilds them all.   (*A*, i. 53–82)

As the Logos in the beginning reified the ideal forms of things in the mind of God, so Dulness, as Aubrey Williams observes, 'is seen introspecting a chaos out of chaos',[76] calling forth the 'motley Images' conceived in her 'fancy'. And as God, his work concluded, 'saw every thing that he had made, and, behold, *it was* very good' (Genesis I: 31), so Dulness, her own labours done, 'With self-applause her wild creation views'.

The general correspondence here between Dulness and the 'Omnific Word' is clear enough. What has not been observed about the parody is that it is meant, in its details, specifically to evoke Milton's account of creation in *Paradise Lost*. The Chaos which Dulness beholds, 'Where nameless somethings in their causes sleep', recalls Milton's 'wilde Abyss' wherein the elements 'in thir pregnant causes mixt / Confus'dly' (ii. 910–14). In particular, her works of creation burlesque God's on the third, fifth, and sixth days, when the sea was separated from the land and all living things were made. As God on the third day divided the sea from the land, so, with reference to the productions of Grub Street, the largesse of Tonson the bookseller and the playwright's hope of a lucrative benefit 'Call forth each mass, a poem or a play'. The pun on 'Third-day' points to Genesis, but Pope's choice of adjectives ('*genial* Jacob . . . a *warm* Third-day') and his earlier reference to Dulness as 'the Great Mother' (*A*, i. 33) seem drawn from *Paradise Lost*, where on the third day of creation God causes the ocean to flow 'with warme / Prolific humour', softening the earth and fermenting 'the great Mother to conceave, / Satiate with genial moisture' (vii. 279–82). On the fifth day God created the fish of the sea and the fowl of the air, commanding them to be fruitful and multiply (Genesis I: 20–2); but Pope's version, in which 'Hints, like spawn, scarce quick in embryo lie', parodies Milton's account, in which the waters 'generate / Reptil with Spawn abundant, living Soule' (vii. 387–8). On the sixth day God bade the earth 'bring forth the

living creature after his kind, cattle, and creeping thing' (Genesis
1: 24); so, as Dulness works, 'Maggots half-form'd . . . learn to
crawl upon poetic feet', and, in travesty of the Logos, 'one poor
Word', teeming under the influence of the goddess's generative
powers, 'a hundred clenches makes'. Again Pope's 'Maggots' recall
Milton's account of the sixth day, when 'At once came forth whatever creeps the ground, / Insect or Worme' (vii. 475–6). In Milton,
of course, the Word is not merely prolific; its creatures are perfectly
formed and move through Eden in well-matched pairs:

> The Earth obey'd, and strait
> Op'ning her fertil Woomb teem'd at a Birth
> Innumerous living Creatures, perfect formes,
> Limb'd and full grown . . .
> Among the Trees in Pairs they rose, they walk'd. (vii. 453–9)

But Dulness's progeny are neither well-formed nor companionable;
they are 'motley Images', 'Figures ill-pair'd, and Similes unlike',
a 'Mob' of advancing metaphors. In her paradise, Milton's 'Dance'
of 'stately Trees' (vii. 324) becomes mad and 'mazy'. Whereas God
commanded the creatures each to generate 'by thir kindes' (vii. 393),
at Dulness's bidding the literary kinds, 'Tragedy and Comedy',
'Farce and Epic', produce only 'a jumbled race', in violation both of
poetic decorum and of Nature's laws. Dulness, indeed, having like
Ambrose Philips performed her own 'poetical Creation', abolishes
Time and the natural Order at a stroke, and undoes even the
separation of the elements ordained by divine fiat on the third day:
'Realms shift their place, and Ocean turns to land'. This is *her*
Nature, 'the *materials* or *stock*'[77] which she affords *her* poets for
imitation. Their world, like their art, being without form and void,
Dulness and her dunces have effectually reduced creation to chaos,
the type and symbol, according to the tradition in which Pope was
writing, 'of an unregenerate graceless Soul'.[78] At one level Pope's
intention in this passage may be seen simply as an elaboration of
Horace's complaint, who characterized lack of decorum in the
arts as a distortion of the natural order of things.[79] But Pope goes
much further than this. By choosing to represent such incompetence in terms of a travesty of the first chapter of Genesis, he
implies that bungling and presumption in the arts are a kind of
blasphemy against creation.

The parody of Genesis is not quite complete until (in *A*, ii. 31–46)
Dulness makes man, or rather a 'Poet's form', in her own image—

a phantom shaped 'of well-bodied air', with feather brain and
leaden heart, and for the gift of speech graced with 'empty words . . .
and sounding strain'. But the climactic instance of the motif of
mock-creation as it pertains to Pope's idea of Nature and aesthetic
form occurs in Book III, as Settle envisions Theobald's reign pre-
cipitating the mad denouement of the *theatrum mundi*. If the stage
according to a traditional analogy[80] is the image of the world, then
the stage of contemporary London, delighting in the harlequinades
of John Rich and the preposterous dramaturgy of Theobald, implies
'a new world, to Nature's laws unknown'—a new creation,
glorious in its consummate Disorder and predicated upon the confusion of the old. God is to his world as the playwright is to the play:
so Dulness, the Deity of Rich and Theobald, having engendered her
'wild creation' in Book I, is seen in Book III plotting the progress of
her saints through history and leading them toward a triumphant
catastrophe. In his role as Faustus, the 'sable Sorc'rer', John Rich
is her St. John the Divine, revealing the signs and portents of the
apocalypse, as 'one wide Conflagration swallows all' and 'a new
world' is ushered in. Settle addresses Theobald:

> 'See now, what Dulness and her sons admire;
> See! what the charms, that smite the simple heart
> Not touch'd by Nature, and not reach'd by Art.'
>
>   He look'd, and saw a sable Sorc'rer rise,
> Swift to whose hand a winged volume flies:
> All sudden, Gorgons hiss, and Dragons glare,
> And ten-horn'd fiends and Giants rush to war.
> Hell rises, Heav'n descends, and dance on Earth,
> Gods, imps, and monsters, music, rage, and mirth,
> A fire, a jig, a battle, and a ball,
> Till one wide Conflagration swallows all.
>   Thence a new world, to Nature's laws unknown,
> Breaks out refulgent, with a heav'n its own:
> Another Cynthia her new journey runs,
> And other planets circle other suns:
> The forests dance, the rivers upward rise,
> Whales sport in woods, and dolphins in the skies,
> And last, to give the whole creation grace,
> Lo! one vast Egg produces human race.   (*A*, iii. 226–44)

Pope's art of ambiguity, his remarkable ability to compress
several levels of meaning within a single statement or narrative
line, is here brilliantly on display. By couching the absurdities of

the contemporary stage[81] within the Christian context of apocalypse, he ironically enforces the analogy between the productions of Art and the divine works of creation. Rich's 'winged volume' is his own Book of Revelation. His vision of a 'war' involving 'Dragons' and 'ten-horn'd fiends' recalls St. John's (Rev. 12: 3, 7), as do the spectacle of hell rising and heaven descending (Rev. 12: 9, 17: 8; 12: 4, 13: 13), and that of the 'Conflagration' which signals the beginning of 'a new world' (Rev. 20: 9, 21: 1).[82] These lines—as indeed the vision as a whole of the historical progress of Dulness that Settle reveals to Theobald—are also calculated to recall Michael's instruction of Adam in *Paradise Lost* (xi–xii). At the end of time, the angel relates, Christ will come again 'to dissolve' this 'perverted World',

> then raise
> From the conflagrant mass, purg'd and refin'd,
> New Heav'ns, new Earth . . .   (xii. 546–9)

In *The Dunciad* the marvels of Rich's theatre furnish most of the materials for the lawless world that succeeds the conflagration; other features are supplied by the advice of Horace and Du Fresnoy on how *not* to represent Nature in art.[83] But, as in Book I, Pope's basic strategy is to imply the relationship between aesthetic form and natural order by describing this new 'creation' in terms of the first chapter of Genesis and Book VII of *Paradise Lost*. The works of the Logos on the six days of creation, from the *fiat lux* to the making of man, are ludicrously duplicated on Theobald's stage, as the 'new world . . . / Breaks out refulgent' and 'one vast Egg produces human race'.[84] The notion of the forests dancing, furthermore, recalls Milton (vii. 324), as does the image of sporting whales and dolphins (vii. 410 ff.).

Theobald stands in admiration of these marvels in a manner appropriately reminiscent of the way in which Satan's joy at spoiling God's work (*PL*, x. 350–6) ironically parallels Adam's delighted response to Raphael's account of the creation (*PL*, viii. 10–13). As Pope presses home the analogy between the divine and human artists, it is the 'Immortal Rich', in his role as theatrical producer *extraordinaire*, who emerges as the Creator of these 'worlds', working their 'wonders' and providentially managing the machinery. Deepening still further the motif of mock-creation, Pope's language recalls another of the sublime moments in scripture: God's answering Job out of the whirlwind, the Author of Nature declaring his Omnipotence through his works.

> Joy fills his soul, joy innocent of thought:
> 'What pow'r', he cries, 'what pow'r these wonders wrought?'
> 'Son! what thou seek'st is in thee. Look, and find
> Each monster meets his likeness in thy mind.
> Yet would'st thou more? In yonder cloud, behold!
> Whose sarcenet skirts are edg'd with flamy gold,
> A matchless youth: His nod these worlds controuls,
> Wings the red lightning, and the thunder rolls.
> Angel of Dulness, sent to scatter round
> Her magic charms o'er all unclassic ground:
> Yon stars, yon suns, he rears at pleasure higher,
> Illumes their light, and sets their flames on fire.
> Immortal Rich! how calm he sits at ease
> Mid snows of paper, and fierce hail of pease;
> And proud his mistress' orders to perform,
> Rides in the whirlwind, and directs the storm.   (*A*, iii. 245–60)

As he appears in Settle's vision, Rich resembles the Deity described by Elihu in The Book of Job (37). Like God, who 'scattereth his bright cloud' and causes 'the light of his cloud to shine' (vv. 11, 15, 21), Rich sits perched on high, resplendent. As Rich's nod controls the theatrical world at Covent-Garden, winging its lightning and rolling its thunder, such is God's power over Nature (vv. 2–4, 12). As Rich hangs up his spangled heavens, so God, as he reminds Job (38) can 'bind the sweet influences of Pleiades' and 'guide Arcturus with his sons' (vv. 31–2). Rich, however imperturbable, knows only too well 'the treasures of the snow' and 'hail' (v. 22). Like Job's God, he 'directeth' the storm and his element is 'the whirlwind' (37: 3, 38: 1).

Even in its first form, then, *The Dunciad* implied, if rather playfully, the vision of Nature inverted which is so starkly presented fourteen years later, when Pope, in his masterpiece, imaginatively proclaimed the final dissolution of civilization—the coming of Dulness, in fulfilment of Settle's hopeful prophecies, 'To blot out Order, and extinguish Light' (iv. 14). But though this vision is implicit in 1728–9, it is not convincing. The early poem is so patently the vehicle for its author's personal animus that its larger theme seems strained or merely hyperbolic. In 1728, when he is not simply relishing his skill at making his enemies 'die sweetly', Pope's concern, as in the early poems, is chiefly aesthetic;

and though a logical application of the analogy between Art and ideal Nature that he cherished, the suggestion that the incompetent productions of Grub Street pose a threat to the divinely appointed order of things can hardly be taken seriously. However gravely Pope may have regarded the lack of taste and poetic talent in his society, he cannot have feared that it presaged universal chaos. By 1742, however, bungling and presumption in the arts have become for him part of a greater theme, only one more inevitable manifestation of the general demoralization of an age; for what has been lost according to *The New Dunciad* is not merely respect for an aesthetic ideal, but belief in the philosophical and theological grounds that made that ideal tenable. The dunces now not only fail to understand Art; they have no adequate conception of Nature, because, succumbing to the neo-epicureanism of Hobbes, Descartes, and the Deists, they have no adequate conception of Nature's Author. Their world is in fact our world, anarchic because it rejects any objective basis for Order, benighted because the light of faith has gone out. Though Newton and the physico-theologians had succeeded in postponing the moment when Nature's soothing harmony could be heard no more, what Donne had feared in the *Anniversaries*—a world in pieces, all coherence gone—is realized when, in Pope's last and most prophetic work, Dulness speaks her 'uncreating word / . . . And Universal Darkness buries All'. It is the world implied in Genesis, and with it the Christian humanist tradition, that lies in ruins.

Like every other normally positive value, the idea itself of Harmony, presented in 'Spring' and *Windsor Forest* as the essential attribute of creation, has in *The Dunciad* been converted into its opposite, Cacophony and Discord, the unifying principles of Dulness's world. These are the laws by which Dulness, as Warburton remarks, works consistently 'to promote the harmony of the whole',[85] making 'ONE MIGHTY DUNCIAD OF THE LAND'. Through her domains howl 'Keen, hollow winds . . . / Emblem of Music caus'd by Emptiness' (*A*, i. 29–30), not the spiritual music of the spheres but a kind of cosmic flatulence. In parody of the pastoral singing contest which had served Pope earlier to dramatize the *concordia discors* of the Golden Age, an echo of Nature's harmony, the dunces in Book II celebrate 'the wond'rous pow'r of Noise' (*A*, ii. 214) and are

gladdened by the 'Harmonic twang' as 'Ass intones to Ass'
(*A*, ii. 243–4):

> Now thousand tongues are heard in one loud din:
> The Monkey-mimicks rush discordant in.
>
> 'Twas chatt'ring, grinning, mouthing, jabb'ring all,
> And Noise, and Norton, Brangling, and Breval,
> Dennis and Dissonance; and captious Art,
> And Snip-snap short, and Interruption smart.   (*A*, ii. 227–32)

This is the music to which Dulness's ears are tuned. Like Damon,
the unerring arbiter of 'Spring' who will not choose between the
singing of Daphnis and Strephon, she reconciles the contending
elements of *her* world, whose characteristic is *discordia*, universal
hubbub: 'Hold (cry'd the Queen) A Catcall each shall win, / Equal
your merits! equal is your din!' (*A*, ii. 233–4).[86]

The climax of this theme occurs in *The New Dunciad* as Pope
inverts the hopeful vision of universal concord that he had presented earlier in *Messiah* (l. 42) and *Windsor Forest* (l. 414), where
'new Musick' charms 'th'unfolding Ear', and 'barb'rous Discord'
dwells in 'Brazen Bonds'. First to do homage before Dulness's throne
in Book IV is 'a Harlot form', the personification of Italian opera,
dressed in 'discordant pride' (iv. 47) and delighting in 'Chromatic
tortures' (iv. 55) calculated to drive the Muses to distraction:
'O *Cara! Cara!* silence all that train: / Joy to great Chaos! let Division
reign' (iv. 53–4). She stands to Dulness and her world as the principle of Music to God's creation, substituting 'Another Phœbus, thy
own Phœbus', for the true god of Harmony (iv. 61 and n.) and
effecting her own excruciating *concordia discors*: 'One Trill shall
harmonize joy, grief, and rage' (iv. 57).[87] In such a context there
is no place for the 'new Musick' promised in Pope's poem and performed in Handel's oratorio on the Messiah. Handel, indeed, whose
music 'borrows aid from Sense' (iv. 64), is banished to Ireland as
a blast from 'Fame's posterior Trumpet' (iv. 71), another sort of
apocalyptic fanfare, heralds Dulness's own Doomsday.

Implicit in this cacophony of a world untuned is Pope's true
subject in *The New Dunciad*: the vision, all too prophetic, of an age
in which the traditional grounds of belief in the providential Order
of things have collapsed under the pressure of a new materialism.
Dulness is, essentially, a god 'Such as Lucretius drew' (iv. 484),
her religion 'Divinity without a *Νοῦς*' (iv. 244).[88] Dulness's 'Force
inertly strong' is, as Pope explains, nothing less than 'the *Vis*

inertiæ of Matter . . . the Foundation of all the Qualities and Attributes of that sluggish Substance' (iv. 7 and n.), and the 'new World' it moulds is that imagined by Epicurus (iv. 15 and n.). In its final form, in other words, *The Dunciad* records the triumph of a philosophical system that Pope, together with the Christian humanist tradition, regarded as the type and paradigm of atheistical thought down through the centuries—a system predicating a Godless universe, a world of matter only, created and governed by chance. It is this system, thought to have been revived by Hobbes, Descartes, and the Deists, which the whole weight of contemporary polemical divinity—from the Cambridge Platonists to the Boyle lecturers and Warburton—was meant to demolish. Thus it is that for Pope's dunces as for those atheistical materialists whom Cudworth laboured so encyclopedically to expose in all their guises, 'Night and Chaos, senseless and stupid matter, fortuitously moved' are 'the highest of all numens'.[89]

Throughout *The Dunciad* the attributes of Dulness are those of matter, inert and lifeless. The offspring of Chaos, she is 'Gross as her sire' (*A*, i. 12), and *her* 'Saturnian age' is 'of Lead' (*A*, i. 26). The heads of her children and the works therein conceived are 'impenetrably dull'—massive, ponderous, heavy.[90] They most nearly resemble bowls and bullets, clock-weights and rolling stones.[91] It is his extraordinary density of skull that enables one of Dulness's champions to distinguish himself in the mud-diving contest, 'With all the Might of gravitation blest' (*A*, ii. 296).

This motif, already present in the original version of the poem, becomes in *The New Dunciad* a principal clue to Pope's deeper intent. As Dulness's 'posterior Trumpet' summons 'all the Nations' to her throne, the goddess and her satellites are seen themselves literally to constitute the 'new World' of their own devising: they *are*, as it were, the universe posited by the materialist philosophers—a universe consisting of blind and senseless matter, devoid of spirit or will, obedient only to the physical laws of mass and motion, governed not by Providence but by Necessity:

> The young, the old, who feel her inward sway,
> One instinct seizes, and transports away.
> None need a guide, by sure Attraction led,
> And strong impulsive gravity of Head:
> None want a place, for all their Centre found,
> Hung to the Goddess, and coher'd around.

> Not closer, orb in orb, conglob'd are seen
> The buzzing Bees about their dusky Queen.
> The gath'ring number, as it moves along,
> Involves a vast involuntary throng,
> Who gently drawn, and struggling less and less,
> Roll in her Vortex, and her pow'r confess.   (iv. 73–84)

As the notes make clear, the 'new world of Dulness' functions according to the laws of physics adduced to explain the mechanical operation of the solar system.[92] The passage, furthermore, seems deliberately modelled on the *Essay on Man* (iii. 7–26); but there, how different is Pope's conception of the material universe, which, though its parts cohere according to the laws of attraction, yet owes the life and harmony of the whole to divine love:

> Look round our World; behold the chain of Love
> Combining all below and all above.
> See plastic Nature working to this end,
> The single atoms each to other tend,
> Attract, attracted to, the next in place
> Form'd and impell'd its neighbour to embrace.
> See Matter next, with various life endu'd,
> Press to one centre still, the gen'ral Good . . .
>
> Nothing is foreign: Parts relate to whole;
> One all-extending, all-preserving Soul
> Connects each being, greatest with the least;
> Made Beast in aid of Man, and Man of Beast;
> All serv'd, all serving! nothing stands alone;
> The chain holds on, and where it ends, unknown.

An empty travesty of the natural order, the dunces' world is all mass and mechanism. What it lacks is everything: 'the all-extending, all-preserving Soul'.

Like that of Epicurus it is also a world capricious and irrational. Dulness's creations, when they succeed at all, are 'lucky' hits (*A*, ii. 43), and in the works of 'her Chosen' we can observe only 'How random Thoughts now meaning chance to find' (*A*, i. 229). This theme, too, Pope heightened in revision. One of the many traits of character that make Cibber so admirable a prince of Dulness's anarchic domains is his love, chiefly unfortunate, of gaming. On his first appearance in Book I, he is the picture of despair, abandoned by his darling Fortune and, a less patient Job, cursing his gods in affliction:

> Now (shame to Fortune!) an ill Run at Play
> Blank'd his bold visage, and a thin Third day:
> Swearing and supperless the Hero sate,
> Blasphem'd his Gods, the Dice, and damn'd his Fate.   (*B*, i. 113–16)

Later, appealing to Dulness for guidance in the choice of career, he is more sanguine. Like Virgil's Mezentius, indeed, he disclaims dependence on any god, trusting instead to his own skill at the tables, which he compares to God's power over Nature. Or, in his proper element amidst the false dice at his favourite gaming-house, he sits like Christ among the rabbis, teaching his fellow priests of Fortune the only form of prayer he knows. 'What can I now?' he asks,

> Or tread the path by vent'rous Heroes trod,
> This Box my Thunder, this right hand my God?
> Or chair'd at White's amidst the Doctors sit,
> Teach Oaths to Gamesters, and to Nobles Wit?   (*B*, i. 201–4)

Cibber's devotion to the dice—a faith he shares with such other modern epicures as Bladen and Knight (iv. 560 and n.)—should be seen as one more aspect of Pope's satire against the new epicureanism of his age. In his preface on 'The Hero of the Poem', Warburton makes this point explicitly. As the classical poets claim divine lineage for their heroes, finding a son of Mars in a mighty warrior or a son of Phoebus in a skilful poet, so Cibber's 'Pedigree' may be derived 'from a Goddess of no small power and authority amongst men . . .'. We have here, Warburton continues, 'a Son of FORTUNE in an artful *Gamester*. And who fitter than the Offspring of *Chance*, to assist in restoring the Empire of *Night* and *Chaos*?'[93]

Cibber and his kind assist in the destruction of civilization merely by *being* what they are, mindless and self-indulgent. They are formidable chiefly because they are legion. Pope's keenest indignation is reserved for the ideologues of the new epicureanism, those heterodox divines and free-thinking philosophers who, by presuming to redefine Nature and Nature's God according to their own private systems, have engineered the collapse of the old Order and undermined the grounds of faith and morality. As he presents it in a crucial passage, the godless system constructed by the new

philosophy is a pastiche of ideas drawn from various sources—
from Hobbes and Mandeville, Spinoza and Descartes, Tindal and
Shaftesbury and the whole tribe of Deists and rationalizing
divines.[94] As Pope notes, having exhorted her philosophers 'to
amuse themselves in Trifles, and rest in Second causes, with a total
disregard of the First', Dulness gratefully receives the assurances
of 'a gloomy Clerk':

> 'Be that my task (replies a gloomy Clerk,
> Sworn foe to Myst'ry, yet divinely dark;
> Whose pious hope aspires to see the day
> When Moral Evidence shall quite decay,
> And damns implicit faith, and holy lies,
> Prompt to impose, and fond to dogmatize:)
> Let others creep by timid steps, and slow,
> On plain Experience lay foundations low,
> By common sense to common knowledge bred,
> And last, to Nature's Cause thro' Nature led.
> All-seeing in thy mists, we want no guide,
> Mother of Arrogance, and Source of Pride!
> We nobly take the high Priori Road,
> And reason downward, till we doubt of God:
> Make Nature still incroach upon his plan;
> And shove him off as far as e'er we can:
> Thrust some Mechanic Cause into his place;
> Or bind in Matter, or diffuse in Space.
> Or, at one bound o'er-leaping all his laws,
> Make God Man's Image, Man the final Cause,
> Find Virtue local, all Relation scorn,
> See all in *Self*, and but for self be born:
> Of nought so certain as our *Reason* still,
> Of nought so doubtful as of *Soul* and *Will.*
> Oh hide the God still more! and make us see
> Such as Lucretius drew, a God like Thee:
> Wrapt up in Self, a God without a Thought,
> Regardless of our merit or default.
> Or that bright Image to our fancy draw,
> Which Theocles in raptur'd vision saw,
> While thro' Poetic scenes the Genius roves,
> Or wanders wild in Academic Groves;
> That NATURE our Society adores,
> Where Tindal dictates, and Silenus snores.'   (iv. 459–92)

Like those strangely congenial antagonists the deist Tindal or the
mathematical divine Samuel Clarke, Dulness's philosophers are

sworn foes to the Christian mysteries; and, as 'higher critics', they
seek to explode the historical foundations of Christianity. Rejecting
the more arduous *a posteriori* approach to truth—pursued, for
example, by the Boyle lecturers, who inferred the being and attributes of God from the empirical observation of design in Nature—
Dulness's mental travellers trip down 'the high Priori Road',
making Nature conform to their preconceptions of her. Along the
way God has been lost from the creation; all that remains is
the universal machinery, a world in which matter and space are
the only realities. As Professor Sutherland remarks, 'the Creator
of the Book of Genesis [has been] deprived of His creative acts'.[95]
Pope, indeed, presents these system-builders in parody of the first
chapter of Genesis. They are shown *actively* reconstituting the
world according to their own ideas: at their bidding Nature
encroaches on God's plan; they 'shove him off', 'thrust' a mechanic
cause into his place, 'bind' him in matter, 'diffuse' him in space;
or, in the fundamental act of disorder epitomizing Pope's complaint
against them, they invert the relationship between Creator and
creature, making 'God Man's Image, Man the final Cause'.

As Hobbes knew, the disappearance of God removes any
absolute basis for a moral imperative. The consequence is solipsism,
the assertion of the self as the centre of creation. But in such a context the self, like all Nature, is merely a mechanism; without soul
or will, it seeks only power and pleasure. In the *Leviathan*, good
and evil are seen as 'local', the names each individual gives to
those acts which gratify his appetites or cause him pain. The
world of *The Dunciad* is the world implicit in the new philosophy
as Pope saw it, a solipsistic materialism for which Epicurus
provides the type and model:

> Oh hide the God still more! and make us see
> Such as Lucretius drew, a God like Thee:
> Wrapt up in Self, a God without a Thought,
> Regardless of our merit or default.

As the 'gloomy Clerk' concludes his speech, Pope presents the
moral consequences of this philosophy in the plump figure of
Silenus, the well-fed, 'bowzy Sire', who stirs from sleep at the
mention of his name. Hedonist without a peer, Silenus is also, as
Pope's note reminds us, the 'Epicurean Philosopher' who in
Virgil's *Sixth Eclogue* 'sings the Principles of that Philosophy in his
drink'. 'Rosy and rev'rend, tho' without a Gown' (iv. 496), he

serves as priest of Dulness's secular religion. In travesty of the sacrament of Confirmation, he leads up the youth to be initiated into her *'greater Mysteries'* (iv. 517 n.), the celebration of which culminates in a mock-eucharist—the venal *'Cup'* proferred by her *'Magus'* (iv. 517 ff.), or, for those stricter epicures more interested in gratifying their palates than in lining their pockets, a gourmet's supper presided over by 'Priest succinct in amice white' (iv. 549 ff.). These ceremonies observed, Dulness's children, apostles all, go forth to 'MAKE ONE MIGHTY DUNCIAD OF THE LAND'. The world thus prepared is ready for 'the all-composing Hour' (iv. 627) of her Second Coming—for the stultifying yawn, universal and irresistible, that quells 'All Nature' (iv. 605) and drowns all 'Sense, and Shame, and Right, and Wrong' (iv. 625).

> Lo! thy dread Empire, CHAOS! is restor'd;
> Light dies before thy uncreating word:
> Thy hand, great Anarch! lets the curtain fall;
> And Universal Darkness buries All.

Here, in the concluding lines of Pope's last poem, the *fiat lux* of Genesis gives way to *fiat nox*. The idea of creation, with all it meant to him of the Order of Nature and the harmony of Art, succumbs to the fact of spreading anarchy. But not quite. It still informs the poet's own values, controlling his choice of analogy and allusion, and it is felt in the formal perfection of his verse. *The New Dunciad* envisions the demise of the Christian humanist tradition, now long since accomplished, but it is itself very much a product of that tradition.

IV

Gay: The Meanings of Art and Artifice

IT might be said that, long before Pater, the poets of the Augustan mode affirmed the fundamental tenet of aestheticism: for Pope, certainly, art was necessary because life was deficient in form. This, too, is the essential point about Gay, not only about the manner of his verse—that 'delicate and sophisticated craftsmanship', as Professor Sutherland has remarked, producing *objets* as precious and frail as Chelsea china[1]—but about his meaning as well. His best-known poems—the *Fables*, *The Shepherd's Week*, *Rural Sports*, *Trivia*—are characteristically witty and finely wrought, apparently frivolous and fragile. It is perhaps not surprising that Dr. Johnson should dismiss their author as lacking the '*mens divinior*, the dignity of genius',[2] or that this estimate should have survived through nearly two centuries. One of the very best of modern critics, though delighting in what he calls Gay's 'artistic coquetry', regrets that he wanted 'the moral earnestness' of his friends Swift and Pope, that his goodness is that of 'a witty child . . . who has read about or even seen the world, the flesh, and the devil, without ever experiencing their desperate allure'.[3] Since Professor Armens's study,[4] it is no longer possible to dismiss Gay quite so easily on these grounds—to see him, as we had grown accustomed to seeing him, as an affable dabbler in verse, in life as a sort of ineffectual and improbably indolent Puck. If life was a jest to Gay (as his epitaph assures us it was), the joke was too often grim and disconcerting, cracked in a 'biting' spirit akin to that of Swift's Jove.

Form and artifice are the distinguishing features of Gay's verse, as they are of the Augustan mode in general. These poets prized the virtues of elegance and proportion, the virtues of a highly mannered art, not because of any easy complacency about the eventual triumph of sanity and decorum, but because they everywhere saw the forces of Chaos and Dark Night threatening to overwhelm them. Such is Pope's meaning in the grotesque apocalypse of *The Dunciad*, where, in parody of classical and Christian poems that celebrate the establishment of Order, Dulness and her legions undo the work of creation. Though Pope is the greater poet (perhaps even because he is), Gay's verse is more clearly representative of this basic assumption both of the Augustan aesthetic and of the Augustan world view. In *Trivia*, especially, we will find embodied the controlling paradox of this mode: the idea—seldom openly expressed but nearly always implied in the poetry itself—that in the poem, as indeed in life, Nature must be made to imitate Art.

Of all the poetic kinds, the one most suited to this theme—and the one in which Gay worked most comfortably—is that of the pastoral. The 'first rule of Pastoral', as Pope more than once insisted, is that 'its Idea should be taken from the manners of the *Golden Age*, and the Moral form'd upon the representation of *Innocence*'.[5] Fundamental here, as we have seen, is the contrast between an Age of Gold nostalgically evoked and an Age of Iron all too present, between a bright, ideal world—ordered, healthy, virtuous—and a world fallen, sick, depraved. A variation on this theme is the constant motif of Gay's poetry: the contrast between the country and the town. Under Gay's hand, however, this conventional thematic polarity of the pastoral (and of the related mode of the georgic) takes on a further significance—one already perhaps implicit in this most stylized, most self-consciously formal of the genres. The art of the pastoral poet, like that of Virgil's husbandman, does not imitate Nature as she actually appears in this degenerate world, but rather subdues and improves her, restoring her as far as possible to her original perfection. In that ideal state, as Sir Thomas Browne remarked, Nature was not at variance with Art, nor Art with Nature, 'they being both servants of his Providence'. In Eden, the perfect handiwork of God, Art and Nature were one; the extreme artfulness of the pastoral style is, in effect, an attempt to express this fact. In Gay's idiom the familiar antitheses of this mode—the country versus the town, the ideal versus the real—are constantly being rendered, not in the conventional terms of the natural as opposed to the civilized worlds as is commonly asserted, but rather in terms symbolizing the basic opposition in this fallen world between Art and Actuality.

By reading the pastoral motif too literally, by seeing Gay's poetry as a celebration of the Natural as opposed to the Artificial and Civilized, the accepted critical view has prevented an appreciation of the peculiar quality and true significance of Gay as a poet. It has committed the ultimate violence upon the poetry by proposing, in effect, a separation between its manner and meaning which is absolute. One reason for this confusion is that we have regarded only what the poem (in certain conventional passages) *says*, and not at all attended to what it *is*. A further problem is the ambiguity of the terms *natural* and *artificial*, which may have both positive and pejorative connotations in Gay. As they are typically used in the pastoral, these words suggest, respectively, the simplicity, purity, and innocence of the Golden Age as opposed to the duplicity and affectation introduced after the Fall in the service of human greed and vanity: these are the 'subtil arts'[6] of city whores and pickpockets and politicians, or the 'art' of the painted belle, Sylvia, which repairs 'her roses and her charms'.[7] Alternatively, and more essentially in Gay, art is the sum of every human virtue: it is the affirmation of civilization in the face of vulgarity and savagery; it is the hard-earned means by which the man of reason and sensibility—the poet and the gentleman—disciplines the wilderness in nature and in himself. With the triumph of art the human situation, however grim in actuality (one thinks, for example, of *Trivia* and *The Beggar's Opera*), is seen as ultimately comic, because the human mind has learned to cope with it, to transcend it. This is not to say that the poet, like the meretricious painter of *Fable XVIII*, enacts a lie by showing deformity in the likeness of beauty; it is rather that in imitating the actual, he asserts by his manner the redeeming values of form and harmony.

The country in Gay's poetry is important, then, primarily as a symbol of an ideal order irrevocably lost in actuality, but attainable through art. Gay's Age of Gold is not to be sought after in time or in space, or in any easy retreat into rural or primitive regions; the Devonshire of his youth was no Eden, and it is likely to have been dull. The ideal in Gay's poetry is found rather in that curious discrepancy between his subject-matter, which can be gross and sordid enough, and his elegant, witty manner. It is an ideal achieved, aesthetically, in the poem itself, in which all the devices of artifice—the polished, balanced couplet, the music and symmetry of the line, the circumlocution of the diction, the allusion

to myth and to the classics—conspire to triumph over the messy
and intractable and too often tragic stuff of life. It is achieved,
ethically and socially, in the practice of benevolence and in what
he refers to as the strict payment of 'due civilities',[8] in those polite
rituals of courtesy and charity which enable us not to exalt, but
to vanquish, the natural man. It is achieved, in other words, by
attaining the condition of art. Form, decorum are *everything*; they
are the ultimate values, for they enable us to survive and function
in a world too often hostile and unmanageable.

Variations on this theme occur throughout Gay's poetry. Consider, for instance, the functional art of the 'skilful angler' in *Rural
Sports* (1720), a poem usually said (I think mistakenly) to celebrate
the Natural as opposed to the Artificial. The angler, who is also
Gay the poet, has left the noisy, noxious city behind, if only
temporarily. Now in 'a calm retreat' (i. 23) in the country, he must
with care and judgement select the 'proper bait' (i. 160), and then
'Cleanse them from filth, to give a tempting gloss' (i. 167); with
his eye on Nature to improve upon her, he fashions his lure with
such patient dexterity 'That nature *seems* to live again in art'
(i. 208; italics mine). There is a correct procedure for casting, for
playing the fish, and for drawing him to shore 'with artful care'
(i. 249). Perhaps the closest modern analogue to Gay's meaning in
this poem occurs in Hemingway's story, 'Big Two-Hearted River'.
Having crossed the burned-over land and 'left everything behind',
Nick Adams found his own 'good place' to fish in the woods.[9] In
both the poem and the story, the art of fishing and the purity of
the style serve the same function, affording a means of controlling
experience, of imposing on life an order and a discipline that it does
not *naturally* have. There are rules to be observed, limits to be
self-imposed, a ritual to be performed. One does not stray into the
swamp, where, as Nick Adams observes, 'fishing was a tragic
adventure' (p. 231); nor does one, in Gay's words,

> wander where the bord'ring reeds
> O'erlook the muddy stream, whose tangling weeds
> Perplex the fisher . . .   (i. 259–61)

It is not Nature that Gay (or Hemingway) celebrates, but nature
controlled and subdued, set in order by art and artifice.

This motive of Gay's poetry is evident even in *The Shepherd's
Week* (1714), which continues to be regarded as 'firmly con-

temporary and realistic',[10] though the poem itself burlesques those very qualities in a mode so splendidly artificial as pastoral. As Pope's admirer and fellow Scriblerian, Gay's purpose in these 'trim' eclogues is not to endorse, but to ridicule, the 'realistic' school of Thomas Tickell and Ambrose Philips, who opposed Pope's own theory and practice.[11] Like Pope himself in *The Guardian*, No. 40, or like Swift in 'A Pastoral Dialogue' (1729), Gay's strategy is through parody to reduce the position of Tickell and Philips to its essential absurdity. If the rules of pastoral are to be drawn from Philips, Gay implies, *these* are the sort of poems we may expect, in which English clowns replace Virgil's elegant shepherds and the coarseness of actuality replaces the sophisticated simplicity of the Golden Age. If pastoral is a poetry of real, rather than of ideal, Nature, then the eclogues of Virgil and Pope 'are by no means *Pastorals*, but *something better*'.[12]

Enforcing this point in 'The Proeme', Gay's homely bard, in prose as quaint and foolish as his ideas, denounces the '*critical gallimawfry*' of Pope and his circle '*concerning, I wist not what, Golden Age, and other outragious conceits, to which they would confine Pastoral*' (p. 28). He is staunchly of Philips's party, rejecting Virgilian refinements for the rustications of Theocritus, who '*maketh his louts give foul language, and behold their goats at rut in all simplicity*'. For Pope—and, we may be sure, for Gay—the true country of pastoral is Arcadia, like the vanished 'Groves of *Eden*' a symbolic region of the spirit accessible only through the idealizing power of the imagination and the transforming power of art. For the poet of *The Shepherd's Week*, who prefers life and human nature as they are, Arcadia is an all too alien land; he will instead set before his English reader '*a picture, or rather lively landschape of thy own country, just as thou mightest see it, didest thou take a walk into the fields at the proper season*' (p. 29). Accordingly, though he follows Pope in attempting his own adaptation of Spenser's calendar, he is quite unaware of its meaning. To make the point clear, Gay contrives to have his bard offer his own redaction of Pope's scheme for the *Pastorals*. The situation in 'Monday; or, The Squabble' ludicrously inverts that in Pope's 'Spring', where Damon's arbitration of the singing contest is presented as an expression of *concordia discors*, the condition of ideal Nature in the Golden Age. Staking a tobacco pouch and an oaken staff, Gay's shepherds Lobbin Clout and Cuddy dispute the virtues of

Blouzelinda and Buxoma while Cloddipole, 'wisest lout of all the
neighbouring plain' (l. 22), attempts the hopeless task of distinguishing the proportion of cacophony between them. Predictably, he
can only end the discord, not, as Damon had done, resolve it into
harmony:

> Forbear, contending louts, give o'er your strains,
> An oaken staff each merits for his pains . . .
> Your herds for want of water stand adry,
> They're weary of your songs—and so am I.   (ll. 119–24)

Similarly, the subject of 'Friday; or, The Dirge', like that of Pope's
'Winter', is death—the death, however, not of Love and Beauty in
a fallen world, but of Blouzelinda, whose loss, lamented by the disconsolate Bumkinet and Grubbinol, is soon forgotten in Susan's
kisses and a mug of ale. As Pope rounded off his pastoral of the
world's Great Year with the 'Messiah', so in 'Saturday; or, The
Flights' Gay's bard ends his week in the country by attempting his
own 'SUBLIMER strains'.[13] For his model, however, he chooses not
Virgil's *Fourth* but his *Sixth Eclogue*, the eclogue not of Christ but
of Silenus, the bibulous epicure who, as Pope would later remark
when introducing him in *The Dunciad*, 'sings the Principles of that
Philosophy in his drink' (iv. 492 n.). Silenus, Pope's 'bowzy Sire',
appears in 'Saturday' as Bowzybeus, who—preferring the cup that
cheers *and* inebriates to the sacred Muse 'Who touch'd *Isaiah*'s
hallow'd Lips with Fire'—carols of 'nature's laws' (l. 51) and
worldly joys, lapsing at last into stupor: 'The pow'r that guards
the drunk, his sleep attends, / 'Till, ruddy, like his face, the sun
descends.' The bard's decision to end his pastorals with the
analogues of Silenus and epicureanism is well suited to the view
of poetry which Pope and Gay attributed to Philips—a poetry
dedicated to the 'realistic' imitation of the things and pleasures of
this world.

Seen in this way, hilariously, as a parody of Philips, *The
Shepherd's Week* seems related only obliquely to the idea of the
Golden Age or to the peculiarly Augustan conception of art's
transforming power. But even here—in a way perhaps comparable
to the counterpoint that obtains in *The Dunciad* between the image
projected of chaos and the music of Pope's couplets—Gay's control
of form and the exquisite artificiality of his diction reveal the
essential impulse of his art. Unlike Swift, neither Gay nor Pope
ever wholly adopts the *style* of the enemy; for to them style is the

way of asserting that *they* are within, the enemy outside, the Palace of Art. Gay's shepherds and shepherdesses do fill their songs with homely references to the business of their daily lives, but his mannered verse has refined away the crudeness even of Philips's swains and milk-maids. Despite the burlesque, Arcadia from time to time encroaches upon Devon. Like Gay's own polished couplets, his rural lasses are 'tidy' and 'clean', dressed in 'kerchief starch'd' and sporting straw-hats 'trimly lin'd with green'.[14]

Though they are comic figures, these shepherds are also poets— poets, moreover, who understand the lesson that Gay's own verse imparts: 'Numbers, like Musick, can ev'n Grief controul.'[15] In 'Friday; or, The Dirge', Gay involves his shepherd-poets in situations that are emblematic of the relationship between the artist and the rude, recalcitrant material of life. In the first of these, Bumkinet and Grubbinol retire to a sheltered vantage-point from which, having gained the necessary detachment from the business of life, they may mourn the death of Blouzelinda, and 'with trim sonnets *cast away our care*' (l. 16). In the second, Grubbinol recalls the ceremonies of her burial:

> With wicker rods we fenc'd her tomb around,
> To ward from man and beast the hallow'd ground,
> Lest her new grave the Parson's cattle raze,
> For both his horse and cow the church-yard graze. (ll. 145–8)

In like manner, the artifice of the verses to follow fences us off from the incursions of nature, by a refining process removing us from its rough force and coarseness, turning bulls into fragile china figments:

> While bulls bear horns upon their curled brow,
> Or lasses with soft stroakings milk the cow;
> While padling ducks the standing lake desire,
> Or batt'ning hogs roll in the sinking mire;
> While moles the crumbled earth in hillocks raise,
> So long shall swains tell *Blouzelinda's* praise. (ll. 153–8)

The meaning of art and artifice in Gay, however, is more clearly represented in the preceding poem, which may be seen as a comic dramatization of the poet's function. In 'Thursday; or, The Spell' Hobnelia uses magic to lure her errant lover 'from the faithless town' (l. 88). The verse itself—with its frequent alliteration, its

repetitions and antitheses—imitates the formal, circular movement
of her dance and incantatory refrain:

> Hobnelia, seated in a dreary vale,
> In pensive mood rehears'd her piteous tale,
> Her piteous tale the winds in sighs bemoan,
> And pining eccho answers groan for groan.
> I rue the day, a rueful day, I trow,
> The woful day, a day indeed of woe!
> When *Lubberkin* to town his cattle drove,
> A maiden fine bedight he hapt to love;
> The maiden fine bedight his love retains,
> And for the village he forsakes the plains.
> Return my *Lubberkin*, these ditties hear;
> Spells will I try, and spells shall ease my care.
> *With my sharp heel I three times mark the ground,*
> *And turn me thrice around, around, around.*   (ll. 1–14)

Like his comic shepherdess, Gay employs his own potent forms and
incantations to discipline the wayward circumstances of life.

In proposing the identity of form and meaning in Gay, I do not
at all wish to imply that he was the advocate and exponent of any
empty aestheticism. The meaning is that art, of a highly conscious
and deliberate sort, is necessary not only to the making of the
poem, but also to the shaping of Gay's hero, who is not the natural,
but rather the truly *civilized*, man. The artist, in life as in poetry, is
supremely skilful, for he has learned to control, even to transform,
his material; he is not the victim of life, but its master. An awareness of this fact will help to reveal that Gay's verse has precisely
that 'third dimension', that 'prismatic depth', which it has been
thought to lack.[16] The superficiality of Gay's verse is illusory; it
exists because the poetry itself is the substantiation of Gay's belief
that art must order, refine, simplify—that the poem must not (as
T. S. Eliot once averred that it must) itself reflect the dominion of
Chaos and Dark Night in this fallen world, but that it must
redeem this world, introducing elegance and form, harmony and
humour, in the very absence of these things. According to Addison, Virgil in the *Georgics* 'breaks the clods and tosses the dung
about with an air of gracefulness'.[17] The image applies equally
well to Gay in his mock-georgic, *Trivia* (1716), a poem that stands
as a kind of extended parable of the relation between actuality
and art.

Despite Professor Sutherland's insistence that 'if we want the actual movement and stench and uproar of the London streets' we must go to Ned Ward, not to Gay,[18] the notion still occurs that Gay's motive in *Trivia* is 'mild satire' of London life, and that his method is a detailed and photographic 'realism'.[19] The usual comparison is with Hogarth in such works as *Gin Lane*. Gay's purpose, however, is not at all to photograph the squalor and the crowded alleys of mid-winter London; he has no desire to make us *feel* the crush of the mob or the biting chill of the weather; he does not wish us to smell the stench of Fleet-ditch or to witness the filth of the kennels. His subject-matter, his material, may be the same as that of Hogarth; but thrust deliberately between us and the reality, removing us from it, insulating us against it, are Gay's tone and his style—with his music and elevated diction, the correctness of his numbers, and those neat couplets patting everything into place, smoothing things over, rendering them, as it were, harmless.

The point can be clearly seen, I think, if we place side by side passages from *Trivia* and from Swift's own burlesque georgic, *A Description of a City Shower* (1710); the subjects are identical, but the treatment and effect are entirely opposite. Here is Swift:

> Now from all Parts the swelling Kennels flow,
> And bear their Trophies with them as they go:
> Filth of all Hues and Odours seem to tell
> What Streets they sail'd from, by the Sight and Smell.
> They, as each Torrent drives, with rapid Force
> From *Smithfield*, or St. *Pulchre's* shape their Course,
> And in huge Confluent join at *Snow-Hill* Ridge,
> Fall from the *Conduit* prone to *Holborn-Bridge*.
> Sweepings from Butchers Stalls, Dung, Guts, and Blood,
> Drown'd Puppies, stinking Sprats, all drench'd in Mud,
> Dead Cats and Turnip-Tops come tumbling down the Flood.[20]

This is realism. The grossness of the imagery, the cacophony of the closing triplet with its final, ponderous alexandrine, function pitilessly to make the reader confront the muck and horror of actuality—almost, indeed, to overwhelm him with it. Listen now to Gay:

> But when the swinging signs your ears offend
> With creaking noise, then rainy floods impend;
> Soon shall the kennels swell with rapid streams,
> And rush in muddy torrents to the *Thames* . . .

Then *Niobe* dissolves into a tear
And sweats with secret grief: you'll hear the sounds
Of whistling winds, e'er kennels break their bounds;
Ungrateful odours common-shores diffuse,
And dropping vaults distill unwholesome dews,
E'er the tiles rattle with the smoking show'r,
And spouts on heedless men their torrents pour.   (i. 157–60, 168–74)

A crucial difference here is Gay's tone, which departs radically
from Swift's and reflects a very different attitude toward the
material. The sense of outrage is gone. Instead, the extravagance
of Gay's method implies a certain wry detachment; the poet is
aloof, arch if not exactly comic, as if he were sure of his ability to
dispel the curse of the scene's noisome reality. Gay's lines—with
their predominantly ordered rhythm of regular iambics and with
their ostentatious use of the devices of allusion, alliteration, and
assonance—call attention to themselves: not to *what* is being
described, but to *how* it is being described. They call attention, in
other words, to the conscious art of the poet. With respect to the
principle that in a successful poem 'The *Sound* must seem an
Eccho to the *Sense*', Swift's treatment looks to be superior; certainly
if Gay were trying for an Hogarthian effect, for 'realism', one can
say only that he bungled the job egregiously. Gay's manner in this
passage is, however, precisely the embodiment of his meaning in
this poem: which is that, though life can be hideous, art offers us
a way of coping with it.

Trivia; or, The Art of Walking the Streets of London will of course
remain interesting and useful as one of our chief documents of
London life in the days of Anne and George I; however, as far as
Gay's thematic intention is concerned, the symbolic meaning of
the city is paramount. Together with the title and the Virgilian
epigraph (which I shall discuss later), the exordium of the poem
provides the necessary clues. Gay begins by declaring his subject
and his very practical purpose; he then proceeds to celebrate the
votaries of the Muse:

Through winter streets to steer your course aright,
How to walk clean by day, and safe by night,
How jostling crouds, with prudence to decline,
When to assert the wall, and when resign,
I sing: Thou, *Trivia*, Goddess, aid my song,
Thro' spacious streets conduct thy bard along;

By thee transported, I securely stray
Where winding alleys lead the doubtful way,
The silent court, and op'ning square explore,
And long perplexing lanes untrod before.
To pave thy realm, and smooth the broken ways,
Earth from her womb a flinty tribute pays;
For thee, the sturdy paver thumps the ground,
Whilst ev'ry stroke his lab'ring lungs resound;
For thee the scavinger bids kennels glide
Within their bounds, and heaps of dirt subside.
My youthful bosom burns with thirst of fame,
From the great theme to build a glorious name,
To tread in paths to ancient bards unknown,
And bind my temples with a Civic crown;
But more, my country's love demands the lays,
My country's be the profit, mine the praise.

These lines suggest Gay's broadly allegorical intention. As in an overture, the dominant motifs of 'the great theme' are sounded, to be developed in the body of the poem. The season is winter; the streets of London are the setting: together they will come to represent the inimical conditions of life itself, the natural and man-made forces opposing the wayfarer who seeks to pass without injury or stain through the City of this World. Art, Gay implies, is the key to survival. At one level his theme is moral, for in *Trivia* the 'Art of Walking the Streets' is synonymous with 'prudence' (l. 3)—the supreme rational virtue of the Christian humanist tradition, which Cicero had called the *ars vivendi* and which Fielding and Goldsmith would consider 'the Art of Life'.[21] Prudence is the art that must be mastered before the wayfarer can thread the labyrinth. Helping him along the way is Art of another kind—the art of pavers and scavengers, cobblers and bootblacks, of 'useful' poets (ii. 1) and painters, musicians and architects. So it is that, like those other practical artists who 'smooth the broken ways' and keep filth within bounds, Gay includes himself among the followers of the Muse.[22]

The poem takes its title from the Roman name for Diana or Hecate, whose shrine was situated at the meeting of three roads; it is Trivia, goddess both of virgin forests and of the underworld, whom Gay invokes to conduct him safely through 'the muddy dangers of the street' (i. 194), just as Aeneas had been guided by her priestess through the infernal regions. Gay's characterization of London transforms the brawling town into something analogous to Virgil's underworld—into another Babylon, the City of this World, corrupt, treacherous, contaminating, where on every side 'smutty dangers' (ii. 36) threaten to besmirch the traveller who has not mastered 'the Art of Walking the Streets'. London is Gay's emblem for actuality, for Life itself. Patterns of recurring images function co-operatively to give the town this symbolic character. The poem opens, as we have seen, with a metaphor comparing the 'winding alleys' and 'perplexing lanes' of the city to a maze, through which the muse must safely conduct the poet. In Book II (ll. 77–90) the figure is resumed and its implications extended: the 'doubtful maze' that bewilders the innocent peasant who has strayed into London from a better country, is now associated with 'the dang'rous labyrinth of *Crete*', the story of which, etched on the walls of the temple of Phoebus by Daedalus himself, Aeneas had read at the entrance to the underworld.

The quality of life that waits within these streets is as predatory and violent, as monstrous, as that which Theseus found. Coaches clash in a snarl of traffic, provoking 'the sturdy war' (iii. 36); the drivers lash each other and grapple in the mud of the street. Chaos and brutality prevail:

> Forth issuing from steep lanes, the collier's steeds
> Drag the black load; another cart succeeds,
> Team follows team; crouds heap'd on crouds appear,
> And wait impatient, 'till the road grow clear.
> Now all the pavement sounds with trampling feet,
> And the mixt hurry barricades the street.
> Entangled here, the waggon's lengthen'd team
> Cracks the tough harness; here a pond'rous beam
> Lies over-turn'd athwart; for slaughter fed
> Here lowing bullocks raise their horned head.
> Now oaths grow loud, with coaches coaches jar,
> And the smart blow provokes the sturdy war;
> From the high box they whirl the thong around,
> And with the twining lash their shins resound:
> Their rage ferments, more dang'rous wounds they try,
> And the blood gushes down their painful eye.
> And now on foot the frowning warriors light,
> And with their pond'rous fists renew the fight;
> Blow answers blow, their cheeks are smear'd with blood,
> 'Till down they fall, and grappling roll in mud.

So when two boars, in wild *Ytene* bred,
Or on *Westphalia*'s fatt'ning chest-nuts fed,
Gnash their sharp tusks, and rous'd with equal fire,
Dispute the reign of some luxurious mire;
In the black flood they wallow o'er and o'er,
'Till their arm'd jaws distil with foam and gore.   (iii. 25–50)

The utter capitulation to rage and swinish brutality characterizes the spiritual condition of the citizens.

Equally significant are the recurrent references in the poem to filth of all kinds—mud, offal, soot, ashes, grease, blood. It is not merely that this filth exists in the town, but that it threatens constantly to bespatter and befoul the wayfarer, just as the moral corruption in which the city wallows threatens to soil and stain his spirit:

> oft in the mingling press
> The barber's apron soils the sable dress;
> Shun the perfumer's touch with cautious eye,
> Nor let the baker's step advance too nigh . . .
> The little chimney-sweeper skulks along,
> And marks with sooty stains the heedless throng;
> When small-coal murmurs in the hoarser throat,
> From smutty dangers guard thy threaten'd coat:
> The dust-man's cart offends thy cloaths and eyes,
> When through the street a cloud of ashes flies;
> But whether black or lighter dyes are worn,
> The chandler's basket, on his shoulder born,
> With tallow spots thy coat; resign the way,
> To shun the surly butcher's greasy tray,
> Butchers, whose hands are dy'd with blood's foul stain,
> And always foremost in the hangman's train.
> Let due civilities be strictly paid.   (ii. 27–45)

Considering the character of the world that Gay describes, that last exclamation is a more than perfunctory appeal. In this world deceit and duplicity, sham and gaudy surfaces prevail. Very little is what it appears to be. The lost, looking for a guide, have their pockets picked; ballad-singers like '*Syrens* stand / To aid the labours of the diving hand' (iii. 79–80); the link-man's torch, meant as a beacon, serves as a lure to trap the unwary; beggars turned thieves use their crutches to fell their victims; whores, promising love, spread infection. In contrast to the honest walker are the riders, rich by rapine and fraud, who loll in coaches, their gaudy insignia belying the rottenness within: 'The tricking gamester insolently rides, / With *Loves* and *Graces* on his chariot's sides' (i. 115–16). Civility and charity are the moral virtues that the poem recommends in the face of pride and inhumanity so widespread as to suggest the ignoble savagery of Hobbes's natural man. Amidst the weak and the poor, the walker practises benevolence while 'Proud coaches pass, regardless of the moan / Of infant orphans, and the widow's groan' (ii. 451–2). The piling up of such scenes and images is relentless, and the ultimate effect is to present the city as the very type and habitation of moral disorder, depravity, and disease.

If, as Gay implies, London is a metaphor for the world, the walker's journey through winter streets is presented as a parable of life. Though, as in Joyce's story of another wayfarer's urban odyssey, Gay's time-scheme for the poem covers just twenty-four hours, a single day and night, yet, like Joyce, he deepens the temporal dimension of the narrative by placing the walker's progress within the larger contexts of human life and history. In Book II the walker's imagination ranges beyond the present moment to encompass 'the periods of the week' (ii. 411), 'the season's change', and 'the monthly progress of the year' (ii. 425–6). Recalling the cries of the town that distinguish the several seasons, he carries us swiftly through the year as Pope had done in the *Pastorals*, moving through spring and summer and autumn to 'the festival of *Christmas*' (ii. 439). In this way, the walker's journey through the city is made to seem perpetual, the wayfaring of Everyman through life within the context of Christian time. Having returned us to the season of the poem's setting, Gay's survey of the year concludes with Christmas and the festival of the Saviour's birth— the event which alone gives meaning to Time and which promises release from the condition of mortality symbolized by the town and winter weather. This is 'the joyous period of the year' (ii. 440) when the Christian message of love fulfilled in Christ is commemorated and expressed in the lives of those who feed the hungry and clothe the naked:

> Now, heav'n-born Charity, thy blessings shed;
> Bid meagre Want uprear her sickly head:
> Bid shiv'ring limbs be warm; let plenty's bowle
> In humble roofs make glad the needy soul.
> See, see, the heav'n-born maid her blessings shed;
> Lo! meagre Want uprears her sickly head;

Cloath'd are the naked, and the needy glad,
While selfish Avarice alone is sad.   (ii. 443–50)

The contrast that follows between the walker's benevolence and
the riders' callous indifference to human suffering dramatizes the
moral theme of the poem, and leads to a final image relating the
message of charity and the hope of salvation to the fact of mortality.
Passing 'the brass knocker, wrapt in flannel band' (ii. 467), the
walker is reminded that for all men death is the end of the journey:
'Here canst thou pass, unmindful of a pray'r, / That heav'n in
mercy may thy brother spare?' (ii. 473–4).

For the poet and his 'associate walkers' (ii. 501) there are certain
compensations for braving the perils of the streets: the friendship,
for example, of civilized men such as Fortescue and Burlington,
the good health that comes with exercise, easy access to those
physicians and shopkeepers who will minister to their needs. Not
least of these are the booksellers whose stalls offer the opportunity
for browsing among the works of Plutarch and Bacon and Aristotle,
Congreve and Pope and Garth—good authors all who can nourish
the mind, affording wise counsel and the consolations of art to
ease life's journey. This, too, is Gay's ambition:

O *Lintot*, let my labours obvious lie,
Rang'd on thy stall, for ev'ry curious eye;
So shall the poor these precepts *gratis* know,
And to my verse their future safeties owe.   (ii. 565–8)

Just how necessary to his reader's safety are the practical arts
of life and poetry that comprise Gay's theme is soon apparent. In
Book III the spectacle darkens with nightfall, and there is less
relief from Gay's levity of tone. Threatened from above by falling
shop windows and 'dashing torrents' from gutters (iii. 205), and
from below by the filth of the streets, the wayfarer finds himself
like Ulysses 'Pent round with perils' (iii. 178), calling for aid in
vain. He is cautioned to avoid the fate of Oedipus, archetypal
victim of the *tri-via*, who came to grief 'Where three roads join'd'
(iii. 217): 'Hence wert thou doom'd in endless night to stray /
Through *Theban* streets, and cheerless groap thy way' (iii. 223–4).
The scenes that follow recapitulate the themes that have characterized the city throughout—the corruption of innocence and the
triumph of deceit and misrule: whores use their 'subtil arts' to

despoil the Devonshire yeoman of his money, his health, and his
virtue; the cause of justice and order finds its hopeless champions
in the ineffectual watchman and the mercenary constable, who
attends only to 'the rhet'rick of a silver fee' (iii. 318). Rakes kindle
riots, beacons are extinguished—the city is given over completely
to disorder and darkness.

As the walker's journey and the poem itself near an end, Gay
enforces the analogy between his particular subject and the universal drama, between the walker's (and the reader's) progress
and the journey of Everyman to the end of Time. The grim tableau
culminates in a scene that places this spectacle of worldly folly
and vice within the larger contexts of history and eternity, asserting the ultimate victory of divine justice. As with Gay's method
throughout, the local and particular image is given universal
significance by the use of analogy and allusion. The total darkness
—in which the chariots of the town's proud riders have been
broken, to sink in the gulf of common-shores—is interrupted by
the outbreak of fire in the city. Here Gay's allusive technique serves
to relate this conflagration both to those which signalled the
destruction of Sodom and Troy, and to the lurid prodigies that
presaged the fall of Caesar. The 'blazing deluge', the tiles descending 'in rattling show'rs' (iii. 359–60), recall God's judgement
against the iniquitous cities of the plain (Genesis 19: 24). But as
the burning building 'sinks on the smoaky ground' (iii. 386),
Gay's final simile shifts the frame of reference from past to future
time, envisioning the fiery collapse of still another city, this time
Naples:

> So when the years shall have revolv'd the date,
> Th' inevitable hour of *Naples'* fate,
> Her sapp'd foundations shall with thunders shake,
> And heave and toss upon the sulph'rous lake;
> Earth's womb at once the fiery flood shall rend,
> And in th' abyss her plunging tow'rs descend.   (iii. 387–92)

Few of Gay's first readers would have failed to see in this image the
Christian conception of the holocaust that will signal the apocalypse
and the dissolution of the world. For, according to Thomas
Burnet's celebrated explanation,[23] the Conflagration would begin
in Italy, the peculiar domain of Antichrist, with the eruption of
Vesuvius and Ætna and the combustion of the inflammable
materials of the earth causing the cities of Rome to sink into lakes

of fire and brimstone. With this vision of the end of Time, the walker concludes his survey of the town. Gay's reassuring burlesque tone is subdued by these vivid reminders of the precarious grandeur of empires and the certain doom of the cities of this world. To render the meaning of the city clear, the penultimate paragraph universalizes Gay's depiction of 'the perils of the wintry town' (iii. 394), likening his own experience and didactic intent to those of other bold travellers, from the deserts of Arabia to the frozen wastes of Greenland, who have witnessed the savagery of man and the hostility of nature:

> Thus the bold traveller, (inur'd to toil,
> Whose steps have printed *Asia*'s desert soil,
> The barb'rous *Arabs* haunt; or shiv'ring crost
> Dark *Greenland*'s mountains of eternal frost;
> Whom providence in length of years restores
> To the wish'd harbour of his native shores;)
> Sets forth his journals to the publick view,
> To caution, by his woes, the wandring crew.   (iii. 399–406)

Barbarism and bitter weather are the conditions in this world, in which all men are travellers. Charity and the strict payment of 'due civilities' are the duties we owe along the way; prudence, the *ars vivendi*, is the means of safe passage. The walker's wayfaring through the winter streets of London is Gay's parable of life.

A final aspect of Gay's art in *Trivia*, and of the meaning of art in the poem, remains to be considered. It is conventional to say that Gay's answer to the corruption and artificiality of the town is the purity and naturalness of the country. This contrast, which certainly appears elsewhere in his poetry, is found in *Trivia* as well: 'On doors the sallow milk-maid chalks her gains; / Ah! how unlike the milk-maid of the plains!' (ii. 11–12). As we have already seen, however, references to the country in Gay do not function as they do in a primitivist or romantic work (in Smollett's *Humphry Clinker*, let us say, or in Wordsworth's 'Michael'), to recommend a return to rural regions. They serve rather to establish a *symbolic* antithesis to the meanings of the city that we have previously discussed, keeping just at the back of our minds—as of the thoughts of Gay's wayfarer through life—the memory of a better country left behind, a distant Eden forever lost. In the same way, the fact that *Trivia* is a mock-georgic establishes a continually implicit comparison between Virgil's happy husbandmen and the sordid denizens of the town. If the pastoral is a symbolic mode, an artful imitation of the Golden Age, *Trivia* reflects its opposite, the Age of Iron—the Age, more specifically, of Georgian England. To read *Trivia* as an assertion of natural values as against the values of art and civilization is to miss the point. These are *winter* streets; Gay's choice of the harshest, darkest season was quite deliberate. Nature, as she appears in *Trivia*, affords no refuge from the grim conditions of life; she is rather *part* of them and very nearly as pitiless as the town itself—drenching the traveller with winter rain, making him wince with the biting cold. The imprudent walker who has not learned 'to know the skies' (i. 122) runs the danger of succumbing to the malevolence of the weather—of being 'Surpriz'd in dreary fogs or driving rain' (i. 124), of having to gasp for breath in 'suffocating mists' (i. 125) that blot out the sun, of being threatened by 'the piercing frost . . . the bursting clouds . . . the drenching show'r' (i. 130–2). Significantly, the Mall lies 'in leafy ruin' (i. 27), and the Thames, frozen over, reflects the death of every vital force.

Gay's answer to the 'smutty dangers' and bitter climates of life is, then, not an escape into rural regions, not a return to Nature. More constructively, it is rather an assertion of the redeeming value of art and artifice in enabling us to cope with the shock of experience, to wrest from the dominion of Chaos and Dark Night a measure of grace, a private terrain where order and joy prevail. In this sense the art of the poem is not merely decorative, but completely functional: it is as useful in helping us to survive as the 'art' referred to in Gay's sub-title, or as those practical artefacts which, following Virgil, he celebrates at length in Book I—shoes, surtouts, umbrellas—implements devised by men as protection against a hostile environment. Something like this is the meaning of *Georgics I*, where the invention of every art is said to have been occasioned by the fall of Saturn and the end of the Golden Age: before the Fall, as Virgil asserts, Nature and Man were in complete harmony; now art is necessary to enable us to control a harsh and inimical world. It is our one way of reclaiming a part at least of our former relationship to an ideal order. It is the Muse who enables Gay, through winter streets, 'to walk clean by day, and safe by night', who conducts him 'securely' through the labyrinth. Gay includes himself among the other votaries of Trivia, because—like the paver, whose 'art / Renews the ways' (ii. 309–10), and the scavenger, who 'bids kennels glide / Within their bounds'—the poet smooths and disciplines the crude material of life.

Gay's redaction of the *Georgics* includes the burlesque of Virgil's account of the invention of implements for subduing and cultivating the earth; the travesty is not the less appropriate to his theme for being comic. The mock-myth of Vulcan's invention of pattens, for example, symbolizes precisely Gay's conception of the function of art. Spying Patty, the country girl in whom he saw for the first time 'Sweet innocence and beauty meet in one' (i. 244), Vulcan, the artificer god, descends to earth in the guise of a blacksmith to woo her. Winter weather threatens to despoil the mortal girl of her health and beauty, until the god, who once fashioned the invulnerable shield of Achilles, forges another practical artefact designed to ease her way along muddy country lanes that prove as treacherous in their way as the streets of London:

> Yet winter chill'd her feet, with cold she pines,
> And on her cheek the fading rose declines;
> No more her humid eyes their lustre boast,
> And in hoarse sounds her melting voice is lost.
>   This *Vulcan* saw, and in his heav'nly thought,
> A new machine mechanick fancy wrought,
> Above the mire her shelter'd steps to raise,
> And bear her safely through the wintry ways.
> Strait the new engine on his anvil glows,
> And the pale virgin on the patten rose.
> No more her lungs are shook with drooping rheums,
> And on her cheek reviving beauty blooms.   (i. 267–78)

As functional as the 'mechanick fancy' of Vulcan, the art of Gay's poetry lifts us, so to speak, out of the mire that threatens to overwhelm us, and restores the bloom of the fading rose on the cheek of innocence. Equally relevant is the burlesque myth depicting the genesis of the bootblack's 'beneficial art' (ii. 152), whom the gods make

> useful to the walking croud,
> To cleanse the miry feet, and o'er the shoe
> With nimble skill the glossy black renew.   (ii. 154–6)

Trivia and her fellow deities aid 'the new japanning art' (ii. 166)— 'The foot grows black that was with dirt imbrown'd' (ii. 209). The bootblack joins Gay's paver and crossing-sweep, as well as the poet himself, in the company of those whose function it is to introduce a measure at least of order and beauty in the face of squalor.

A crucial passage in the development of this theme occurs in Book II, where Gay and his friend William Fortescue stroll along the Strand passing sites formerly inhabited by men of taste, but now claimed by the forces of vulgarity. Only the name Arundel, famed connoisseur and collector of art, remains to mark the street where once his mansion stood as a monument to an aesthetic ideal:

> Where *Titian*'s glowing paint the canvas warm'd,
> And *Raphael*'s fair design, with judgment, charm'd,
> Now hangs the bell'man's song, and pasted here
> The colour'd prints of *Overton* appear.
> Where statues breath'd, the work of *Phidias*' hands,
> A wooden pump, or lonely watch-house stands.
> There *Essex*' stately pile adorn'd the shore,
> There *Cecil*'s, *Bedford*'s, *Viller*'s, now no more.   (ii. 485–92)

In a world thus given over to barbarism and depravity, one sanctuary alone remains, one bastion against the ugly and the vulgar: the Palladian house of the Earl of Burlington, whose good taste Pope would later compliment in his *Moral Essays* (IV). This is Gay's Palace of Art, embodying in the correctness of its outward form and in the works of art cherished within its walls, the aesthetic ideal which the poem itself asserts:

> Yet *Burlington*'s fair palace still remains;
> Beauty within, without proportion reigns.
> Beneath his eye declining art revives,
> The wall with animated picture lives;
> There *Hendel* strikes the strings, the melting strain
> Transports the soul, and thrills through ev'ry vein;
> There oft' I enter (but with cleaner shoes)
> For *Burlington*'s belov'd by ev'ry Muse.   (ii. 493–500)

Here alone, where Beauty and Proportion reign, can the wayfarer find refuge from the mud of winter streets.

While Gay in such passages 'often [as Addison said of Virgil in the *Georgics*] conceals the precept in a description, and represents his Countryman performing the action in which he would instruct his reader',[24] the poem is itself the substantiation of the theme. Gay's tone and that ostentatious artificiality of style that we have remarked, never permit the actual world to intrude, even though that world—grim, unpredictable, violent—is his subject.

A splendid illustration of this triumph of manner and artifice is the story of Doll, the ill-fated apple-woman. In itself the situation Gay describes is horrid: one day, as Doll is hawking pippins on the frozen Thames, the ice opens and swallows her, cutting off her head. (One can imagine what Hardy would have done with this!) But Gay's treatment cancels out the horror, transforming a grotesque and potentially tragic accident into a formal object of comic harmony and grace:

> 'Twas here the matron found a doleful fate:
> Let elegiac lay the woe relate,
> Soft as the breath of distant flutes, at hours
> When silent evening closes up the flow'rs;
> Lulling as falling water's hollow noise;
> Indulging grief, like *Philomela*'s voice.
>   *Doll* ev'ry day had walk'd these treach'rous roads;
> Her neck grew warpt beneath autumnal loads
> Of various fruit; she now a basket bore,
> That head, alas! shall basket bear no more.
> Each booth she frequent past, in quest of gain,
> And boys with pleasure heard her shrilling strain.
> Ah Doll! all mortals must resign their breath,
> And industry it self submit to death!
> The cracking crystal yields, she sinks, she dyes,
> Her head, chopt off, from her lost shoulders flies;
> Pippins she cry'd, but death her voice confounds,
> And pip-pip-pip along the ice resounds.
> So when the *Thracian* furies *Orpheus* tore,
> And left his bleeding trunk deform'd with gore,
> His sever'd head floats down the silver tide,
> His yet warm tongue for his lost consort cry'd;
> *Eurydice* with quiv'ring voice he mourn'd,
> And *Heber*'s banks *Eurydice* return'd.   (ii. 375–98)

The mock formality of Gay's 'elegiac lay'; the too delicious repetition of the liquid *l* sounds in 'Lulling as falling water's hollow noise'; the forced exclamation of grief ('That head, alas!') and the strained platitudes on mortality; Doll's ludicrously abbreviated cry resounding across the ice; the absurdly incongruous allusions to Philomela and to Orpheus—every touch conspires to turn pathos into laughter, to remove us from any involvement in the scene. By his skill as a craftsman and rhetorician, Gay has transformed the grotesque into the exquisite, imposing on the chaos of life a certain form and comic grace. In such passages, having managed to make life conform to the principles of art, he holds it up at arm's length, as it were, for our admiration and diversion. Like the magic of Hobnelia or the art of the paver, Gay's style, his manner, continually controls or remakes the crude material of experience, no matter how terrifying and intractable. What occurs in Gay's best poems is not the imitation of Nature or reality, but its metamorphosis, leaving the object still recognizable—witness Doll's fate or the city shower or the bull in the 'Friday' eclogue—but harmless; and not merely harmless, but aesthetically pleasing. Gay's characteristic tone of impish laughter has cost him the serious attention of more than one reader in our time, as it appears to have done in his own, because we have not seen that, far from being frivolous or irrelevant, the note he strikes is that of a hard-won affirmation: the poet's assertion of the redeeming value of his art. Gay does not imitate reality; because he is its master, he mocks it.

For his epigraph to *Trivia* Gay chose the opening line of Virgil's *Ninth Eclogue*: '*Quo te Mæri pedes? An, quo via ducit, in Urbem?*' (which Dryden renders: 'Ho *Mœris*! whither on thy way so fast? / This leads to Town'). The theme and the situation in Virgil's poem help, I think, to illuminate Gay's own meaning. The shepherd Mœris and his friend, the poet Menalcas, have been dispossessed of their pastures, and very nearly deprived of their lives, by the soldiers of the emperor. Mœris is journeying toward the town, bearing forced tribute to his oppressors. Lycidas, who hails him, is at first surprised:

> Your Country Friends were told another Tale;
> That from the sloaping Mountain to the Vale,
> And dodder'd Oak, and all the Banks along,
> *Menalcas* sav'd his Fortune with a Song.   (ll. 11–14)

Like the song of Menalcas, the poetry of John Gay makes, so to speak, this same attempt to redeem the land. Menalcas, 'in these hard iron times' (l. 16), failed; in *Trivia* at least—and in those other poems we have been considering—Gay succeeded.

V

Fielding: The Argument of Design

FROM a certain point of view—the one I have been taking in this study—*Tom Jones* (1749) is at once the last and the consummate literary achievement of England's Augustan Age: an age whose cast of mind saw the moral drama of the individual life enacted within a frame of cosmic and social Order, conceived in the then still compatible terms of Christian humanism and Newtonian science, and whose view of art, conditioned by the principles of neo-aristotelian aesthetics, saw the poem as fundamentally mimetic of this universal Design. For the Augustan writer—for Gay or Pope, let us say—the poem was a highly finished artefact: a 'product', as Northrop Frye has put it, rather than a 'process'.[1] The philosophical and aesthetic assumptions of the age are, we have remarked, most explicitly and memorably expressed in Pope's complementary poems, the *Essay on Criticism* and the *Essay on Man*. These assumptions, moreover, are the implicit affirmation behind the ironic correspondences and desperate paradoxes of *The New Dunciad*, in which the triumph of Dulness is seen as a dark apocalypse, a grotesque parody of classical and Christian ideals of Order and of Art. As a rationale for literature, however, these ideals are perhaps more appropriate to comedy than to Pope's favourite mode of satire, because the cosmic system they assume and celebrate is ultimately benign—comic in the profoundest sense. It is a universe not only full and various, but regular, created by a just and benevolent Deity whose genial Providence governs all contingencies, comprehends every catastrophe, from the bursting of a world to the fall of a sparrow. This creation, as opposed to the one with which we are familiar, is characterized not only by Energy, but by Order.

The idea is most succinctly stated in these familiar lines which have been our theme from the beginning:

> All Nature is but Art, unknown to thee;
> All Chance, Direction, which thou canst not see;

All Discord, Harmony, not understood;
All partial Evil, universal Good . . .

Significantly for our present purposes, for Fielding, as for many of his contemporaries, Pope was '*the inimitable Author of* the Essay on Man', who '*taught me a System of Philosophy in* English *Numbers*'.[2] Although, to be sure, Fielding had other teachers besides Pope—from Plato and Cicero to Locke and the Latitudinarians—there is, as we shall see, an essential agreement between the doctrine of the *Essay on Man* and the meaning of Fielding's masterpiece. As a comic novel—that is, as a fictional imitation of Life, of Nature—*Tom Jones* stands as an elaborate paradigm of those correlative tenets of the Augustan world-view: the belief in the *existence of* Order in the great frame of the universe, and in the *necessity for* Order in the private soul. Its special triumph as a work of art is that it does not merely declare these values explicitly in the narrator's commentary and in the dialogue, but embodies them formally in the structure of its periods and its plot, and in the function of its narrator, and expresses them figuratively through the controlled complexities of its language and the emblematic significance of many of its scenes and principal characters. The meaning of *Tom Jones* is, in other words, inseparable from its form and rhetorical texture: the novel itself is the symbol of its author's universe.

To state this proposition in other, more schematic terms, the meaning of *Tom Jones* turns upon the presentation of two major and complementary themes: these are the doctrines of Providence with respect to the macrocosm and of Prudence, the analogous rational virtue within the microcosm, man. Together with charity and good-nature, always the essential and indispensable qualifications of Fielding's moral men, Providence and Prudence define the specific ethos of *Tom Jones*. These concepts are what Fielding particularly intended when he declared in his Dedication to George Lyttelton that he had written his novel with 'the Cause of Religion and Virtue' firmly in mind.[3] One reason why *Tom Jones* is the salient example of literary art in Augustan England is that Art, in a fundamental and philosophic sense, is its subject: thus the Creation and that Providence which presides over it are, according to the language of traditional Christian theology, 'the Art of God'; and Prudence, as Cicero had insisted in a phrase Fielding was to borrow in *Amelia* (I. i), is 'the Art of Life'. For all its generous exuberance and cheerful, bumptious energy, *Tom Jones* is the celebration of the rational values of Art, of the controlling intelligence which creates Order out of Chaos and which alone gives meaning to vitality, making it a source of wonder and of joy.

Although Fielding's twin themes are closely (even etymologically)[4] related, they will require chapters to themselves. Here we shall consider the doctrine of Providence, the argument of the book's design.

i. *The Meaning of Design*

The relationship between Fielding (or, if we prefer, the narrator or 'implied author', Fielding's 'second self')[5] and his book *Tom Jones* has more than once been likened to God's providential supervision and superintendence of his creation. 'Such a literary *providence*, if we may use such a word,' declared Thackeray in admiration at Fielding's artful conduct of his story, 'is not to be seen in any other work of fiction.'[6] More recent critics have urged the same analogy, Wayne Booth among them, for whom the idea of Providence becomes a way of describing the unique *effect* of Fielding's narrator: not so much the sense we have of his presiding over and manipulating the action of the book (to which Thackeray had reference), but more especially the sense we have of the narrator's 'voice', the expression of an eminently urbane, judicious, and benevolent intelligence, himself the principal 'character' of the novel, who more than any other *within* the world of his book— more even than Allworthy—provides us with a moral 'norm' and centre, conditioning our attitudes toward and judgement of his people, benignly reassuring us about their ultimate fates, even, finally, redeeming 'Tom's world of hypocrites and fools'.[7] That Fielding's example should have given currency to the term 'omniscient' author is more appropriate, perhaps, than we have thought. What Thackeray and Booth regard as a useful analogy for describing the effect of the narrative in *Tom Jones* is with Fielding himself a deliberate metaphor: the author-narrator of *Tom Jones* stands in relation to the world of his novel as the divine Author and His Providence to the 'Book of Creation'—not like Joyce's artist or his God, 'invisible, refined out of existence, indifferent, paring his fingernails',[8] but rather very much interested and involved.

With its genial and omniscient author, its intricate yet symmetrical design, its inevitable comic denouement, *Tom Jones* offers itself as the paradigm in art of cosmic Justice and Order, at once the mirror and embodiment of its author's Christian vision of life. In the opening chapter Fielding declares that he has chosen 'no other than HUMAN NATURE' as his subject—its whole range and variety, from the 'more plain and simple Manner in which it is found in the Country' to all the 'Affectation and Vice which Courts and Cities afford'. To apply his own figure, he was setting out to purvey the feast of life, or, as he had earlier remarked of Cervantes' achievement in *Don Quixote*, to present 'the History of the World in general'.[9] Several passages in *Tom Jones* encourage this interpretation: that Fielding consciously understood his task as an author to be the creation, by aesthetic and rhetorical means, of a symbolic 'world' which would faithfully represent the nature of that actual world which God created and providentially controls. The narrator himself repeatedly calls attention to the very characteristic of his plot which critics, according to their prejudices, have either lauded or deplored: namely, that intricate concatenation of little trivial events which either bring his characters together or keep them apart and which lead, finally, to the comic resolution of every difficulty. Such, for example, are Sophia's snatching from the fire the muff which Tom had cherished, thereby revealing her love for him (V. iv); or Partridge's failing to see Mrs. Waters at Upton, when he might thus have prevented Tom's apparently incestuous affair (IX. iii–iv). 'Instances of this Kind', the narrator remarks of the latter unlucky situation, 'we may frequently observe in Life, where the greatest Events are produced by a nice Train of little Circumstances; and more than one Example of this may be discovered by the accurate Eye, in this our History' (XVIII. ii). Similarly, in commenting upon the episode of the muff, he had earlier compared the mechanism of his plot to the great machine of the universe itself, invoking a favourite metaphor of the rationalist divines:[10] 'The World may indeed be considered as a vast Machine, in which the great Wheels are originally set in Motion by those which are very minute, and almost imperceptible to any but the strongest Eyes' (V. iv). In passages like these the controlling analogy between the two creations, that of the comic novelist and that of the Deity, is implied throughout the book; but in the introductory chapter to Book X Fielding declares it explicitly, albeit with a decorous apology for the brashness of the comparison. In language echoing such works as Cudworth's

True Intellectual System of the Universe and Pope's *Essay on Man*, Fielding applies to his own book a metaphorical compliment which his friend John Upton had reserved for the supreme achievement of Shakespeare.[11]

First, then, we warn thee not too hastily to condemn any of the Incidents in this our History, as impertinent and foreign to our main Design, because thou dost not immediately conceive in what Manner such Incident may conduce to that Design. This Work may, indeed, be considered as a great Creation of our own; and for a little Reptile of a Critic to presume to find Fault with any of its Parts, without knowing the Manner in which the Whole is connected, and before he comes to the final Catastrophe, is a most presumptuous Absurdity. The Allusion and Metaphor we have here made use of, we must acknowledge to be infinitely too great for our Occasion; but there is, indeed, no other, which is at all adequate to express the Difference between an Author of the first Rate, and a Critic of the lowest.

What Fielding has here done—and what he intended throughout *Tom Jones* to be the basic point and symbol of the novel—is to invert the terms of a familiar analogy, as old at least as Plotinus: God is to his creation as the poet to his poem. Those qualities which we have already remarked in the novel—the intrusive, genial, omniscient narrator; the shaped periods and logical syntax of the prose;[12] the intricate yet symmetrical structure; the final distribution of rewards and punishments—make *Tom Jones* the image and emblem of its author's universe, as the universe had been understood by countless philosophers and divines of the Christian humanist tradition. On one level, the design of *Tom Jones* is the argument of the novel; and this argument is, in sum, the affirmation of Providence—a just and benign, all-knowing and all-powerful Intelligence which orders and directs the affairs of men toward a last, just close. The usual form of the analogy may be seen in Cudworth, who compares the design of the creation to that of a dramatic poem:

But they, who, because judgment is not presently executed upon the ungodly, blame the management of things as faulty, and Providence as defective, are like such spectators of a dramatick poem, as when wicked and injurious persons are brought upon the stage, for a while swaggering and triumphing, impatiently cry out against the dramatist, and presently condemn the plot; whereas, if they would but expect the winding up of things, and stay till the last close, they should then see them come off with shame and sufficient punishment. The evolution of the world, as

Plotinus calls it, is . . . a *truer poem* . . . [and] God Almighty is that skilful
dramatist, who always connecteth [our actions and his designs] into good
coherent sense, and will at last make it appear, that a thread of exact
justice did run through all, and that rewards and punishments are
measured out in geometrical proportion.[13]

Or consider Thomas Burnet, who found the world itself a far more
exquisite work of art than any poem or romance, however well
plotted:

. . . Where there is variety of Parts in a due Contexture, with something
of surprising aptness in the harmony and correspondency of them, this
they will call a Romance; but such Romances must all Theories of Nature,
and of Providence be, and must have every part of that Character with
advantage, if they be well represented. There is in them, as I may so say,
a *Plot* or *Mystery* pursued through the whole Work, and certain Grand
Issues or Events upon which the rest depend, or to which they are subordinate; but these things we do not make or contrive our selves, but find
and discover them, being made already by the Great Author and Governour
of the Universe: And when they are clearly discover'd, well digested, and
well reason'd in every part, there is, methinks, more of beauty in such
a Theory, at least a more masculine beauty, than in any Poem or Romance;
And that solid truth that is at the bottom, gives a satisfaction to the Mind,
that it can never have from any Fiction, how artificial soever it be.[14]

To cite only one other of many possible examples, the same analogy
was developed by Samuel Boyse in *Deity* (1740), a poem on the
attributes of God which Fielding praised and quoted at some length,
both in *The Champion* (12 February 1739/40) and in *Tom Jones*
(VII. i). For Boyse, celebrating God's Providence in the lines Fielding quoted, the world is 'the vast theatre of time' in which God's
creatures 'Perform the parts thy Providence assign'd, / Their
pride, their passions to thy ends inclin'd' (viii. 617, 621–2).

The theatre—or for that matter the 'comic Epic-Poem in Prose'—
was a fit emblem of the world, because it was, as Fielding observed
earlier in this same chapter, 'nothing more than a Representation,
or, as *Aristotle* calls it, an Imitation of what really exists' (VII. i).
The fundamental problem for the critic, therefore, is the one we
undertook to solve at the beginning of this study: to define the
particular conception of Nature which the poet has attempted to
express in his work. What, in other words, is the *poet's* understanding of 'what really exists'? For Fielding, as for Pope and
those other poets, philosophers and divines whose views we considered at length in Chapter I, Nature was 'the Art of God': its

characteristics were Order and Design, harmony and symmetry and proportion; its Author the great Artificer who supervised its operation and presided over the most trivial acts of His creatures, conducting them at last to that final catastrophe at which the divine analogue of poetic justice would be meted out to all. The two artists, human and divine, thus bear to each other an obvious analogy and relationship, the one creating Nature, the other imitating and reflecting that creation. This relationship is a basic principle of Augustan aesthetics—one which may be sensed, for example, in the delicate formalism of Gay's poetry and in the nice symmetry and exquisite tensions of Pope's couplets. The notion, once more, is this: since Nature is herself the supreme artefact— harmonious, symmetrical, skilfully contrived and designed to express the divine Idea—the artist who imitates her will reflect and embody this comely order in his own creation. The very form of the poem—or of the painting, the building, the cantata—thus assumes a symbolic, even an ontological significance. Form *is* meaning.

Keeping in mind these mutually dependent assumptions of theology and aesthetics in the Augustan period, we may better appreciate the meaning of form in *Tom Jones*. Form, a sense of significant design, is one of Fielding's chief contributions to the art of the novel. Even in *Joseph Andrews* character and action were made to imply a dimension of meaning larger than their literal reality: the twin heroes of that novel—representatives of the cardinal Christian virtues of chastity and charity—embark on a pilgrimage which leads them away from the City of this World toward a life of simplicity and love in a better country.[15] In *Tom Jones* Fielding fully realized the possibilities of the symbolic form he had tentatively explored in his first novel. As we have seen, he was setting out to represent in art the feast of life, the 'History' and emblem of the world in little. Since *design*—not merely fulness, but regularity; not merely variety, but symmetry, proportion, relationship—was the characteristic of that world, his own fiction would embody, and therefore symbolically assert, that principle of life.

Although critics have acknowledged, even marvelled at, the balanced architecture of *Tom Jones*, they have failed to grasp its value as symbol of the book's total philosophical meaning. Here, for example, is the one major inadequacy of R. S. Crane's otherwise brilliant and illuminating anatomy of the plot of *Tom Jones*.[16]

Though Professor Crane defined the organic interrelationship of character and action in the novel, he ignored an equally essential fact of the book's structure: Fielding's schematic arrangement of his materials according to principles which may best be described not in literary terms—not, that is, in terms of the interaction of the characters and the probable sequence of events (though these are, of course, fundamental considerations)—but in terms of contemporary aesthetics. It is awkward that the theory of literature espoused by the Chicago critics should have found its chief example in an author whose greatest work contradicts an essential axiom of that theory: namely, that meaning and form in fiction are determined exclusively from *within* the work by the developing organic interrelationship of character, thought, and action which of course, in one sense, *is* the novel.[17] This is true enough if we are to consider only the literal level of the narrative; but in *Tom Jones*—as in countless other novels from Richardson to Joyce and Faulkner—meaning and even the shape of the action are in large part determined by certain extrinsic, non-organic principles which may be generally termed *figurative* or *analogical*. Characters, scenes, the action itself—while maintaining an autonomous 'reality' within the world of the novel—may owe their conception to some ulterior, abstract intention of the author. When the abstraction becomes so obtrusive that it dispels the illusion of reality in a fiction, we no longer have a novel, but an allegory or parable. The two levels of meaning may, however, and often *do*, exist concomitantly, character and action preserving their literal identity and integrity, while at the same time implying values more universal and conceptual. Thus, by means of such devices as allusion and analogy, Fielding could shape an entire episode in his novel—Tom Jones's encounter with the gypsy king—into a complex political parable,[18] or, as we shall see in Chapter VI, by means of certain emblematic techniques in the presentation of Sophia Western and in the description of his hero's ascent of Mazard Hill, he could imply a broadly allegorical significance in the story of Tom Jones's pursuit of his mistress.

This same principle of ulteriority affects the structure of the novel. Design is the matrix of plot in *Tom Jones*; it is the primary (if not the only) determining factor in the structure of the book. The elements of the plot have been organized within an artificial and schematic framework imposed upon them from without.

Nothing inherent in Fielding's *story* necessitated the geometrical arrangement of its parts according to what may be called the Palladian[19] principles of proportion, balance, and symmetry. To speak of the 'architecture' of *Tom Jones* is not merely a gratuitous critical elegancy; on one significant level, Fielding's novel demands to be considered in terms of this analogy. The same axioms that determined the form of Ralph Allen's 'stately House' at Prior Park or Lord Pembroke's bridge at Wilton[20] have, in a sense, determined the form of *Tom Jones*. Thus, as is well known, the novel is divided into three equal parts of six books: Parts I and III, containing the adventures in Somerset and in London, comprise the twin 'stationary' bases of the structure; Part II, serving as a sort of arch between the two, carries the reader, together with Fielding's hero and heroine, from Paradise Hall and its immediate environs to the Great City. The adventures at Upton, where the lines of the plot converge and separate again, stand as the keystone of the arch in the mathematical centre of the novel, and are balanced on either side by the narratives of the Man of the Hill and Mrs. Fitzpatrick, the one serving as a foil to the character and story of Jones, the other performing the same function for Sophia.

There is, of course, more than one way to account for such a balanced and proportionate arrangement of parts: 'every thing that is perfect and regular', declared Robert South, 'is a credit and a glory to itself, as well as to its author';[21] and in his widely read work, *Reflections on Aristotle's Treatise of Poesy*, René Rapin insisted that 'the *Design*' of a heroic poem, like that of a great painting or palace, must evince a '*Proportion* and *Symmetry* of Parts'.[22] There is a pleasure, pure and simple, in the apprehension of harmony. But the Palladian design of *Tom Jones* has a deeper, more functional significance. Like the Order of the 'great Creation' to which Fielding compared his book, the symmetrical frame of *Tom Jones* becomes apparent only after we have 'come to the final Catastrophe' and have broadened our perspective, stepping back from the consideration of the part to comprehend the plan of the whole. In this sense the design of *Tom Jones* is an essential aspect of Fielding's imitation of 'what really exists', the emblem of a similar pattern in the cosmic architecture of Nature, a similar artistry in the Book of Creation.

ii. *Fortune and Providence*

Design, as we have seen, implies an artificer. The assertion of Order and Harmony in the Creation entails the correlative belief in God's superintending Providence: as Pope has it, Nature is Art; Chance, Direction. Whereas the *Essay on Man* declares this doctrine discursively, a fundamental purpose of *Tom Jones* is to *demonstrate* it in the dramatic and representational mode of a comic fiction, which is—at least as Fielding practised the form— the symbolic imitation and epitome of life. Just as the methods of historical criticism help to clarify the meaning of design in *Tom Jones*, enabling us to grasp the full implication of Aristotle for the Augustan artist, so they may help us to come to terms with the vexed question of 'probability' in Fielding's plot—as, indeed, in other fictions of the period from Congreve's *Incognita* and his plays[23] to Smollett's *Roderick Random* and Goldsmith's *Vicar of Wakefield*.

Fielding declares in *Tom Jones* (VIII. i) that the true province of the novelist is the 'probable', not the 'marvellous', even averring that he would rather see his hero hang than rescue him by unnatural means (XVII. i). But few critics have taken him seriously. In response to Coleridge's famous dictum that, together with *Oedipus Tyrannus* and *The Alchemist*, *Tom Jones* has one of the most perfect plots in literature, Austin Dobson long ago protested that

progress and animation alone will not make a perfect plot, unless probability be superadded. And though it cannot be said that Fielding disregards probability, he certainly strains it considerably. Money is conveniently lost and found; the naïvest coincidences continually occur; people turn up in the nick of time at the exact spot required, and develop the most needful (but entirely casual) relations with the characters.[24]

Although Professor Crane has gone far toward demonstrating that the action of *Tom Jones* may be seen as an 'intricate scheme of probabilities', yet his inclusion of so many 'accidents of Fortune' within this scheme does indeed strain, as Dobson put it, the definition of what is 'probable'.[25] Certainly Fielding's practice in the novel seems often to belie his professions. What, we may well wonder, is perfect and probable about a plot which depends for its complication and happy resolution upon such a remarkable series of chance encounters and fortunate discoveries? Fleeing from her father's house, Sophia happens upon the one person who can direct her along the road that Tom has taken. Tom happens to find himself in that isolated region where both the Man of the Hill and Mrs. Waters are threatened by ruffians, and so is able to rescue them. Having been seduced by this rustic Circe, he later discovers that she is (as he has been told) his mother! Disconsolate when he learns that Sophia knows of his infidelity and has spurned him, he resolves to lose his life in defence of Hanover, but his plans are changed when he chances to fall into the same road his mistress has taken and chances to meet a beggar who has found the pocketbook she inadvertently dropped. Later, languishing in prison, he finds that he has not, after all, committed incest and that Mr. Fitzpatrick has not, after all, died of his wounds. Indeed, the incidence of such happy casualties in Fielding's plot has led critics deeper and more recent than Dobson to pronounce 'Fortune' the sovereign diety of *Tom Jones*,[26] 'Fantasy' the wishful refuge of its author.[27] Fielding *knew* the hard realities and tragic consequences of life, wherein handsome young men, however good-natured, are ruined by knaves and hanged for their indiscretions; but his sanguine humour was forever compelling him to turn the nightmare of actuality into a cheerful dream of Eden: something like this is the drift of too many modern readers.

What I wish here to suggest is that the fortunate contingencies and surprising turns which affect the course of events in *Tom Jones* are neither the awkward shifts of incompetency nor the pleasant fantasies of romance; rather, they have an essential function in the expression of Fielding's Christian vision of life. As the general frame and architecture of *Tom Jones* is the emblem of Design in the macrocosm, so the narrative itself is the demonstration of Providence, the cause and agent of that Design. Unlike Defoe or Richardson, Fielding rejected the methods of 'formal realism'[28] for a mode which verges on the symbolic and allegorical: his characters and actions, though they have a life and integrity of their own, frequently demand to be read as tokens of a reality larger than themselves; his novels may be seen as artful and highly schematic paradigms of the human condition. For Fielding, and for the great majority of his contemporaries, no assumption about the world, and about man's place in the world, was more fundamental than the doctrine of a personal and particular Providence: 'The belief of this', Tillotson had insisted, 'is the great foundation of religion.'[29] This is the theme of countless discourses and homilies, most of which base their arguments on the discernible Order in the natural world and on the precepts of scripture. If we are to understand the significance of certain crucial recurrent themes in *Tom Jones*—the question of *probability* in the action of the novel and of *fortune* as it affects the lives of the characters—it will be useful to consider the doctrine of Providence as it appears in such representative authors as William Sherlock, whose *Discourse Concerning the Divine Providence* (1694) was a standard treatise on the subject, and those influential divines, Barrow, South, Tillotson, and Clarke, whose works Fielding is known to have read and admired.[30]

Deriving ultimately from Aristotle and Horace, the critical principle of 'probability' was first systematically applied to the novel by Fielding himself in *Tom Jones* (VIII. i), and—with the notable exception of the literature of the absurd—it has remained a basic operative principle with critics and novelists alike. Unlike the writer of romance, the novelist must decline the favours of gods from machines; his plot must work itself out by means of the natural interaction of the characters, the plausible and inevitable sequence of cause and effect. Fielding presents the doctrine most clearly in the prefatory chapter to Book XVII, as he considers the difficulties of extricating his hero from 'the Calamities in which he is at present involved, owing to his Imprudence':

> This I faithfully promise, that notwithstanding any Affection, which we may be supposed to have for this Rogue, whom we have unfortunately made our Heroe, we will lend him none of that supernatural Assistance with which we are entrusted, upon Condition that we use it only on very important Occasions. If he doth not therefore find some natural Means of fairly extricating himself from all his Distresses, we will do no Violence to the Truth and Dignity of History for his Sake; for we had rather relate that he was hanged at *Tyburn* (which may very probably be the Case) than forfeit our Integrity, or shock the Faith of our Reader.

Yet what is 'natural' or 'probable' about the extraordinary chain of events by which Jones is redeemed from prison and reconciled to his friend and mistress, his 'crimes' undone, his enemies exposed, his true identity revealed? As we have seen, the 'faith' of more than one reader has been 'shocked' by the apparent contrivance of Fielding's story. In another sense, however, the reader's faith—both in the ingenuity and kindly art of the author (his wonderful ability to make everything come right in the end) and in a corresponding benignity and design in the world he is imitating —is confirmed and substantiated by this very contrivance. Though Fielding spurned the good offices of the *deus ex machina*, he warmly affirmed the benevolent Providence of the god *in* the machine, that 'vast Machine' to which he had earlier compared the world. He could do so, moreover, without violating the critical principle he had himself laid down. In a universe ultimately 'comic' and Christian, the occurrence of what William Turner called '*the Most Remarkable Providences, both of Judgment and Mercy*'[31] was both natural and probable. To write a novel—at least a comic novel— and fail to imply them would be, in effect, to misrepresent the creation, to belie 'what really exists'.

Consider, for example, Tillotson's analysis in his sermon, 'Success not always Answerable to the Probability of Second Causes': though 'prudence', that virtue which Tom Jones so notably lacked, is necessary in human life, since 'GOD generally permits things to take their natural course, and to fall out according to the power and probability of second causes',[32] yet 'GOD hath reserved to himself a power and liberty to interpose, and to cross as he pleases, the usual course of things; to awaken men to the consideration of him, and a continual dependance upon him; and to teach us to ascribe those things to his wise disposal, which, if we never saw any change, we should be apt to impute to blind necessity'.[33] When prudence fails—prudence, which is the judicious weighing of means to accomplish a desired end according to the probability of second causes—then we must 'look above and beyond these to a superior cause which over-rules, and steers, and stops, as he pleases, all the motions and activity of second causes . . . For the providence of GOD doth many times step in to divert the most probable event of things, and to turn it quite another way: and whenever he pleaseth to do so, the most strong and likely means do fall lame, or stumble, or by some accident or other come short of their end.'[34] This, too, is the burden of Samuel Clarke's sermon, 'The Event of Things not always answerable to Second Causes': 'The *Providence of God*, by means of *natural Causes*, which are all entirely of *His* appointment, and *Instruments only* in *His* hand; does often for wise reasons in his government of the World, disappoint the most probable expectations.'[35] With characteristic shrewdness, Robert South, whose wit Fielding could on occasion prefer to that of Congreve,[36] managed his own extreme formulation of this doctrine. In his sermon, 'On the Mercy of God', he presents a sort of Sartrean universe, wherein the accidental and adventitious are the rule rather than the exception: paradoxically, the improbable is the probable. Only the benevolent supervention of God prevents human life from being a monstrous succession of unpredictable calamities:

> . . . how many are the casual unforeseen dangers, that the hand of Providence rescues [men] from! How many little things carry in them the causes of death! and how often are men that have escaped, amazed that they were not destroyed! Which shows that there is an eye that still watches over them, that always sees, though it is not seen; that knows their strengths and their weaknesses; where they are safe, and where they may be struck; and in how many respects they lie open to the invasion of a sad accident . . . In a word, every man lives by a perpetual deliverance; a deliverance, which for the unlikelihood of it he could not expect, and for his own unworthiness, I am sure, he could not deserve.[37]

In another well-known sermon, 'All Contingencies under the Direction of God's Providence', South further insists that what men call Fortune and Chance are in fact nothing more than agents of God's wise government of the world, affecting everything that happens to us down even to the casting of lots.[38]

The idea of Fortune is, indeed, a controlling theme in *Tom Jones*. It affects every stage in the hero's life from his birth to his imprisonment to his final redemption and marriage. To Allworthy, Tom is 'a Child sent by Fortune to my Care' (XVIII. iii). Before accepting his own responsibility for the calamities which have befallen him, Tom exclaims against the fickle goddess who has tormented him: 'Sure . . . Fortune will never have done with me, 'till she hath driven me to Distraction' (XVIII. ii). As we have remarked, the direction of Fielding's plot is frequently determined by the most unlikely coincidences, to which the narrator calls our attention in wry tribute to the goddess who 'seldom doth Things by Halves' (V. x). As we follow what Professor Crane has called the 'intricate scheme of probabilities' leading through complication to final resolution, we are never allowed to forget another, equally significant aspect of the plot: that it is Fielding who is contriving the circumstances and manipulating the characters, violating the rules of probability in a deliberate and self-conscious manner, introducing into his own story an element of the improbable analogous to those unexpected and inexplicable occurrences in the actual world which come under the category of 'luck'. It is 'Fortune', who, 'having diverted herself, according to Custom, with two or three Frolicks, at last disposed all Matters to the Advantage of' Sophia as she plans to flee her father's house (VII. ix). It is 'luck' which brings her to the same town and inn from which Jones had started on his journey, and which causes her to stumble on the same guide who had conducted him toward Bristol (X. ix). It is the 'lucky Circumstance' of Western's arrival in the nick of time that prevents Lord Fellamar's rape of Sophia (XV. v). It is 'Fortune', who, 'after so many Disappointments', brings Tom and Sophia together again in Lady Bellaston's house (XIII. xi), and 'Fortune' again who appears 'an utter Enemy' to their marriage (XV. x). As he introduces his hero's ill-timed visit to Mr. Nightingale, the narrator summarizes this theme in the novel:

> Notwithstanding the Sentiment of the *Roman* Satirist, which denies the Divinity of *Fortune*, and the Opinion of *Seneca* to the same Purpose; *Cicero*, who was, I believe, a wiser Man than either of them, expressly holds the contrary; and certain it is, there are some Incidents in Life so very strange and unaccountable, that it seems to require more than human Skill and Foresight in producing them (XIV. viii).

As Tillotson, as well as Cicero, was aware, there are limits to the efficacy of human prudence, an unpredictable and *apparently* irrational shape to circumstances.

Nowhere in the novel is this point more clearly and deliberately made than in the sequence of events which befall Fielding's hero immediately after Upton. Aware that his indiscretion with Mrs. Waters is known to Sophia, who has consequently abandoned him in dismay and indignation, Jones sets out from the inn convinced that his love is hopeless and resolved to give his life in the war against the Jacobites. Fortune, however, intervenes to change his purpose and lead him in pursuit of his mistress. The operation of Chance in human affairs is first demonstrated, appropriately enough, at a crossroads. Western, arriving at this junction in his efforts to overtake his daughter, 'at last gave the Direction of his Pursuit to Fortune, and struck directly into the *Worcester* Road', which leads him away from Sophia (XII. ii); confronted with the same choice, Jones, still determined to join the King's forces, 'immediately struck into the different Road from that which the Squire had taken, and, by mere Chance, pursued the very same thro' which *Sophia* had before passed' (XII. iii). Reaching another cross-way, Jones and Partridge there encounter an illiterate beggar who, in travelling the same road Sophia had taken, happened to find the little pocket-book containing a £100 bank-note which she had accidentally dropped. This chance discovery provides Jones both with a motive to pursue Sophia and with the guide he needs to resolve the difficulty of the crossroads. Of this fortunate coincidence—and a later one equally lucky—Partridge points the obvious moral: '"two such Accidents could never have happened to direct him after his Mistress, if Providence had not designed to bring them together at last." And this [the narrator observes] was the first Time that *Jones* lent any Attention to the superstitious Doctrines of his Companion' (XII. viii).

The episode of the beggar at the crossroads serves as a sort of parable of the doctrine of Providence which Fielding affirms throughout *Tom Jones*. Finding himself by chance in that remote place where the Man of the Hill is threatened by thieves, Jones comes to the rescue and acknowledges himself to be the instrument of God: '"Be thankful then," cries *Jones*, "to that Providence to which you owe your Deliverance"' (VIII. x). As he takes his leave of the Old Man, Jones's 'providential Appearance' (IX. vii) at the scene of Northerton's attempted murder of Mrs. Waters enables him to perform a similar office, no less pious than gallant, by rescuing the damsel from distress, and confessing himself 'highly pleased with the extraordinary Accident which had sent him thither for her Relief, where it was so improbable she should find any; adding, that Heaven seemed to have designed him as the happy Instrument of her Protection' (IX. ii). Such 'extraordinary accidents' and happy improbabilities are not so much a convenience to Fielding the author, providing him with easy escapes from the difficulties of his plot, as they are a calculated demonstration of providential care and design in the world. Most of these coincidences in *Tom Jones* are so gratuitous that an author of Fielding's inventive skill could easily have avoided them: Jones's rescue of the Old Man, for example, serves no real function either in advancing the plot or in allowing the two characters to meet, since Jones and Partridge have already settled themselves in the Old Man's house before the attack occurs; and there were a score of devices more probable than the chance encounter with a lucky beggar at a crossroads which Fielding might have used to put his hero on the trail of Sophia. Jones in the first case and the beggar in the second are agents not only of their author in administering the narrative, but also of that higher Providence for which, within the symbolic microcosm of the novel, the author stands as surrogate. Fielding's contrivances imply those of the Deity.

The theme of Providence is—somewhat paradoxically it may seem to us—enforced by those recurrent, intrusive references to Fortune that we have earlier remarked. For the modern reader the two concepts appear contradictory. For Fielding and his contemporaries—unless of course, like Pope's dunces, they happened to share Cibber's epicurean faith in the goddess Fortune[39]—there was only one explanation for that 'more than human Skill and Foresight' which alone could produce the 'strange and unaccountable' casualties of life. Fortune (or Chance) was, indeed, no more than a figure of speech, a convenient vulgarism, enabling one to talk of Providence while avoiding the note of pious sobriety—a note well lost in the pages of a comic novel. 'As to *Chance*', declared Samuel Clarke, ''tis evident That is nothing but a *mere Word*, or an *abstract Notion* in our manner of conceiving things. It has no real Being; it is Nothing, and can *do* nothing.'[40] Or again, in his sermon, 'The Event of Things not always answerable to Second Causes', Clarke denounces the epicurean notion that Chance, not Design, governs the world: 'We may observe, that what men vulgarly call *Chance* or unforeseen *Accident*, is in Scripture always declared to be the *determinate Counsel and Providence of God*. What careless and inconsiderate men ascribe in common Speech to *Chance* or *Fortune*; that is, to *nothing at all*, but a mere empty word, signifying only their *Ignorance* of the true Causes of things; this the Scripture teaches *Us* to ascribe to the all-seeing and all-directing Providence of God.'[41] Perhaps the most illuminating gloss on the theme of Fortune and Providence in *Tom Jones*, however, is found in William Sherlock's *Discourse Concerning the Divine Providence*, a work popular enough to have gone through nine editions by 1747. Sherlock's third chapter, 'Concerning God's Governing Providence', anticipates Fielding's parable of the lost-and-found banknote, using the same example to illustrate the dominion of Fortune over the affairs of men and the dominion of Providence over Fortune:

> . . . Let us consider God's Government of accidental Causes, or what we call Chance and Accident, which has a large Empire over human Affairs: Not that Chance and Accident can do any Thing, properly speaking; for

whatever is done, has some proper and natural Cause which does it; but what we call Accidental Causes, is rather such an Accidental Concurrence of different Causes, as produces unexpected and undesigned Effects; as when one Man by Accident loses a Purse of Gold, and another Man walking in the Fields without any such Expectation, by as great an Accident finds it. And how much of the Good and Evil that happens to us in this World, is owing to such undesigned, surprizing, accidental Events, every Man must know, who has made any Observations on his own, or other Mens Lives and Fortunes . . . *Time and Chance*, some favourable Junctures, and unseen Accidents, are more powerful than all human Strength, or Art, or Skill.

Now what an ill State were Mankind in, did not a wise and merciful Hand govern what we call Chance and Fortune? How can God govern the World, or dispose Mens Lives and Fortunes without governing Chance, all unseen, unknown, and surprizing Events, which disappoint the Counsels of the Wise, and in a Moment unavoidably change the whole Scene of Human Affairs? Upon what little unexpected Things do the Fortunes of Men, of Families, of whole Kingdoms turn? And unless these little unexpected Things are governed by God, some of the greatest Changes in the World are exempted from his Care and Providence.

This is Reason enough to believe, That if God governs the World, he governs Chance and Fortune; that the most unexpected Events, how casual soever they appear to us, are foreseen and ordered by God.

Such events as these are the properest Objects of God's Care and Government; because they are very great Instruments of Providence; many times the greatest Things are done by them, and they are the most visible Demonstration of a superior Wisdom and Power which governs the World . . .[42]

As Sherlock postulates and Fielding in *Tom Jones* dramatizes, a lost purse, a dropped pocket-book—however adventitious they may appear—find a place in God's benevolent ordering of things.

Sherlock also anticipates Fielding in defining the relationship between Fortune and human foresight, Providence and Prudence— the one sustaining the frame of the world and guiding the affairs of men according to the dictates of perfect Wisdom, the other imitating the example of this divine wisdom, however fallibly, in the sphere of the individual life. As the passage opens, we may recall Fielding's allusion to Cicero:

The Heathens made Fortune a Goddess, and attributed the Government of all Things to her . . . Whereby they only signified the Government of Providence in all casual and fortuitous Events; and if Providence governs any Thing, it must govern Chance, which governs almost all Things else, and which none but God can govern. As far as Human

Prudence and Foresight reaches, God expects we should take care of our-selves; and if we will not, he suffers us to reap the Fruits of our own Folly; but when we cannot take care of ourselves, we have reason to expect and hope, that God will take care of us. In other Cases, human Prudence and Industry must concur with the Divine Providence: In Matters of Chance and Accident, Providence must act alone, and do all itself, for we know nothing of it; so that all the Arguments for Providence, do most strongly conclude for God's Government of all casual Events.[43]

Though God allows scope for the voluntary acts of men—who, in so far as they conduct themselves virtuously, with charity and prudence, have fulfilled their duty to their neighbours and them-selves—he none the less controls the whole Creation with unerring wisdom and omniscience, ordering even the bungling and malicious deeds of human beings within the fabric of his wise design. As Clarke expressed it, ''tis impossible but he must actually direct and appoint every particular thing and circumstance that is in the World or ever shall be, excepting only what by his own pleasure he puts under the Power and Choice of subordinate Free Agents'.[44] 'Nor is there *in Nature* Any *Other Efficient* or proper *Cause* of any Event . . . but only the *Free Will of rational and intelligent* Creatures, acting within the Sphere of their limited Faculties; and the *Supreme Power of God,* directing, by his omnipresent Providence . . . the inanimate Motions of the whole material and unintelligent World.'[45] Within *Tom Jones* both these assumptions about reality are accommodated: on the one hand, we may trace, with Professor Crane, what might be termed the 'naturalistic' determination of events through the probable and predictable interaction of the characters; yet, on the other hand, we are aware of what seems best described as the 'artificial' determination of events through the arbitrary and quite improbable contrivances of the author, who presides like Providence over the world of the novel, distant yet very much involved, omniscient and all-powerful, arranging the elements and circumstances of his story according to a pre-conceived scheme as symmetrical and benevolent as the Design of that larger Creation he mirrors.

The shape of Fielding's narrative in *Tom Jones* and his choice of a narrative method may thus be seen as, in a sense, inevitable: the perfect vehicles for his theme. This theme, the assertion of Design and Providence in the world, is indeed the basis of Fielding's comic vision. It echoes in his writings from *The Champion* to that refutation of Bolingbroke which he died too soon to finish. God was always for him 'the only true, great Ruler of the Universe, who is a Being of infinite Justice',[46] a Being 'supremely wise and good', who was concerned to reward the virtuous and punish the guilty,[47] and 'in whose Power is the Disposition of all Things'.[48] He could scoff at those atheists and free-thinkers who, like Epicurus or Mandeville, preferred to believe against the dictates of reason 'that this vast regular Frame of the Universe, and all the artful and cunning Machines therein were the Effects of Chance, of an irregular Dance of Atoms'.[49] Such perfection in the works of Nature, he declared in another leader, was 'infinitely superior to all the little Quackery, and impotent Imitation of Art'.[50] But always for Fielding this nice Design in the Creation implied the continuing care of the Artificer, whose hand controlled the fates of nations and of individual men: in *The Jacobite's Journal* (19 March 1748) he printed with approval a letter from a correspondent who observed that it was God's 'good and all-directing Providence' which had freed England from Stuart tyranny and established her Constitution; and a similar conviction informs his little chronicle of divine retribution, *Examples of the Interposition of Providence in the Detection and Punishment of Murder* (1752). What Fielding himself affirms is, moreover, reiterated by the good men and women of his fiction, who express their trust in Providence in their adversity or their gratitude to God for their timely deliverances. Appropriately enough, it is Parson Adams who best summarizes this doctrine when, echoing Tillotson and a score of other divines,[51] he admonishes Joseph Andrews in affliction: with Joseph we are reminded that 'no Accident happens to us without the Divine Permission', that 'the same Power which made us, rules over us, and we are absolutely at his Disposal'; but, while acknowledging God's omnipotence, we may take comfort in the knowledge that every accident, every event, is 'ultimately directed' to some benevolent purpose (III. xi). In Fielding's last novel it is Amelia who echoes the parson's faith, acknowledging 'that Divine Will and Pleasure, without whose Permission at least, no Human Accident can happen' (VIII. iv).[52]

As in the world at large, the 'ultimate direction' of events in *Tom Jones*—and, indeed, in all Fielding's novels—is a comic apocalypse: that last, improbable, joyous catastrophe in which true identities are discovered, the innocent redeemed, an unerring justice meted out to one and all. To use South's fine phrase, the 'perpetual deliverance' of Fielding's characters from rape, murder, imprisonment, disgrace, is the essential pattern of his fiction— a pattern culminating in the final distribution of poetic justice. Yet one of the absurdities which Fielding found in *Pamela* was Richardson's insistence that virtue was rewarded and vice punished in this world: 'A very wholesome and comfortable Doctrine,' Fielding remarked in *Tom Jones* (XV. i), 'and to which we have but one Objection, namely, That it is not true.' Why, one may well ask, should the happy conclusion of Fielding's own fiction be considered any less intellectually reprehensible than that of *Pamela*? The answer, I believe, is implicit in what we have been saying so far about the relation of form to meaning in *Tom Jones*. Whereas Richardson offers *Pamela* to us as a literal transcription of reality, Fielding's intention is ultimately symbolic. In the Preface to *Joseph Andrews* Fielding saw the business of the comic novelist, as he saw that of his friend Hogarth, the 'Comic History-Painter', as 'the exactest copying of Nature'; but he meant this in an Aristotelian, not a Baconian, sense. He would have agreed with Imlac that the poet was not concerned to number the streaks of the tulip; his subject was 'not Men, but Manners; not an Individual, but a Species'.[53] Richardson's eye is on the fact, Fielding's on the abstraction which the fact implies. The happy ending of *Pamela* is unacceptable because the novel asks to be taken as a faithful (even in a pious sense) representation of actuality. Fielding's fiction makes no such claim. Ultimately he asks us to consider not Tom Jones, but 'HUMAN NATURE', not so much the story of his hero's fall and redemption as that rational and benign scheme of things which the story and its witty, genial author imply. *Tom Jones* asks to be taken as a work of Art, as paradigm and emblem of that wise Design which Pope celebrated, and in terms of which, 'partial Evil', however real, however terrible, may be seen as 'universal Good'. Given this assumption of an order and meaning to life, there must be, as Samuel Clarke put it, a

final vindication of the Honour and Laws of God in the proportionable reward of the best, or punishment of the worst of Men. And consequently 'tis certain and necessary . . . there must at some time or other be such a Revolution and Renovation of Things, such a *future State* of existence of the same Persons, as that by an exact distribution of Rewards or Punishments therein, all the present Disorders and Inequalities may be set right;

and that the whole Scheme of Providence, which to us who judge of it by only one small Portion of it, seems now so inexplicable and much confused; may appear at its consummation, to be a Design worthy of Infinite Wisdom, Justice and Goodness.[54]

Within the microcosm of the novel, this is precisely the function of Fielding's comic denouements, at which, miraculously, every difficulty is swept away, every inequity redressed. What appeared confusion, both in the conduct of the story and in the lives of the characters, is, after all, a wise design: the mighty maze is not without a plan. And a principal instrument of this revelation is an astonishing sequence of what Fielding calls 'those strange Chances, whence very good and grave Men have concluded that Providence often interposes in the Discovery of the most secret Villainy' (XVIII. iii). Sharing Allworthy's admiration at the 'wonderful Means' by which mysteries have been dispelled and justice has triumphed, the reader may wish to apply to Fielding himself what the good squire exclaims of the Deity: 'Good Heavens! Well! the Lord disposeth all Things' (XVIII. vii).

In the deliberate, philosophic use of coincidence, if in no other respect, Fielding reminds us of no one so much as Thomas Hardy —though, to be sure, the intentions of the two novelists are antithetical. Whereas the grotesque improbabilities of Hardy's plots are meant to mirror a universe hostile, or at best indifferent, to man, Fielding's happy turns and fortunate encounters reflect a very different, appropriately Augustan world. His contrivances, as we have remarked, imply those of the Deity. Fielding was not, of course, alone among his contemporaries in enforcing this analogy. As Richard Tyre has shown, it was a fundamental argument with such critics as John Dennis, for whom poetic justice in the drama was necessary as the reflection of 'meaning, order, and coherence' in the universe.[55] Neither Dennis nor Fielding was blind to the tragic circumstances of life, but both conceived the function of art to be the imitation of a reality more comprehensive and rational than our limited experience could disclose: 'Poetick Justice', Dennis observed, 'would be a Jest if it were not an Image of the Divine, and if it did not consequently suppose the Being of a God and Providence'.[56] A similar rationale, as we shall see, underlies that extraordinary series of calamities and fortunate restorations which modern critics have deplored in the plot of Goldsmith's Christian fable, *The Vicar of Wakefield*; and Smollett, too—though in a much more arbitrary and perfunctory fashion— attempts to justify the preposterous turns and discoveries of *Roderick Random* by attributing them all to the marvellous workings of Providence.[57] Written from a comparable belief in a Christian universe, such works as *Troilus and Criseyde*, *Paradise Lost*, and *Clarissa* attempt to reconcile the tragedy of existence with the consoling doctrine of the Church by resorting, variously, to a final apotheosis of the hero or to the reassurances of a ministering angel.

Happily, no such solution is possible or necessary to the comic novelist. As the example of Smollett in *Roderick Random*, or of Osborne in the film of *Tom Jones*,[58] makes clear, nothing, of course, is less artistically satisfying than a happy ending incoherently imposed on a story, whereby chance medley at a stroke becomes a wedding feast. The marriage of Tom and Sophia, however, is the *telos* of Fielding's novel, standing in the same relation to the world of *Tom Jones* as that 'Great Day' toward which life itself was tending, 'when', as Clarke expressed it, 'the Reasons of things and the whole Counsel of God shall be more perfectly disclosed'.[59] In accord with the Augustan conception of the ways in which Art imitates Nature, Fielding here may be seen to offer his own variation of a structural strategy we have already observed in Pope's *Pastorals* and *Dunciad* and in Gay's *Trivia*, whose time-schemes imply the progress of history toward apocalypse: his comic denouement reflects the purposeful movement of Time itself. *Tom Jones* has been cherished for many reasons, but its special triumph is as a work of art: the form of the novel—its symmetry of design; the artful contrivance of its plot; the intrusive, omniscient narrator; and that final, miraculous resolution of every complication—is the expression and emblem of its author's coherent, Christian vision of life.

VI

Fielding: The Definition of Wisdom

IF from one point of view the form of *Tom Jones* may be said to express the Augustan faith in Order most memorably articulated in the *Essay on Man*, Fielding's plan for the novel resembles Pope's in yet another way. In Epistle II of the *Essay*, Pope had turned from a consideration of design in the macrocosm to define the nature of order in the microcosm, implying as he did a traditional analogy between the rational powers that govern the universe and control the passions. As the Deity in his wisdom orders the world at large, so Reason was for Pope 'The God within the mind'.[1] It was also that faculty of moral vision and foresight which, as we shall see presently, was in the Christian humanist tradition synonymous with *prudentia*, chief of the cardinal virtues and the one virtue parallel in the human sphere to the *providentia* of God. Indeed, so close was the analogy that the two terms are etymologically related.[2] This function of Reason is what Pope has in mind when distinguishing between the 'moving' and 'comparing' principles of the soul:

> Self-love still stronger, as its objects nigh;
> Reason's at distance, and in prospect lie:
> That sees immediate good by present sense;
> Reason, the future and the consequence. (ii. 71–4)

In *Tom Jones*, too, Fielding's twin themes are Providence, the theological argument of the book's design, and Prudence, the moral doctrine of its fable. Though this schematic conception of his subject is never so obtrusive as to interfere with our enjoyment of the story as story—as is generally true in a more strictly allegorical work—it is nevertheless the key to Fielding's deeper intent and one of the special qualities of his craft as a novelist. It had, furthermore, the sanction of neo-classical critical theory: according to Le Bossu, for example, whom both Fielding and Pope regarded as the principal modern authority on the genre, the action of an epic poem—and therefore presumably of a 'comic Epic-Poem in Prose'— must '*Allegorically*' contain the moral, which was primary.[3] In *Tom Jones* Fielding's moral purpose was nothing less than the definition of Wisdom. By exploring the substance and form of this, the novel's most important ethical theme—and, later, by exploring the similar intentions behind Goldsmith's *Vicar of Wakefield*—we may better appreciate the implications of Bossu's doctrine for eighteenth-century fiction. In *Tom Jones*, especially, the relation of narrative method to meaning is one more, and perhaps the most remarkable, instance of the principle of expressive form which we have proposed as a distinguishing characteristic of Augustan art.

In dedicating the book to Lyttelton, Fielding himself provides the clue both to his moral purpose in *Tom Jones* and (in part at least) to his method of implementing that purpose. He declares

that to recommend Goodness and Innocence hath been my sincere Endeavour in this History. This honest Purpose you have been pleased to think I have attained: And to say the Truth, it is likeliest to be attained in Books of this Kind; for an Example is a Kind of Picture, in which Virtue becomes as it were an Object of Sight, and strikes us with an Idea of that Loveliness, which *Plato* asserts there is in her naked Charms.

Besides displaying that Beauty of Virtue which may attract the Admiration of Mankind, I have attempted to engage a stronger Motive to Human Action in her Favour, by convincing Men, that their true Interest directs them to a Pursuit of her.

The dominant ethical theme of *Tom Jones* turns upon the meaning of 'Virtue' and of the phrase, our 'true Interest'—what Squire Allworthy calls 'the Duty which we owe to ourselves' (XVIII. x). One method Fielding chooses to present this theme is implicit in the platonic figure of Virtue's irresistible 'Charms' and in the metaphor of the 'Pursuit of her'. Fielding's statement, then, is schematic, pointing both to the doctrine of the novel and to the means, which may be described as iconomatic, by which the novelist transforms the abstraction of his theme into 'an Object of Sight'.

Tom Jones, in a sense, is an exercise in the fictive definition of Virtue, or moral Wisdom—just as Fielding's earlier novels, *Joseph Andrews* and *Jonathan Wild*, may be regarded as attempts to represent through word and action the true meaning of such concepts as Charity, Chastity, and Greatness. To achieve this purpose,

Fielding employs many devices—characterization, for one, by which certain figures in the novel become 'Walking Concepts', as Sheldon Sacks has observed,[4] acting out the meaning of various virtues and vices. At present, however, I am concerned with only two of these techniques: Fielding's exploitation of verbal ambiguity —the power of the word, as it were, to define the moral vision or blindness of character and reader alike—and his attempt to delineate emblematically the meaning of true Wisdom. The problem for the critic, fundamentally, is to ascertain the nature of that Wisdom which Fielding, together with the philosophers and divines of the Christian humanist tradition, wished to recommend. For this we may conveniently recall Cicero's distinction in *De Officiis* (I. xliii) between the two kinds of wisdom, the speculative and the practical, *sophia* and *prudentia*:

> And then, the foremost of all virtues is wisdom—what the Greeks call σοφία; for by prudence, which they call φρόνησις, we understand something else, namely, the practical knowledge of things to be sought for and of things to be avoided.[5]

The apprehension of *sophia* was the goal of Plato's philosopher; the acquisition of *prudentia*—which begins with the intimation that the Good, the True, and the Beautiful are one—is the quest of the *vir honestus*. Fielding's intention in *Tom Jones* is to demonstrate the nature, function, and relationship of these correlative ethical concepts.

i. *Prudence: The Function of Ambiguity*

The importance of Prudence, the *ars vivendi*, to the Augustan ethos we have already obliquely glimpsed in Gay's *Trivia*. In *Tom Jones* our understanding of the concept deepens, for Prudence (together with the more or less synonymous word *discretion*) is there Fielding's central moral theme.[6] The term recurs and reverberates throughout the novel, acquiring something of the quality and function of a musical motif. Yet its meanings are curiously ambivalent; according to the context, which Fielding carefully controls, prudence is either the fundamental vice, subsuming all others, or the essential virtue of the completely moral man. It exists, as the exegetical tradition might express it, *in malo et in bono*. At the very start of the narrative Bridget Allworthy, the prude of easy virtue, is said to be remarkable for 'her Prudence'

and 'discreet . . . in her Conduct' (I. ii); but on the last page of the
novel Tom Jones himself is represented as a fit partner for Sophia
only because he has 'by Reflexion on his past Follies, acquired
a Discretion and Prudence very uncommon in one of his lively
Parts'. In one sense, prudence is the summarizing attribute of
Blifil, the villain of the piece, and it is the distinguishing trait of
a crowded gallery of meretricious and self-interested characters
from every rank of society—of Deborah Wilkins (I. v, vi), Jenny
Jones (I. ix), Mrs. Seagrim (IV. viii), Mrs. Western (VI. xiv),
Partridge (VIII. ix), Mrs. Honour (X. ix), Lady Bellaston (XIII. iii,
XV. ix). Antithetically, however, the acquisition of prudence is
recognized by the good characters of the novel—by Allworthy,
Sophia, and ultimately by Jones—as the indispensable requisite of
the moral man. 'Prudence', Allworthy maintains, 'is indeed the
Duty which we owe to ourselves' (XVIII. x). Sophia alone, of all
the characters in the novel, is possessed of prudence in this posi-
tive sense (XII. x). And the lack of it in Jones is the source of all his
'Calamities' (XVII. i), all his 'miserable Distresses' (XVIII. vi).

References to prudence, understood in either the positive or
pejorative sense, may be found elsewhere in Fielding's writings;
but only in *Tom Jones* does the word recur with such frequency and
insistence. Indeed, as I wish to suggest, Fielding's intention to
recommend this virtue affected the very shape and character of
Tom Jones: the choice and representation of the principal characters,
the organization of the general movement of the narrative, and
the content of particular scenes were determined in significant ways
in accordance with a broadly allegorical system designed both to
define the virtue of prudence and to demonstrate its essential
relevance to the moral life. Unfortunately for modern readers, the
passage of time has obscured the meaning of this concept in the
novel. To repair that disadvantage, it will be necessary to recover
the classical, Christian, and contemporary contexts which Fielding
drew upon.

Prudentia in the Christian humanist tradition is practical
wisdom—the chief of the four cardinal virtues: prudence, justice,
temperance, and fortitude. According to Cicero, who was principally responsible for its meaning during the period in question,
prudence is essentially the ability to distinguish between good and
evil. It is a rational faculty, therefore, which depends on the proper
functioning of memory, intelligence, and foresight: memory

enabling us to recall what has happened, so that we may learn from experience; intelligence enabling us to discern the truth of circumstances as they really are; and foresight enabling us, on the basis of past knowledge and with the aid of a penetrating judgement, to estimate the future consequences of present actions and events.[7] Prudence is, in other words, that perspicacity of moral *vision* which alone permits us to perceive the truth behind appearances and to proceed from the known to the obscure; it implies, furthermore, the power to *choose* between good and evil and to determine the proper and effective means of achieving the one and avoiding the other.[8] As such it is the *ars vivendi*—the 'Art of Life', as Fielding calls it in *Amelia* (I. i)—the supreme rational virtue and the most hard won, the possession only of the *vir honestus*.

Although by the seventeenth century a curious process of redefinition had begun which resulted eventually in our present perverse understanding of the term—a process by which the noblest virtue of antiquity has come to signify nothing more than a mean-spirited and cautious expediency—prudence in its original sense continued to find advocates among poets, moralists, and divines who cherished the humanist values. Following the examples of George Turberville and Alexander Barclay, John Denham in 1668 published a poem on the subject based on the Latin of Mancinus.[9] As Denham represents it, the primary function of prudence is to distinguish the essential characters of things to determine 'What's decent or un-decent, false or true' (l. 2):[10]

> Hee's truly Prudent, who can separate
> Honest from Vile, and still adhere to that;
> Their difference to measure, and to reach,
> Reason well rectify'd must Nature teach.   (ll. 3–6)

Since the prudent man has given over the government of himself to 'Clear-sighted Reason' (l. 13), he recognizes that the passions, the irrational impulses of the natural man, are his enemies. Reminiscent of Aristotle's characterization of youth in the 'Three Ages of Man', the imprudent are rash and incontinent, 'To their Wills wedded, to their Errours slaves' (l. 39). Accordingly, Denham exhorts his readers: 'Let not low Pleasures thy high Reason blind' (l. 147). For Denham and Mancinus, as for Cicero, prudence is identical with clarity of moral vision and with the pragmatic ability to act upon this knowledge. The prudent man carefully weighs 'Things past, and future with the present' (l. 175), and he understands 'the means, the manner, and the end' (l. 186) of any course of action:

> Some secrets deep in abstruse Darkness lye;
> To search them, thou wilt need a piercing Eye.
> Not rashly therefore to such things assent,
> Which undeceiv'd, thou after may'st repent; . . .   (ll. 21–4)

> Look forward what's to come, and back what's past,
> Thy life will be with Praise and Prudence grac'd:
> What loss, or gain may follow thou may'st guess,
> Thou then wilt be secure of the success; . . .   (ll. 207–10)

Prudence thus instructs us in true values and desirable ends, and she discloses the most expedient and efficacious means of attaining them. She is Fortune's foe and champion of 'the Golden Mean' (ll. 249–50).

For 'the Classical Reader' of the next century, as Fielding called his more literate contemporaries in the Preface to *Joseph Andrews*, this exalted understanding of prudence still obtained. For Fielding's friends Christopher Smart and James Harris, prudence was 'the Queen and Directress of all the other Moral Virtues',[11] the faculty 'instructing us how to discern the *real Difference of all Particulars*, and suggesting the proper Means, by which we may either *avoid* or *obtain* them'.[12] In *Polymetis* (1747) Joseph Spence noticed, with special reference to Cicero, that 'PRUDENCE, (or Good Sense) stands in the front of all the virtues', being the faculty by which emperors keep 'the whole world in order', and by which in 'lower life . . . all the affairs of human life are regulated and disposed, as they ought to be' (p. 138).

One of the fullest contemporary expositions of this virtue occurs in an article 'On Prudence' appearing in Sir John Hill's *British Magazine* for March 1749, one month after the publication of *Tom Jones*. This essay, Number XLI in the series called 'The Moralist', begins by celebrating the dignity and antiquity of the concept:

PRUDENCE is at once the noblest and the most valuable of all the qualifications we have to boast of: It at the same time gives testimony of our having exerted the faculties of our souls in the wisest manner, and conducts us through life with that ease and tranquillity, that all the boasted offices of other accomplishments can never give us. The ancient Moralists with great reason placed it in the first rank of human endowments, and called it the parent and guide of all the other virtues. Without prudence, nothing in our lives is good, nothing decent, nothing truly agreeable or permanent: It is the rule and ornament of all our actions; and is to our conduct in this motly world of chances, what physick is to the body, the surest means of preventing disorders, and the only means of curing them.[13]

To further define the nature and function of this virtue, 'the Moralist' invokes the traditional metaphor of sight, opposing the unerring perspicacity of the rational, to the blindness and brutishness of the passionate man: 'Prudence is the just estimation and trial of all things; it is the eye that sees all, and that ought to direct all, and ordain all: and when any favourite passion hoodwinks it for the time, man ceases to be man, levels himself with the brutes, and gives up that sacred prerogative his reason, to be actuated by meanest [sic] of all principles.'[14] The special provinces of prudence are the judgement and the will: seeing what is right and how to attain it, the prudent man translates this knowledge into action—deeds 'which will make ourselves and our fellow-creatures most happy, and do the greatest honour in our power to our nature, and to the great creator of it'. Again, the prudent man looks to the past (memory), the present (judgement), and the future (foresight); his own and others' past experiences inform his perception of present exigencies and enable him to predict the probable consequences of actions and events.[15] The prudent man alone is equipped to survive in a world of deceitful appearances and hostile circumstances, for only he 'sees things in their proper colours, and consequently expects those things from them which ruin others by the surprize of their coming on'; only he 'is guarded against what are called the changes and chances that undo all things'.[16] Although, as Tillotson and William Sherlock observed,[17] not even prudence can always foresee the improbable casualties which occur under the direction of Providence, yet she is, however fallible, our only proper guide.

Prudence in this positive sense is indeed, as Allworthy insists, 'the Duty which we owe to ourselves', that self-discipline and practical sagacity which Fielding's open-hearted and impetuous hero must acquire. But as Tom Jones has his half-brother Blifil, or Amelia her sister Betty, so every virtue has its counterfeit, its kindred vice which mimics it. The result is a kind of sinister parody of excellence. Thus Cicero warns against confusing false prudence and true, a vulgar error by which the clever hypocrite, bent only on pursuing his own worldly interest, passes for a wise and upright man. Such are the scoundrels of this world who—practised in what Fielding liked to call 'the *Art of Thriving*'[18]—wear the mask of prudence, separating moral rectitude from expediency.[19] It is 'wisdom [*prudentia*]', Cicero writes, 'which cunning [*malitia*] seeks to counterfeit',[20] so as the better to dupe and use us. The distinction between the two prudences, true and false, is clearly drawn in this passage from Isaac Barrow's sermon, 'Of the Virtue and Reasonableness of Faith':

> With faith also must concur the virtue of prudence; in all its parts and instances: therein is exerted a sagacity, discerning things as they really are in themselves, not as they appear through the masks and disguises of fallacious semblance, whereby they would delude us; not suffering us to be abused by the gaudy shews, the false glosses, the tempting allurements of things; therein we must use discretion in prizing things rightly, according to their true nature and intrinsick worth; in chusing things really good, and rejecting things truly evil, however each kind may seem to our erroneous sense; therein we must have a good prospect extending itself to the final consequences of things; so that looking over present contingencies we descry what certainly will befal us through the course of eternal ages.
>
> In faith is exercised that prudence, which guideth and prompteth us to walk by the best rules, to act in the best manner, to apply the best means, towards attainment of the best ends.
>
> The prudence of faith is indeed the only prudence considerable; all other prudence regarding objects very low and ignoble, tending to designs very mean, or base, having fruits very poor or vain; to be wise about affairs of this life (these fleeting, these empty, these deceitful shadows) is a sorry wisdom; to be wise in *purveying for the flesh*, is the wisdom of a beast, which is wise enough to prog for its sustenance; to be wise in gratifying fancy, is the wisdom of a child, who can easily entertain and please himself with trifles; to be wise in contriving mischief, or embroiling things, is the wisdom of a fiend; in which the old serpent, or grand politician of hell, doth exceed all the *Machiavels* in the world; this (as St. *James* saith) is earthly, sensual, *devilish wisdom*; but the wisdom of faith, or that *wisdom, which is from above, is first pure, then peaceable; gentle, easy to be entreated, full of mercy and good works.*[21]

This passage from Fielding's 'favourite' divine[22] provides an admirable gloss on the antithetical meanings of prudence in *Tom Jones*, though we need not consider Barrow's sermon a 'source' for

Fielding's ideas on the subject. As we have seen, the concept of true prudence was a commonplace among those well-read in the classics or their modern commentators. So, too, was the notion of its shadow and opposite, false prudence, the 'mock Wisdom' of this world.²³ This is the characteristic of the whole 'tribe' of hypocrites and politicians, of whom, as Robert South declared, Machiavelli was 'the great patron and *coryphœus*'.²⁴ Thus, in language anticipating Fielding's anatomy of hypocrisy in 'An Essay on the Knowledge of the Characters of Men', Tillotson warned that 'The politicians of the world' pretend to wisdom; 'but theirs is rather a craftiness than a wisdom. Men call it prudence; but they are glad to use many arts to set it off, and make it look like wisdom; by silence, and secrecy, and formality, and affected gravity, and nods, and gestures. The scripture calls it "the wisdom of this world", I Cor. ii. 6 and a "fleshly wisdom", 2 Cor. i. 12. It is wisdom misapplied, it is the pursuit of a wrong end.'²⁵ Similarly, Bishop Hoadly cited 'the *Instance* of *Wisdom* and *Cunning*' to illustrate his observation that: 'THERE is hardly any one Vertue, or Excellence in the *Best* Part of Mankind, but what is attempted to be imitated, or mimicked, by Something in the *Worst*; designed to make the same Appearance, but in reality as distant in Nature from it, as a *Shadow* from a *Substance*; nay, as contradictory to it, as *Evil* is to *Good*, or as a monstrous *Defect* is to *Perfection* itself.'²⁶ And to adduce one other of many possible examples, only a few months before *Tom Jones* went to press an essay by 'the Moralist' in Hill's *British Magazine* defined 'that species of wit, which we, to distinguish it from real prudence, whose form it affects to appear in, call *Cunning*', the author regretting that the 'many often miss the distinction between this shadow of wisdom and wisdom itself; and the vile successful villain is too often said to have rais'd himself to all his happiness and honours by his wisdom'.²⁷

This, then, is the point of Fielding's deliberately ambiguous use of the term in *Tom Jones*: the difficulty of distinguishing true prudence from false, wisdom from cunning. Even an Allworthy can mistake the characters of men, can fail to penetrate the pious disguises of the Blifils of this world. True prudence, Fielding would assert in *Amelia*, was 'the Art of Life'; false prudence, he had declared in 'An Essay on the Knowledge of the Characters of Men', was 'the *Art of Thriving*', the signal talent and virtue of Blifil and Jonathan Wild, of Shamela and Stephen Grub,²⁸ indeed of a host of self-serving hypocrites and worldly politicians who threaten to defeat the good-natured children of his comedies, to confound his cheerful vision of charity and order. These are the Enemy, whom he made it his business, as ironist and as magistrate, to expose and punish.

As we have seen, these meanings of prudence, true and false, were commonplaces of the Christian humanist tradition. By the eighteenth century, however, this noblest of the cardinal virtues of the Ancients had suffered from reinterpretation by writers of bromidic conduct books addressed chiefly to a middle-class audience of shopkeepers and schoolboys. Debased and vulgarized, *prudentia*, the hard-earned wisdom of the *vir honestus*, had become —if in name only—the property of the *vir œconomicus*. In the process, ironically, its counterfeit and shadow came, in effect, to be taken for the thing itself: self-discipline, discretion, foresight, expediency came to be valued for mercenary reasons—not as the way to self-knowledge and a virtuous conduct, but as the surest means of prospering in the world. This modern definition of prudence deepens the ambiguities of the term in *Tom Jones*. In this new context, the prudent person is coolly self-interested—even, in fact, hypocritical: he prizes the reputation of virtue more than virtue itself, since a good name can be profitable to him, will enable him more easily to use others to his own advantage; he is seldom open or candid (and then only by design), since he must conceal his true motives from those he hopes to gain by; he is never passionate, since only the man who is in control of himself can hope to manipulate others.

Though the difference is great between the grasping malevolence of Blifil, let us say, and the desire of his mother to conceal her indiscretions, both characters are 'prudent' in this new sense. Consider, for example, the worldly counsel of Balthazar Gracian in *The Art of Prudence: or, A Companion for a Man of Sense.*[29] In a series of three hundred maxims Gracian provides a sort of *vade mecum* for the aspiring hypocrite, a layman's guide to 'the *Art of Thriving*': thus, to adduce a random sample of his wisdom, he advises his readers, variously, '*Not to be too free, nor open*' (Maxim III), '*To find out a Mans* Foible, *or weak side*' (XXVI), '*Never to be disorder'd with Passion*' (LII), '*Under the Veil of another Man's Interest, to find one's Own*' (CXLIV (misnumbered CLXIV)), '*To be able to Cast the Blame and Misfortunes upon Others*' (CXLIX), '*To know how to use*

Friends' (CLVIII), '*never [to] lose the Favour of him that is Happy, to take Compassion on a Wretch*' (CLXIII), '*To Act all that is agreeable by one's Self, and all that's Odious by others*' (CLXXXVII), '*To take Advantage of another Man's Wants*' (CLXXXIX), '*Not to make one's Self too Intelligible*' (CCLIII). The Blifils, indeed the Iagos, of this world have clearly heeded Gracian's exhortation to proceed in all things with 'Pious Craft' (CXLIV). We may recognize each of Fielding's villains in the master's delineation of the 'expert Person', who 'uses for Weapons the stratagems of Intention': 'He never does, what he seems to have a mind to do. He takes aim, 'tis true, but that only to deceive the Eyes of those that look upon him. He blurts out a word, and afterwards does what no body dreamt of' (XIII). Another maxim, explaining the necessity for the prudent man '*To Dissemble*' (XCVIII), makes clear why Fielding's hearty and good-natured heroes—a Tom Jones or a Parson Adams, let us say—are so ill equipped for the business of life, so vulnerable to the designs of their predatory neighbours:

> PASSIONS are the Breaches of the Mind. The most useful Knowledge is the Art of Disguising one's Thoughts. He that shews his Game, runs the risque of losing it . . .
> . . . he that disguises [his passions], preserves his Credit, at least in appearance. Our Passions are the Infirmities of our Reputation.

Gracian's work is only one of several handbooks on prudence addressed to a public apparently eager to penetrate the mysteries of worldly prosperity and '*Pollitricks*', to use Fielding's fine coinage in *Jonathan Wild* (II. v). Among the most popular of these was William de Britaine's *Humane Prudence: or, The Art by which a Man may Raise Himself and His Fortune to Grandeur* (1680), which reached a twelfth edition by 1729. In a piece of typical advice De Britaine admonishes the reader 'to try in the first Place to subdue your Passions, or at least so artificially to disguise them, that no Spy may be able to unmask your Thoughts; here to dissemble, is a great Point of Prudence; for by this means you so cunningly hide all your Imperfections, that no Eye shall be able to discover them'.[30] Applying the general precept to the particular case of his most promising disciples, De Britaine concludes with a section entitled, '*Sententiæ Stellares*: or, Maxims of Prudence to be observed by Artisans of State'. A similar work was Thomas Fuller's *Introductio ad Prudentiam: or, Directions, Counsels, and Cautions, tending to prudent Management of Affairs in Common Life*, which had gone through three editions by 1731. Fuller, a physician of Queen's College, Cambridge, designed this collection of 1,761 apothegms to direct his son (as Mentor had directed Telemachus!) in the ways of flourishing in the world. Fuller's motive was shared by several other writers who attempted to anatomize the modern art of prudence for the benefit of schoolboys[31]—most of them appealing to the selfish interests of their readers in pious language formerly reserved for nobler themes. The terms prudence, wisdom, and virtue were, in effect, emptied of their original significance and euphemistically made to refer to the practice of duplicity and the pursuit of personal gain. By such means the middle-class mind achieved a comfortable reconciliation between morality and Mammon. Though published five years after *Tom Jones*, James Burgh's discussion of prudence in Book I of *The Dignity of Human Nature* (1754) not only serves to clarify Fielding's use of the term, but also illustrates some of the subtler ways by which the *prudentia* of the Christian humanist tradition became transmuted into the cardinal virtue in the pantheon of middle-class values. Burgh, a schoolmaster by profession, represents prudence as

a turn of mind, which puts a person upon looking forward, and enables him to judge rightly of the consequences of his behaviour, so as to avoid the misfortunes into which rashness precipitates many, and to gain the ends which a wise and virtuous man ought to pursue.

It is evident to the meanest understanding, that there is a fitness or unfitness, a suitableness or unsuitableness of things to one another, which is not to be changed, without some change presupposed in the things, or their circumstances. Prudence is the knowledge and observance of this propriety of behaviour to times and circumstances, and probable consequences, according to their several varieties.[32]

In itself this definition is close enough to Cicero's or Barrow's and could well serve as a description of that rational temper which Tom Jones requires. In context, however, Burgh differs from Fielding in identifying the function of prudence with the attainment of selfish ends; the language the philosophers had used to define the *ars vivendi* now comfortably justifies the modern art of prospering in the world. Prudence is 'indispensably necessary', Burgh advises, not so much for the health of the private soul, but to frustrate the designs of the envious and to enable us to move profitably through life. Here, as in other works on the subject, the great enemies of

prudence are inexperience and rashness: the lack of 'a due knowledge' of mankind, together with that 'natural vivacity and warmth
of youth' which lead us, with Tom Jones, to behave in a 'forward
and precipitate manner . . . [to] the disappointment of our designs'.[33]
Through the colours and devices of such rhetoric, Right Reason is
transmogrified into shrewdness, a politic circumspection; and the
ideal of self-discipline becomes the rationale for thriving. Prudence
in this sense is that virtue which a Robinson Crusoe or a Pamela
so well understands.

The concept of prudence in *Tom Jones* is deliberately complex, as
significant yet as elusive as the meaning of wisdom itself. The single
term carries with it at least three distinct meanings derivative
from the ethical and historical contexts we have been exploring:
(1) it may signify *prudentia*, the supreme rational virtue of the
Christian humanist tradition, that practical wisdom which Tom
Jones, like the *vir honestus*, must acquire; (2) it may signify the
shadow and antithesis of this virtue—reason in the service of
villainy—that malevolent cunning which characterizes the hypocrite Blifil; or (3) it may signify that prostitute and self-protective
expediency, that worldly wisdom, which, owing to the influence
of Gracian, De Britaine, Fuller, and the other pious-sounding per-
petrators of a middle-class morality, replaced the humanist concept
of *prudentia* in the popular mind. These are the basic variations on
the theme. According to the context in *Tom Jones*, one of these
meanings will be dominant, but the others echo in the reader's
memory effecting a kind of ironic counterpoint and ultimately, as
it were, testing his own sense of values, his own ability to make
necessary ethical distinctions between goods real or merely
apparent.

In Book XII, Chapter iii, Fielding protests: 'If we have not all
the Virtues, I will boldly say, neither have we all the Vices of a
prudent Character.' The vices of the prudent characters in *Tom
Jones*—of Blifil, Bridget Allworthy, Lady Bellaston, and their kind—
should now be sufficiently evident. The positive meaning of
prudence in the novel, however, is perhaps less obvious, for the
virtue which Fielding recommends is essentially synthetic, combining the *prudentia* of the philosophers with certain less ignoble
features of the modern version. What Tom Jones fundamentally
lacks, of course, is *prudentia*: moral vision and self-discipline.
Although he intuitively perceives the difference between Sophia

and the daughters of Eve, he is too much the creature of his passions to be able to act upon that knowledge. He moves through life committing one good-natured indiscretion after another, unable to learn from past experiences or to foresee the future consequences of his rash behaviour. Only in prison, at the nadir of his misfortunes, does the full meaning of his imprudence appear to him. To Mrs. Waters, Jones 'lamented the Follies and Vices of which he had been guilty; every one of which, he said, had been attended with such ill Consequences, that he should be unpardonable if he did not take Warning, and quit those vicious Courses for the future', and he concludes with a 'Resolution to sin no more, lest a worse Thing should happen to him' (XVII. ix). When, moments later, he is informed that Mrs. Waters, the woman he had slept with at Upton, is his own mother, Jones arrives at last at that crucial moment of self-awareness toward which the novel has been moving. Rejecting Partridge's suggestion that ill luck or the devil himself had contrived this ultimate horror, Fielding's hero accepts his own responsibility for his fate: 'Sure . . . Fortune will never have done with me, 'till she hath driven me to Distraction. But why do I blame Fortune? I am myself the Cause of all my Misery. All the dreadful Mischiefs which have befallen me, are the Consequences only of my own Folly and Vice' (XVIII. ii). Here is at once the climax and the resolution of the theme of *prudentia* in the novel—a theme to which Fielding would return in *Amelia*, where, in the introductory chapter, he propounded at length the lesson Tom Jones learned: 'I question much, whether we may not by natural means account for the Success of Knaves, the Calamities of Fools, with all the Miseries in which Men of Sense sometimes involve themselves by quitting the Directions of Prudence, and following the blind Guidance of a predominant Passion; in short, for all the ordinary Phenomena which are imputed to Fortune; whom, perhaps, Men accuse with no less Absurdity in Life, than a bad Player complains of ill Luck at the Game of Chess.'[34] Prudence in this sense is the supreme virtue of the Christian humanist tradition, entailing knowledge and discipline of the self and the awareness that our lives, ultimately, are shaped less by circumstances, than by reason and the will. This, Fielding concludes, echoing Cicero, is 'the Art of Life'.

Although this is the fundamental positive meaning of prudence in *Tom Jones*, Fielding extends the concept to accommodate a nobler, purified version of that worldly wisdom so assiduously inculcated by the moderns. Since the business of life was a matter not simply of preserving the moral health of one's soul, but also of surviving in a world too quick to judge by appearances, it was necessary to have a proper regard to one's reputation. In Maxim XCIX Gracian warned that 'THINGS are not taken for what they really are, but for what they appear to be . . . It is not enough to have a good Intention, if the Action look ill' (see also CXXX), and Fuller's apothegms (for example, Nos. 1425 and 1590) similarly emphasize that 'a fair Reputation' is necessary to all men. Fielding, however, is careful to distinguish his own version of prudence from that of the cynical proponents of a self-interested dissimulation—those who cared not at all for virtue, but only for the appearance of virtue. Good nature and charity are the indispensable qualifications of Fielding's heroes—of Parson Adams, Heartfree, Tom Jones, Captain Booth—who demand our affection despite their naïveté, their foibles and indiscretions. But Fielding was concerned that the good man preserve his good name; otherwise he became vulnerable to the malicious designs of his enemies and subject to the disdain of his friends. The difficulty of distinguishing truth from appearances is Fielding's constant theme: the classical *prudentia* enables us to make these crucial discriminations; prudence in the modern sense, on the other hand, is in part the awareness that such distinctions are rarely made by the generality of men, that we are judged by appearances and must therefore conduct ourselves with discretion. As early as *The Champion* (22 November 1739) Fielding had insisted on this point: 'I would . . . by no Means recommend to Mankind to cultivate Deceit, or endeavour to appear what they are not; on the contrary, I wish it were possible to induce the World to make a diligent Enquiry into Things themselves, to withold them from giving too hasty a Credit to the outward Shew and first Impression; I would only convince my Readers, *That it is not enough to have Virtue, without we also take Care to preserve, by a certain Decency and Dignity of Behaviour, the outward Appearance of it also.*'[35] This, too, is the 'very useful Lesson' Fielding sets forth in *Tom Jones* for the benefit of his youthful readers, who will find

. . . that Goodness of Heart, and Openness of Temper, tho' these may give them great Comfort within, and administer to an honest Pride in their own Minds, will by no Means, alas! do their Business in the World. Prudence and Circumspection are necessary even to the best of Men. They are indeed as it were a Guard to Virtue, without which she can never be safe. It is not enough that your Designs, nay that your Actions, are intrinsically good, you must take Care they shall appear so. If your Inside be never so beautiful, you must preserve a fair Outside also. This must be constantly looked to, or Malice and Envy will take Care to blacken it so, that the Sagacity and Goodness of an *Allworthy* will not be able to see thro' it, and to discern the Beauties within. Let this, my young Readers, be your constant Maxim, That no Man can be good enough to enable him to neglect the Rules of Prudence; nor will Virtue herself look beautiful, unless she be bedecked with the outward Ornaments of Decency and Decorum. (III. vii)

Like Virtue herself, Sophia is concerned to preserve her good name, the outward sign of her true character (XIII. xi). And Allworthy more than once echoes his author's sentiments in advising Jones that prudence is 'the Duty which we owe to ourselves' (XVIII. x), that it is, together with religion, the sole means of putting the good-natured man in possession of the happiness he deserves (V. vii).

As the recommendation of Charity and Chastity is the underlying purpose of Fielding's first novel, *Joseph Andrews*, the dominant ethical concern of *Tom Jones* is the anatomy of Prudence. It is a process as essential as the discrimination of vice from virtue, of selfishness from self-discipline, and as significant to life as the pursuit of wisdom. Lacking prudence, Tom Jones is a prey to hypocrites and knaves and too often the victim of his own spontaneities, his own generous impulses and extravagancies. For Fielding in this his greatest novel, virtue was as much a matter of the understanding and the will as of the heart. Prudence, he implies, is the name each man gives to that wisdom, worldly or moral, which he prizes. This is the fundamental paradox of the novel as of life. Fielding's rhetorical strategy—his ironic use of the same word to convey antithetical meanings—forces the reader to assess his own sense of values, to distinguish the true from the false. We, too, are implicated, as it were, in Tom Jones's awkward progress toward that most distant and elusive of goals—the marriage with Wisdom herself.

ii. *Sophia and the Functions of Emblem*

Since it is a *practical* virtue, Fielding may thus define prudence, negatively and positively, by associating the word with various examples of moral behaviour chosen to illustrate those disparate meanings of the concept which he meant either to ridicule or recommend. In action the 'prudence' of Blifil or Mrs. Western may be distinguished from the 'prudence' of Sophia; the deed to which the word is applied controls our sense of Fielding's intention, whether ironic or sincere. The nature of *speculative* wisdom, on the other hand, is less easily and effectively conveyed by means of the counterpoint of word and action: *sophia* was a mystery even Socrates could describe only figuratively—a method to which Fielding alludes in the Dedication to *Tom Jones* when he invokes the platonic metaphor of the 'naked Charms' of Virtue imagined as a beautiful woman.[36] In *Tom Jones* the meaning of *sophia* is presented to the reader as 'an Object of Sight' in the character of Fielding's heroine.

Although it has apparently escaped the attention of his critics, the emblemizing technique Fielding here employs—which it is our present purpose to consider in its various manifestations in *Tom Jones*—is one of the most distinctive resources of his art as a novelist. In co-operation with such other strategies as allusion, analogy, and design, one of the functions of this technique is to complicate the literal level of the story and to deepen its significance. As we have already seen, an impulse akin to, if not identical with, the allegorical or parabolic is among the characteristic features of the Augustan mode, evident, for example, in Pope's handling of the episode of Vulcan's shield or in Gay's manner of suggesting in *Trivia* that the walker's journey through London's winter streets implies the wayfaring of Everyman through life. A similar motive informs Fielding's fiction. Indeed, more than any other writer of the period—unless, perhaps, one accepts J. Paul Hunter's provocative interpretation of Defoe's method in *Robinson Crusoe*[37]— Fielding organized his novels schematically, choosing his characters and shaping his plots so as to objectify an abstract moral theme which is the germ of his fiction. There is what may be called an iconomatic impulse behind much of Fielding's art: many of his most memorable episodes and characters, and the general design and movement of such books as *Joseph Andrews* and *Tom Jones*, may be seen to function figuratively as emblem or allegory, as the embodiment in scene or character or action of Fielding's themes. *Tom Jones* is not of course an allegory in the same sense or in the same way that *The Faerie Queene*, let us say, is an allegory; nevertheless, both these works have certain schematic intentions and certain narrative and scenic techniques in common. *Tom*

Jones differs from the conventional allegory in that Fielding's *story* is primary and autonomous: characters, events, setting have an integrity of their own and compel our interest in and for themselves; they do not require, at every point in the narrative, to be read off as signs and symbols in some controlling ideational system. Whereas Una is 'the One', Sophia Western is the girl whom Tom Jones loves and her family bullies. Spenser's heroine engages our intellect; Fielding's our affection and sympathy. Yet at the same time Fielding shares with the allegorist the desire to *render* the abstractions of his theme—in this instance, to find the particular shape and image for the complementary concepts of Providence and Prudence, of divine Order and human Virtue, which were the bases for his comic vision of life. What Charles Woods observed of Fielding's plays, invoking a favourite term of the critic Sneerwell in *Pasquin*, pertains as well to the novels, where Fielding deserts the 'realistic' mode for the 'Emblematical'.[38]

The general figurative strategy in *Tom Jones* is implicit in the passage from Fielding's Dedication comparing 'Virtue' (i.e. *sophia*) to a beautiful woman and our 'true Interest' (i.e. *prudentia*) to the 'Pursuit of her'. Although Sophia Western is first of all a character in Fielding's novel, she is also the emblematic redaction of the platonic metaphor. After his expulsion from Paradise Hall, Tom Jones's journey is at first aimless and uncertain: '*The World*, as *Milton* phrases it, *lay all before him*; and *Jones*, no more than *Adam*, had any Man to whom he might resort for Comfort or Assistance' (VII. ii). After the crisis at Upton, however, his pursuit of Sophia will symbolize his gradual and painful attainment of *prudentia*, of self-knowledge and clarity of moral vision. The marriage of Tom and Sophia is thus the necessary and inevitable culmination of Fielding's theme: it is a symbolic union signifying the individual's attainment of true wisdom.

To illustrate the quasi-allegorical dimension of *Tom Jones*, we may consider, first of all, the ways in which Fielding renders the platonic metaphor of Virtue—in which the idea of *sophia* becomes associated with the girl Sophy Western. Without forgetting his heroine's role and function in the story itself, from time to time in the course of the narrative Fielding makes the reader aware that Sophia's beauty is ultimately the physical manifestation of a spiritual perfection almost divine, that she is for him as for Tom Jones, the Idea of Virtue incarnate. Like much of his comedy

Fielding's introduction of Sophia '*in the Sublime*' style (IV. ii) is both playful and serious, mocking the extravagancies of romance while at the same time invoking the old values of honour and virtue which romance celebrates. By a process of allusion—to mythology, art, poetry, and his own more immediate experience—Fielding presents his heroine as the ideal woman, the representative of a beauty of form and harmony of spirit so absolute as to be a sort of divine vitalizing force in man and nature alike. She is like 'the lovely *Flora*', goddess of spring-time, whom every flower rises to honour and who is the cause of the perfect harmony of the birds that celebrate her appearance: 'From Love proceeds your Music, and to Love it returns.' Her beauty excels that of the Venus de Medici, the statue considered by Fielding's contemporaries to be 'the standard of all female beauty and softness'.[39] She is the idealization in art of his dead wife Charlotte, 'whose Image never can depart from my Breast'. But what is clear above all is that her beauty is only the reflection of her spiritual nature: 'the Outside of *Sophia* . . . this beautiful Frame', is but the emblem of her 'Mind', which diffuses 'that Glory over her Countenance, which no Regularity of Features can give'. Like Elizabeth Drury, Donne's ideal woman in *The Anniversaries*, to whom Fielding here expressly compares her, Sophy Western is also the image and embodiment of '*Sophia* or the *Divine Wisdom*'.[40]

For Jones, of course, Sophia *is* the perfection of beauty and virtue that her name implies: she is 'my Goddess', he declares to Mrs. Honour, 'as such I will always worship and adore her while I have Breath' (IV. xiv). And he can scarcely think of her except in terms of divinity itself: he stands in awe of her 'heavenly Temper' and 'divine Goodness' (V. vi); she is his 'dear . . . divine Angel' (XVIII. xii). Such sentiments are, to be sure, the usual effusions and hyperbole of the adolescent lover, but they work together none the less to reinforce the reader's sense of Sophy's perfections. In answer to the landlady's insipid description of his mistress as 'a sweet young Creature', Jones supplies a truer definition, applying to Sophia alone Jaffeir's apostrophe to Woman in *Venice Preserved* (I. i):

> 'A sweet Creature!' cries *Jones*, 'O Heavens!
> *Angels are painted fair to look like her.*
> *There's in her all that we believe of Heaven,*
> *Amazing Brightness, Purity and Truth,*
> *Eternal Joy, and everlasting Love.*   (VIII. ii)

Like his author, Jones insists that Sophia's physical beauty is only
the imperfect manifestation of her essential spiritual nature. It is
her 'charming Idea' that he dotes on (XIII. xi). Thus, when his
friend Nightingale inquires if she is 'honourable', Jones protests
that her virtues are so dazzling as to drive all meaner considerations from his thoughts; it is not her body but the spiritual reality
it expresses which demands his love:

> 'Honourable?' answered *Jones* . . . 'The sweetest Air is not purer, the
> limpid Stream not clearer than her Honour. She is all over, both in Mind
> and Body, consummate Perfection. She is the most beautiful Creature in
> the Universe; and yet she is Mistress of such noble, elevated Qualities, that
> though she is never from my Thoughts, I scarce ever think of her Beauty;
> but when I see it.' (XV. ix)

Twice during the novel Fielding symbolically dramatizes the
distinction he wishes his readers to make between the girl Sophy
Western and her 'Idea'—that is, in a platonic sense, the mental
image or form of that essential spiritual Beauty of which his
heroine's lovely face is but an imperfect manifestation.[41] As
Socrates had regretted that mortal eyes were able to behold only
the shadow of *sophia*, reflected as in a glass darkly,[42] so Fielding
uses the conventional emblem of the mirror to dramatize the nature
of his allegory, to demonstrate that what is ultimately important
about Sophia is not her physical charms, but her spiritual reality.
The use of the mirror as an emblem of the mind's powers to con-
ceptualize and abstract was common among iconographers. 'The
Glass', writes a commentator upon Ripa's emblems, 'wherein we
see no real Images, is a Resemblance of our *Intellect*; wherein we
phancy many Ideas of Things that are not seen'; or it 'denotes
Abstraction, that is to say, by Accidents, which the Sense comprehends; the Understanding comes to know their Nature, as we, by
seeing the accidental Forms of Things in a Glass, consider their
Essence'.[43] Fielding introduces this emblem at the moment when
his hero, having pursued Sophia from Upton, is reunited with her
in Lady Bellaston's town house (XIII. xi). The first sight the lovers
have of each other is of their images reflected in a mirror:

> . . . *Sophia* expecting to find no one in the Room, came hastily in, and
> went directly to a Glass which almost fronted her, without once looking
> towards the upper End of the Room, where the Statue of *Jones* now stood
> motionless.—In this Glass it was, after contemplating her own lovely Face,

that she first discovered the said Statue; when instantly turning about, she perceived the Reality of the Vision . . .

The vision in the mirror that has momentarily turned Jones to a statue is the visible projection of the ideal image of Sophia he has carried in his mind. Whatever his indiscretions, he assures her that his '*Heart* was never unfaithful': 'Though I despaired of possessing you, nay, almost of ever seeing you more, I doated still on your charming Idea, and could *seriously* love no other Woman.'

Still clearer, perhaps, is Fielding's use of the mirror emblem toward the close of the novel (XVIII. xii), in a scene designed both to stress the allegorical identity of Sophia and to dramatize Socrates' declaration in the *Phaedrus* (250D) that 'wisdom would arouse terrible love, if such a clear image of it were granted as would come through the sight'. But, as Fielding observed in *The Champion* (5 July 1740), few there are 'whose Eyes are able to behold Truth without a Glass'. Protesting that 'No Repentance was ever more sincere', and pleading that his contrition 'reconcile' him to his 'Heaven in this dear Bosom', Jones attempts to overcome Sophia's doubts as to his sincerity by making her confront the vision of her own beauty and virtue reflected in a mirror. To behold and possess not the image merely, but the reality itself, would, as Socrates had said, convert even the most inveterate reprobate to the love of virtue:

[Jones] replied, 'Don't believe me upon my Word; I have a better Security, a Pledge for my Constancy, which it is impossible to see and to doubt.' 'What is that?' said *Sophia*, a little surprized. 'I will show you, my charming Angel,' cried *Jones*, seizing her Hand, and carrying her to the Glass. 'There, behold it there in that lovely Figure, in that Face, that Shape, those Eyes, that Mind which shines through those Eyes: Can the Man who shall be in Possession of these be inconstant? Impossible! my *Sophia*: They would fix a *Dorimant*, a Lord *Rochester*. You could not doubt it, if you could see yourself with any Eyes but your own.' *Sophia* blushed, and half smiled; but forcing again her Brow into a Frown, 'If I am to judge,' said she, 'of the future by the past, my Image will no more remain in your Heart when I am out of your Sight, than it will in this Glass when I am out of the Room.' 'By Heaven, by all that is sacred,' said *Jones*, 'it never was out of my Heart.'

Such passages demand to be read on more than one level: Sophy Western's image in the glass is the literalizing of the platonic metaphor, the dramatization of Fielding's meaning in the broadly allegorical scheme of the novel. Ultimately, her true identity is ideal, an abstraction.

Within the paradigmatic universe of *Tom Jones*—in which the values of Fielding's Christian humanism are systematically rendered and enacted—Sophy Western is both cynosure and avatar, the controlling centre of the theme of Virtue and its incarnation. Though she is, above all, the woman that Tom loves, she is also, as Fielding's Dedication implies, the emblem and embodiment of that ideal Wisdom her name signifies. Without her Paradise Hall and the country from which Tom has been driven are unbearable, meaningless (XII. iii)—an Eden empty of grace. To win her in marriage is the supreme redemptive act, a divine dispensation which for Jones, as for every man, restores joy and order to a troubled world: 'To call *Sophia* mine is the greatest . . . Blessing which Heaven can bestow' (XVIII. x). But for one of Jones's passionate nature the conditions upon which she may be won are exacting, nothing less, indeed, than the acquisition of *prudentia*: Tom must perfect his 'Understanding', as Sophia herself insists (XI. vii), must learn not only to distinguish between the values of the spirit and those of the flesh, between the true and the false, but to discipline his will so that this knowledge may govern his life. Having learned this lesson at last, Jones is able to withstand the blandishments of such sirens as Mrs. Fitzpatrick, for, as the narrator observes, 'his whole Thoughts were now so confined to his *Sophia*, that I believe no Woman upon Earth could have now drawn him into an Act of Inconstancy' (XVI. ix). On the eve of their wedding, as the company of brides and grooms convenes, Sophia is revealed presiding over the feast of virtuous love, eclipsing the beauty of the women, adored by every man: she 'sat at the Table like a Queen receiving Homage, or rather like a superiour Being receiving Adoration from all around her. But it was an Adoration which they gave, not which she exacted: For she was as much distinguished by her Modesty and Affability, as by all her other Perfections' (XVIII. xiii). In its way not unlike the banquet of Socrates, the wedding dinner of Tom and Sophia celebrates the power of Beauty and Virtue. In the light of such passages, Jones's 'Quest' for 'his lovely *Sophia*' (X. vii) takes on a symbolic dimension: it is the dramatization of Fielding's expressed concern in the novel to convince 'Men, that their true Interest directs them to a Pursuit of [Virtue]'.

Fielding's method of projecting the abstractions of his theme in image and action is comparable, in a way, to the Augustan poet's favourite device of personification. It is also the correlative in fiction of the graphic artist's use of emblem and allegorical design. Following Horace, Fielding recognized the sisterhood of the two art forms.[44] In this respect, as in others, he may be compared with Pope, many of whose descriptions—that of the triumph of Vice in the *Epilogue to the Satires, Dialogue I* (ll. 151 ff.), for example, or of Dulness holding court in *The Dunciad* (iv. 17 ff.)—have the effect of allegorical *tableaux*, pictorially conceived and composed in order to carry the poet's meaning before the visual imagination. Fielding himself more than once observed the relationship between his own satiric art and that of his friend Hogarth, the 'comic History Painter', who well understood the use of symbolic detail to render and characterize abstractions.[45] Particularly 'Hogarthian' in conception and effect, for instance, is the image Fielding presents of the philosopher Square after his hilarious exposure in Molly Seagrim's bedroom (V. v). At the critical moment the rug behind which he has concealed himself falls away, and the august metaphysician—who has made a career of denouncing the body—is revealed in the closet, clad only in a blush and Molly's nightcap and fixed 'in a Posture (for the Place would not near admit his standing upright) as ridiculous as can possibly be conceived':

> The Posture, indeed, in which he stood, was not greatly unlike that of a Soldier who is tyed Neck and Heels; or rather resembling the Attitude in which we often see Fellows in the public Streets of *London*, who are not suffering but deserving Punishment by so standing. He had a Night-cap belonging to *Molly* on his Head, and his two large Eyes, the Moment the Rug fell, stared directly at *Jones*; so that when the Idea of Philosophy was added to the Figure now discovered, it would have been very difficult for any Spectator to have refrained from immoderate Laughter.

The distinctive quality of this passage is graphic. It is as close to the pictorial as the artist in words can bring it: the sense of composition, of attitude is there; the subject has been frozen at the critical moment in time, his chagrin economically defined by the two features, the nightcap and the astonished stare, which explain and characterize it. What is more, the scene has an emblematic effect: it serves as the pictorial projection of an *idea*—namely, of the theory of 'the true Ridiculous', which, as the Preface to *Joseph Andrews* makes clear, Fielding thought to consist principally in the comic disparity between what we are and what we profess to be. As the literal revelation of the naked truth behind the drapery of pretension, the exposure of Square is the quintessential scene in Fielding's fiction.

Other scenes in the novel are pictorially conceived, and for a variety of effects. Most obvious of these is Fielding's ironic imitation of one of the most celebrated historical *tableaux* of the period: Plate VI of Charles Le Brun's magnificent series depicting the victories of Alexander.[46] As Le Brun had represented the vanquished King Porus being carried before the magnanimous conqueror, so Fielding, with due regard to the arrangement and attitudes of his figures, describes the scene after Jones's and Western's bloody victory over the forces of Blifil and Thwackum (V. xii):

At this time, the following was the Aspect of the bloody Field. In one Place, lay on the Ground, all pale and almost breathless, the vanquished *Blifil*. Near him stood the Conqueror *Jones*, almost covered with Blood, part of which was naturally his own, and Part had been lately the Property of the Reverend Mr. *Thwackum*. In a third Place stood the said *Thwackum*, like King *Porus*, sullenly submitting to the Conqueror. The last Figure in the Piece was *Western the Great*, most gloriously forbearing the vanquished Foe.

Analysis of Fielding's mock-heroicism must clearly extend beyond his burlesque allusions to Homer and Virgil to such skilful imitations of specific masterpieces of historical art.

Certain other scenes in *Tom Jones* recall the art of the painter of 'prospect' pieces, wherein, however, Fielding has chosen and arranged the features of the landscape for their allegorical or emblematic suggestiveness. Such are the descriptions, almost iconological in effect, of Allworthy's estate and of the view from Mazard Hill. The prospect at Paradise Hall (I. iv), while apparently a static landscape, is carefully organized so as to carry the reader's eye, and hence his imagination, from the immediate and local outward to the distant and infinite, thereby implicitly presenting the characteristic quality and intention of Fielding's art in the novel, which is a continual translation of particulars into universals: the spring, gushing from its source at the summit of the hill, flows downward to a lake in the middle distance, from whence issues a river which the eye follows as it meanders for several miles before it empties itself in the sea beyond. The scene takes on yet another significant dimension once we are aware that it is

composed of elements associating Paradise Hall, the place of Tom
Jones's birth and the home of his spiritual father, both with the
estates of Fielding's patrons, George Lyttelton and Ralph Allen,
and with Glastonbury Tor, which rises fully visible from the
threshold of Sharpham Park, Fielding's own birthplace and the seat
of his maternal grandfather.[47] Paradise Hall is very much the product of Fielding's symbolic imagination; it is his own, as well as
his hero's, spiritual home. Equally suggestive, and more obviously
emblematic, is the subsequent description of Allworthy walking forth
to survey his estate as dawn breaks, bathing the creation in light.
The glory of this good man—who is, more than any other character
except Sophia herself, the centre of the novel's moral universe—is
rendered in terms of the sun, traditional symbol of the deity:[48]

It was now the Middle of *May*, and the Morning was remarkably serene,
when Mr. *Allworthy* walked forth on the Terrace, where the Dawn opened
every Minute that lovely Prospect we have before described to his Eye.
And now having sent forth Streams of Light, which ascended the blue
Firmament before him, as Harbingers preceding his Pomp, in the full Blaze
of his Majesty up rose the Sun; than which one Object alone in this lower
Creation could be more glorious, and that Mr. *Allworthy* himself presented;
a human Being replete with Benevolence, meditating in what Manner he
might render himself most acceptable to his Creator, by doing most Good
to his Creatures.

A final illustration of Fielding's emblematic art in *Tom Jones*
will serve to return us to the theme of Wisdom. As in presenting
the 'Idea' of *sophia*, Fielding, at one significant moment in the
novel, also drew upon conventional iconological techniques in
order visually to project the meaning of *prudentia*. The scene occurs
at the opening of Book IX, Chapter ii, as Tom Jones contemplates
the prospect from atop Mazard Hill. Structurally, the scene holds
a crucial position between the narrative of the Old Man of the Hill
and the pivotal events at Upton; thematically, it is the emblematic
statement of the nature of true prudence and of Tom's progress
along the way to acquiring that virtue. Fielding's basic device was
entirely familiar. We will recall that it was conventional for poets
and philosophers alike to translate the notion of the prudent man's
intellectual apprehension of past, present, and future into physical
and spatial terms: to look in the direction from whence one has
come is to contemplate the meaning of the past; to look in the
direction one is going is to consider what the future holds in store.

15. From Le Brun's *Alexander and the Vanquished King Porus*

16. Titian's *Allegory of Prudence*

17. Ripa's Emblem of Prudence

The iconology of Prudence traditionally represented this virtue in the likeness of a figure with two (or three) faces—one, often the face of an old man, looking to the left or behind; the other, that of a young man or woman, looking to the right or ahead. Titian's *Allegory of Prudence*—the symbolism of which Professor Panofsky has brilliantly explicated[49]—depicts a head with three faces and bears a Latin inscription reading: 'The prudent man of today profits from past experience in order not to imperil the future.'[50] Following the design by Caesar Ripa, whose *Iconologia* (1593) was the standard work well into the eighteenth century, most emblematists represented Prudence with two faces, while retaining the sense of Titian's symbolism. George Richardson explains the significance of the design as follows: 'The ancients have represented this virtue with two faces, the one young, and the other old, to indicate that prudence is acquired by consideration of things past, and a foresight of those to come.'[51] The persistence of this metaphor, associating Prudence with the vision of distant things, is further suggested by Pope's personification of this virtue in *The Dunciad* (i. 49), where the image of Prudence with her perspective glass was drawn from a different, but obviously related, iconological tradition.

As we have already remarked, what Tom Jones must acquire before he is ready to marry Sophia and return to the country of his birth is prudence—the ability to learn from past experience, both his own and others', so as to distinguish the true from the false and to estimate the future consequences of his present behaviour. To invoke the Aristotelian notion of the 'Three Ages of Man',[52] at this juncture in Tom's progress toward maturity he is presented with the extreme alternatives of youth and age—the rashness and passion which characterize his own adolescence, and which define all that is most and least admirable about him, as opposed to the cowardly cynicism of the Old Man of the Hill. Having heard the wretched history of the Old Man and rejected his misanthropy, Tom has profited from one lesson that experience has to teach him; but, as events in Upton will soon prove, he has not yet mastered the more difficult test of his own past follies. As Upton represents the apex of the rising action of the novel and the turning-point in Tom's progress, so at this stage in the narrative Fielding's hero stands literally at the summit of a high hill, from which he can survey the vast terrain that separates him from his home and mistress, and, by facing in the opposite direction, regard the obscure and tangled wood which, it will appear, contains the woman who will abruptly dislodge Sophia from his thoughts and involve him in the near fatal consequences of his own imprudence. The prospect Fielding describes, with a warning that we may not fully 'understand' it, allegorizes the theme of prudence in the novel, rendering spiritual and temporal matters in terms of physical and spatial analogues: the view southward toward 'Home' representing the meaning of the past, the view northward toward the dark wood imaging the problem of the future. As the Old Man shrewdly remarks to his young companion: 'I perceive now the Object of your Contemplation is not within your Sight':

Aurora now first opened her Casement, *Anglicè,* the Day began to break, when *Jones* walked forth in Company with the Stranger, and mounted *Mazard* Hill; of which they had no sooner gained the Summit, than one of the most noble Prospects in the World presented itself to their View, and which we would likewise present to the Reader; but for two Reasons. *First,* We despair of making those who have seen this Prospect, admire our Description. *Secondly,* We very much doubt whether those, who have not seen it, would understand it.

Jones stood for some Minutes fixed in one Posture, and directing his Eyes towards the South; upon which the old Gentleman asked, What he was looking at with so much Attention? 'Alas, Sir,' answered he with a Sigh, 'I was endeavouring to trace out my own Journey hither. Good Heavens! what a Distance is *Gloucester* from us! What a vast Tract of Land must be between me and my own Home.' 'Ay, ay, young Gentleman,' cries the other, 'and, by your Sighing, from what you love better than your own Home, or I am mistaken. I perceive now the Object of your Contemplation is not within your Sight, and yet I fancy you have a Pleasure in looking that Way.' *Jones* answered with a Smile, 'I find, old Friend, you have not yet forgot the Sensations of your youth.—I own my Thoughts were employed as you have guessed.'

They now walked to that Part of the Hill which looks to the North-West, and which hangs over a vast and extensive Wood. Here they were no sooner arrived, than they heard at a Distance the most violent Screams of a Woman, proceeding from the Wood below them. *Jones* listened a Moment, and then, without saying a Word to his Companion (for indeed the Occasion seemed sufficiently pressing) ran, or rather slid, down the Hill, and without the least Apprehension or Concern for his own Safety, made directly to the Thicket whence the Sound had issued.

Occurring midway through Jones's journey—and through his progress toward maturity, toward the acquisition of prudence—the scene atop Mazard Hill is the emblematic projection of Fielding's theme. Essentially, Fielding's method and his meaning are comparable to Pope's in distinguishing between the functions of passion and reason in the soul:

> Self-love still stronger, as its objects nigh;
> Reason's at distance, and in prospect lie:
> That sees immediate good by present sense;
> Reason, the future and the consequence.

The past and its meaning are plain and clear to Jones, but not plain and clear enough; the future is obscure and tangled, fraught with sudden and unforeseen dangers. Sophia is abruptly supplanted in his thoughts by the more immediate appeal of another woman, in whose arms at Upton Tom will forget, for the moment at least, the lesson of his past follies and the claims of his true mistress. It is his affair with Jenny Jones at Upton that will result in his estrangement from Sophia and, eventually, in the anxious knowledge that his behaviour, however generous and gallant, has apparently involved him in the sin of incest. What Tom sees looking south from Mazard Hill reassures us about his essential health of spirit, about those values he ultimately cherishes. His precipitous descent, however, reflects those qualities of character which are both his greatest strength and his weakness: on the one hand, courage and selflessness, prompting him to the assistance of injured frailty; on the other, that rashness which is the source of his vulnerability as a moral agent.

The climax of this theme occurs in Book XVIII, ch. x, wherein Fielding's '*History begins to draw towards a Conclusion*', as Jones, after his long estrangement from his home and spiritual father, is 'restored' to Allworthy's 'Presence' and 'Favour'. It is here that Allworthy defines true Prudence as 'the Duty which we owe to ourselves'. The dialogue between the Squire and Jones, who has now reached maturity as a moral agent, turns upon the nature of wisdom, described in language that recalls the iconographic tradition of *prudentia*. Since Prudence entails the proper operation of memory, judgement, and foresight—the proper estimation of past, present, and future—Jones assures his uncle that, having reflected on the 'Follies and Vices' of his 'past Life' which have brought him to 'the Brink of Destruction', he will make it 'the whole Business of my future Life to deserve that Happiness you now bestow on me'. Jones having 'seen' his errors, Allworthy's advice is to 'Remember them only yourself so far, as for the future to teach you the better to avoid them . . .' As Allworthy, with the faults of Jones and his half-brother in mind, proceeds to distinguish between the characters of the imprudent man and the villain, his words ironically evoke the very situations in which Jones had found himself atop Mazard Hill and in the Gatehouse—now, however, in contrast to Jones's present happiness, the iconography of Prudence defines the benighted and desperate condition of Blifil's soul:

> 'Where-ever he turns his Eyes, Horror presents itself; if he looks backward, unavailable Repentance treads on his Heels; if forward, incurable Despair stares him in the Face; till, like a condemned Prisoner, confined in a Dungeon, he detests his present Condition, and yet dreads the Consequence of that Hour which is to relieve him from it. Comfort yourself, I say, my Child, that this is not your Case; and rejoice, with Thankfulness to him who hath suffered you to see your Errors, before they have brought on you that Destruction to which a Persistance in even those Errors must have led you. You have deserted them, and the Prospect now before you is such, that Happiness seems in your own Power.'

Allworthy's metaphors dispel the ambiguities of the novel's dominant ethical theme by disclosing the essential nature and ultimate consequences of Prudence, false and true—of Blifil's malicious cunning and Jones's hard-earned wisdom. Throughout Fielding's narrative true Prudence is what Jones lacks and what he must acquire. For Prudence, the cardinal virtue of antiquity, was for Fielding—as for those other Augustan moralists, Gay and Pope and Goldsmith, who shared with him the heritage of Christian humanism—pre-eminently the 'Art of Life'.

Despite the number of illuminating studies in recent years, the technical resources of Fielding's art as a novelist have not yet been fully disclosed, nor have we as yet adequately appreciated the degree to which Fielding applied the devices of his craft to the communication of his serious concerns as a moralist. If the structure of *Tom Jones* is organic in an Aristotelian sense—as Professor Crane has shown it to be—it is also schematic, the expression through emblem, parable, and significant design of Fielding's controlling themes. If *Tom Jones* is the playful celebration of the feast of life—as Andrew Wright has insisted—it is also the expression in art of Fielding's Christian vision. The ways in which such devices as ambiguity, allegory, and emblem function together to define the theme of Wisdom in the novel may be taken as one more measure of Fielding's intention and his achievement.

VII

Goldsmith: The Comedy of Job

HENRY JAMES doubtless made the essential point about *The Vicar of Wakefield* (1766) when he admired its amenity of tone.[1] Indeed, something like what T. S. Eliot remarked of the Master might more properly be applied to Goldsmith: to read through his works is to become comfortably acquainted with a mind so genial, so splendidly equanimous, that few ideas could violate it. There was more to him, of course—much more—than his obtuse contemporaries saw, for whom he was '*un étourdi*', 'an inspired idiot', 'an inexplicable existence in creation'.[2] For one thing, as Garrick knew, he 'wrote like an angel': in *The Citizen of the World* (1762) an essayist of unexampled ease and delicate humour; in *The Traveller* (1764) and *The Deserted Village* (1770) a poet of sufficient skill in managing the couplet to deserve comparison with Pope; in *The Good Natur'd Man* (1768) and *She Stoops to Conquer* (1773) a dramatist witty enough to rival Farquhar and, in an age of mawkish propriety, to refresh the theatre with laughter. 'Whether, indeed, we take him as a poet,—as a comick writer,—or as an historian', declared Johnson, Goldsmith 'stands in the first class'.[3] Johnson and Garrick, as well as James, have the emphasis right: perhaps no other major author in English may be so completely defined in terms of the stylistic virtues of grace and lucidity, charm and an unfaltering amenity of tone. No one who knew him—not even Reynolds, his most loyal apologist—chose to remark Goldsmith's profundity of vision; still less would they have been disposed to question his sincerity in matters of religion, or to relish a crypto-Swiftian archness in his estimate of human nature. It has remained for modern criticism—in search, presumably, of ways to make Goldsmith acceptable to admirers of Melville and *The Sacred Fount*—to discover dark corners and labyrinthine depths in, for example, the fine and airy fabric of *The Vicar of Wakefield*.[4]

There are, I believe, dimensions to *The Vicar of Wakefield* which have not yet been appreciated, but they are supplied by the aesthetic and theological assumptions implicit in the Augustan mode as we have been defining it, not by the anachronistic rhetorical expectations of present-day 'close readers'. Goldsmith enjoyed a good practical joke on occasion; but though he once seems to have tricked an acquaintance into eating a candle,[5] his notion of literary comedy did not extend to hoodwinking his audience, as one recent critic supposes.[6] This much we can assert about *The Vicar of Wakefield* without denying an important element of irony in the work directed at Dr. Primrose, an element to which he himself calls attention by reflecting as narrator upon his own vanities and foibles: his 'blindness', for example, to the real worth of Mr. Burchell or to the predatory intentions of Squire Thornhill. At one level, as Curtis Dahl has shown,[7] the work is about disguise and duplicity, but it is also, finally, about illumination: the moral and spiritual enlightenment not only of Dr. Primrose, but of the reader. So, too, though there is burlesque and parody aplenty in the book, it is offered with the intention less of exploding the literary genres or the characters in question than of affording pleasure to the literate reader, and at times of enhancing through analogy (chiefly with Job, as we shall see) our sense of the essential dignity and humanity of the hero. Still less, if we understand the kind of work Goldsmith was writing and his thematic intentions, are the conspicuous narrative contrivances of the *Vicar*—the use of coincidence, the abrupt turns and reversals in the fortunes of the characters, the happy ending—to be dismissed as the effects of the author's incompetency in conducting the story, or regarded as a satiric strategy to discredit the romances and 'weeping' comedies of the day. All these are indeed distinctive features of Goldsmith's book, but to understand how they function we must reconstruct the aesthetic and didactic premisses that controlled his choice of fable and character, and helped to define his manner as well.

As a writer of fiction, Goldsmith may be said to stand in the same relation to Fielding, from whom he learned most, as in poetry Gay stands to Pope: similar assumptions about the nature, function, and efficacy of literary form and artifice help to determine the character and meaning of their works. With respect to texture and style, for example, Goldsmith is with Fielding, at the farthest remove from the 'formal realism' that distinguishes the novels of Defoe and Richardson. Like Fielding—though without the advantage of Fielding's 'omniscient' narrator, a device which contributes so much to our sense of the artificial world of *Joseph Andrews* and *Tom Jones*—Goldsmith in *The Vicar of Wakefield* manipulates his style and plot in such a way as to parody the conventions of a whole range of literary modes, making us continually aware of his work as an artefact, a 'Tale', as he preferred to call it, *made* as well as told. Thus, in an astute analysis, D. W. Jefferson has called attention to various passages in which Goldsmith imitates such traditional forms as the comedy of manners, the pastoral romance, the novel of the road, and the 'cony-catching' narrative, as well as such fictional conventions as the interpolated tale and the didactic digression.[8] Everywhere Goldsmith deliberately softens the potentially tragic or pathetic impact of the calamities which befall the Primrose family by abrupt modulations of tone and reductions of scale effected by means of the most self-conscious artifice: by means of parody and narrative acrobatics. 'Everywhere', as Jefferson puts it, 'we meet the familiar and the archetypal, neatly scaled down', and the effect of such manipulation is very close to what we have already observed in *Tom Jones*, or in Gay's *Trivia*: Goldsmith's method is to emphasize 'the story as story, to call attention to the difference between it and life, and to place it at a certain distance from life'.[9]

The self-conscious manipulation of rhetorical conventions to achieve comic, and at times therapeutic, effects of distancing is one characteristically Augustan feature of Goldsmith's art. Another, which it will be our present purpose to explore in detail, is Goldsmith's reliance on a controlling analogy to unify and to universalize his theme. Again, though there are obvious differences between them, the most helpful comparison is with Fielding, who in *Joseph Andrews* had adapted the favourite contemporary theory of the biblical epic to a new genre, the 'comic Epic-Poem in Prose', effecting, in the adventures of a virtuous footman and a good-natured country parson, a mock-heroic redaction of the stories of the patriarchs Joseph and Abraham.[10] In *Tom Jones*, as we have seen, he had devised an even tighter schematic frame within which to develop the themes of Providence and Prudence, traditionally the supreme rational attributes of the great and little worlds whose history, 'in general', he was writing. In *The Vicar of Wakefield* Goldsmith's didactic purpose is similar, the assertion of the doctrines of Providence and Prudence; but for the hint he needed to frame his own parable of human life, he reverted to Fielding's earlier, simpler solution in *Joseph Andrews*. Dr. Primrose is not only spiritual kin to Parson Adams, as has often been remarked; like his predecessor, he also recapitulates—and in a much more comprehensive and faithful way than Fielding's Abraham—the story and character of a biblical prototype: the patriarch Job. Though the similarity between the vicar and Job is sufficiently striking to have been often noticed,[11] no one has proposed what I take to be the crucial function of the analogy in serving not only as the matrix of Goldsmith's fable, but also as the means of harmonizing his curiously disparate thematic intentions, which critics have regretted as an unresolved medley of motifs:[12] prudence and fortitude, disguise and moral vision, fortune and providence. But before we begin using the Job story to gloss the *Vicar*, we had better make clear both the reasons for doing so and the particular meanings the story had for Goldsmith's contemporaries.

That Goldsmith found in the Book of Job a model for his own tale of Christian suffering and redemption may be inferred, first of all, from the number of salient situational and structural parallels between the two works. Like the patriarch Job, in whom were comprised the roles of priest and prince, the vicar, according to Goldsmith's 'Advertisement', 'unites in himself the three greatest characters upon earth . . . a priest, an husbandman, and the father of a family', that well-ordered 'little republic' to which he gives laws.[13] Though basically a good man, he is yet a man— inclined to be proud and contumacious in his piety, like Job, who, though 'perfect and upright' (1 : 1), nevertheless deserves the trials that he undergoes because of his vanity and blindness to his own defects, a point stressed by Elihu the arbiter (32–33) and, as we shall see, emphasized in the numerous eighteenth-century commentaries on the book. The vicar's prosperity resembles Job's, consisting in considerable property, a loving (if sometimes intractable) wife, and a large and devoted family. Like Job, the vicar is precipitately plunged from this happy state into the depths of adversity, his afflictions increasing as his trials become progressively more grievous: the loss of his fortune and home, the debauching of his daughter, the burn to his arm—stages, as the commentators on Job remark, which define ever more intense degrees of suffering, from material loss to spiritual grief to bodily pain.[14] What is especially remarkable is that the calamities which befall both protagonists are not only manifold, but entirely unexpected, the tranquillity they enjoy being broken by the sudden arrival of messengers bearing unwelcome news: thus the vicar, while celebrating the prospective marriage of his eldest son (cf. Job 1: 18), is called out by one of his relations, who has no other function in the story, to be told of the loss of his fortune (IV. 24); and news of Olivia's ruin interrupts him as he consoles himself with thoughts of the virtue and harmony of his family:

> 'But where is my darling Olivia? That little cherub's voice is always sweetest in the concert.'—Just as I spoke Dick came running in. 'O pappa, pappa, she is gone from us, she is gone from us, my sister Livy is gone from us for ever'—   (IV. 91)

As we shall see, the messenger device in Job was regarded as particularly significant, since it heightened the reader's sense both of the sufferings of the hero and of the supernatural character of his afflictions. Like Job, too, the vicar is tormented by a malevolent and powerful antagonist whose ability to do harm, however, is limited by a superior agent on whose will he is 'entirely dependant' (IV. 29), one indeed who as *deus ex machina* eventually—after the lessons of adversity have been learned—delivers him from affliction and justifies him. Finally, the vicar's 'latter end' is blessed, his property recovered, his children miraculously restored to life and virtue. And the tale concludes in a joyous festival.

Such an impressive pattern of correspondences is strong presumptive evidence that Goldsmith wished to enforce the analogy between the two stories, though he has not, like Fielding in *Joseph Andrews*, obligingly clinched the case by giving his hero the name of his biblical prototype. (To have done so, surely, in a tale of this idyllic character would have been gauche and heavy-handed.) On at least two occasions, furthermore, the analogy is made explicit as the vicar applies to his own situation passages from Job which the commentaries cite as key texts, establishing the grounds of the hero's patience and final justification: these are Job 1: 21 and 42: 7–8. In the first instance, after initially succumbing to grief and anger at the news of Olivia's seduction, the vicar acknowledges his duty as a Christian to endure misfortune with patience and fortitude: '"Blest be his holy name for all the good he hath given, and for all that he hath taken away"' (IV. 92). What he here affirms is one of the central themes both of the *Vicar* and of Job, namely, the doctrine of a particular Providence: that every event in life, good or evil, happens by divine permission.[15] In the second instance, the vicar reproves his wife and children for urging him to avoid utter penury and ruin by condoning Squire Thornhill's intended marriage to Arabella Wilmot, a marriage he regards as morally, if not technically, bigamous. His words echo those with which God justified Job and rebuked his false comforters: '"Why, my treasures," cried I, "why will you thus attempt to persuade me to the thing that is not right!"' (IV. 139). Again, the allusion directs us to one of the chief themes of the two works, expounded at length in the vicar's climactic sermon to the prisoners (ch. XXIX), namely, the doctrine of futurity: that, though the dealings of Providence are unequal in this life, the sufferings of good men will be abundantly recompensed in the hereafter.[16] Indeed, the vicar's sermon enforcing this doctrine may itself be seen as an elaboration on Job's hope to find in death relief from his sufferings (3: 17–18):

There the wicked cease *from* troubling; and there the weary be at rest.
There the prisoners rest together; they hear not the voice of the oppressor.

This, surely, is one of the texts to which Dr. Primrose alludes when he assures his wretched congregation that religion ' "has promised peculiar rewards to the unhappy; the sick, the naked, the houseless, the heavy-laden, and the prisoner, have ever most frequent promises in our sacred law" ' (IV. 161).[17] Even when the vicar turns from scripture to philosophy for the wisdom to comprehend the tribulations of virtuous men, he is likely to recall a maxim adduced by the commentators in applying the predicament of Job to the general human condition. Thus, as he distinguishes in a famous passage between the virtues of patience and charity—the distinction, that is, between his own stoicism and Sir William Thornhill's benevolence—Dr. Primrose recalls Seneca in *De providentia* (ii. 6): 'The greatest object in the universe, says a certain philosopher, is a good man struggling with adversity; yet there is still a greater, which is the good man that comes to relieve it' (IV. 167). The relevance of this quotation to the story of Job is clear from Charles Peters's commentary: 'THE Character of *Job* . . . affords us such a Spectacle, as *Seneca* (alluding to the Shews of Gladiators so common amongst the *Romans*) says, was worthy of the Deity himself, to look upon, viz. that of *a pious and good Man combating Adversity. . . .*'[18]

Not only the implicit scheme of situational correspondences, then, but also the explicit echoes of texts either drawn from or applied to the Book of Job, would seem to declare Goldsmith's intention to establish a functional analogy between the biblical story and his own tale of Christian piety and fortitude. A further clue suggesting the controlling importance of this device in *The Vicar of Wakefield* may be found in the epigraph displayed on the title-page: *'Sperate miseri, cavete fœlices'* ('Hope, ye unhappy ones; ye happy ones, fear'). On the last page of *The Anatomy of Melancholy* (1621), these words conclude Burton's discussion of the 'Cure of Despair' in those afflicted with religious melancholy—a discussion, as one might suppose, in which Job figures as the type of true faith and patience in adversity. The lesson Burton, as well as Goldsmith, is at pains to inculcate is that affliction, teaching a man humility and self-knowledge, 'comes by God's permission and providence'. 'Faith, hope, repentance, are the sovereign cures and remedies, the sole comforts in this case; confess, humble thyself, it is sufficient'.[19]

Such, briefly, is the internal evidence for Goldsmith's having intended to evoke the Job analogy in *The Vicar of Wakefield*. That he should have done so, given the nature of his theme, will perhaps strike no one as particularly remarkable; the appeal of Job remains strong even in our own, less pious times, as MacLeish's drama *J.B.* (1958) attests. It would have seemed still less surprising to Goldsmith's first readers, considering the special prominence of the story in the middle decades of the eighteenth century, when it became the focus of a strenuous theological debate concerning the implications of the doctrine of an unequal providence—a debate which Goldsmith himself apparently followed with interest, if with a certain impatience at the pomposity and pedantry of the contestants. Thus, at approximately the moment when he began writing the *Vicar*, Goldsmith was (probably)[20] the author of an article in *The Critical Review* (August 1759), reviewing the *Works* of William Hawkins, one of these disputacious divines, who sided with the Bishop of London against the followers of Warburton by maintaining that, even before the Christian dispensation, Job took comfort in the expectation of a life hereafter in which the good man would be recompensed for his sufferings in this world. The reviewer deplores the effects of such polemical divinity—'The Bangorian controversy', he declares, 'has not more divided our speculative divines' (I. 200)—yet his acceptance of the essential doctrines involved, the doctrine of immortality and a future state, is clear. This, as he asserts resuming the subject in March 1760, 'it is our duty to believe' (I. 226).[21]

The dispute which elicited these remarks involved Thomas Sherlock and William Warburton as the chief antagonists and centred on the interpretation of Job 19: 25–6:

> For I know *that* my redeemer liveth, and *that* he shall stand at the latter *day* upon the earth:
> And *though* after my skin *worms* destroy this *body*, yet in my flesh shall I see God . . .

In *The Sense of the Ancients before Christ on the Circumstances and Consequences of the Fall* (1725) Sherlock had affirmed that this 'famous passage', part of the burial offices of the Church, pointed surely, if mysteriously, to Christ and the resurrection;[22] Warburton on the contrary, proposing in *The Divine Legation of Moses* (1742) an allegorical reading of Job, rejected this orthodox view to argue that the text referred only to a 'temporal Deliverance' from affliction.[23] To many divines the distinction seemed crucial, since Warburton, while subscribing to the received notion that Job taught the doctrine of an unequal providence, had cast doubt on one of the principal Old Testament texts generally taken as supporting the doctrine of futurity. The sides were soon drawn. Those who followed Bishop Sherlock included Richard Grey, Richard Brown, Charles Peters, William Hawkins, and Richard Parry;[24] among those who inclined toward Warburton were George Costard, John Garnett, and John Towne.[25] In the same period appeared several other, more or less neutral, treatises reflecting the widespread interest in the subject which the controversy had generated. These include a variety of studies by Daniel Bellamy, William Worthington, Walter Hodges, Leonard Chappelow, Thomas Heath, and Bishop Lowth.[26] None of these works need be regarded as a 'source' for Goldsmith's treatment of the Job theme, but from them emerges a certain pattern of assumptions about the nature and meaning of Job which will, I believe, help us to see *The Vicar of Wakefield* more clearly—to see it, in fact, as a more interesting and much more coherent book than we have thought.

Goldsmith in *The Vicar of Wakefield* may be said to offer his own variation on favourite Augustan themes: like his friend Johnson he depicts the vanity of human wishes and exhorts his readers to turn their thoughts to eternity; like Pope he writes to 'vindicate the ways of God to Man'. What Pope and Johnson had attempted in poetry and apologue, Goldsmith essayed in that 'new species of writing' whose potential for instruction and delight Fielding had demonstrated in *Joseph Andrews*. If he wished to emulate Fielding's practice in that novel by presenting his own Christian comedy of contemporary low-life in terms of a controlling analogue which would at once universalize his theme and satisfy the theorists of the biblical epic, he could have found no more appropriate model than the story of Job. For one thing, the story of the patriarch's sufferings within a scheme of providential order harmonized the themes of Johnson and Pope so congenial to his audience; it was said, indeed, that the author of Job (whom many supposed to be Job himself)[27] shared a common purpose with the poet of the *Essay on Man*.[28] Furthermore, though critics disagreed as to its 'kind', whether epic or dramatic,[29] and its character, whether historical or parabolic,[30] the Book of Job was generally acknowledged as the greatest and most ancient of poems. Its setting and mood of primitive simplicity are pastoral, a mode well suited to Goldsmith's tale, whose hero, priest and patriarch, tends his flocks and governs his 'little republic' against the bucolic background of rural England.[31] But the poem itself, according to the canons of neo-classical criticism, is of the high heroic order. Since, as Le Bossu had decreed,[32] the aim of heroic poetry is didactic, the moral being conveyed within an allegorical fable, the subject of the Book of Job is the loftiest imaginable: namely, the demonstration and vindication of divine Providence, whose dispensations, while apparently unequal with respect to this life, will be proved just in the hereafter. To enforce this great argument, the poet availed himself of the most awesome machinery, involving Satan and the Supreme Being in the trials and ultimate redemption of the hero. Job himself, though a passive figure—a man of moral fortitude rather than martial prowess—appears superior to all the heroes of the pagan poets, his courage being preferable to that of Achilles or Aeneas in the same measure as the ordeals of the spirit are more exacting than those of the body.[33] Paradoxically, though Job is the very type of the Christian hero, he is not without faults. Indeed, it is his very frailty as a human being—his pride and petulance and partial vision—which gives value to his eventual triumph over adversity by making his example worthy of the emulation of other imperfect men.

Stressed by critics and commentators alike, this feature of the contemporary estimate of Job is particularly notable in view of the ambivalency associated with Goldsmith's hero, who, though he endures and is justified, is yet for most of the tale gently satirized for petty vanities which blind him to the true character of the world. Taking Job as a species of epic poetry designed to move and instruct its readers, Blackmore explains the necessity for the hero's imperfections: 'a perfect Idea of Virtue, which is never to be found in any meer Man, offends against the establish'd Rule in Epick Writings, which excludes all things improbable, so instead of promoting, it rather obstructs the End of that Poetry: For a perfect Idea of Virtue and Excellency may amaze and dazle us, but when propounded for our Imitation, it will rather discourage than excite us.'[34] (This same rule, we may remark, was extended to the characters of the comic epic by Fielding in *Tom Jones* (X. i), who, in the figure of Parson Adams, had earlier supplied a working model of the principle which served for Dr. Primrose.) Blackmore is entirely conventional in identifying Job's faults as his pride and obduracy in rashly censuring 'the Divine Administration' (p. lvii) and his limited vision (pp. lxvi–lxviii). In his own analysis of the poem more than fifty years later, Bishop Lowth, taking Job as a dramatic performance, similarly justified the hero's imperfections by referring to Aristotle's notion that the design of tragedy is to excite the passions of pity and terror and to promote the cause of virtue, which last function, however, the spectacle of a very good man under affliction was ill calculated to achieve. On this point Lowth disagreed:

This opinion of the philosopher seems to result from an unjust and visionary estimation of human virtue, to repress which appears to have been the very design and object of the book of Job. The character of Job indeed, though approaching so near to the perfection of virtue, seems, notwithstanding, to have a considerable alloy of human infirmity, so as neither to want probability, nor to lose its effect in exciting terror.[35]

Job is meant to stand as 'an example of perfect virtue', but only 'as far as is consistent with human infirmity' (II. 407). He is pious, devout, patient; yet he succumbs to despair and complains against his fate, giving in 'to the dictates of nature' (II. 408). What is more, as Elihu points out, he is guilty of pride and arrogance and contumacy, and glories in his own righteousness (II. 371 ff., 394–7). According to Lowth, 'The design of the poem is, therefore, to teach men, that having a due respect to the corruption, infirmity, and ignorance of human nature, as well as to the infinite wisdom and majesty of God, they are to reject all confidence in their own strength, in their own righteousness, and to preserve on all occasions an unwavering and unsullied faith, and to submit with becoming reverence to his decrees' (II. 383).

For theological reasons, other commentators went far beyond Blackmore and Lowth in stressing Job's faults. Walter Hodges is perhaps the most egregious example, who strains to find support for Article XI of the Church in Job's 'self-idolatry' and 'spiritual pride', that corrupt nature which he shares with all other men and which may be expiated only through the imputed righteousness of Christ.[36] Richard Grey and John Garnett, while less extreme in their orthodoxy, nevertheless find that until the denouement the hero is not at all a model of patience and humility, but rather a *negative* example of those virtues, exhibited by the author in the same spirit as the Spartans did their drunken slaves to children, to warn them against vice![37] Keeping in mind the recent critical view that Goldsmith's attitude toward the vicar is consistently ironic, one may profitably attend to Garnett's analysis of the technique of Job, wherein the poet, 'by exposing the vice of impatience, in so ridiculous a figure, as Job cuts in that character, has effectually recommended its reverse; and shewn where the true merit as well as the true beauty of that virtue lies, by those admirable strokes of raillery and reproof' which Job's friends level at him. The method, which is indeed admirably suited to the taste of an age that relished satire and mock-heroics, may be compared to caricature in painting; the distortions in such figures

. . . have a surprising effect, suited exactly to the character, they are designed to expose, and shew how far they are deviated beyond natural proportion. A warrior like Achilles, at the toilette; a Sampson, making sport for the Philistines; a David, concerting an intrigue; a Solomon, in a state of infatuation; are so many instructive lessons of the virtues, they had deserted, as they place the several weaknesses or vices of so distinguished characters, in a point of light, which at the same time shew their obliquity, and make them supremely ridiculous. A Job, impatient, and an Edomite, humane, are figures equal to the best of them. (pp. 294–5)

That Goldsmith achieved something of the same effect in presenting his own comic figure of Job is, from the drift of recent criticism, sufficiently obvious. What he did not intend, surely, is that, while enjoying Dr. Primrose's foibles, we should forget quite so completely his proper character.

The commentaries, moreover, provide the key to a further significant dimension of Goldsmith's characterization of the vicar, and of the bewildering world of shifting appearances which nearly defeats him. As in *Tom Jones*, an important purpose of *The Vicar of Wakefield* is the definition of prudence, the most elusive and ambiguous of the moral virtues, implying on the one hand a false and narrow shrewdness in the ways of the world, or, on the other, that true sagacity which enables one to penetrate disguises and to estimate judiciously the real worth of things. The importance of this theme has been sensed, in part at least, by Michael Adelstein, who observes that the idea of prudence runs 'like a motif throughout the early part of the novel',[38] and by Curtis Dahl, who interprets the tale as 'a parable of unmasking'.[39] No one, however, has as yet suspected the connection Goldsmith intended between the theme of prudence and the controlling symbol of disguise.

Traditionally, we will recall, true prudence was regarded as precisely that perspicacity of moral vision which enabled one to distinguish between appearances and reality. Accordingly, Barrow insisted,

with faith also must concur the virtue of prudence; in all its parts and instances: therein is exerted a sagacity, discerning things as they really are in themselves, not as they appear through the masks and disguises of fallacious semblance, whereby they would delude us; not suffering us to be abused by the gaudy shews, the false glosses, the tempting allurements of things; therein we must use discretion in prizing things rightly, according to their true nature and intrinsick worth; in chusing things really good, and rejecting things truly evil, however each kind may seem to our erroneous sense . . .[40]

Prudence in this sense is what Job was thought to lack—as Worthington puts it, 'a due sense of his own blindness'.[41] Having been misled by the opinion of his innocence and righteousness, he must acknowledge his own frailty and the justice of divine providence; only then, as Thomas Heath observes of Job's final affirmation of that wisdom which only God can impart, will he have acquired 'prudence' and 'vision'.[42] In developing this point, the commentators represented both Job and his antagonists as taking part in a troubled drama of disguise and self-delusion. Before Job may be justified and restored to his former prosperity with 'decency and probability', the poet, according to Garnett, must bring his hero 'to a proper sense both of God and of himself', must 'pull the mask off from him, and discover a secret, which had hitherto laid unobserved, and that was, that in fact he was not the man he had hitherto passed upon the world for, but that his sins had brought upon him all the calamities he labored under . . .'[43] As for his false friends, Job himself accuses them of 'acting a part only, and then asks of them, *will it be good for you that God* search you out? i.e. can you stand this personated character of yours out to the very last, when God shall strip as he shortly will, the mask from off your face?' (p. 243). When that climactic moment occurs, writes Heath, 'at the blaze of his all-piercing eye all disguises fall off, all glosses vanish, every heart is lain open, every motive to action is discovered' (p. 154 n.).

A very similar relationship between prudence and false appearance informs the story of that latter-day Job, the Vicar of Wakefield. The ambiguity of prudence—that virtue which Fielding variously called the 'Art of Thriving' or the 'Art of Life'—is established at the start of the tale, and the two meanings of the term resound in counterpoint throughout the narrative until they are implicitly resolved in Chapter xxviii, which, together with Chapter xxix on the idea of Providence, comprises the conceptual climax of Goldsmith's thematic concerns. In Chapter ii, prudence is used three times in the narrow pragmatic sense of frugality and expediency in the management of one's worldly affairs, virtues for which the vicar commends his wife (IV. 22) and Mr. Wilmot (IV. 25) and which he is himself urged to practise by the messenger who brings news of his loss of fortune (IV. 24). In the following chapter, on the other hand, Goldsmith presents the meaning of prudence that it will be his purpose to recommend: that wisdom which surely distinguishes between goods real and only apparent, and which finds true honour and contentment in the pursuit of virtue. The point is clear as the vicar comforts his family in affliction:

'You can't be ignorant, my children,' cried I, 'that no prudence of ours could have prevented our late misfortune; but prudence may do much in disappointing its effects. We are now poor, my fondlings, and wisdom bids us conform to our humble situation. Let us then, without repining, give up those splendours with which numbers are wretched, and seek in humbler circumstances that peace with which all may be happy . . . let us from this moment give up all pretensions to gentility; we have still enough left for happiness if we are wise, and let us draw upon content for the deficiencies of fortune.' (IV. 26)

During most of the tale, however, Dr. Primrose is himself incapable of heeding this sound advice. Like Job in Matthew Henry's interpretation, the vicar has 'Knowledge and Wisdom' in general, but often his words are 'without Prudence' with respect to his own folly: 'Sometimes', Henry remarks, 'we need and deserve those Reproofs our selves which we have given to others . . . [Job] did not rightly *understand himself.*'⁴⁴ Though Dr. Primrose rallies his wife for allowing worldly interests to blind her to the real worth of Mr. Burchell and Squire Thornhill as prospective husbands for her daughters (IV. 31, 43–4), his own vanity leads him into the same error (e.g. IV. 40, 52, 81–2). For prudential reasons, he hopes Sophia has been '"taught to judge properly"' of poor men who affect to disparage the goods of this world: '"Your mother and I have now better prospects for you. The next winter, which you will probably spend in town, will give you opportunities of making a more prudent choice"' (IV. 71). In all this—whether in misjudging the intent of Burchell's letter (ch. xv) or in missing the irony of Squire Thornhill's role in the allegorical portrait, where he plays Alexander to Olivia's Amazon (ch. xvi)—the vicar's vanity and pride distort his vision of reality, leading him to mistake the semblance for the truth of things. His fault, as he comes to see, is precisely that moral blindness which, in his own words, characterizes all those who embrace error to gratify their own false hopes and desires:

'The vice does not lie in assenting to the proofs they see; but in being blind to many of the proofs that offer. Like corrupt judges on a bench, they determine right on that part of the evidence they hear; but they will not hear all the evidence. Thus, my son, though our erroneous opinions be involuntary when formed, yet as we have been wilfully corrupt, or very negligent in forming them, we deserve punishment for our vice, or contempt for our folly.'⁴⁵

The 'pattern of disguise' in *The Vicar of Wakefield*, so exhaustively analysed by Dahl, is in a sense the inevitable expression, the 'objective correlative', of the book's major ethical theme. Goldsmith ingeniously developed and elaborated the metaphor of vision and blindness, disguise and unmasking, which, as we have seen, was traditionally associated with the idea of prudence—and which, in the mid eighteenth century certainly, was very much a part of the interpretation of Job.

The climax of this theme—and its connection with the theme of providence and futurity, which are the chief theological concerns of both Job and the *Vicar*—occurs in Chapter xxviii, entitled: 'Happiness and misery rather the result of prudence than of virtue in this life. Temporal evils or felicities being regarded by heaven as things merely in themselves trifling and unworthy its care in the distribution.' The ambiguity of prudence is here finally demonstrated and resolved, for though the heading appears to distinguish between prudence and virtue, it identifies prudence (either true or false) as the only source of earthly contentment or misery, while the chapter itself depicts the vicar's painful education to the meaning of true prudence. In one of its aspects, of course, prudence in the *Vicar*, as in *Tom Jones*, is that worldly wisdom, the serpent's cunning, which even the innocent must acquire if they would not be gulled by the sharpers of Vanity Fair or debauched by honest-seeming scoundrels; it will soon appear that the vicar's world is in part redeemed through the kindly duplicities of Jenkinson the confidence man, who by an artful contrivance has transformed the Squire's mock marriage into a true one, preserving Olivia's chastity. More essentially, however, as Chapter xxviii makes clear, prudence implies that self-knowledge and moral perspicacity on which virtue itself depends. Through adversity, the vicar's pride has been humbled ('"Heaven be praised . . . there is no pride left me now"' (IV. 154)), and his eyes have been opened to the highest wisdom:

'I am now [he declares to George] raised above this world, and all the pleasures it can produce. From this moment I break from my heart all the ties that held it down to earth, and will prepare to fit us both for eternity.' (IV. 159)

Like Job, the vicar has been chastened to an awareness of his own folly and presumption. And he has come to understand—a felt conviction now, no longer a merely abstract and perfunctory notion—how far the essential values of the spirit are preferable to the delusive pleasures of the world. Having experienced the vanity and inequity of the human condition, wherein all men are prisoners together, he prepares with Job to affirm the wisdom and justice of Providence.

H

This, the assertion of the doctrines of providence and futurity, is the point of the vicar's sermon in Chapter XXIX and the major didactic motive of the tale as a whole—an emphasis, it is worth noting, which Hugh Kelly at once discerned in reviewing the book for *The Babler* (10 July 1766), where he applauded Goldsmith for 'a masterly vindication of that exterior disparity in the dispensations of providence, at which our modern infidels seem to triumph with so unceasing a satisfaction'.[46] To this purpose, no document was so apposite as the Book of Job, which, according to the expositors of the 'common system', was written expressly to refute the heterodox opinions of those who argued from the wretchedness of the human condition to deny the efficacy and justice of Providence. The design of the Book of Job was thought to be threefold: (1) to discredit the Manichean doctrine of 'two independent principles' by showing that every event in life, evil as well as good, is ordered by divine Providence, Satan being powerless to test Job without God's permission; (2) to affirm the doctrine of an 'unequal Providence', according to which the virtuous may suffer and the vicious prosper in this life; and (3) to assert the goodness of God by reference to a future state in which rewards and punishments will be equitably distributed. An anonymous follower of Sherlock against Warburton thus conveniently summarizes the orthodox view: the 'grand Points' which the author of Job 'endeavours to prove, in Opposition to the superficial Tenets of Deists and Infidels, are these; That God Almighty is immediately concerned in the Government of human Affairs, in the Disposal of all Events, which brought Happiness and Misery to each Individual, in their respective Conditions and Circumstances of Life; and That the Dispensations of an unequal Providence were not reconcileable with the moral Character of God, but upon the Supposition of a future State'.[47]

Each of these 'grand Points' influenced *The Vicar of Wakefield* in important and surprising ways, affecting Goldsmith's conception of certain characters and his handling of episode and plot. Though Goldsmith's curious use of 'fairy-tale motifs and archetypal patterns'[48] has been remarked by recent critics, no one has quite suspected the extent to which he drew upon the Job myth to raise his story to the level of parable. The same conspicuous system of narrative improbabilities that led commentators to interpret Job not as a true history, but as an allegory of the life of man, has puzzled or annoyed readers of the *Vicar* ever since Macaulay:[49]

They affirm likewise [writes Blackmore of Job], that it has an Air of Contrivance to sink a Man so suddenly from the most prosperous Condition, and to lay him under such grievous Sufferings and the very Extremity of Misery, and by a no less sudden and surprizing Revolution, in so short a space of time, to make him again the most happy Man in the World. They urge, that in the Catastrophe when this patient Man is rewarded for his inflexible Perseverance, the allotting him just the same Number of Children as he had lost, and just a double Quantity of Riches as he enjoy'd before, seems too nice to be a real Fact.[50]

As in Job, the improbable suddenness of the calamities that befall the vicar—emphasized by the messengers who abruptly disturb his contentment, bringing news of his loss of fortune or the ruin of his daughter—is one device which enhances our sense of the author's deliberate contrivance. In the fictional worlds of both Job and the vicar, such contrivance serves to enforce the impression that there is 'something supernatural'[51] in the hero's ordeal, that he has been singled out by Providence for special testing.[52] Job's misfortunes are dramatically foreshortened so as to intensify these effects, whereas Goldsmith, striving for a balance between the parabolic and the probable more in keeping with the demands of his form, distributes the vicar's trials over twenty-eight chapters, following his model chiefly in the suddenness of the blows and in their regular modulation from less to more severe.

In the world of the *Vicar*, as in the world of Job, the hero's very human struggle for self-knowledge and redemption is merely the specific focus of a larger drama in which the real antagonists are abstractions, what Sherlock refers to as the 'two principles' of good and evil. As Blackmore observes, discussing the machinery of Job, 'the chief Apostate Angel and the Divine Being himself' are interested in the action.[53] In the *Vicar* these principles find their avatars in Squire Thornhill and Sir William Thornhill. Just as Satan in Job is powerless to act without the divine permission, so the arch marplot of Goldsmith's tale is from the first said to be 'entirely dependant on the will of his uncle' (IV. 29), his actions observed and at last controlled by Sir William. Sir William, indeed, is the tale's most extraordinary figure. Though he is the Lord of the Manor which defines the vicar's world and the *deus ex machina* of the vicar's tragi-comedy, who will serve at last as judge and

mediator, resolving every complication, Sir William moves about
the country impersonating an indigent vagabond, Mr. Burchell.
In this his role is analogous to that of Elihu in the Job story, whom
some commentators construed as the type and figure of the
incarnate Christ, the Redeemer himself who condescended to move
among men in disguise, testing and judging them.[54] The spectacle
of critics in determined pursuit of Christ figures from *Beowulf* to
Giles Goatboy is already crowded and droll enough; one feels no
particular disposition to add to the fun in an essay on *The Vicar
of Wakefield*. But Goldsmith plainly invites some such interpretation
of Sir William. The analogy between Burchell and Christ is early
made, for example, as the vicar, without knowing the true identity
of his guest and certainly without suspecting his later role in
delivering him from affliction, praises his children for their
hospitality to a stranger: ' "The greatest stranger in this world, was
he that came to save it. He never had an house, as if willing to see
what hospitality was left remaining amongst us" ' (IV. 39). When,
like the Duke in *Measure for Measure*, Sir William finally puts off
his disguise and reveals himself, he appears as the 'deliverer' of
the vicar and his family, forgiving transgressions, judging the true
and the false, healing the sick, dispensing justice and charity 'with
a countenance open as the sun' (chs. xxx–xxxi). The transformations and reversals in these last chapters are so thick and so
astonishing that critics have been uncertain whether to deplore
them as an egregious violation of probability or to enjoy them as
a delicious travesty of the romance *finale*. They may be better
accounted for, I suspect, by reference to the miraculous denouement of Job, which was universally regarded as a notable and
philosophic instance of the *deus ex machina* convention—that
'common Expedient of Dramatic Writers' by which, according to
Horatian precept, the tangled skein of the plot is unravelled and
'the mysterious Ways of Providence' are revealed.[55] Garnett, for
example, justifies the device on both aesthetic and didactic grounds,
citing the intervention of Apollo in Euripides' *Orestes*: when the
drama 'seems to threaten nothing less than a tragical conclusion',
the sudden interposition of the deity functions both 'to enhance the
surprise, as it should when at last we find all the parties reconciled',
and to manifest God's 'power and providence, in retrieving [men]
from ruin, when they are as incapable of recovery, from all human
means, and to all human appearance' as Job was.[56]

But Job's justification and his restoration to prosperity could not occur, according to Sherlock and the advocates of the 'common system', until, his pride chastened by adversity, he had learned the principal lesson which his story was designed to inculcate: namely, as Hawkins summarizes, that 'the acknowledged Inequality of present Distributions throughout this Book, and the utter Inconsistency of the divine Dispensations with our Ideas of Justice in the Case of Wickedness successful, or Goodness distrest *throughout Life*' argues for 'the final Adjustment of all Difficulties and Irregularities in a *future State*'.[57] Job's maintaining this view against the remonstrances of his false and incredulous friends is what earns him God's praise for having said 'the thing that is right'.[58] This, too, is the point of Dr. Primrose's sermon to the prisoners in Chapter XXIX, the true climax and peripeteia of Goldsmith's tale. But to gauge the distance that originally separates the vicar from this saving knowledge, we must return to Chapter III and recall his advice to George as the young man, the family fortune lost, sets out to make his way in the world. Presenting his son with a bible to be his 'comfort on the way', the vicar draws his particular attention to Psalm 37: 25—'*I have been young, and now am old; yet never saw I the righteous man forsaken, or his seed begging their bread*'—a text, as Bishop Sherlock observes, which was often mistakenly construed as contradicting the doctrines of providential inequality and futurity.[59] The trials of adversity which the vicar endures are calculated both to humble his pride and complacency and to convince him of his error in thus mistaking the scheme of Providence. That he learns at last the lesson attributed to Job is clear in Chapter XXIX: 'The equal dealings of providence demonstrated with regard to the happy and the miserable here below. That from the nature of pleasure and pain, the wretched must be repaid the balance of their sufferings in the life hereafter.' The vicar's sermon, addressed to his fellow prisoners, develops the paradox that the very inequality of the distribution of good and evil in this world is the basis, ultimately, for vindicating the equality and justice of Providence, which 'has given the wretched two advantages over the happy in this life, greater felicity in dying, and in heaven all that superiority of pleasure which arises from contrasted enjoyment' (IV. 162). Like Job, and Rasselas, Dr. Primrose comes to understand that in this life there is more to suffer than to enjoy; the balance will be redressed, but only hereafter. It is this lesson that the homilists on Job sought to impart: 'The true principle then of patience, or fortitude properly so called, is faith, a firm persuasion of the being and providence of God, and a steady reliance upon the assurances he has vouchsafed us, of a future state, in which, shall finally be adjusted all the seeming inequalities of the present; in which, all tears shall be wiped away from the good man's eyes, and death and sorrow shall be no more . . .'[60]

In Chapters xxviii and xxix, Dr. Primrose has reached the nadir of his worldly fortunes: penniless and imprisoned, painfully burned; Olivia dishonoured and dead; Sophia abducted; George condemned to death—he is 'a wretched survivor in the midst of ruin' (IV. 159). But affliction, as Robert Burton remarked, 'is a school or academy, wherein the best scholars are prepared to the commencements of the Deity',[61] and the vicar's arduous education to the meaning of Providence and Prudence is now complete; the dominant, complementary themes of the tale are resolved. As in those other parabolic narratives exploring these same motifs, the Book of Job and *The History of Tom Jones*, this lesson once learned precipitates the miraculous descent of the god from the machine, and the tale concludes in a joyous festival of love and reconciliation. Olivia is restored to life and virtue; George is reprieved; Sophia is exalted; the vicar is justified and redeemed, his body healed, his lost wealth recovered.

In Goldsmith as in Fielding,[62] such flagrant disregard of the principle of probability has been deplored by critics as a weak and meretricious capitulation to the popular taste for romance. But Goldsmith, no less than Fielding, condemned the authors of romance on these same grounds: 'Those paint beauty in colours more charming than nature, and describe happiness that man never tastes. How delusive, how destructive therefore are those pictures of consummate bliss, they teach the youthful mind to sigh after beauty and happiness which never existed, to despise the little good which fortune has mixed in our cup, by expecting more than she ever gave.'[63] From the same motives he advised the fair author of *The Fair Citizen* to stick to her kitchen: 'one good Pudding is worth fifty modern Romances.'[64]

What, then, are we to make of his own improbable fiction? Though he condemned the practice as immoral, was he incapable himself of refraining from the delusive escapist fantasies of romance? Or, to take a more charitable line, did he see himself as a parodist, poking fun at a preposterous genre? Neither explanation will do. Parody and satire are a part of Goldsmith's intention in *The Vicar of Wakefield*, but only a part; and he was not writing a 'romance' in the conventional sense at all. What distinguishes Goldsmith from the writers of romance—and what distinguishes Fielding from Richardson in *Pamela*—is the belief that fiction should be neither an escapist entertainment nor an exercise in the 'realistic' depiction of actuality (Fielding found *Pamela* especially exasperating because it managed, insidiously, to be *both* things). Like Fielding, Goldsmith saw the craft of fiction as the creation of deliberately artificial paradigms of the general human condition— works in which contrivance and ostentatious artifice imply the highest truth: that the artist, whether human or divine, controls and comprehends his materials within the flow of time, that there is an order and a meaning to life which men may perceive and which, in art, they may emulate. Accordingly, Goldsmith's happy ending in *The Vicar of Wakefield*, like Fielding's in *Tom Jones*, is consonant with Dennis's defence of poetic justice in the drama: it is a reflection of the faith of his age in Order. On these grounds Matthew Henry interpreted the conclusion of the Book of Job as prefiguring that greater denouement of the Book of Life: God, he writes

. . . has the *entire* Plan and Model of Providence *before him*, and knows what he *will do*, which we do not, and therefore understand not what *he doth*. There is a Day of *Judgment before him*, when all the seeming Disorders of Providence will be set to rights, and the dark Chapters of it will be expounded: Then thou shalt see the full Meaning of these dark Events, and the final Period of these dismal Events . . .[65]

The cosmic analogue of poetic justice, he continues, is parabolically shadowed in Job's final reward:

And the extraordinary Prosperity which *Job* was crown'd with after his Afflictions, perhaps was intended to be to us Christians a Type and Figure of the Glory and Happiness of Heaven, which the *Afflictions of this present time* are *working for us*; and in which they will issue at last, and what will be *more than double* to all the Delights and Satisfactions we now enjoy, as *Job*'s after-Prosperity was to his former . . . (p. 135)

Though the special quality of *The Vicar of Wakefield* is owing in large part to that unfailing amenity of tone which James remarked, and to those playful effects of parody and verbal artifice which D. W. Jefferson observes, it is also founded in a characteristically

Augustan assumption about the nature of narrative: the idea that fiction, like all art, is an imitation of ideal nature, a rendering by means of analogy, type, and figure of the universal human comedy, whose author is Providence, whose actors, however faulty their performance, confess the efficacy of the rational virtues, and whose formal character is the product of the highest artifice—harmony, symmetry, the full consent of things. In the Book of Job, Goldsmith found the essential Christian paradigm to express this faith.

VIII

Swift and Sterne: The Disturbance of Form

As Celsus, the true physician in Garth's *Dispensary* (1699), descends through Nature to the underworld, he glimpses Chaos confined in his lair, sulking because deprived of dominion by Order, yet comfortable and complacent because 'undisturb'd by Form'.[1] The passage brings neatly into focus the tension felt throughout the period between the Augustan faith in a rational universe and those subterranean pressures which, as the century progressed, worked ever more effectually to undermine the foundations of that faith. In 1742 Pope closed his poetic career prophetically with the image of the 'great Anarch' unconfined, restored to dominion over Nature and the minds of men. But still the poet's mastery of form disturbs that empire, serving as a reproach to confusion and affirming both the validity and the efficacy of the old ideals. The victory of Chaos Pope foresaw would not be accomplished until later in the century, when, the ontological and epistemological assumptions of Christian humanism having been discredited by the proponents of a new scepticism, a new subjectivism, the forms themselves that expressed those ideals in art would come to seem merely arbitrary and quaint, and new forms would reflect a new belief that the highest Reality was neither Nature nor Nature's God, but the troubled consciousness of individual men.

Throughout this study I have chosen to define the special character of literature and the arts in Augustan England by stressing the ways in which the idea of Order affected the theory and practice of aesthetic Form in the period. But the gulf between the world Pope and Fielding celebrated and the 'new world' foreseen in *The Dunciad* may best be measured by turning now to the idea of Chaos as it occupied two of the greatest writers of the century.

Swift in *A Tale of a Tub* (1704) and Sterne in *Tristram Shandy* (1759–67) employ a similar narrative strategy to very different ends: in both, the formal principles of Augustan art are deliberately violated, on the one hand to affirm the norms the author has apparently abandoned, on the other to reveal them as a pointless irrelevancy. In *A Tale of a Tub* the image of madness projected implicitly declares the nature of sanity and the value of rational order; in *Tristram Shandy* the mind is presented as an autonomous, irrational mechanism preventing rather than promoting knowledge of any objective reality. In Swift, typically, the old ideals of Order and Right Reason are known through their contraries; in Sterne they have been replaced by the Hobby-horse, those private systems for survival that enable us to Shandy-it through life without succumbing completely to the muddle of things.

i. *Swift: Order from Confusion*

Before considering the place of *A Tale of a Tub* within the Augustan mode as we have been defining it, we should be clear that in certain respects Swift consciously disowned the aesthetic assumptions and conventions to which Pope and Gay, Fielding and Goldsmith, subscribed. His verse is an obvious case in point. The remark attributed to Dryden—'Cousin Swift, you will never be a poet'—might be said to apply not only to Swift's questionable competence as a prosodist, but to his arch repudiation of the Augustan idea of poetry itself. After the half-dozen odes of the early 1690s in which he brought himself, awkwardly enough, to be grave in verse, his poetry for forty years strikes the more congenial note of irony, ridiculing the pride and pretensions of men and mocking the forms—especially the poetic forms—which dignified them. In both respects his aim, in so far as it was seriously meant at all, was to expose man's indomitable capacity for self-delusion and self-flattery, to remind him of his mortality and his weakness as a moral agent. For Swift the Augustan formulation that Art was the imitation of '*la belle Nature*' seemed morally irresponsible because calculated to conceal, even indeed to deny, the truth of things as they are: the plain truth that Eden is irrecoverable and that *human* nature, at least, is fallen. 'For fine

Ideas', like fine poems, 'vanish fast, / While all the gross and filthy last.'[2] If his friends Pope and Gay were poets in the Augustan mode, then Swift, one must say, was its 'Anti-Poet'.[3] Even in the mock-forms in which they excelled, Pope and Gay do not mean to break windows and overturn foundations; the ridicule, as Warburton observed of *The Dunciad*,[4] 'falls not on the thing *imitated*, but *imitating*'. In Swift's parodies the mode itself comes under attack, both its theoretical basis and its forms and favourite metaphors.

From one point of view, what Norman O. Brown has called Swift's 'excremental vision'[5] may be seen as his way of inverting (to the antipodes!) the traditional 'poetic' conception of man's relationship to Nature, Time, and Art. It is the 'Necessities of Nature'[6]—the idea not of Order but of ordure—that substitute in Swift's verse for her imagined perfection. The secret of the riddle entitled '*The* Gulf *of all* human Possessions' (1724) is that neither reason nor art, let us say, but defecation is the common denominator and perpetual memorial of the human condition. Excrement, 'the Fruits, / Vain Man, of all thy vain Pursuits' (ll. 1–2), is here the universal substance, like Nature without a *Noῦς* another Chaos to which all things are reduced and from which all things begin:

> YET from this *mingled Mass* of Things,
> In Time a new Creation springs.
> These *crude* Materials once shall rise,
> To fill the Earth, and Air, and Skies:
> In various Forms appear agen
> Of Vegetables, Brutes, and Men.
> So *Jove* pronounc'd among the Gods,
> *Olympus* trembling as he nods.   (ll. 89–96)

This, too, is Strephon's rude epiphany, the eminently curable romantic lover of 'The Lady's Dressing Room' (1730). As the contents of Celia's elegant close-stool dispel his cherished delusion that mortal women are goddesses, Strephon, repeating Milton's description of the primordial Abyss (*PL*, ii. 890–1), perceives that Order itself, like most idealisms, is founded precariously on Confusion: 'O may she better learn to keep / "Those Secrets of the hoary deep!"' (ll. 97–8). Celia 'in her Glory' is for Swift a type of all human 'perfections'—a beauty hard-won (and therefore not quite to be despised), but at best ephemeral and illusory, disguising the essential fact of mortal frailty. If Strephon, who has missed the point by turning misogynist,

> . . . would but stop his Nose . . .
> He soon would learn to think like me,
> And bless his ravisht Sight to see
> Such Order from Confusion sprung,
> Such gaudy Tulips rais'd from Dung.   (ll. 136, 141–4)

Echoing absurdly behind these lines may be heard Uriel's account of the creation of the world:

> Confusion heard his voice, and wilde uproar
> Stood rul'd, stood vast infinitude confin'd;
> Till at his second bidding darkness fled,
> Light shon, and order from disorder sprung.   (*PL*, iii. 710–13)

The analogy between divine and human art seriously proposed by Pope and other Augustans was for Swift preposterous, one more measure of man's irrepressible vanity. Celia at her toilet, through artful applications masking corruption, is his own sardonic tribute to the ways in which men and women emulate 'th'Omnific Word'.

Swift's scatological reduction of the assumptions and metaphors of contemporary aesthetics is so thoroughgoing that it takes on the appearance of a deliberate satiric programme. Two of the more outrageous examples occur in 'A Panegyrick on the Dean' (1730), where, alluding to his erection of a pair of privies—'Two Temples of magnifick Size' (l. 201) dedicated to the goddess Cloacina—he demands to be compared with the architect whom the Burlington circle most esteemed: '*Palladio* was not half so skill'd in / The Grandeur or the Art of Building' (ll. 199–200). Still more audacious in the same poem is his version of the myth of the Ages of Man which in Pope's *Pastorals* had come to symbolize our sad estrangement from the innocence and ideal loveliness of Eden. For Swift what made 'That *golden* Age' (l. 234) preferable to the present is that then—all Nature was a jakes! The 'daily Vot'ries' (l. 239) of Cloacina performed their acts of worship by purling streams and in shady groves and, for their convenience, 'many a Flow'r abstersive grew' (l. 249). Now, alas, 'in our degen'rate Days' (l. 287), the more fastidious resort to out-houses and chamber-pots, forgetting that 'Nature never Diff'rence made / Between the Scepter and the

Spade' (ll. 289–90). How fitting, then, that Swift's 'Pastoral Dialogue' (1729), his own essay in the mode that Pope regarded as presenting a 'perfect image' of that happier time, should conclude with Dermot's welcome advice to Sheelah: 'But see, where *Norah* with the Sowins comes— / Then let us rise, and rest our weary Bums.'

If for critics such as Dennis and Jonathan Richardson the studio of the poet or painter 'must be like Eden before the fall, like Arcadia',[7] for Swift, apparently, construing the analogy in his own original way, it more nearly resembled another sort of closet. Typically, he recalls the conventions of Augustan neo-platonism only to scoff at them. In his verses on 'Vanbrug's House' (1703) consider, for example, what becomes of the Pythagorean notion, implicit in the myth of Amphion, that the same numbers which govern harmony in music and poetry govern architecture as well:

> In times of old, when Time was young,
> And Poets their own Verses sung,
> A Song would draw a Stone or Beam,
> That now would overload a Team,
> Lead them a Dance of many a Mile,
> Then rear 'em to a goodly Pile,
> Each Number had it's diff'rent Power;
> Heroick Strains could build a Tower;
> Sonnets and Elegyes to Chloris
> Would raise a House about two Storyes;
> A Lyrick Ode would Slate; a Catch
> Would Tile; an Epigram would Thatch.   (ll. 1–12)

To carry the joke still farther, in 'Apollo: or, A Problem Solved' (1731) the god himself of Harmony and Poetry is found to be, like the celebrated *castrato* Nicolini, impotent. One reason, surely, for all this iconoclasm is that Swift saw what we have called the transforming power of poetic artifice not as a virtue, bringing actuality closer to ideal Nature, but as a sort of intellectual cosmetics, comparable, at another level, to Corinna's 'Arts', which 'by the Operator's Skill'[8] conceal flaws and blemishes not merely of the body, but of the mind. For Swift, as '*A Love Song* in the *Modern* Taste' (1733) suggests, it was not the glory but the folly of Augustan aesthetics that it was founded on the premiss that 'Nature must give Way to Art' (l. 4).

As we have in part already seen in considering the travesty of the fiat motif in 'The Lady's Dressing Room', Swift's mockery extends to an even more fundamental assumption of his age: the notion that there is a meaningful analogy between macrocosm and microcosm, that men, in so far as they are rational, will imitate in their own lives the Order of universal Nature. In one sense, of course, the Houyhnhnms are Swift's comment on this belief—since the Fall, the only truly rational animals we are likely to meet. In his poetry the image of the *human* condition that emerges is one of a world irrational and disintegrated, a jumble of jarring atoms and discrete particles.[9] The image is especially effective because accomplished by a systematic inversion of the favourite themes and poetic strategies of his more optimistic contemporaries, for whom elemental discord was resolved into a larger harmony, an ideal realized in human life and art through emulation of the original act which brought Order out of Chaos. As Ralph Cohen has shown,[10] a conventional method in the period for expressing this view of universal Order was the poetic survey of creation: in Thomson's *Seasons* or in Pope's *Windsor Forest* the panoramic cataloguing of contrasted elements in Nature—hills and valleys, the woodland and the plain, light and shadow—conduces to the impression of the unity of the Whole, a vision redounding to the glory of the Creator. In satire Pope, describing Belinda at her dressing table, can use the convention ironically to present his heroine as the cynosure and deity of her circle, for whom 'The various Off'rings of the World appear'.[11] In Swift the device is less playful. His surveys are not of Nature, but of those little worlds which men and women have made their own—city streets, the rooms of prostitutes and belles—places whose disarray attests to the moral character of their inhabitants.

In 'The Lady's Dressing Room', which may serve as the paradigmatic example, Swift's travesty of the method and intention of the Augustan 'prospect' poem results in the image of total chaos. Like Strephon, Swift takes a 'Survey' of Celia's chamber, the 'world' of the poem, which is at once 'grand' in its comprehensiveness and 'strict' (ll. 7, 115) in its relentless particularity, presenting the contents of the room to our view in the way that Celia's 'magnifying Glass' discloses the 'smallest Worm' in her nose (ll. 60, 64). In *Windsor Forest* or *Cooper's Hill*, let us say, the prospect of general Nature is soothing because seen from a distance and idealized, the impression of harmony reinforced in the balanced,

orderly movement of the verse. Swift's 'survey' affords a different
sort of spectacle altogether, a noisome 'Inventory' of 'all the Litter
as it lay' (ll. 8, 10): a dirty smock, disgusting combs, a greasy fore-
head cloth, obscene gallipots and vials and basins, culminating in
the inevitable reeking close-stool. This, too, is the effect of the
brutal conclusion of 'A Description of a *City Shower*' (1710), in
which the storm, like another 'Deluge' purging the '*Devoted* Town'
(l. 32), flushes away offal from every corner of the city:

> Sweepings from Butchers Stalls, Dung, Guts, and Blood,
> Drown'd Puppies, stinking Sprats, all drench'd in Mud,
> Dead Cats and Turnip-Tops come tumbling down the Flood.

Once, indeed, in each of these poems the flowers of Milton's
Paradise (cf. *PL*, iv. 256) and the ideal of *concordia discors* merge
grotesquely to characterize a very un-Edenic sort of reality, as
'Filth of all Hues and Odours' join 'in huge Confluent' (ll. 55, 59)
and the contents of Celia's basin are revealed, 'A nasty Compound
of all Hues' (l. 41).

The achievement of Order and Beauty in such a world is for
Swift a hopeless, though not an unsympathetic, undertaking. In
several of his most effective poems he recalls with derision the old
analogy between divine and human art. The miracle of Celia 'in
her Glory' is, as we have seen, a triumph of art eliciting echoes of
Milton's account of the creation. Indeed, in some respects she has
outdone 'th'Omnific Word', since *her* Order, sprung from Confusion,
has not been six days in the making:

> FIVE Hours, (and who can do it less in?)
> By haughty *Celia* spent in Dressing;
> The Goddess from her Chamber issues,
> Array'd in Lace, Brocade and Tissues.   (ll. 1–4)

In 'A Beautiful Young Nymph Going to Bed', an excruciating study
in disintegration, Corinna is such another work of art. Having
submitted to the painful nocturnal ritual of disassembling herself,
she must as another day begins bring a precarious Order out
of Chaos:

> THE Nymph, tho' in this mangled Plight,
> Must ev'ry Morn her Limbs unite.
> But how shall I describe her Arts
> To recollect the scatter'd Parts?
> Or shew the Anguish, Toil, and Pain,
> Of gath'ring up herself again?   (ll. 65–70)

Night and Chaos being associate deities, daybreak is the time when the inhabitants of the city resume the impossible task of ordering their world. In 'A Description of the Morning' (1709), prentices, charwomen, and scavengers perform, like Celia and Corinna, those artful labours designed to keep confusion at bay:

> The Slipshod Prentice from his Masters Door,
> Had par'd the Dirt, and Sprinkled round the Floor.
> Now *Moll* had whirl'd her Mop with dext'rous Airs,
> Prepar'd to Scrub the Entry and the Stairs.
> The Youth with Broomy Stumps began to trace
> The Kennel-Edge, where Wheels had worn the Place.   (ll. 5–10)

In Gay's *Trivia* these same humble activities are dignified through association with those other practical arts—the arts of living and of poetry—which enable men to cope with actuality, introducing order into the mess of things. Swift, too, is aware that art is necessary if life is to be endured: despite their moral failings, one senses a certain sympathy for Corinna's 'mangled Plight'[12] or for 'haughty' Celia's wish to raise a tulip from dung, a certain gratitude for those who tidy the streets and houses of the city. But the dominant note of his verse is that the attempt itself to disguise corruption is at worst, as in the case of pastoral poets or of painted belles, a snare and a delusion, motivated by pride and falsifying the truth of things as they are; at best, merely futile. In 'A Description of the Morning', Swift's superb and disconcerting travesty of the pastoral aubade, the efforts of Moll and her fellow workers to tidy up the town are lost in the sense conveyed of physical and moral disorder. Betty's stealing from her master's bed 'to discompose her own', the venal turnkey conspiring to promote robbery in the streets, the bailiff on the watch for prey, the cacophonous shouts of coalmen and chimney-sweeps—the images are discrete and discordant, affirming not, certainly, the harmony of things, but the separateness and muddle of the human condition.

As a poet, then, Swift was something of an anomaly in his age, who found in travesty and burlesque his true, scoffing vein, and who looked for a model not to Dryden and Pope, but to Butler and Scarron. What sets him apart, of course, is not that he practised the mock-forms—the best mock-poems of the period are by Dryden and Pope and Gay—but that he could take neither the forms themselves seriously nor the assumptions and conceits behind them. The premiss of Augustan aesthetics—that Art is the imitation of ideal Nature—is essentially neo-platonic, and platonism in most of its guises he derided as an elegant irrelevancy, perhaps the fundamental intellectual expression of man's irrepressible determination to prefer beautiful idealisms to awkward realities. If Pope's careful art would revive the 'Groves of *Ĕden,* vanish'd now so long', Swift's jarring rhymes and repugnant images remind us that they are irrecoverable and that a poetry which obscures this plain and Christian truth is frivolous, even pernicious.

The special character of Swift's art is partially attributable to the kind of Christian he was: in theology Augustinian, believing in the depravity of man unredeemed by grace; in religion High Church.[13] In both respects, though he was 'orthodox' (the Articles of the Church being thoroughly Augustinian in tenor), he was also unfashionable;[14] for the dominant theological impulse of the age, conditioned by the rationalism of the Cambridge Platonists and the Latitudinarian divines, was, relatively speaking, optimistic about human nature and tolerant toward non-conformity. For Swift, as later for William Law and George Whitefield, this was not Christianity at all but a particularly complacent species of moral philosophy scarcely distinguishable, in its apparent emphasis on the self-sufficiency of men in matters of salvation, from the deism of a Shaftesbury or Tindal, or the stoicism of a Cicero. It described men not as they are, proud and corrupt, but men as they liked, in their vanity, to think of themselves: reasonable and benevolent. His aim as priest and as satirist is to remind us of what we are.

The form of *A Tale of a Tub*—or rather its deliberate formlessness— is one expression of this purpose: it is the mirror of man, especially of Modern man, as Swift saw him. Yet its very eccentricities imply a centre, a core of belief which defines confusion and which reveals the satirist to be the advocate, rather than the opponent, of traditional forms and values. In narratives such as the *Tale* or *Gulliver's Travels* and in such essays as 'An Argument against Abolishing Christianity' or 'A Modest Proposal', Swift's stance as an author is the dramatic equivalent of his favourite rhetorical device of irony, whose way to Truth is inversion, affirming the opposite of what is said. It is also the equivalent of one of his favourite strategies as a homilist, which is to define virtue through the anatomy of vice: thus by describing the several kinds of false witnesses, he explained in his sermon on that subject, 'I have made it less necessary to dwell much longer upon this Head; because a faithful Witness, like every Thing else, is known by his contrary . . .'[15] The teller of the *Tale* is, as it were, Truth's false witness, by whom her proper character may be known. Unlike Pope or Fielding (except, perhaps, in *Jonathan Wild*), who are also skilful ironists, Swift in employing this technique of 'contraries' chooses to adopt the style of the Enemy the better to disclose his essential character. Though, if we are attentive, Swift is there plainly enough behind the mask, the voices we hear, particularly in the prose satires, are those of a mad Modern author or a too-well-travelled surgeon, a fatuous astrologer, an economic projector, a mercenary defender of the faith. Among the prominent satirists of the period only Defoe, most notably in *The Shortest Way with the Dissenters* (1702), carried this method of ironic impersonation so far, and Defoe was so little master of the device that he seems to *be* the inflexible bigot he abhors. Swift was not so inept: we can distinguish readily enough the ventriloquist from the dummy. We know the teller of the *Tale* for a fool not only because he smugly acknowledges his membership in the 'honourable Society' of Bedlam,[16] but because his book, the mirror of his mind, is hopelessly out of control and because, irrepressible egoist and epicurean that he is, he is the proper secretary of a philosophy which his author despises.

Throughout this study we have been concerned with the ways in which form in Augustan literature and the arts may be said to express certain ontological assumptions about the nature of reality. In *A Tale of a Tub* Swift, too, accepts this premiss of contemporary aesthetics, but, since his aim is to define Truth by her contrary, his own form becomes the image not of Order, but of Chaos. If, as the teller of the *Tale* invites us to do (p. 54), books may be compared to buildings, Swift's is a gothic temple without symmetry, proportion, or design, entered through a swollen '*Porch*' of disconnected members, its 'nave' broken into fragments at the whimsy of the architect by crazy corridors leading nowhere, its 'apse' merely terminating the process of aimless agglomeration. From one point of view, of course, the form of the work—the proliferation of prolegomenous materials, the digressions, the footnotes, the hiatuses—appears as a satire on modern pedantry; in this sense, it is the most glaring of all those '*Parodies*', as Swift remarks in his 'Apology' to the 1710 edition, '*where the Author personates the Style and Manner of other Writers, whom he has a mind to expose*'

(p. 7). This Scriblerian aspect of the book anticipates Pope's strategy in *The Dunciad Variorum* (1729), where, though the poetry itself is there to remind us of the alternative to duncery, it seems in danger of being overwhelmed by the paraphernalia of prefaces, annotations, appendices. From another point of view, however, the form of the *Tale* may best be understood in terms of Swift's graver purpose, the satire of '*the numerous and gross Corruptions in Religion*' (p. 4)—a purpose that anticipates Pope's 'deep Intent' in *The New Dunciad* of 1742. The mockery in both these works is meant not merely to embarrass the pedants and hackney authors of the age, but, at the profoundest level, to expose the essential character of heterodoxy, in particular of that 'new *Modish System* of reducing all to sense' which threatened to deprive the world of its Creator and man, his Maker's image, of a soul. Fifty years before Pope would do the same, Swift in the 'Ode to the Athenian Society' (1692) identified the Enemy as atheistical materialism:

> *The Wits*, I mean the Atheists of the Age,
> Who fain would rule the Pulpit, as they do the Stage,
> Wondrous *Refiners* of Philosophy,
> Of Morals and Divinity,
> By the new *Modish System* of reducing all to sense,
> Against all Logick and concluding Laws,
> Do own th' Effects of Providence,
> And yet deny the Cause.   (ll. 103–10)

What was here revived, he continues, is the doctrine of Epicurus—the insistence that the world, though manifestly a work of '*wondrous Wit*' (l. 125), was the lucky production of Chance, the effect of

> . . . a *Crowd of Atoms* justling in a heap,
> Which from Eternal Seeds begun,
> Justling some thousand years till ripen'd by the Sun . . .
> (ll. 127–9)

The new epicureanism, contrived in the image of Hobbes, Descartes, and Spinoza, denied the mysteries of religion and the spiritual basis of reality, reducing the world to a machine and man, in Rochester's phrase, to a 'reasoning engine'.[17] Swift's creed was different: 'I believe in much', he declares, 'I ne're can hope to see' (l. 134). Philosophy, the 'beauteous Queen' meant by Heaven 'To be the great Original / For Man to *dress and polish* his Uncourtly Mind' (ll. 216–18), he saw as having been long since corrupted through

pride into scepticism and the quibbling of chop-logic meta-
physicians:

> In what *Mock-habits* have they put her, since the Fall!
> More oft in Fools and Mad-mens hands than Sages
> She seems a *Medly of all Ages* . . .   (ll. 219–21)

Of all ages, to be sure, 'But always with a stronger relish of
the Last' (l. 215). Written shortly after the ode, the *Tale* reflects
these same intellectual concerns: the controversion of atheistical
materialism, that 'new *Modish System*' which is the darling of
madmen masquerading as wits. For Swift, as for the age in general,
this was the quintessential heterodoxy, as ancient as Epicurus and,
what is more to the point, as modern as the Sage of Malmesbury.

The Teller of the *Tale* is just such a wit—a materialist and a madman, the very glass of fashion. By now, after a quarter of a century
of debate with no consensus yet in view, the whole question of the
persona in the *Tale* should be thoroughly *non grata*: did Swift mean
to parody the Enemy or to impersonate him?[18] Either term, perhaps,
will serve since Swift himself appears to have regarded them as
interchangeable.[19] What must be clear if we are to understand
the work, however, is the impression, deliberately created, that
a character by no means to be identified with Swift himself is the
'author' of the *Tale*. Even before we actually hear the Teller's voice
for the first time in the 'Epistle Dedicatory' to Prince Posterity, we
are apprized of this strategy in a footnote: '*the Author*', Swift
remarks, '*begins in a way very frequent with him, by personating other
Writers* . . .' (p. 30 n.).

It is not a matter of parody only, by which is usually meant the
imitation of a particular literary style for satiric effect, but of the
invention of a fully realized *dramatis persona*. As he proceeds in his
labyrinthine rambles to the end of his work, the Teller reveals himself to us at virtually every step of the way. Unabashed exhibi-
tionist that he is, he seems in fact to regard himself as his most
interesting subject, his egoism (in the rhetorical sense) being the
inevitable expression of his solipsism and megalomania. The
'*freshest Modern*' (p. 130) of them all, he shares 'the *Modern*
Inclination to expatiate upon the Beauty' of his own productions
(p. 132), and resents the injustice of Time's enmity toward 'our
vast flourishing Body' (p. 31), the swarming authors of the age
whom he calls his 'Brethren' (p. 42). He is an indefatigable reader
of 'our Noble *Moderns*', whose 'most edifying Volumes'—when he

is not himself adding to their number with panegyrics on '*the World*' and '*the Proceedings of the* Rabble', or with histories of 'Ears' and descriptions of '*the Kingdom of* Absurdities' (p. 2)—he pores over 'Night and Day, for the Improvement of my Mind, and the good of my Country' (p. 96). He hugely admires Bentley (p. 125), is chummy with Wotton (pp. 128, 169), and knows Dryden well enough to be able to reveal his confidences to the world (p. 131)—an intimacy he finds especially flattering, since he is aware 'how exceedingly our Illustrious *Moderns* have eclipsed the weak glimmering Lights of the *Antients*' (p. 124). We are scarcely surprised, then, that he shares with Swift 'neither a Talent nor an Inclination for Satyr', seeing that he is 'so entirely satisfied with the whole present Procedure of human Things' (p. 53).

We learn, too, not only about his attitudes and dubious predilections, but about 'the Circumstances and Postures' of his private life, knowledge of which, he trusts, will enable us better to understand his book. The 'shrewdest Pieces' of his treatise—which presumably are quite shrewd indeed, since he regards himself as 'Secretary' of the universe (p. 123) and his work as 'a faithful Abstract drawn from the Universal Body of all Arts and Sciences' (p. 38)—were 'conceived in Bed, in a Garret', where he sharpened his 'Invention' with hunger: 'In general', he confides, 'the whole Work was begun, continued, and ended, under a long Course of Physick, and a great want of Money' (p. 44). The enforced abstemiousness of his way of life, together of course with his taste and talent, has eminently well qualified him, therefore, for 'the Honor' recently conferred upon him of his election to membership in 'that Illustrious Fraternity', the '*Grub-street* Brotherhood' (pp. 63–4). Not long since, indeed, the qualities of his mind made him eligible for a place in another fraternal order, the 'honourable Society' of Bedlam, 'whereof', he reveals with becoming modesty, 'I had some Time the Happiness to be an unworthy Member' (p. 176). It may prove, however, a little disconcerting to his readers to discover that the writing of this treatise—which he humbly offers 'for the Advancement of Universal Knowledge' and the great 'Emolument' it will bring to 'this whole Globe of Earth' (p. 106), and which he variously describes as 'Divine' (pp. 124, 181), 'miraculous' (pp. 184, 203), 'wonderful' (p. 186)—was in fact undertaken as a kind of occupational therapy, enabling him to exchange his cell in Bedlam for a garret in Grub Street. He concludes

his 'Digression concerning the Original, the Use and Improvement of
Madness in a Commonwealth' with the touching confession

. . . That even, I my self, the Author of these momentous Truths, am
a Person, whose Imaginations are hard-mouth'd, and exceedingly disposed to run away with his Reason, which I have observed from long
Experience, to be a very light Rider, and easily shook off; upon which
Account, my Friends will never trust me alone, without a solemn Promise,
to vent my Speculations in this, or the like manner, for the universal
Benefit of Human kind . . .   (p. 180)

If egoism is the Teller's natural vein, other aspects of the Tale's
form are attributable to his membership in the societies of Grub
Street and Bedlam. In so far as he is capable at all of consciously
determining the shape of his book, he is, as 'a most devoted Servant
of all Modern Forms' (p. 45), cautious 'upon all Occasions, most
nicely to follow the Rules and Methods of Writing, laid down by the
Example of our illustrious Moderns' (p. 92). Though he is not quite
a match for Dryden, whose 'forty or fifty Pages' of prefatory self-
congratulation have set the standard, yet he is by no means con-
temptible in this respect, taking care to provide his own inordinate
series of 'Prefaces, Epistles, Advertisements, Introductions, Prolego-
mena's Apparatus's, To-the-Reader's' (p. 131). As for that other distinctive feature of the Tale's organization—the digressions and
digressions within digressions which cause the book to resemble
'a Nest of Boxes' (p. 124) and fit it up to make 'a very comely
Figure on a Bookseller's Shelf' (p. 148)—it, too, is acknowledged
a 'great Modern Improvement' in the art of narrative (p. 143). But
in matters of form as in other things the Teller is most a man of his
time in declining all constraint, whether of reason or convention.
Though his 'Digression in the Modern Kind' should have been the
preface of his treatise, he will not be bound by precedent, claiming
'an absolute Authority in Right, as the freshest Modern, which
gives me a Despotick Power over all Authors before me' (p. 130).

Such generic explanations of the Tale's form in terms of the
eccentricities of contemporary literary practice are of course an
essential part of Swift's parody of Modernism. With reference to
the persona himself, however, they are merely academic. With or
without modern 'Rules' to guide him, the Teller could only have
produced the confused and disconnected work which he sets
before us for our edification; for there can be no method in madness,
and the Teller, though a 'Modern Wit' (p. 148), is mad. Bringing

his treatise to an end, he reveals that his 'art', like his mind, has all along been out of control:

> IN my Disposure of Employments of the Brain, I have thought fit to make *Invention* the *Master*, and to give *Method* and *Reason*, the Office of its *Lacquays*. The Cause of this Distribution was, from observing it my peculiar Case, to be often under a Temptation of being *Witty*, upon Occasions, where I could be neither *Wise* nor *Sound*, nor any thing to the Matter in hand.   (p. 209)

Lacking the power to dispose his thoughts rationally, he has also been prevented by a 'short Memory' (p. 134) from keeping them in order. Well along in his tale of the three brothers, it accidentally occurs to him, as Martin and Jack are about to reform their coats, that he 'ought in Method, to have informed the Reader about fifty Pages ago' (p. 135) of Peter's having forbidden them to do so. Later, concluding his '*Digression in Praise of Digressions*' which he has as usual inserted in his book at random, he invites the more 'judicious' reader 'to remove it into any other Corner he pleases' (p. 149). What has produced all this muddle in which the Teller glories is not modern precedent alone, but the extravagancies of his own unruly brain, avoiding at any cost 'the fatal Confinement of delivering nothing beyond what is to the Purpose' (p. 144). Protesting at last his determination to press on to his journey's end, he is yet in no hurry to be home ('having never so little Business' as when he is there), and when 'Accident' provides the opportunity for digressing along the way, he is not one to decline:

> AFTER so wide a Compass as I have wandred, I do now gladly overtake, and close in with my Subject, and shall henceforth hold on with it an even Pace to the End of my Journey, except some beautiful Prospect appears within sight of my Way; whereof, tho' at present I have neither Warning nor Expectation, yet upon such an Accident, come when it will, I shall beg my Readers Favour and Company, allowing me to conduct him thro' it along with my self. For in *Writing*, it is as in *Travelling* . . .   (p. 188)

What began as a promise to close with his subject develops inevitably into a simile spun out for two long paragraphs, after which he stumbles into the main road, picking his way along through the scraps and blanks of his commonplace book, pausing to give us a taste of his '*general History of Ears*' (p. 202), and stopping at last only because he has mislaid his notes.

This same inability to order his thoughts in logical sequence is apparent not merely in the absence of any controlling design in the

Tale, but, still more essentially, in the Teller's rambling, para-tactical style. As in the passage quoted above, for example, ideas and images are set down at random as one thought suggests another, and sentences are formed by a process of accretion, clause following clause, parenthesis piled upon parenthesis. We are in the presence, indeed, of a prose that might have served Hobbes as a case-book example of literary insanity: 'But without steadiness, and direction to some end [Hobbes observes], a great fancy is one kind of madness; such as they have, that entering into any dis-course, are snatched from their purpose, by every thing that comes in their thought, into so many, and so long digressions, and parentheses, that they utterly lose themselves . . .'[20] What the *Tale*, in short, lacks are precisely those qualities of rational dis-course which Swift regarded as essential, but which the Teller looks upon as entirely superfluous: '*Method*, and *Style*, and *Grammar*, and *Invention*' (p. 148). For Swift, no less than Hobbes, such a style was the stamp and signature of a deranged mind. In 'Some Thoughts on Free-Thinking' (1713?) he repeats with approval the remark of an Irish bishop:

> that the difference betwixt a mad-man and one in his wits, in what related to speech, consisted in this: That the former spoke out whatever came into his mind, and just in the confused manner as his imagination presented the ideas. The latter only expressed such thoughts, as his judg-ment directed him to chuse, leaving the rest to die away in his memory. And that if the wisest man would at any time utter his thoughts, in the crude indigested manner, as they come into his head, he would be looked upon as raving mad.[21]

The expression of the Teller's mind, the *Tale* is the literary approximation of chaos. Formally, its characteristic is not unity and a coherent design, but disintegration; not an organic whole-ness, but a jumbled multiplicity of discrete parts and fragments. Throughout the work, it is in precisely these terms that Swift dis-tinguishes between order, health, and sanity on the one hand and disorder, disease, and madness on the other. Thus, in one of his rare and ever ineffectual moments of lucidity the Teller remarks in his Preface that, 'as Health is but one Thing, and has been always the same, whereas Diseases are by thousands, besides new and daily Additions; So, all the Virtues that have been ever in Mankind, are to be counted upon a few Fingers, but his Follies and Vices are innumerable, and Time adds hourly to the Heap' (p. 50). A similar distinction between unity and multiplicity informs the symbolism of the tale itself: since he intends the advancement of '*Unity*' (p. 139) through moderation, Martin's coat is whole, its 'Substance' uninjured (p. 136); in contrast, the coats of Peter and Jack show the effects, respectively, of their vanity and zeal, Peter's being 'a Medley, the most Antick' conceivable (p. 135), Jack's 'a Meddley of *Rags*, and *Lace*, and *Rents*, and *Fringes*' (p. 141). No less antic and confused is the medley the Teller has made of his tale, for which, however, Swift chooses a gastronomic metaphor, comparing such modern books to the 'Refinements' epicures have made upon plain and wholesome food, preferring 'various Compounds . . . *Soups* and *Ollio's*, *Fricassées* and *Ragousts*' (p. 143) to more substantial fare. The *Tale* is the literary analogue to 'the Fashion of jumbling fifty Things together in a Dish . . . in Compliance to a depraved and *debauched Appetite*, as well as to a *crazy Constitution*' (p. 144). 'Method', Swift advised Stella, 'is good in all things. Order governs the world. The Devil is the author of confusion.'[22] In *A Tale of a Tub*, as the Teller assures us, it is 'as hard to get quit of *Number*, as of *Hell*' (p. 55).

Also affecting the form of the *Tale*—particularly with reference to its sylistic texture—is another disposition of the Teller's mind that points toward Swift's profoundest satiric intentions, which extend beyond the anatomy of madness and the parody of literary Modernism to the characterization of atheism. Related to the Teller's pride and his rage for novelty is his thoroughgoing materialism:[23] he is an egregious instance of that 'new *Modish System* of reducing all to sense' which Swift, together with Pope and the great majority of their contemporaries, regarded as the chief threat to the faith of the age in providential Order. Like his fellow Moderns who, emulating the epicurean account of creation, prefer to 'strike all Things out of themselves, or at least, by Collision, from each other' (p. 135), the Teller in his egoism has repudiated tradition, exalting the self over those 'common Forms' and that 'common Sense' (p. 171) which in this fallen, fallible world must comprise the basis of order in all things, whether in art or morality, society or religion. A complete solipsist, he is confident of his ability to encompass the universe, to fathom every mystery. Whereas reason dictates humility in the face of 'things agreed on all hands impossible to be known' (p. 166), his more sanguine imagination devises 'new Systems' that explain them all away. His author's professed belief in much 'I ne're can hope to see' the Teller disdainfully dismisses as the vulgar faith of timorous and dull-witted men: what the world calls 'madness'—the quality of mind that distinguishes the projectors and system-builders of the world from the common herd—he vastly prefers to wisdom, for without it 'even all Mankind would unhappily be reduced to the same Belief in Things Invisible' (p. 169).

Consequently, though reason and religion declare that the highest realities are both spiritual and ultimately inscrutable, to the Teller every mystery may be known because all things are reducible to sense, to body or to symbol. On the one hand he delights in occult systems—numerology, cabbalism, Rosicrucianism, hermeticism—whose adepts profess to explain and control the world by manipulating arcane signs and symbols of their own devising. This is 'the Republick of *dark* Authors' (p. 186) who boast their own peculiar transforming power, mistaking shadows for substances or turning plain and simple truths into shadows. So, as he labours to bring Jack's story to a close, the Teller primes those readers especially 'whose converting Imaginations', like his own, 'dispose them to reduce all Things into *Types*; who can make *Shadows*, no thanks to the Sun; and then mold them into Substances, no thanks to Philosophy; whose peculiar Talent lies in fixing Tropes and Allegories to the *Letter*, and refining what is Literal into Figure and Mystery' (pp. 189–90).

Mysticism in this sense is merely a subtler form of materialism, like all the Teller's favourite 'Physico-logical' schemes substituting 'a Type, a Sign, an Emblem, a Shadow, a Symbol' (p. 61) for spiritual essences. He compulsively objectifies every abstraction. It is not just that he delights in allegories and metaphors, which for others exist as rhetorical means to an end, implying conceptual truths beyond the power of discursive reason to define, but that he sees them as ends in themselves, as *literal* explanations of the world.[24] For him God *is* the 'Father' who has 'died' (p. 73); religion *is* a coat, embellished with shoulder-knots or torn to shreds; the soul *is* wind; madness, a vapour. Abstract speculations he finds too painful to pursue. As he expounds his theory of the physical basis of madness, for instance, the niceties of his argument lead him out of his proper element: he must by logical discrimination account for the 'Individuation' between such renowned lunatics as '*Alexander the Great, Jack of Leyden,* and

Monsieur *Des Cartes*'. Perplexed, he pauses in an agony of intel-
lection, resolving the difficulty at last by plunging into the void—
that corner of his mind where, in other men, the faculty of reason
resides:

> The present Argument [he complains] is the most abstracted that ever
> I engaged in, it strains my Faculties to their highest Stretch; and I desire
> the Reader to attend with utmost Perpensity; For, I now proceed to
> unravel this knotty Point.
> * THERE is in Mankind a certain * * * * * * * * * *
> *
> *Hic multa* * * * * * * * * * * * * * * * *
> *desiderantur.* * * * * * * * * * * * * * * *
> *
> * * * And this I take to be a clear Solution of the Matter.   (p. 170)

To a mind such as his, in which all concepts must be objectified to
be grasped, the *hiatus in manuscriptis*, the dead blank on the page,
is the literal equivalent for 'abstraction'. In terms of the Teller's
'Physico-logical' system, therefore, it *is* the solution he requires.

His usual shift when confronted with such '*Metaphysical Cob-
web Problems*' (p. 170 n.) is to avoid them altogether by reducing
them to analogous physical terms. To account, for example, for
the pride of priests and politicians and poets who (figuratively
speaking) exalt themselves over other men in order to convert us
to their private views, the Teller renders the verbal arts as oratorical
'Machines'—the pulpit, the ladder, the stage-itinerant—by which
wits of every variety may literally raise themselves above the
multitude. Having translated the idea of spiritual *hauteur* into
a physical equivalent, by an identical procedure he explains why
a position of eminence is effective in communicating knowledge
from speaker to audience. Appealing to 'the System of *Epicurus*',
his favourite philosopher, he construes both the medium and the
message as material substances: not only is air, the acoustical
element, 'a heavy Body', but words themselves, the vehicles of
ideas, are physical objects, having 'Weight' and 'Gravity' and
causing 'deep *Impressions*' when swallowed and digested.

> The deepest Account, and the most fairly digested of any I have yet met
> with, is this, That Air being a heavy Body, and therefore (according to the
> System of *Epicurus*) continually descending, must needs be more so, when
> loaden and pressed down by Words; which are also Bodies of much
> Weight and Gravity, as it is manifest from those deep *Impressions* they
> make and leave upon us; and therefore must be delivered from a due

Altitude, or else they will neither carry a good Aim, nor fall down with a sufficient Force.

Corpoream quoque enim vocem constare fatendum est,
Et sonitum, quoniam possunt impellere Sensus.
Lucr. Lib. 4.

AND I am the readier to favour this Conjecture, from a common Observation; that in the several Assemblies of these Orators, Nature it self hath instructed the Hearers, to stand with their Mouths open, and erected parallel to the Horizon, so as they may be intersected by a perpendicular Line from the Zenith to the Center of the Earth. In which Position, if the Audience be well compact, every one carries home a Share, and little or nothing is lost.   (pp. 60–1)

Or, if Epicurus should prove inadequate to explain the ways in which proselytizers achieve a common understanding with their audience, he may resort to another branch of physics:

For, there is a peculiar *String* in the Harmony of Human Understanding, which in several individuals is exactly of the same Tuning. This, if you can dexterously screw up to its right Key, and then strike gently upon it; Whenever you have the Good Fortune to light among those of the same Pitch, they will by a secret necessary Sympathy, strike exactly at the same time.   (p. 167)

Indeed, so complete a physico-logician is the Teller, it is hardly surprising to learn that the *Tale* itself, like the mind-expanding visions of more recent Moderns, has been chemically induced. With characteristic modesty he informs us that he could never have surpassed Homer in producing 'an universal System in a small portable Volume of all Things that are to be Known, or Believed, or Imagined, or Practised in Life' (p. 125), if he had not ingested a certain curious nostrum, the recipe for which, culled from 'a great Philosopher of O. Brazile', he generously divulges:

YOU take fair correct Copies, well bound in Calfs Skin, and Lettered at the Back, of all Modern Bodies of Arts and Sciences whatsoever, and in what Language you please. These you distil in balneo Mariæ, *infusing* Quintessence of Poppy Q.S., *together with three Pints of* Lethe, *to be had from the Apothecaries. You cleanse away carefully the* Sordes and Caput mortuum, *letting all that is volatile evaporate. You preserve only the first Running, which is again to be distilled seventeen times, till what remains will amount to about two Drams. This you keep in a Glass Viol, Hermetically sealed, for one and twenty Days. Then you begin your Catholick Treatise, taking every Morning fasting, (first shaking the Viol) three Drops of this* Elixir, *snuffing it strongly up your Nose. It will dilate it self about the Brain (where there is any) in fourteen Minutes, and you immediately perceive in your Head an infinite Number of* Abstracts,

Summaries, Compendiums, Extracts, Collections, Medulla's, Excerpta quædam's, Florilegia's *and the like, all disposed into great Order, and reducible upon Paper.* (pp. 126–7)

In the world the Teller inhabits, all things are corporeal, and therefore all things are explicable by number, weight, and measure. It is the world of Epicurus made all too familiar to Swift's con- temporaries in the pages of Hobbes's *Leviathan.*

The climax of this theme in the *Tale* is Section IX, the *'Digression concerning the Original, the Use and Improvement of Madness in a Commonwealth'*, in which the Teller defines happiness, the philo- sopher's *summum bonum*, as *'a perpetual Possession of being well Deceived'* (p. 171). That this is also his author's definition—at least of true happiness, which is founded on Christian self-knowledge, as distinct from 'what is generally understood' by happiness—is most unlikely, since Swift's constant purpose as moralist and divine was to disabuse us of precisely those comfortable delusions about human nature and human life that the Teller cherishes. The felicity the Teller recommends is that which Gulliver so tenaciously clings to, even after the searing epiphany of the Fourth Voyage: a felicity founded on ignorance and pride—on the com- placent belief that men are better than they are, or, if plain experience should prove otherwise, that *we* at least have escaped the universal taint. If to shape our understandings 'by the Pattern of Human Learning' is to become instructed in our 'private Infirmities' (p. 171), the Teller, no less than Gulliver or the reader, inclines to a less disconcerting curriculum.

His definition of happiness is the inevitable consequence of his materialism and solipsism. Only by preferring 'that Wisdom, which converses about the Surface, to that pretended Philosophy which enters into the Depth of Things' (p. 173) can we attain 'the sublime and refined Point of Felicity, called, *the Possession of being well deceived*; The Serene Peaceful State of being a Fool among Knaves' (p. 174). The Teller attributes value only to those things which gratify his senses directly or which submit to the flattering transformations of his fancy. Not memory, which reminds us only too well of what things have been, or reason, which tells us what in fact they are, but imagination is the faculty of mind he prizes, for it 'can build nobler Scenes, and produce more wonderful Revolutions than Fortune or Nature will be at Expence to furnish' (p. 172). Kin to those romantic lovers, painted belles, and idealizing poets whom Swift mocked in verse, he thus refines upon actuality:

> How fade and insipid do all Objects accost us that are not convey'd in the Vehicle of *Delusion?* How shrunk is every Thing, as it appears in the Glass of Nature? So, that if it were not for the Assistance of Artificial *Mediums,* false Lights, refracted Angles, Varnish, and Tinsel; there would be a mighty Level in the Felicity and Enjoyments of Mortal Men.   (p. 172)

But the Teller's idealism is itself a kind of sensuality of the mind, converting unpalatable truths into soothing fantasies. As such it is the psychological extension of his essential epicureanism, reducing reality to what may be apprehended by the senses, which 'never examine farther than the Colour, the Shape, the Size, and whatever other Qualities dwell, or are drawn by Art upon the Outward of Bodies' (p. 173). If reason for such accomplished epicures as Hobbes and Rochester, let us say, is the servant of man's sensual nature, instructing him how best to avoid pain and enhance his enjoyments, it was for Swift the instrument of a higher principle: self-knowledge in the context of Augustinian Christianity. Reason in this sense the Teller rejects, as usual, on hedonistic and aesthetic grounds, for what it reveals is unlovely. Indeed, since it implies moral and spiritual values of which he has no conception, he can deal with it only by means of a physical analogy: the anatomist's dissection of 'Corporeal Beings', a repulsive operation leading predictably to the conclusion that 'the *Outside*' is 'infinitely preferable to the *In*', and therefore a practice to be avoided at all costs (p. 173). As in anatomy, the science of the body, so in philosophy, the science of human nature, the Teller favours those 'projectors'— deists or stoics or Latitudinarian divines, we may suppose—who have found out 'an Art to sodder and patch up the Flaws and Imperfections of Nature'; but he is most at home with the patron and pattern of all those who substitute secular for spiritual explanations of reality:

> And he, whose Fortunes and Dispositions have placed him in a convenient Station to enjoy the Fruits of this noble Art; He that can with *Epicurus* content his Ideas with the *Films* and *Images* that fly off upon his Senses from the *Superficies* of Things; Such a Man truly wise, creams off Nature, leaving the Sower and the Dregs, for Philosophy and Reason to lap up. This is the sublime and refined Point of Felicity, called, *the Possession of being well deceived*; The Serene Peaceful State of being a Fool among Knaves.   (p. 174)

In the wonderland world the Teller inhabits, then—a world apprehended entirely through sense and the imagination—only matter and fantasy are real. Allegories, analogues, metaphors— though '*the Men of Wit and Tast*' (p. 20) for whom Swift wrote will discern their figurative significance, just as they will follow the '*Irony*' that runs through '*the Thread of the whole Book*' (p. 8)— have for the Teller only a literal reference; for abstractions, the Christian mysteries, all things of the spirit are in his system inconceivable, as meaningless as the soul itself, that '*immaterial substance*', was for Hobbes. The Teller is Swift's *reductio ad absurdum* of epicureanism, reducing all to sense in defiance of the Christian belief in 'Things Invisible' or 'impossible to be known'. Twice during his narrative of the three brothers—to Swift's intended audience an allegory of the secularization and disintegration of the Church through worldliness and pride, to the Teller a history pure and simple—he pauses to expound the curious theologies on which his own faith is founded: Sartorism, whose tenets obtained 'especially in the *Grand Monde*, and among every Body of good Fasion' (p. 76), is the physico-logical equivalent of materialism, what Swift had called 'the new *Modish System*'; Æolism, for whose devotees the Teller has 'a peculiar Honour' (p. 161), is the equally physico-logical redaction of spiritualism.

As Pope in *The Dunciad* would render the new epicureanism by parodying the Christian doctrine of creation, Swift in the account of the Tailor-God renders 'material'-ism literally,[25] by spinning out an analogy between Christian ontological conceptions and the 'world' of fashion: since clothes not only make but *are* the man, cloth alone is substance, and the tailor who gives form to this material, daily creating men 'by a kind of Manufactory Operation' (p. 76), is the only Demiurge. As in the little world of man, so in the macrocosm:

THE Worshippers of this Deity had also a System of their Belief, which seemed to turn upon the following Fundamental. They held the Universe to be a large *Suit of Cloaths*, which *invests* every Thing: That the Earth is *invested* by the Air; The Air is *invested* by the Stars; and the Stars are *invested* by the *Primum Mobile*. Look on this Globe of Earth, you will find it to be a very compleat and fashionable *Dress*. What is that which some call *Land*, but a fine Coat faced with Green? or the Sea, but a Wastcoat of Water-Tabby? Proceed to the particular Works of the Creation, you will find how curious *Journey-man* Nature hath been, to trim up the *vegetable* Beaux: Observe how sparkish a Perewig adorns the Head of a *Beech*, and what a fine Doublet of white Satin is worn by the *Birch*. To conclude from all, what is Man himself but a *Micro-Coat*, or rather a compleat Suit of Cloaths with all its Trimmings? As to his Body, there can be no dispute; but examine even the Acquirements of his Mind, you will find them all contribute in their Order, towards furnishing out an exact Dress: To instance no more; Is not Religion a *Cloak*, Honesty a *Pair of Shoes*, worn out in the Dirt, Self-love a *Surtout*, Vanity a *Shirt*, and Conscience a *Pair of Breeches*, which, tho' a Cover for Lewdness as well as Nastiness, is easily slipt down for the Service of both.   (pp. 77–8)

Sartorism, it would seem, accounts not merely for the body, but for the true and spiritual man, his essential being as a moral and rational agent. Its subtlest professors, moreover, refine it still farther, supplying physico-logical proof that the soul itself is the 'outward Dress', the fairest and least corruptible part, by which men are distinguished from all other corporeal animals. These adepts held

that Man was an Animal compounded of two *Dresses*, the *Natural* and the *Celestial Suit*, which were the Body and the Soul: That the Soul was the outward, and the Body the inward Cloathing; that the latter was *ex traduce*; but the former of daily Creation and Circumfusion. This last they proved by *Scripture*, because, *in Them we Live, and Move, and have our Being*: As likewise by Philosophy, because they are *All in All, and All in every Part*.
(pp. 79–80)

St. Paul's definitions of God sartorially applied to man strike the Teller as cogent proof of the clothes theology, but Swift's Christian readers who recall the contexts in scripture will find them an implicit refutation of the materialist philosophy couched in the allegory. In Acts 17, Paul insists before 'certain philosophers of the Epicureans, and of the Stoicks' who had erected an altar to 'the Unknown God', that God, who 'made the world and all things therein . . . dwelleth not in temples made with hands' (not made, that is, like the Tailor's creations, 'by a kind of Manufactory Operation'); since, Paul continues, God 'giveth to all life, and breath, and all things', it is 'in him we live, and move, and have our being'. In 1 Corinthians 15, Paul's purpose is similarly to remind men of the spiritual basis of reality: since we are creatures with immortal souls for whom Christ died, we shall not perish with the body; for though death vanquishes the body, God through Christ has vanquished death and will reign at last 'all in all'.

Sartorism, the systematic objectification of the doctrine of a spiritual creation, is the glorification of man and material substance. Having paused to expound it for us, the Teller resumes his narrative, which, like all good Augustan poets, he sees as the imitation in art of the Logos—in this case, of the sartorial Word: 'And so leaving these broken Ends, I carefully gather up the chief Thread of my Story, and proceed' (p. 81). As the Tailor weaves the world, so the *Tale*-or fashions the crazy fabric of his own creation. The episode is Swift's sardonic parable of the materialization of the world *à la mode*. The *Tale* itself, the Teller's own 'outward dress', is the formal expression of this theme.

In Section VIII the process of universal secularization which the Teller finds so congenial is carried still farther, to include those who, ostensibly despising the body, profess to believe in the spirit, and in inspiration as the way to truth. Primarily, of course, Swift's satire is directed against religious enthusiasm: the persuasion, leading to the proliferation of sects and to the contempt of the 'common Forms' of worship, that the Holy Spirit communicates directly with individuals without the mediation of the Church. This for Swift was fanaticism, a kind of madness: the delusion of presumptuous and self-serving men that they were prophets and apostles all. Here, as in *The Mechanical Operation of the Spirit* (1704), he insinuates that all such 'Spiritual' ecstasies are the sublimation of 'Carnal' impulses (p. 157). By the physico-logical method which is the key to ontology in the Teller's world, the Æolists arrive at their religion by reducing the terms '*Spiritus, Animus, Afflatus . . . Anima*' (p. 151) to their literal significations only: hence spirit becomes wind, the soul becomes breath, physical substances. 'THE Learned *Æolists*, maintain the Original Cause of all Things to be *Wind*, from which Principle this whole Universe was at first pro-duced, and into which it must at last be resolved . . .' (p. 150). The gods of their religion, therefore, 'whom they worshipped, as the Spirits that pervade and enliven the Universe' (p. 154), are the four winds, the physical equivalent of a spiritual Providence. Esteeming flatulence the greatest good, their priests induce this happy state by both natural and artificial means, gaping into storms or applying bellows to the breech in order at last to edify their disciples with farts and belches. Like all things in the Teller's world, the divine essence itself is physical, and therefore con-veniently transportable for distribution among the faithful: being trapped by priests, it may be fetched 'from the Fountain Head, in certain *Bladders*' and disploded 'among the Sectaries in all Nations,

who did, and do, and ever will, daily Gasp and Pant after it'
(p. 155). As with the spirit, so with the cultivation of the mind, since
words, the instruments of learning, may be reduced to airy nothing
by syllogism: '*Words are but Wind; and Learning is nothing but
Words*; Ergo, *Learning is nothing but Wind*' (p. 153). The episode of
Æolism completes utterly the Teller's corporealization of the
universe.

Materialism and that particular species of megalomania which
makes self the centre of creation, despising 'common Forms' and
'common Sense', are Swift's principal targets in *A Tale of a Tub*.
For the Anglican community in the second half of the seventeenth
century, these evils were pre-eminently embodied in Hobbes's
Leviathan, 'from whence the terrible Wits of our Age are said to
borrow their Weapons', threatening the safety of the ship of state,
the established order in 'Religion and Government' (pp. 39–40).
Swift's method is obliquely to endorse the order of things by
exposing to our view the image and consequences of disorder,
both the nature of confusion and its form. If, according to the
Christian humanist tradition, an analogy obtained between
macrocosm and microcosm, the souls of wits and philosophers
might be said to mirror their worlds. Since he denied Providence
and a rational Order to the universe, mind for Epicurus must be
the chaos from which cogent thought fortuitously springs; and
Descartes himself is the vortex of a world created in his own
image:

> *Epicurus* [the Teller assures us] modestly hoped, that one Time or other,
> a certain Fortuitous Concourse of all Mens Opinions, after perpetual
> Justlings, the Sharp with the Smooth, the Light and the Heavy, the Round
> and the Square, would by certain *Clinamina*, unite in the Notions of *Atoms*
> and *Void*, as these did in the Originals of all Things. *Cartesius* reckoned to
> see before he died, the Sentiments of all Philosophers, like so many lesser
> Stars in his *Romantick* System, rapt and drawn within his own *Vortex*.
>
> (p. 167)

The world of the *Tale* similarly reflects the 'realities' in which
the Teller, its 'Secretary', believes: solipsism, corporealism, the
irrational. The form of the *Tale*, in accordance with the Augustan
doctrine of imitation, is the expression and embodiment of that
world: in style egoistical, conceited, rambling; in texture concrete;
in design confused. In strictest logic, perhaps, the Augustan
analogy between literary and ontological form as applied to

epicureanism would best be served by the word-machine that Gulliver finds at the Academy of Lagado, by which, through the chance arrangements of linguistic elements, the operator hopes to produce 'a compleat Body of all Arts and Sciences', though unhappily he has succeeded only in accumulating several large folio volumes of broken sentences.[26] The Teller's book will do, however, as an approximation of the Book of Nature according to Epicurus, Hobbes, and Descartes. Swift's intention in the *Tale*, like that of the true critic, is to 'divide every Beauty of Matter or of Style from the Corruption that Apes it' (p. 92), and so to distinguish reason from madness, the spirit from the letter, order from confusion.

ii. *Sterne: The Poetics of Sensibility*

Well into his ninth and final volume, Tristram Shandy openly invites comparison of his autobiography with Swift's equally zany masterpiece, claiming an immortality for his *Life and Opinions* as deserved as that which 'the *Legation of Moses*, or the *Tale of a Tub*'[27] will enjoy. In this, as 'Posterity' has proved by confirming half the prediction, he was a better prophet than Dr. Johnson,[28] for, though sufficiently 'odd' by neo-classical standards, *Tristram Shandy* has lasted. Indeed—to apply a more recent standard of literary merit, no less infallible—it appears in retrospect the most 'relevant' production of the age, the age which marked, as Leo Spitzer put it, 'the great caesura'[29] between the old ideology and the new. It was Sterne, Earl Wasserman observes,[30] not Johnson or Burke or Gibbon, who sensed most surely the intellectual currents stirring in the latter half of the eighteenth century, currents that soon enough would sweep away the traditional grounds of faith and morality which had nourished and, as we have seen, in a sense determined the forms of art.

From the viewpoint of Augustan aesthetics, certainly, *Tristram Shandy* and *A Tale of a Tub* seem 'odd' in similar ways. As a narrator, Tristram is as obstinate as the Teller in straying from the straight road: there are so many irresistible 'views and prospects' (p. 28) that beckon him, and he 'will not balk' his fancy (p. 55) for the mean considerations of method and regularity. His style, too, is 'wild' (p. 398), a rhapsody (p. 27) of broken sentences, interjections, interruptions, non-sequiturs—in short, a philosopher's nightmare. For Hume at mid century, as earlier for Hobbes and

Swift, prose such as this, lacking all order and design, resembled 'the ravings of a madman'.[31] Tristram also seems to share with the Teller the conviction that men are irrational, creatures more of the senses than of the spirit:

> I said, 'we are not stocks and stones'—'tis very well. I should have added, nor are we angels, I wish we were,—but men cloathed with bodies, and governed by our imaginations;—and what a junketting piece of work of it there is, betwixt these and our seven senses, especially some of them, for my own part, I own it, I am ashamed to confess.   (p. 273)

'REASON is', for him, 'half of it, SENSE' (p. 376). For Swift, as we have seen, this was the fatal syndrome of Modernism, the disease of an age whose idols were self and the body; and the Teller, who personifies these corruptions of the Christian humanist ideal, is the object of his author's devastating mockery. In *Tristram Shandy*, however, the ethos that informed Swift's irony has given way to a new understanding of the human condition for which the appropriate literary response is no longer satire, but farce and pathos. It is because he is a 'modern' man that Tristram Shandy— like Sterne, like his reader—is a 'small HERO', 'the continual sport of what the world calls Fortune' (p. 8). Not pride, but the mind itself isolates the Shandys within themselves; not reason, but the heart and senses and imagination offer the hope of release and communion. In the different attitudes of Swift and Sterne to method and confusion, judgement and fancy, mind and body, we may discern the passing of traditional values and the emergence of a new conception, based on a new definition of human nature, of the ways in which the literary artist imitates life. As eccentric in its architecture (whose unevenness annoys Walter, the man of reason (p. 251)) as in the lives of its inhabitants, Shandy Hall is the theatre of the modern world.

It is not, of course, 'modern' in all its appearances. For one thing, the Shandys themselves profess to believe in a providential universe. To Toby, the pious warrior, 'providence brings good out of every thing', even gunpowder (p. 435); and the Deity is both 'the Father' of compassion (p. 437), and the perfect judge whose wisdom will at last distinguish the hypocrite from the honest man (p. 320). Man in affliction, he counsels Walter, despondent over the accident to Tristram's nose, is 'upheld by the grace and the assistance of the best of Beings' (p. 208). Even Walter, to whom such religious comforts merely cut 'the knot' of life's tangled skein when an ingenious hypothesis or two might untie it, can use a Christian argument on occasion (p. 455). And Tristram, though he doubts, shrewdly enough, that the Christian religion will survive another half century (p. 377), pays his respects to 'the Disposer of all things' (p. 375), whose 'infinite wisdom . . . dispenses every thing', including the proportions of wit and judgement in the human mind, 'in exact weight and measure' (p. 146).

But what is remarkable, and finally ominous, about Tristram's autobiography is that in it the Shandys, good and faithful Christians though they may be, are seen to inhabit a world defined in *human* terms alone. The idea of Providence that helped to determine the special character of *Tom Jones* and *The Vicar of Wakefield* as works of art is in *Tristram Shandy* merely incidental and perfunctory. The Shandys act out the bumbling comedy of their lives not against the generous and reassuring background of cosmic Order, but within a frame as constricted as a country parish and as muddled as the mind of man. Their 'world', like that of the village midwife, is no more 'than a small circle described upon the circle of the great world, of four *English* miles diameter, or thereabouts, of which the cottage where the good old woman lived, is supposed to be the centre' (p. 9)—a circle, Tristram continues, 'of which kind every soul living, whether he has a shirt to his back or no,—has one surrounding him' (p. 27). In *Tristram Shandy* not Nature or Nature's God, but the self is the hub of the universe. This was the lesson that, first among contemporary novelists, Sterne drew from Locke, whose 'glory' it was 'to free the world from the lumber of a thousand vulgar errors' (pp. 149–50).[32] Since, as Locke argued, there are no innate ideas, it might be seen to follow that our apprehension of the world, and therefore our understanding of ourselves, will be relative and problematical, differing for each individual according to his experience. Nature, which Pope and his fellow Augustans had regarded as 'One *clear, unchang'd,* and *Universal* Light'—the 'just Standard' by which reasonable men regulated their lives and the ideal pattern for the artist's imitation— could now no longer be confidently regarded as an objective and uniform phenomenon, divinely ordained and for all men at all times 'still the same'.[33] Reality is now no longer something external to the individual—something 'out there' to which he must relate in prescribed ways; it has become internal and subjective, a world, as it were, of his own involuntary creating whose tenuous order, imposed by the mechanical operations of the mind organizing a multiplicity of sensations, is for each man private and arbitrary and unique.

This is one implication of Sterne's epigraph from Epictetus: 'It is not things themselves that disturb men, but their judgments about these things.' As the title-page warns us, we are not to expect adventures and certainties in this book, but the life and especially the *opinions* of one individual man, 'Tristram Shandy, Gentleman'. *Tom Jones* and *The Vicar of Wakefield* may be read as paradigm and parable because they were written from the conviction that Truth, like human nature, is one and ever the same, that the drama of each individual life, however unique in its particular circumstances, recapitulates the drama of the human condition in general unfolding under the eye of Providence. Through the 'Individual' Fielding implies the 'Species'. Though Tristram expects his book to be 'no less read than the *Pilgrim's Progress* itself' (p. 5), his own life is no allegory because there is no longer any common system of belief, no 'higher' reality beyond itself, to which it can relate. If Vanity Fair was Bunyan's emblem for the world, whose proper character all men might recognize if they would, for Tristram the metaphor has another significance, connoting the separateness and relativism of life: 'every man will speak of the fair as his own market has gone in it;—for which cause I affirm it over again to be one of the vilest worlds that ever was made' (p. 8). The world is indeed a different and ultimately a private place for each of the Shandys. By his own admission, Tristram is 'a most tragicomical completion of his [father's] prediction, "That I should neither think, nor act like any other man's child . . ."' (p. 462). Walter, too, is unique, his peculiar angle of vision distorting his perception of the world so that he becomes, in effect, the creator of his own private universe:

> The truth was, his road lay so very far on one side, from that wherein most men travelled,—that every object before him presented a face and section of itself to his eye, altogether different from the plan and elevation of it seen by the rest of mankind.—In other words, 'twas a different object,—and in course was differently considered . . .   (p. 289)

Our 'preconceptions', Tristram observes as Toby misconstrues another of his brother's metaphors, have 'as great a power over the sounds of words as the shapes of things . . .' (p. 450). The most explicit statement in the novel of this subjectivism, however, is

Walter's dissertation on time and duration, that invaluable, though regrettably abortive, contribution to 'the *Ontologic treasury*' (p. 142) which he has borrowed from Locke:

> *For if you will turn your eyes inwards upon your mind,* continued my father, *and observe attentively, you will perceive, brother, that whilst you and I are talking together, and thinking and smoaking our pipes: or whilst we receive successively ideas in our minds, we know that we do exist, and so we estimate the existence, or the continuation of the existence of ourselves, or any thing else commensurate to the succession of any ideas in our minds, the duration of ourselves, or any such other thing, co existing with our thinking,—and so according to that preconceived*—You puzzle me to death, cried my uncle Toby.— (p. 141)

The Shandys find life puzzling in more ways than one. It remains an enigma despite Walter's hypotheses or Toby's simple piety or Tristram's desperate efforts to encompass it within the nine volumes of his autobiography:

> But mark, madam, we live amongst riddles and mysteries—the most obvious things, which come in our way, have dark sides, which the quickest sight cannot penetrate into; and even the clearest and most exalted understandings amongst us find ourselves puzzled and at a loss in almost every cranny of nature's works . . . (p. 219)

Though a different place for each of them, the world bears nevertheless a common aspect: inexplicable even when it appears most obvious, overwhelming in its multiplicity, unpredictable in its contingencies, it bewilders and eludes them all—and they themselves, as Tristram protests to the commissary at Lyons, are the heart of the enigma:

> —My good friend, quoth I—as sure as I am I—and you are you—
> —And who are you? said he.—Don't puzzle me; said I. (p. 400)[34]

In *Tristram Shandy* traditional explanations of the human condition have given way to a distinctly 'modern' view of man based on Lockean epistemology. As *Tom Jones* is the fictional embodiment of the Augustan ethos most memorably articulated in *An Essay on Man*, Sterne's remarkable book is the objectification in art of the new subjectivism implicit in *An Essay Concerning Human Understanding*, the work that Tristram calls 'a history-book . . . of what passes in a man's own mind' (p. 66) and that his author valued next to the Bible.[35] However orthodox he may have been as a priest, as a novelist Sterne conceived the curse of Adam not in Christian terms, according to the Augustinian doctrine of innate depravity, but in terms of the new philosophy: as the nature of the mind itself, whose mechanism, beyond our power to control, limits our knowledge of the world to our experience of it, isolating the individual within the prison of the self. Solipsism, which for Swift or Fielding, let us say, is the consequence of pride and self-love, is for Sterne a condition of life which can be mitigated neither by the will nor by the reason, but by feeling and the imagination. The mind itself has become the marplot of Eden. Mechanically associating 'ideas which have no connection in nature' (p. 7)—ideas such as the winding of a clock and the act of sexual intercourse—it inhibits, at times prevents, communion and relationship with other human beings. From one point of view, the hilarious opening chapter of *Tristram Shandy* may be seen as Sterne's arch reinterpretation of the Augustinian doctrine that the Children are victimized by the mistakes of the Parents: it is not 'sin' which spoils Tristram's conception—'the effects of which I fear I shall carry with me to my grave' (p. 7)—but the mind, its irksome mechanism of confinement and frustration:

> *Pray, my dear*, quoth my mother, *have you not forgot to wind up the clock?—* Good G—*!* cried my father, making an exclamation, but taking care to moderate his voice at the same time,—*Did ever woman, since the creation of the world, interrupt a man with such a silly question?* (p. 4)

Intercourse of a verbal kind is equally unsatisfactory, Sterne implies, either because of the dullness of our understandings—for which reason Walter's conversation with his wife in their 'Bed of Justice' is as one-sided as any Socratic dialogue (pp. 332–3)—or because of the mind's tendency to draw from language only those meanings and connotations which conform to our private prejudices and predispositions. Toby, for example, conditioned past all redeeming to a world of armaments and fortifications, is as apt a demonstration of Bergson's theory of comedy as one could wish. The mechanism of his brain registers only those snatches of discourse that relate to his obsession:

> Now, whether we observe it or no, continued my father, in every sound man's head, there is a regular succession of ideas of one sort or other, which follow each other in train just like—A train of artillery? said my uncle Toby.—A train of a fiddlestick! quoth my father,— (p. 141)

Responding in conversation by preconditioned reflexes, Toby

might serve as a case study from B. F. Skinner's notebook. Dr. Slop's sudden arrival inevitably brings Stevinus to his mind (pp. 83 ff.). Walter's contortions while reaching for his pocket with his opposite hand remind his brother of the returning angle of the traverse where he incurred his wound at Namur (p. 120). As Walter, lamenting the accident to Tristram's nose, asks, 'did ever a poor unfortunate man . . . receive so many lashes?' Toby recalls the flogging of a grenadier in Makay's regiment (p. 206). As Yorick in an unguarded moment uses the phrase 'point blank' metaphorically, Toby rises 'to say something upon projectiles' (p. 240). Though he is the soul of complaisance and wishes to be attentive to please his brother, Toby's mind will not turn upon any subject alien to his private experience and preoccupations. His fancy strays to the bowling-green as Walter lectures upon Prignitz, but it returns, 'quick as a note could follow the touch', when he hears the word 'siege' (p. 178).

Toby is only the most notable instance in the novel of Sterne's view that men are governed not by reason, but by their imagination, which is in turn conditioned by sensuous experience—by those circumstances in life which wound us or give us pleasure. Noting that a thin man like himself must see the world differently from a corpulent philosopher such as Bishop Hall, Tristram professes to admire the Pythagoreans, who sought a life of pure ratiocination; but he is aware that there is no escape from the body, that our estimation of things, our thoughts and our ideals, are determined by our humours and appetites:

> I love the *Pythagoreans* (much more than ever I dare tell my dear *Jenny*) for their . . . *'getting out of the body, in order to think well'*. No man thinks right whilst he is in it; blinded, as he must be, with his congenial humours, and drawn differently aside, as the bishop and myself have been, with too lax or too tense a fibre—REASON is, half of it, SENSE; and the measure of heaven itself is but the measure of our present appetites and concoctions—
>
> (p. 376)

This passage is at the heart of Sterne's philosophy of human life and character in *Tristram Shandy*. He sees the mind as not only imprisoned in the body, but controlled by it—our apprehension of the world and of ourselves determined by our senses. His metaphor for this fact is the Hobby-horse, at once the source of our limitations and frustrations (and therefore of much of the novel's comedy), and a means of our survival in a vexing and incomprehensible world.[36] As Tristram assures us in dedicating his autobiography to the highest bidder, the Hobby-horse is 'a kind of background to the whole' (p. 13). Superficially at least, Sterne's notion of the Hobby-horse seems only another, more whimsical version of the theory of the ruling passion popular in contemporary psychology and most memorably stated in Pope's *Epistle to Cobham* and the *Essay on Man*. 'WHEN a man', Tristram observes, 'gives himself up to the government of a ruling passion,—or, in other words, when his HOBBY-HORSE grows head-strong,—farewell cool reason and fair discretion!' (p. 71). If we would know the characters of men, Pope's advice is to 'Search then the Ruling Passion'.[37] Accordingly, Tristram 'will draw my uncle *Toby*'s character from his HOBBY-HORSE' (p. 57).

Both concepts apparently lend themselves to a deterministic view of human nature: we do not choose to be driven by the appetites that motivate our actions. In the Christian humanist tradition, however, as it was understood by Pope and Swift and Fielding, the passions may be governed by reason and the will, bringing the self into conformity with moral norms divinely sanctioned and accepted by society. In *Tristram Shandy*, on the other hand, the notion of the Hobby-horse does not function in an ethical, but rather in an epistemological and ontological context, as the vehicle for the relativist view of reality which Sterne found to be implicit in Locke's subjectivism. Walter's hypotheses, Toby's military games, Tristram's obsession with capturing his life on paper—each is the manifestation of the mind's instinctive attempt to organize experience, to impose on the painful and disconcerting multiplicity of things an order and a meaning it otherwise would lack. The order his Hobby-horse affords is real enough and necessary to the rider, but in an absolute sense it is illusory and, as a guide to life, continually belied by intractable circumstances and contingencies. In *A Tale of a Tub* this habit of mind is equivalent to madness, for Swift, like those other Augustans we have been considering, believed that the Order of things was objectively founded and discernible to the eye of reason. But if, as Bacon implied, the old cosmology was itself a kind of hobby-horsical construct testifying to man's natural inclination to organize actuality according to his preconceptions;[38] and if, as Locke reasoned, there are no innate ideas, no one and universal conception of reality— then, in Swift's sense, we are all system-builders inhabiting private worlds of our own imagining. In *Tristram Shandy*, for the first time in English fiction, Sterne explored these implications of the new philosophy.

His attitude toward the Hobby-horse is ambivalent. On the one hand, it is an obsession narrowing the range of possible responses to life and, as it affects our relationships with others, potentially destructive. On the other hand, it is the mind's defence against the bewildering and often inimical world that threatens to overwhelm us. Controlling our perception of the world, the Hobby-horse limits and distorts reality, completing the process of self-enclosure which the mechanism of the mind already assures. Walter's way, as Tristram remarks, 'was to force every event in nature into an hypothesis, by which means never man crucified TRUTH at the rate he did' (p. 494). And as Walter's continually abortive efforts to converse with his brother or 'hang up' inferences within his wife's 'head-piece' (p. 111) make clear, the Hobby-horse co-operates with other causes (stupidity, for example) to prevent communication. In *Tristram Shandy*, as Rebecca West has somewhere observed of life, there are no dialogues, only intersecting monologues. Happiness, Swift ironically declared in *A Tale of a Tub*, is '*a perpetual Possession of being well Deceived*'. In *Tristram Shandy* Sterne in effect accepts that definition, for the mind as he sees it, being limited by its dependence on the senses, must find contentment if at all only in a partial and imperfect vision of a world too vast to comprehend, too enigmatic to explain. Our Hobby-horses are based on the delusion—but a delusion necessary to enable us to function at all—that the order we impose on the world and in terms of which we govern and solace our lives, is equivalent to Truth, that our private ontologies may substitute for Reality.

They are, therefore, inevitably a source of our discomfiture, and of Sterne's droll estimation of the farce of life. Walter, whose only happiness is the conviction that he may control the world with an ingenious hypothesis, is perpetually disappointed by circumstances:

Will not the gentle reader pity my father from his soul?—to see an orderly and well-disposed gentleman, who tho' singular,—yet inoffensive in his notions,—so played upon in them by cross purposes;—to look down upon the stage, and see him baffled and overthrown in all his little systems and wishes; to behold a train of events perpetually falling out against him, and in so critical and cruel a way, as if they had purposedly been plann'd and pointed against him, merely to insult his speculations.—In a word, to behold such a one, in his old age, ill-fitted for troubles, ten times in a day suffering sorrow;—ten times in a day calling the child of his prayers TRISTRAM!—Melancholy dissyllable of sound! which, to his ears, was unison to *Nincompoop*, and every name vituperative under heaven.—By his ashes! I swear it,—if ever malignant spirit took pleasure, or busied itself by traversing the purposes of mortal man,—it must have been here;—   (pp. 42–3)

Tristram himself must admit the hopelessness of his own efforts to bend life to his wishes. A year after he completed the first instalment of his autobiography, Tristram, 'having got . . . almost into the middle of my fourth volume—and no farther than to my first day's life', recognizes that he cannot make his pen keep pace with time: 'as at this rate I should just live 364 times faster than I should write—It must follow, an' please your worships, that the more I write, the more I shall have to write' (p. 214). Our Hobby-horses, furthermore, however innocently we mount them, not only increase our own frustrations, but prove troublesome to others. Dr. Slop's darling forceps, Toby's requiring the lead weights of window sashes to cast his toy cannons, Walter's teaching that names and noses have magical powers over the lives of men—all have their awkward and debilitating consequences for Tristram:

Unhappy *Tristram*! child of wrath! child of decrepitude! interruption! mistake! and discontent! What one misfortune or disaster in the book of embryotic evils, that could unmechanize thy frame, or entangle thy filaments! which has not fallen upon thy head, or ever thou camest into the world—what evils in thy passage into it!—What evils since!—   (pp. 221–2)

Paradoxically, though it limits and annoys, the Hobby-horse is also our solace and compensation in a puzzling, injurious world. However absurd and fugitive its pleasures, however inadequate as a means to Truth, it is for each of the Shandys his stay against confusion:

'Tis the sporting little filly-folly which carries you out for the present hour—a maggot, a butterfly, a picture, a fiddle-stick—an uncle *Toby*'s siege— or an *any thing*, which a man makes a shift to get a stride on, to canter it away from the cares and solicites of life—'Tis as useful a beast as is in the whole creation—nor do I really see how the world could do without it—   (p. 450)

As Walter sees it, and as it functions in the lives of all the Shandys, it is something more than a temporary diversion from care; it is the expression of our instinctive desire to endure, to find compensations for the blows and disappointments life deals us. His hopes in Tristram's nose having been dashed, he will offset the evil by christening his son Trismegistus, thereby counterbalancing the failure of one favourite hypothesis by the prompt application of another. So, he observes to Toby, explaining man's resiliency in the 'rugged journey' of life, there is a 'great and elastic power within us of counterbalancing evil, which like a secret spring in a well-ordered machine, though it can't prevent the shock—at least it imposes upon our sense of it' (p. 209).

But it is Toby himself whose Hobby-horse supplies the paradigm of this reflexive capacity of the mind to reduce life, the destructive element, to a form which may be mastered and enjoyed. Toby's obsession with model fortifications grew during his painful recuperation from the groin wound he received at the siege of Namur, and it is the means of his recovery. At first, frustrated in his attempt to beguile the pain of the wound by recounting the history of it, Toby aggravated rather than eased his condition. The inadequacy of language to recreate the experience so that it might be either shared by others or comprehended by himself compounds his perplexity and despair: 'his life', as Tristram expresses it, 'was put in jeopardy by words' (p. 67). Only by objectifying the experience—by turning from words to maps, so that he can 'stick a pin upon the identical spot of ground where he was standing in when the stone struck him' (p. 64)—is he able to master and exorcise it; and this principle once learned he extends to all battles, the activity that once defined his life, procuring plans and histories of the fortified towns of Italy and France, 'all which he would read with that intense application and delight, that he would forget himself, his wound, his confinement, his dinner' (p. 68). His wound is finally cured, however, only when the process of objectification is complete: contracting the theatre of war to the Lilliputian dimensions of a sheltered bowling-green, Toby methodically reenacts Marlborough's campaigns, now towering over and safely controlling the violent world that injured him. Tristram's own Hobby-horse similarly enables him to recreate, to objectify by committing to paper, the experiences of a life which he too, though a 'small HERO', has found a kind of warfare upon earth, suffering the slings and arrows of Fortune—that 'ungracious Duchess' who 'in every stage of my life, and at every turn and corner where she could get fairly at me . . . has pelted me with a set of as pitiful

misadventures and cross accidents as ever small HERO sustained'
(p. 8). His book, he trusts,

. . . shall make its way in the world, much better than its master has done
before it—Oh *Tristram*! *Tristram*! can this but be once brought about—the
credit, which will attend thee as an author, shall counterbalance the many
evils which have befallen thee as a man—thou wilt feast upon the one—
when thou hast lost all sense and remembrance of the other!—   (p. 255)

The Hobby-horse, then, though a mixed blessing, is a way of
ordering life and of coping with it. In a sense that delightfully
anticipates more recent psychological theory, it is also a way of
displacing and sublimating sexual urges that Sterne, rather like
Freud, appears to have regarded as the common denominator of
the human condition.[39] If Toby's groin wound led to his obsession
with military games, it was also the cause of the 'extream and
unparallel'd modesty' of his nature (pp. 50–1); he knows, as
Walter remarks in exasperation, not 'so much as the right end of
a woman from the wrong' (p. 77). As he journeys, eager and blush-
ing, to the country to take possession of his bowling-green, Toby's
Hobby-horse seems surrogate for another kind of passion:

Never did lover post down to a belov'd mistress with more heat and
expectation, than my uncle *Toby* did, to enjoy this self-same thing in
private;—I say in private;—for it was sheltered from the house, as I told
you, by a tall yew hedge, and was covered on the other three sides, from
mortal sight, by rough holly and thickset flowering shrubs; so that the idea
of not being seen, did not a little contribute to the idea of pleasure pre-
conceived in my uncle *Toby*'s mind.   (p. 75)

Only when the Treaty of Utrecht puts an end to his games on the
green does Toby turn his attention to the Widow Wadman and
begin 'to lay siege to that fair and strong citadel' (p. 154). Though
he takes no pleasure in sex, regarding a certain connubial office as
a duty to be performed, as seldom as justice will allow, for the sake
of posterity, Walter, too, can yet find rapture in a prologue on long
noses: 'when my father got home', Tristram relates, 'he solaced
himself with *Bruscambille* after the manner, in which, 'tis ten to
one, your worship solaced yourself with your first mistress,—that
is, from morning even unto night' (p. 167). As for Tristram, among
'the many evils' which have befallen him 'as a man' and for which
his book must serve as compensation, we may recall the time he
was left standing before his Jenny, garters in hand, 'reflecting upon
what had *not* pass'd'—a disaster 'the most oppressive of its kind

which could befall me as a man, proud, as he ought to be, of his manhood—' (p. 395).

None of the Shandys, not even Walter's bull, is very happy in sexual matters: they are interrupted, damaged in tender parts, impotent. The world the novel presents is one of frustration and misadventure in the most essential human relationship. Though Sterne is not quite to be regarded as a precursor of Lawrence, who seems to have shared Walter Shandy's opinion that 'there is no passion so serious as lust' (p. 456), yet his sexual comedy is directly related to the novel's profoundest philosophical theme: the problem, implicit in Locke's epistemology, of human isolation, the imprisonment of the individual within the self. The solution to that problem, also implicit in Locke, Sterne found in the role the senses played in relating the self to the outside world, and in the emphasis on the social affections explicit in Shaftesbury and the Latitudinarian divines. Throughout *Tristram Shandy* the mind constricts, the senses enlarge the soul. Though an agile hypothesizer, Walter's efforts to make his brother understand him are frustrated rather than furthered by the dubious 'gift of ratiocination and making syllogisms'; reason, indeed, is in one sense the measure of our fallen condition, 'for in superior classes of beings, such as angels and spirits,—'tis all done, may it please your worships, as they tell me, by INTUITION' (p. 177). It is 'the weakness and imbecility of human reason' (p. 418) that Sterne's comedy makes us conscious of, opposing the mechanical operations of the mind to the sure knowledge of the heart.

To translate the language of the heart, Tristram assures us as he ponders Slawkenbergius's tale of Diego and Julia, requires 'a sixth sense':

—What can he mean by the lambent pupilability of slow, low, dry chat, five notes below the natural tone,—which you know, madam, is little more than a whisper? The moment I pronounced the words, I could perceive an attempt towards a vibration in the strings, about the region of the heart.— The brain made no acknowledgment.—There's often no good understanding betwixt 'em.—I felt as if I understood it.—I had no ideas.—The movement could not be without cause.—   (pp. 204–5)

Sterne's reputation as a novelist of sentiment is, of course, founded on such passages. Not ratiocination but feeling, not discourse so much as moments of non-verbal, sensuous communion—a gesture, a caress, an attitude of body or a tone of voice—are the means to understanding. Of this the most famous example in the novel is 'the lesson of universal good-will' that Tristram learns from Toby's kindness to a fly:

> I was but ten years old when this happened;—but whether it was, that the action itself was more in unison to my nerves at that age of pity, which instantly set my whole frame into one vibration of most pleasureable sensation;—or how far the manner and expression of it might go towards it;—or in what degree, or by what secret magick,—a tone of voice and harmony of movement, attuned by mercy, might find a passage to my heart, I know not;—this I know, that the lesson of universal good-will then taught and imprinted by my uncle *Toby*, has never since been worn out of my mind: And tho' I would not depreciate what the study of the *Literæ humaniores*, at the university, have done for me in that respect, or discredit the other helps of an expensive education bestowed upon me, both at home and abroad since;—yet I often think that I owe one half of my philanthropy to that one accidental impression.   (pp. 86–7)

Tristram's analysis of how the experience affected him is reminiscent of the corporealism of Swift's Teller: Toby's action was 'in unison' to his nerves, setting his 'whole frame into one vibration'; its meaning was permanently 'imprinted' on his mind.[40] But here there is no irony intended. Reason for Sterne is, 'half of it, SENSE', and the way to the soul is through the body. Though separated by their Hobby-horses and by the general curse of self-enclosure, the Shandys are united in love and communicate through the unspoken language of the body: the tender glance that penetrates the heart (p. 87), the clasp of hands (pp. 87, 410, 451), the tug of a garment (pp. 465–6), a whistle (pp. 52–3), a dance (pp. 410–11), the shedding of a tear (p. 206)—such are the means of communion in the novel, expressions of feeling that the senses convey directly to the heart.

This, surely, is one explanation—another being that he dearly loved a bawdy joke—for Sterne's apparent obsession with sexuality, the most intimate act of knowledge. In the final chapter of the novel, Walter's diatribe against man's sexual nature serves ironically as an apology for his author's theme and method:

> —THAT provision should be made for continuing the race of so great, so exalted and godlike a Being as man—I am far from denying—but philosophy speaks freely of every thing; and therefore I still think and do maintain it to be a pity, that it should be done by means of a passion which bends down the faculties, and turns all the wisdom, contemplations, and operations of the soul backwards—a passion, my dear, continued my

father, addressing himself to my mother, which couples and equals wise men and fools, and makes us come out of our caverns and hiding-places more like satyrs and four-footed beasts than men.   (p. 495)

If the act of procreation is natural, he complains, why should it have offended the delicacy of philosophers and 'wherefore, when we go about to make and plant a man, do we put out the candle?' Why are all its aspects and appurtenances 'to be conveyed to a cleanly mind by no language, translation, or periphrasis whatever?' With society in general, Walter esteems the 'act of killing and destroying a man' more 'glorious', and the phallic instruments of war more 'honourable':

—We march with them upon our shoulders—We strut with them by our sides—We gild them—We carve them—We inlay them—We enrich them—Nay, if it be but a *scoundril* cannon, we cast an ornament upon the breach of it.—

But Sterne is of another opinion and in *Tristram Shandy* intends, like Yorick, who has listened to Walter's reasoning with dismay, 'to batter the whole hypothesis to pieces'.

For the most part sensuality for the Shandys is a matter of embarrassment and frustration. Once, however, in the scene that closes Tristram's narrative of his race against death, it is the source of joy and harmony and communion, dispelling the curse of human limitation and mortality and providing Tristram a glimpse of Eden on the plains of Languedoc:

O! there is that sprightly frankness which at once unpins every plait of a *Languedocian*'s dress—that whatever is beneath it, it looks so like the simplicity which poets sing of in better days—I will delude my fancy, and believe it is so.   (p. 410)

As the scene unfolds, images that in the Augustan tradition had served as metaphors for Nature's abstract Order—the measured dance, the harmony of reconciled opposites—are humanized, rendering the love and concord in the hearts of men and women. Pope's Vulcan, the figure of the artist transforming a painful world into objects of ideal beauty, reappears, as it were, changed into the 'lame youth, whom *Apollo* had recompenced with a pipe', providing simpler pleasures with a momentary music. At the sound, Tristram kicks off his boots and takes hold of Nanette's hands. 'It taught me to forget I was a stranger.' Her dress unpinned, her hair untied, they dance off as the nymphs and swains sing in harmony, affirming the joy of life and expelling sorrow—the meaning of his name:

> The sister of the youth who had stolen her voice from heaven, sung alternately with her brother—'twas a *Gascoigne* roundelay.
>
> VIVA LA JOIA!
FIDON LA TRISTESSA!
>
> The nymphs join'd in unison, and their swains an octave below them—
>
> I would have given a crown to have it sew'd up—*Nanette* would not have given a sous—*Viva la joia!* was in her lips—*Viva la joia!* was in her eyes. A transient spark of amity shot across the space betwixt us—
>
> (p. 411)

If only for the moment, Tristram is admitted to a world far from the clocks and Hobby-horses of Shandy Hall, a world of innocent sensuality, free and vital, where there are no strangers.

The senses, then, are one means of relationship, the imagination is another. In his Preface, addressed to the 'Anti-Shandeans' among his readers (p. 143) and placed with a Shandean disregard for logic in the midst of his third volume, Tristram hints at this view by disputing Locke's preference for judgement over wit in his analysis of the faculties of the mind. Though he freed the world from 'a thousand vulgar errors', in this belief, Tristram insists, the philosopher was 'bubbled' (p. 149). One reason for Sterne's criticism is apparent in Locke's definition of the two faculties, which represents judgement as working to separate 'ideas wherein can be found the least difference' and wit as working to assemble 'ideas . . . wherein can be found any resemblance'.[41] Judgement, in other words, dis-integrates; wit—for which 'fancy' and 'imagination' are synonymous terms—has the opposite purpose of relating and combining the disparate elements of experience. In a world characterized by multiplicity and separateness, it is the mind's unifying power. In *Tristram Shandy*—through puns, analogues, metaphors, *double entendres* confusing ideas which the judgement would force apart—not the least of its functions is to heighten our sense that our sexual natures supply the common denominator of experience, that Sterne and his reader are joint participants in what Robert Alter has called 'the game of love'.[42]

It is the imagination, furthermore, that unifies the world, relating the Self to the Other, and serves therefore to qualify the solipsism of Hobbes and Locke. For by imaginatively generalizing upon his own experience, the individual may escape the self, sharing empathically in the happiness and distress of others and coming at last to the understanding that self-love and social are the same. In part, it is this sense of the individual's capacity for imaginative projection that informs the doctrines of good nature and universal benevolence which Shaftesbury and the Latitudinarians opposed to Hobbes and the Augustinian tradition. Sterne believed that both things were true: that if men were by nature self-enclosed and self-interested, they were also capable of communion, generosity, and love.[43] Serving as an exemplum of this paradox is the scene in which Toby and Corporal Trim dispute whether a wound to the groin or one to the knee causes the more 'intolerable anguish' (p. 438). The argument cannot be resolved rationally, since each man's experience of pain (or pleasure) is his only measure of what is real; but it can be dissolved into harmony by a higher principle:

> The dispute was maintained with amicable and equal force betwixt my uncle *Toby* and *Trim* for some time; till *Trim* at length recollecting that he had often cried at his master's sufferings, but never shed a tear at his own—was for giving up the point, which my uncle *Toby* would not allow—
> 'Tis a proof of nothing, *Trim*, said he, but the generosity of thy temper—
> So that whether the pain of a wound in the groin (*cæteris paribus*) is greater than the pain of a wound in the knee—or
> Whether the pain of a wound in the knee is not greater than the pain of a wound in the groin—are points which to this day remain unsettled.

It is the mind's capacity imaginatively to make another's experience its own that defines the man of sensibility. For Walter, the 'secret spring' that smooths the rough passages of life is his irrepressible Hobby-horse; for Tristram, it is another sort of mechanism by which the happiness of others is made our own and colours our perception of the world, dissolving the boundaries that separate us and harmonizing the self and Nature:

> —For my uncle *Toby*'s amours running all the way in my head, they had the same effect upon me as if they had been my own—I was in the most perfect state of bounty and good will; and felt the kindliest harmony vibrating within me, with every oscillation of the chaise alike; so that whether the roads were rough or smooth, it made no difference; every thing I saw, or had to do with, touch'd upon some secret spring either of sentiment or rapture.   (p. 483)

In this frame of mind Tristram encounters poor Maria. The compassion and benevolence he feels for her are genuine, but, as he is honest enough to sense, they are not his, or any man's, whole character. As he sits between Maria and her goat listening to her melancholy cadences, his sympathy for her sorrow is balanced by a less generous interest in her, making him aware 'of what a *Beast* man is' (p. 484):

> MARIA look'd wistfully for some time at me, and then at her goat—and then at me—and then at her goat again, and so on, alternately—
> —Well, *Maria,* said I softly—What resemblance do you find?

In *Tristram Shandy,* that curious mixture of bawdy comedy and poignant sentiment, Sterne gave expression to what he took to be the paradox of the human condition, at once the stuff of farce and of pathos. Balancing the views of Hobbes and Locke, Shaftesbury and the Latitudinarians, he saw men as both absurd and lovable, enclosed within themselves by the body and the mind, yet capable of being released from that bondage through feeling and the imagination.

Sterne's disturbance of the formal principles of Augustan aesthetics may be seen, then, in part, as the concomitant of a new ontology, defining reality not as the 'Art of God', an objective construct designed by the divine Geometrician and providentially controlled, whose unchanging Order may be rationally apprehended, but as the subjective creation of the human understanding, a world fashioned by the mechanism of the mind imposing on a multiplicity of random sensations an order idiosyncratic and, with reference at least to any absolute conception of truth, illusory. As Sterne sensed, the 'cosmic syntaxes', to use Earl Wasserman's phrase,[44] had been broken. The world would soon enough no longer seem the well-wrought dramatic Poem of history, inscribed by God's Word with measure, rhyme, and reason, unfolding coherently from Genesis to Apocalypse; it would seem instead the product of the private imagination, responding to the whims of circumstance and the exigencies of desire. Inverting, as it were, the old analogy between macrocosm and microcosm, the individual now defined the structure of his universe. The aimlessness that Swift in *A Tale of a Tub* had presented as the shape of chaos, the projection and embodiment of madness, has become in *Tristram Shandy* the formal expression of a new conception of reality, implying not an aberration from Order, but the imitation of Life.

Not method and reason, the Augustan virtues, but impulse and imagination are the test of truth and the means of communication for Sterne; not symmetry and design, but the 'marbled page' is the 'motly emblem' of his book (pp. 168–70). Throughout the novel Tristram mocks the rules that governed Augustan aesthetics, dismissing them as stultifying and irrelevant; for his subject is life, defined not as in other authors by what a man does—he rebukes his readers for their 'vile pruriency for fresh adventures in all things' (p. 44)—but by what he *is*, the sum of his 'opinions' and feelings. And life in this sense is not to be contained by formal principles (seen now, to use Pope's distinction, as 'devised' by officious critics, rather than 'discovered' in Nature), by arbitrary aesthetic considerations of unities, of beginnings, middles, and ends, but only by the limitations of mortality: birth and death, the quality of experience and the mechanism of the mind. Unique and individual, the narrative of his life, unlike those of Bunyan's Pilgrim or Tom Jones or Dr. Primrose, is neither allegory nor paradigm nor analogue, for it 'stands' for nothing beyond itself. Since Tristram's story is coextensive with himself, it begins, properly, with the night of his begetting; he will trace 'every thing in it, as *Horace* says, *ab Ovo*' (p. 6). He is aware that Horace on formal grounds commended Homer for *not* beginning the *Iliad* with the birth of Helen from Leda's egg, but, he insists, 'in writing what I have set about, I shall confine myself neither to his rules, nor to any man's rules that ever lived'. In *Tristram Shandy*, indeed, the only advocate of the rules of art is Slawkenbergius, whose prodigious tale, with 'all the essential and integrant parts' of a Sophoclean drama 'rightly disposed' in 'the order *Aristotle* first planted them', progresses methodically through '*Protasis, Epistasis, Catastasis*' to its '*Catastrophe* or *Peripeitia*' (p. 199).

Tristram's book, on the contrary, has no more structure than the vagaries of his mind provide. He pleads, disingenuously and of course in vain, for assistance from those shaping '*Powers*' of Augustan art,

—which enable mortal man to tell a story worth the hearing,—that kindly shew him, where he is to begin it,—and where he is to end it,—what he is to put into it,—and what he is to leave out,—how much of it he is to cast into shade,—and whereabouts he is to throw his light! (p. 153)

If the powers of art haven't abandoned him altogether, their visitations are infrequent and felt in peculiarly Shandean ways: at one point in his narrative, in order to achieve his own version of the

Augustan ideal of harmony and proportion, he tears out of his book a particularly fine chapter that threatens to disturb the monotony of his style, thereby ingeniously preserving 'that necessary equipoise and balance, (whether of good or bad) betwixt chapter and chapter, from whence the just proportions and harmony of the whole work results' (p. 238). Indeed, in deference to divines and philosophers, cabbage-planters and mathematicians, he will try, he assures us, to bring the divagations of his narrative under control and 'to go on with my uncle *Toby*'s story, and my own, in a tolerable straight line' (p. 359), aspiring to

the excellency of going on even thus;

---

which is a line drawn as straight as I could draw it, by a writing-master's ruler, (borrowed for that purpose) turning neither to the right hand or to the left.   (p. 360)

But Tristram's method, if crazy and capricious by Augustan standards of regularity and symmetry, is faithful enough as a mirror of the fluid, shifting processes of the mind, working by impulse and association. It is even, as he facetiously remarks, 'the most religious' method, 'for I begin with writing the first sentence—and trusting to Almighty God for the second' (p. 415). What matters in *Tristram Shandy* is not pattern, but the flow of soul, the registering of sensation and the movement of thought. As a man of sensibility, Tristram would revise Descartes's essential premiss: 'I think, *and* feel, and therefore I am.' His procedures as an author reflect a new conception of the doctrine of mimesis, of the way in which form recapitulates ontology. Taking a pair of chapters to record the conversation between Walter and Toby as they descend the stairs, he warns that since they are 'in a talking humour', there may be as many chapters as steps:

—let that be as it will, Sir, I can no more help it than my destiny:— A sudden impulse comes across me—drop the curtain, *Shandy*—I drop it— Strike a line here across the paper, *Tristram*—I strike it—and hey for a new chapter?

The duce of any other rule have I to govern myself by in this affair— and if I had one—as I do all things out of all rule—I would twist it and tear it to pieces, and throw it into the fire when I had done—Am I warm? I am, and the cause demands it—a pretty story! is a man to follow rules— or rules to follow him?   (p. 211)

Sterne rejects the rationalist aesthetic of the Augustans for fancy and free form, imitating not Nature's geometry—what the critics and theologians of the preceding hundred years had seen as her fondness for regularity and symmetry—but her profusion, caprice, and infinite variety. It is the 'variety' his perpetual digressions provide that is 'the sunshine . . . the life, the soul of reading', banishing cold winter (p. 55). Sterne's metaphors for his book suggest Nature's vitality, not her intricate design; freedom, organicism are his aim. If authors and gardeners may be compared, he will plant no cabbages 'one by one, in straight lines, and stoical distances'; he is of a party with Launcelot Brown and Humphry Repton, preferring to express in art Nature's wildness and abhorrence of constraint, where at 'every step that's taken, the judgment is surprised by the imagination' (p. 415). He is least of all a builder of Palladian structures:

> And what of this new book the whole world makes such a rout about?— Oh! 'tis out of all plumb, my Lord,—quite an irregular thing!—not one of the angles at the four corners was a right angle.—I had my rule and compasses, &c. my Lord, in my pocket.—Excellent critic!   (p. 134)

Instead of such readers, give him 'that man whose generous heart will give up the reins of his imagination into his author's hands, —be pleased he knows not why, and cares not wherefore' (p. 135). Give him humour and a spark of genius, 'and send *Mercury*, with the *rules and compasses*, if he can be spared, with my compliments to—'.

But the form of *Tristram Shandy* is a more remarkable development than these explanations would suggest. If from one point of view it represents a new conception of how Nature ought to be imitated in a work of art—by impulse rather than by rule—from another point of view it is not so much a celebration of freedom as a protest against the limitations of the human condition.[45] Behind Sterne's bawdy games and verbal antics one may sense a troubled awareness of man's transiency, impotence, and isolation—the irreducible facts of life which his book is designed to oppose and mitigate, not only by turning them to laughter, but by transmuting them into another substance more lasting, vital, mutual: the substance of his art.

Tristram's book, as we remarked earlier, is an attempt to master and make permanent that most fugitive and puzzling thing, his life. It is the objectification, the palpable projection and embodiment, of his subjective self. His writing, he implies, bears the same relation to his life as the body to the mind, and 'exactly like a jerkin, and a jerkin's lining' the two are inseparable and coextensive; living and writing, he assures us, are 'in my case . . . the same thing' (pp. 120–1). His book, he hopes, will contain and encompass him, excluding 'nothing which has touched me', and by it, therefore, he will know himself and be known to others, a relationship that will 'grow into familiarity' and 'terminate in friendship' (p. 8). He intends to write and publish two volumes of his 'life' every year for as long as he lives (p. 29), which procedure—thanks to the digressive-progressive 'machinery' of his work sustaining it, as the world itself is sustained, by the reconciliation of 'two contrary motions'—he trusts will keep it 'a-going these forty years, if it pleases the fountain of health to bless me so long with life and good spirits' (pp. 54–5). Our sense of the identity of Tristram's life and his book is reinforced by his frequent references to the precise moment and place of composition, inviting us to imagine him in the actual process of writing, which, as he constantly insists, is identical with the processes of his thought and feeling. One consequence of this pretence, in fact, is that his book has become more real to him than his life, providing him with a knowable, even a tangible, identity and serving as a compensation for mortality. Whereas Tristram is the sport of Fortune, frustrated by circumstances, impotent, dying of consumption, his *Life and Opinions* will, he trusts, enjoy a better fate and 'shall make its way in the world, much better than its master has done before it—' (p. 255). Though, as Wayne Booth has argued,[46] Sterne may not have intended to continue his novel beyond the ninth volume, it is clear that the illusion he wished to enforce is that the book is open-ended; for from Tristram's point of view, life itself must end with the final sentence.

Tristram's attempt to make his book contain him must of course fail, for, by his own calculation, he is living '364 times faster' than he can write; 'I shall', he laments, 'never overtake myself' (pp. 214–15). As an author he shares his father's fate, who scribbles away at his *Tristra-pædia* while 'every day a page or two became of no consequence' (p. 284). As we are aware from the first chapter, Time—the clock and all it implies of frustration and mortality—is the marplot of Tristram's life and art. If his book offers him the hope of permanence, of objectifying and fixing the flow of consciousness, the hopelessness of his efforts as an author to 'overtake' himself heightens our sense of the limitations of the human condition and, most especially, of the inevitability of death. If Time is always leaving him behind, Mortality is at his back, 'that death-looking, long-striding scoundrel of a scare-sinner, who is posting after me' (p. 371). The finality of death—Yorick's, Bobby's, the threat of Tristram's own—is one of the less cheerful aspects of the Shandean world, rendered by that memorial to utter darkness and annihilation, the black pages (pp. 25–6), and by 'the mortality of *Trim*'s hat' (p. 273), which brings its meaning home even to Susannah:

> —'Are we not here now;'—continued the corporal, 'and are we not'—(dropping his hat plumb upon the ground—and pausing, before he pronounced the word)—'gone! in a moment?' The descent of the hat was as if a heavy lump of clay had been kneaded into the crown of it.—Nothing could have expressed the sentiment of mortality, of which it was the type and forerunner, like it,—his hand seemed to vanish from under it,—it fell dead,—the corporal's eye fix'd upon it, as upon a corps,—and *Susannah* burst into a flood of tears. (p. 274)

As far as the novel would allow—which is, like life, a temporal mode whose effects must be achieved through the arrangement of words in sequence—Sterne's objective in *Tristram Shandy* was to develop a form that would release us from the bondage of Time. He attempts by various devices to stop the clock, by which previous narratives had been regulated[47]—*Tom Jones*, for example, whose every book carries a signature of the years or weeks or days in which the action transpires. Sterne instead leads us into the timeless regions of the consciousness where past and present are one and simultaneously apprehended: 'for in good truth, when a man is telling a story in the strange way I do mine, he is obliged continually to be going backwards and forwards to keep all tight together in the reader's fancy' (p. 351). The illusion of simultaneity is for the most part achieved by Sterne's digressive technique; the movement 'backwards and forwards' by impulse and the association of ideas, enforcing the distinction which Walter found in Locke between chronological and psychological time, the one ticking out our physical existence, the other dependent upon the succession of ideas in the mind, by which '*we know that we do exist*' (p. 141). In this manner Tristram, fleeing from Death across France, may escape the limitations of time and space:

> —Now this is the most puzzled skein of all—for in this last chapter, as far at least as it has help'd me through *Auxerre*, I have been getting forwards

in two different journies together, and with the same dash of the pen—
for I have got entirely out of *Auxerre* in this journey which I am writing
now, and am got half way out of *Auxerre* in that which I shall write hereafter—There is but a certain degree of perfection in every thing; and by
pushing at something beyond that, I have brought myself into such a situation, as no traveller ever stood before me; for I am this moment walking
across the market-place of *Auxerre* with my father and my uncle *Toby*, in
our way back to dinner—and I am this moment also entering *Lyons* with
my post-chaise broke into a thousand pieces—and I am moreover this
moment in a handsome pavillion built by *Pringello*, upon the banks of the
Garonne, which Mons. *Sligniac* has lent me, and where I now sit rhapso-
dizing all these affairs.   (pp. 393–4)

In the attempt to suggest the simultaneity of time past and time
present in the consciousness, Sterne anticipates, however crudely,
certain experimental novelists of our own century. In treating what
might be called the physical dimension of his narrative, recording
actions which in life must necessarily occur in time, he is no less
inventive, achieving an effect analogous to the 'stop-action' technique of modern cinematography. In Chapter XXI of the first
volume, for example, Toby begins to reply to his brother:

I think, replied my uncle *Toby*, taking his pipe from his mouth, and
striking the head of it two or three times upon the nail of his left thumb,
as he began his sentence,—I think, says he:—   (p. 48)

The description is repeated, and Toby finally allowed to complete
the sentence, ten chapters later (II. vi), Tristram having interrupted
the narrative for that space in order to fill in his uncle's character,
leaving him 'all this while . . . knocking the ashes out of his tobacco
pipe' (p. 49). Similarly, the account of Walter and Toby descending the stairs is slowed down to the point virtually of suspended
animation, as Walter takes a step, draws back his leg, takes the
step over again, and the pair are left at last having progressed no
farther than the first landing (pp. 210–14). But the implications
of this device in terms of what might be called the 'metaphysics' of
Sterne's novel are rendered almost paradigmatically in the scene
where news of Bobby's death is reported in the kitchen: after Trim
drops his hat, the 'type' of mortality, Tristram, so to speak, rewinds
the reel to play the action over again, slowing it down to analyse
its meaning and effect. At such moments, Sterne freezes time, holding an act or gesture indefinitely suspended while allowing the
mind to run free. We have the illusion at least that the threat of

Time has been neutralized and fugitive experience made permanent.

If Sterne found the theory of duration useful in opposing the tyranny of Time, we have seen that he was less happy about another implication of Locke's epistemology: solipsism. Perhaps the most striking emblem in Sterne's works of this fundamental limitation of the human condition is the image of Yorick at the start of his sentimental journey through alien countries, sitting alone in the stationary *désobligeant*, with blinds drawn against the solicitations of charity, writing his Preface on the difficulties of communication. In *Tristram Shandy* Sterne is no less interested in the problem of our isolation and separateness, of how we may be known to others and in turn know them. Before beginning to draw his uncle Toby from his Hobby-horse, Tristram regrets that there is no '*Momus*'s glass' to reveal the characters of men, no window in the human breast by which the soul might be viewed 'stark naked' and 'all her motions,—her machinations' observed (p. 55). Unfortunately, he reminds us, 'our minds shine not through the body, but are wrapt up here in a dark covering of uncrystalized flesh and blood' (p. 56). What Sterne attempts, as it were, is to make his narrative of the Shandys substitute for '*Momus*'s glass', to devise a form by which a printed book might serve to disclose character, through words and images uniting author and reader in a mutual and liberating act of imaginative understanding.

If language traditionally is the medium of rational discourse, through words appealing to the judgement, Sterne had doubts about its efficacy. Like Locke in Book III of the *Essay*, he regarded words as imprecise and treacherous; refracted through the distorting lens of our preconceptions and prejudices, they tend to inhibit communication and to confirm us in our private systems of self-enclosure. Unlike Locke, he preferred imagination to judgement as the agency of understanding. Though novels must of course be written in words and appeal to the judgements of their readers, Sterne strives to overcome the inherent limitations of the form by deliberately exploiting the ambiguities of language so as to engage the reader's imagination: writing, Tristram remarks,

. . . when properly managed, (as you may be sure I think mine is) is but a different name for conversation . . . The truest respect which you can pay to the reader's understanding, is to halve this matter amicably, and leave him something to imagine, in his turn, as well as yourself.

For my own part, I am eternally paying him compliments of this kind, and do all that lies in my power to keep his imagination as busy as my own.

(p. 83)

Occasionally, as in the context in which this passage occurs, Sterne eschews words altogether, inviting the reader to 'imagine' speeches, descriptions, events. He may even provide him with a blank page, so that he may please his 'fancy' by painting the Widow Wadman to his own mind (pp. 356–7). More often, however, he relies on the ambiguities of language to achieve some of his most distinctive comic effects. Most things in Shandy-land— words not least among them—have, as Walter puts it, 'two handles' (p. 78): Toby's references to 'curtins and horn-works' provide Dr. Slop with the opportunity for bawdy punning (pp. 84–5); there is confusion about the meanings of mortars (p. 151), and bridges (p. 153), and noses (pp. 161–2)—most especially, noses. For which reason Tristram finds it inexcusable that he should have neglected to define his terms, the obligation of all true philosophers:

> . . . heaven is witness, how the world has revenged itself upon me for leaving so many openings to equivocal strictures,—and for depending so much as I have done, all along, upon the cleanliness of my reader's imaginations.
> —Here are two senses, cried *Eugenius*, as we walk'd along, pointing with the fore finger of his right hand to the word *Crevice*, in the fifty-second page of the second volume of this book of books,—here are two senses,— quoth he.—And here are two roads, replied I, turning short upon him,— a dirty and a clean one,—which shall we take?—The clean,—by all means, replied *Eugenius*. *Eugenius*, said I, stepping before him, and laying my hand upon his breast,—to define is to distrust.   (p. 162)

But Tristram will define, nevertheless—with such scrupulous exactness that we never afterward encounter the word *nose* in his book without applying a phallic interpretation. At other times Sterne's bawdry is the effect of his relying on our imaginations to fill in hiatuses in his text, or to complete syntactical constructions that he has carefully interrupted—a device best remembered from the final abortive sentence of *A Sentimental Journey*.[48] By such means he breaks down our sense of separateness, implicating the reader in his comedy. If ratiocination multiplies distinctions and confirms us in our solipsism, the imagination—and especially the sexual imagination—reminds us of what we have in common, drawing us out of our 'caverns and hiding-places'.

A further distinctive feature of Sterne's art is his attempt to find alternatives to language as a means of communication. Since we are creatures 'cloathed with bodies, and governed by our imaginations', we are most immediately and powerfully affected not by the abstractions that words imply, but by impressions conveyed directly to the heart by the senses. In this respect, the painter or musician has the advantage over the artist in words, as after Locke eighteenth-century aestheticians such as Jonathan Richardson were well aware:

> Words [Richardson writes] paint to the imagination, but every man forms the thing to himself in his own way: language is very imperfect: there are innumerable colours and figures for which we have no name, and an infinity of other ideas which have no certain words universally agreed upon as denoting them; whereas the painter can convey his ideas of these things clearly, and without ambiguity; and what he says every one understands in the sense he intends it.
>
> And this is a language that is universal; men of all nations hear the poet, moralist, historian, divine or whatever other character the painter assumes, speaking to them in their own mother tongue.
>
> Painting has another advantage over words; and that is, it pours ideas into our minds, words only drop them. The whole scene opens at one view, whereas the other way lifts up the curtain by little and little.[49]

Sterne, too, saw words in this way, as impeding rather than promoting intercourse between men. In his dispute with Locke over the function and importance of the imagination, Tristram rejects the philosopher's mode of logical discourse in order to argue by analogy, using wit, the synthesizing power of the mind, to prove that wit is equal at least to judgement as a means to understanding:

> I hate set dissertations,—and above all things in the world, 'tis one of the silliest things in one of them, to darken your hypothesis by placing a number of tall, opake words, one before another, in a right line, betwixt your own and your readers conception,—when in all likelihood, if you had looked about, you might have seen something standing, or hanging up, which would have cleared the point at once . . . [—something, for instance, such as the cane chair he is sitting on:] Will you give me leave to illustrate this affair of wit and judgment, by the two knobs on the top of the back of it,—they . . . will place what I have to say in so clear a light, as to let you see through the drift and meaning of my whole preface, as plainly as if every point and particle of it was made up of sun beams.   (p. 148)

Seeking new strategies to overcome the inherent limitations of his form, Sterne throughout *Tristram Shandy* prefers to 'illustrate' rather than relate, for 'the eye . . . has the quickest commerce with the soul,—gives a smarter stroke, and leaves something more inexpressible upon the fancy, than words can either convey—or sometimes get rid of' (p. 273). One celebrated manifestation of this motive in the novel is his occasional abandonment of words altogether in favour of visual devices—the black and marbled pages, the diagrams of his narrative, the squiggle on the page that makes us see Trim's flourish with his stick (p. 464). Another is his attempt through words to render what recent psychologists have called 'body language': those gestures or postures of the body—such as Toby's freeing the fly, or Trim's dropping his hat, or Walter's physical attitude as he lies sprawled upon the bed in sorrow (pp. 160, 204–8)—which express the sentiments of the heart more vividly than speech can do.

> —There are a thousand unnoticed openings, continued my father, which let a penetrating eye at once into a man's soul; and I maintain it, added he, that a man of sense does not lay down his hat in coming into a room,—or take it up in going out of it, but something escapes, which discovers him.   (p. 315)

This deliberate appeal to the senses includes the ear as well as the eye. At the most trivial level, Sterne will use onomatopoetic devices to help us hear a fiddle tuning up (pp. 280–1), a ditty being hummed (p. 390), the crack of a coachman's whip (p. 379). More important are the ways in which the inarticulate sounds his characters utter reveal their feelings as effectively as their physical movements and attitudes. Toby is a notable example: though he is no match for his brother in a debate, he can silence him by whistling a few bars of *Lillabullero*, his '*Argumentum Fistulatorium*' (p. 53); his 'Humph!' grunted in reply to Dr. Slop's account of Romish doctrine serves 'as well as if he had wrote a whole volume against the seven sacraments' (p. 97). And Sterne is fully aware of another advantage of the spoken as opposed to the written word, since meaning may be determined by tone of voice. 'A fiddlestick!' answers the Widow Wadman in reply to Toby's innocent suggestion that the pleasure of begetting children may be some compensation for the trouble they cause their mothers:

> Now [Tristram observes] there are such an infinitude of notes, tunes, cants, chants, airs, looks, and accents with which the word *fiddlestick* may be pronounced in all such causes as this, every one of 'em impressing a sense and meaning as different from the other, as *dirt* from *cleanliness*—

That Casuists (for it is an affair of conscience on that score) reckon up no less than fourteen thousand in which you may do either right or wrong.
    Mrs. *Wadman* hit upon the *fiddlestick*, which summoned up all my uncle *Toby*'s modest blood into his cheeks—   (p. 487)

Though such strategies contribute to the 'oddness' of *Tristram Shandy* as a work of fiction, there is more to them than mere whimsy. As attempts to circumvent the limitations of the novel form, to render scene and character *physically*, they are the expression of Sterne's belief that life must be felt in order to be known, that the way out of the self is through the senses—the eye, the ear, the touch: those organs by which we relate to and interpret the impingent world. There is in his novel as in the story of Toby's Hobby-horse a sense in which words, though perhaps not quite fatal, perplex the understanding and prevent communication. Like Toby, Tristram attempts to comprehend his world (and to help his reader comprehend it) by objectifying it. By stretching the resources of language so that prose approaches the condition of sensible experience, Sterne makes of his novel a kind of '*Momus*'s glass', disclosing the hearts and souls of his characters. In the sensationalism upon which the new philosophy was based, he found a way of mitigating the solipsism which it implied, a way of reconciling the contradictory views of Locke and the Latitudinarians.

    Appealing to the senses and the imagination rather than the judgement, proceeding by impulse rather than design, rejecting chronological structure for the illusion of the flow of consciousness, Sterne represents a revolutionary conception of the ways in which art imitates, in Fielding's phrase, 'what really exists'. For as the Augustan Age passed into the Age of Sensibility, the object of the artist's imitation was shifting from ideal Nature to the individual consciousness. Despite their resemblances, *A Tale of a Tub* and *Tristram Shandy* violate the formal expectations of their first readers for diametrically different ends. What is in Swift an aberration from the norms of rational order, implying the madness and materialism of the Modern world, has become in Sterne the image of reality. The attitudes of these two writers toward solipsism, imagination, sense, and time serve to define the aesthetic and intellectual contexts of the 'Augustan' and the 'Modern' modes.

Epilogue

THERE are of course many ways of defining the special character of literature and the arts in a given historical period. In this study, I have stressed just one: by exploring the relationship between the idea of Art and the idea of Nature in the hundred years extending from the Restoration to the accession of George III, I have tried to account for some of the distinctive features and implications—and also, I trust, for some of the peculiar pleasures—of aesthetic form in the period, in music, architecture, and gardening, but most particularly in the works of two poets and two novelists who may be taken as representative of the 'Augustan mode'.

In the intellectual history of England, these hundred years are uniquely important, for they marked the end of a continuous and coherent philosophical tradition. As the new spirit of scientific rationalism gained, it was first seen to confirm the old grounds of belief, then it utterly swept them away. The vehemence and persistence with which the divines attacked the materialism of Hobbes and the mechanism of Descartes reflect both a hopeful access of confidence in a providential universe, whose benign and intricate Order had been reaffirmed by Newton and the physico-theologians, and a deepening apprehension that the new philosophy would empty the world of meaning by depriving it of its Creator. This same confidence is evident in the *Essay on Man*; this same apprehension in the grotesque apocalypse of *The Dunciad*.

But before the darkness fell and Chaos was restored to empire, artists and aestheticians shared the faith of the divines in Order and expressed that faith in theory and practice, sophisticating the neo-classical doctrine of mimesis, and in a sense 'perfecting' it, since they believed that Nature, the object of the artist's imitation, was now better understood. For Alexander Malcolm or Robert Morris or the Fairchild lecturers, form in the abstract arts of music, architecture, and gardening was a reflection of Nature's harmony and due proportion. For Pope and Gay in poetry, for Fielding and Goldsmith in fiction, form in the mimetic arts implied a similar confidence in the power of the shaping intelligence not to distort but to transcend actuality, by 'the providence of wit' emulating ideal Nature and the artful design of creation. Pope's balanced couplets, Gay's exquisite artificiality, Fielding's symmetrical architecture, Goldsmith's bold contrivances express, variously, the conviction that Nature is Art, Chance Direction. To these writers, furthermore, who continued to endorse the values and assumptions of Christian humanism, the cardinal virtues were charity and prudence, and life itself an art to be mastered. As the great world was characterized not only by Energy, but by Order, so, too, the little world of man should reflect those essential aspects of creation in an active benevolence and a wise self-control—prudence and providence being regarded as the analogous attributes of order in microcosm and macrocosm. According to this tradition, moreover, the drama of each individual life was seen in relation to the larger drama of Time in which all men are implicated: Pope's shepherds or his dunces, Gay's Walker, Fielding's Tom Jones, Goldsmith's Dr. Primrose are all, for better or for worse, types of Everyman, whose life unfolds under the eye of Providence moving toward a last, just close.

To the Augustan artist, the meaning of creation was inherent in its artful Form and coherent Design, attesting to the wisdom and love of the Creator. On these familiar grounds, newly established, the faith of the age was founded. In art, as in life, the pattern for emulation lay outside the self, a standard fixed, ordered, benign, and to the eye of reason visible in the great frame of Nature. Even Swift, who found both the platonism of contemporary aesthetics and the complacency of contemporary ethics pernicious and absurd, endorsed the Augustan ideals of rationality, method, and order, defining them in *A Tale of a Tub* by their contraries. By the end of the century, however, this fine, coherent fabric, lucid and comprehensible, was in the process of disintegration. The ontological assumptions of the Christian humanist tradition were giving way to the subjectivism implicit in Locke's *Essay Concerning Human Understanding*. The centre of Order was transferred from Nature and Nature's God to the individual consciousness and, as a consequence, a radical reassessment of aesthetic principles was required. This new situation is clearly evident for the first time in *Tristram Shandy*, in which Sterne, offering a revolutionary conception of the ways in which art imitates reality, devised a form to mirror and to mitigate the fact of solipsism—a form that defines the world in terms of the processes of the mind while implying, in its appeal to the senses and the imagination, the means of communication and relationship. Sterne is in many ways the most 'Modern' author of his time, who created in Shandy Hall the comic epitome of a world still quite recognizable as our own.

But if the intellectual assumptions that determined the forms of art for Sterne's predecessors seem no longer valid, the forms themselves have lasted, and, because of those assumptions, answer more surely an enduring human need for order and harmony and grace.

Notes

CHAPTER I

1. 'To My Honored Friend, Sr Robert Howard, On his Excellent Poems' (1660), ll. 29–34; J. Kinsley, ed., *The Poems of John Dryden* (Oxford, 1958), Vol. I.

2. *The History of Tom Jones, a Foundling* (1749), X. i.

3. Quotations from Pope's poetry are taken from the Twickenham Edition, ed. John Butt *et al.*, 10 vols. (London and New Haven, 1939–67).

4. See 'The Parallelism between Literature and the Arts', *English Institute Annual, 1941* (New York, 1942), pp. 40–2.

5. See *An Inquiry into the Principles of Harmony in Language and of the Mechanism of Verse, Modern and Antient* (1804), Section VI, pp. 84 ff. Mitford illustrates his point by analysing the first sixteen lines of *An Essay on Man*.

6. *Mnemosyne: The Parallel between Literature and the Visual Arts* (1970), p. 42.

7. 'Of the Sister Arts; An Essay', in *Works* (1735), pp. 379–80.

8. Fielding, *Joseph Andrews* (1742), III. i.

9. Johnson, *Rasselas* (1759), ch. X.

10. Pope, *An Essay on Criticism*, l. 89.

11. See *The Subtler Language* (Baltimore, 1959), pp. 10–11.

12. Rudolf Wittkower, *Architectural Principles in the Age of Humanism*, 3rd ed., rev. (1962); John Hollander, *The Untuning of the Sky: Ideas of Music in English Poetry, 1500–1700* (Princeton, 1961); Gretchen L. Finney, *Musical Backgrounds for English Literature, 1580–1650* (New Brunswick, N.J. (1962)); Edward Tayler, *Nature and Art in Renaissance Literature* (New York, 1964).

13. See Leo Spitzer, *Classical and Christian Ideas of World Harmony* (Baltimore, 1963); A. O. Lovejoy, *The Great Chain of Being* (Cambridge, Mass., 1936); Wasserman, *Subtler Language*, ch. IV; Maynard Mack, ed., *Pope's Essay on Man* (New Haven, 1951), intro.

14. For a useful discussion of the development of the new conceptions of order, from Donne's despair to Pope's sanguine optimism, see Michael Macklem, *The Anatomy of the World* (Minneapolis, 1958).

15. *The Dunciad* (1743), iv. 475–6.

16. *A Poem Sacred to the Memory of Sir Isaac Newton* (1727), pp. 9, 7.

17. See Robert H. Hurlbutt III, *Hume, Newton, and the Design Argument* (Lincoln, Neb., 1965).

18. *The Harmonies of the World*, trans. C. G. Wallis, in *Great Books of the Western World*, ed. R. M. Hutchins (Chicago, 1952), XVI. 1048.

19. *An Account of Sir Isaac Newton's Philosophical Discoveries*, ed. P. Murdock (1748), pp. 32–3. For MacLaurin's opinion of Kepler, whom he regarded as a genius queerly given to analogizing, see pp. 50–1.

20. *Opticks*, 4th ed. (1730), Bk. II, Pt. i, Obs. 14.

21. Ibid., Bk. III, Pt. i, Qu. 14.

22. Newton's *Correspondence*, ed. J. F. Scott (Cambridge, 1967), IV. 274.

23. Ibid., IV. 275.

24. Hollander, pp. 9, 18–19, and ch. VI. Similarly, after reviewing the use of neo-platonist ideas in English poetry from Shakespeare to the Romantics, James Hutton asserts that Pope in the *Ode for Musick* could not have believed what he was saying! ('Some English Poems in Praise of Music', *English Miscellany*, II (1951), 1–63, esp. p. 61). The reasons for this sort of thinking are presented in Claude V. Palisca's article, 'Scientific Empiricism in Musical Thought', which traces the gradual dis-crediting of Pythagorean theories of harmony by seventeenth-century scientists investigating the physical properties and mathematical proportions that produce music. (See H. H. Rhys, ed., *Seventeenth Century Science and the Arts* (Princeton, 1961), pp. 91–137.) Arguments that undeniably had a profound effect on the musical thought of a few savants, had, however, little or no influence on the poets, divines, and aestheticians of the period down to, roughly, 1750. And in the Age of Newton and Shaftesbury, it would be extremely difficult to find anyone who subscribed to what Palisca strangely represents as 'growing evidence that the universe was not a harmony at all' (p. 93).

25. See E. R. Wasserman, 'Pope's *Ode for Musick*', *ELH*, XXVIII (1961), 163–86; J. A. Levine, 'Dryden's *Song for St. Cecilia's Day, 1687*', *PQ*, XLIV (1965), 38–50; and A. Fowler and D. Brooks, 'The Structure of Dryden's *Song for St. Cecilia's Day, 1687*', in Fowler, ed., *Silent Poetry: Essays in Numerological Analysis* (1970), pp. 185–200.
 There are, of course, limits to the useful application to Augustan literature of modes of analysis which have been profitably employed in the explication of Medieval and Renaissance poetry. As the critics cited above have argued, Dryden does seem to have structured his *Song* according to the conventions of numerological symbolism; but recent attempts to press this approach on Shadwell's *Song for St. Cecilia's Day, 1690* and on Fielding's *Joseph Andrews* have been strained and unpersuasive. (See the essays by H. Neville Davies and Douglas Brooks in Fowler's collection.) Most neo-classical writers and critics would doubtless agree with Thomas Tickell (*Spectator*, No. 632 (13 December 1714)) that, though the 'Love of Symmetry and Order . . . is natural to the Mind of Man', the arcane doctrines of the numerologists were nothing more than 'very whimsical Fancies', having 'no Foundation in Reason'. It is not surprising that, even after a hopeful and exhaustive search for 'numerological structures' in Pope's poetry, Alastair Fowler could find no evidence of them (see *Triumphal Forms: Structural Patterns in Elizabethan Poetry* (Cambridge, 1970), pp. 85–7, 122). Even Sir John Hawkins, no enemy to Pythagorean notions of world harmony, found the doctrines of the numerologists absurd. (See *A General History of the Science and Practice of Music* (1853), I. 6–7; this work was originally published in 1776.)

26. Spitzer, p. 76.

27. Samuel Clarke, 'A Demonstration of the Being and Attributes of God', *Works* (1738), II. 546.

28. *Musick's Monument* (1676), Pt. III, ch. x ('Musick's Mystical and Contemplative Part'); pp. 265, 268.

29. *Davideis*, Bk. I, in *Poems* (1656), Pt. IV, p. 13.

30. *Opticks*, 4th ed., Bk. III, Pt. i, Qu. 31.

31. *The Power of Harmony* (1745), pp. 46, 48.

32. *An Essay on the Universe* (1733), p. 20.

33. *Proposal* (1688), sigs. A2ᵛ, [a]1ʳ, and p. 3.

34. *Treatise of Musick* (Edinburgh, 1721), pp. 67–70.

35. Such, for instance, is the view of Charles Gildon in *The Laws of Poetry* (1721), pp. 83–9, published in the same year as Malcolm's *Treatise*.

36. *The Oration, Anthems & Poems, Spoken and Sung at the Performance of Divine Musick, at Stationers-Hall, for the Month of May, 1702* (1702), p. 20. Somewhat more fanciful than Collier's analogy, but no less to the point, is the following passage from *The Great Abuse of Musick* (1711) by Arthur Bedford, chaplain to the Duke of Bedford:

> Nay, I may venture to add, that perhaps there is not a greater Resemblance of God, as he is a *spiritual* Substance, and enters into the very *Heart* and *Soul*, filling it with Delight and Satisfaction, than *Musick* is; nor any thing that will give us a clearer *Idea* of a *Trinity* in *Unity*, than the *three Concords* join'd together *in one Sound*, as it most usually happens in a *Consort* of *four* Parts, which is always reckon'd as the most compleat and perfect of all. It is worth our Observation, that when any *Words* are repeated, or some particular *Musical Notes*, they are usually mention'd *three* times, and such *Repetitions*, nay, the very *Fuges* in three Parts seem most *natural* and *harmonious*, as if all did direct us of course whither to raise our Thoughts, and where to place our Affections. The *three Concords* united are so pleasant, that did not *God* by his Providence order our Senses to be delighted with Variety, that the same Sound cannot always divert us, we might have been apt to imbibe the Error of some *Heathens*, and think, that the *Godhead* was nothing but *Harmony* it self.   (pp. [256]–7)

Bedford goes on to observe that in heaven, happily, our natures will be so altered that we will not desire variety. Cf. the similar passage in Bedford's sermon, *The Excellency of Divine Musick* (1733), pp. 20–1.

37. See Manfred F. Bukofzer, *Music in the Baroque Era* (New York, 1947), pp. 365–9; 392–3; and Hugo Leichtentritt, *Music, History, and Ideas* (Cambridge, Mass., 1946), pp. 145–6. On the place of symmetry in the Augustan theory of pure form, see below, Section ii.

38. See Bertrand H. Bronson's essay in *Music and Literature in England in the Seventeenth and Eighteenth Centuries* (Los Angeles [1953]), pp. 32–41.

39. Bukofzer, p. 369.

40. Bukofzer, p. 392.

41. Cf. Herbert M. Schueller's summary of the views of such disparate theorists as Avison, Hawkins, Burney, Beattie, and John Gregory: 'Music in many respects, as reflecting the "music" of the spheres, and as typifying the order of the Muses, resembled the harmony of the universe itself. *The pleasure of music could therefore arise from a sense of order inherent in man*; the harmony in music was congenial to the inherent taste for harmony in man' ('The Pleasures of Music: Speculation in British Music Criticism, 1750–1800', *JAAC*, VIII (1950), 170). See also Schueller's article, 'Literature and Music as Sister Arts: An Aspect of Aesthetic Theory in Eighteenth-Century Britain', *PQ*, XXVI (1947), 193–205, esp. pp. 197–8.

42. See above, n. 25.

43. In Husk, p. 189.

44. *Ode for Musick* (1730), pp. 23–4. Though a less explicit treatment of the idea, Christopher Smart's *Ode on Saint Cecilia's Day* assumes that 'From heav'n music took its rise' (in *Carmen Alexandri Pope*, 2nd ed., 1746).

45. Hawkins, I. 63.

46. Ibid., I. xxv, 65–6, 410–11 and n.; and II. 788.

47. Ibid., I. 65–6.

48. See Lipking's discussion in *The Ordering of the Arts in Eighteenth-Century England* (Princeton, 1970), pp. 258–61.

49. Hurlbutt, p. 4.

50. See, for example, the following works, all of which adopt the design argument to discredit the neo-epicurean philosophies and to assert the beneficent Providence of God, the divine Artificer: Isaac Barrow, Sermon VI, 'The Being of God Proved from the Frame of the World', *Works* (1741), II. 66–76; Henry More, *An Antidote against Atheisme* (1653); Ralph Cudworth, *The True Intellectual System of the Universe* (1678); John Ray, *The Wisdom of God Manifested in the Works of the Creation* (1691); William Derham, *Physico-Theology* (1713) and *Astro-Theology* (1715); Richard Bentley, *The Folly and Unreasonableness of Atheism*, the Boyle lectures for 1692; and Samuel Clarke, *A Demonstration of the Being and Attributes of God*, the Boyle lectures for 1704.

51. Though he does not consider this particular aspect of the *Characteristicks*, Ernst Cassirer has suggested Shaftesbury's relationship to the neo-platonic tradition extending from Ficino through the Cambridge theologians. (See *Die platonische Renaissance in England und die Schule von Cambridge* (Leipzig, 1932); trans. J. P. Pettegrove, 1953).

52. *The Moralists* (1709), I. iii; in *Characteristicks*, 5th ed. (1732), II. 214.

53. 'Concerning Beauty, Order, Harmony, Design', Pt. I of the *Inquiry*, 2nd ed. (1726), p. 17.

54. *Soliloquy: or, Advice to an Author* (1710), III. iii; in *Characteristicks*, 5th ed., I. 353.

55. *Miscellaneous Reflections* (1714), III. ii; in ibid., III. 184–5.

56. *Sensus Communis: An Essay on the Freedom of Wit and Humour* (1709), IV. ii; in ibid., I. 136–7.

57. On the dominance of syllabism and stress regularity during this period, see Paul Fussell, Jr., *Theory of Prosody in Eighteenth-Century England*, Connecticut College Monograph, No. 5 (New London, Conn., 1954), pp. 35–6. This is a useful study, to which I am indebted. It should be clear, however, that I do not accept Fussell's contention that there is no metaphysical basis for the order and regularity of verse structure in the period (p. 38), or that Augustan poets enjoyed a 'somewhat morbid thrill of fascination' at the chaos presumably introduced into their once stable universe by the new philosophy (p. 39).

58. *Lectures on Poetry* (1742), pp. 29–30.

59. *The Rambler* (1753), I. 513–14.

60. Ibid., I. 522.

61. In *Of Harmony and Numbers in Latin and English Prose, and in English Poetry* (1744), Manwaring asserts that harmony in literature 'is founded on the Principles of Harmony in Musick' (p. 2) and that poetic numbers, in particular, are to be regarded as an imitation of the 'musical Concords' of the diatonic scale, 'which consists of half and whole Tones' (p. 35). Pope's *Windsor Forest*, he feels, perfectly exemplifies this hypothesis, whereas Milton 'wants this Division of the Verse into musical Concords, where his Verse is composed of Polysyllable Words, which are often an Obstruction to this Division; but then the Grandeur of his Diction and Thoughts, and his most beautiful Transpositions, supply this Harmony, or Want of the Numbers; and the Misfortune is, that whenever this Poet has these Numbers or musical Concords, they are generally confounded by prosaic Stops' (p. 43). Say, though he proceeds from similar premisses concerning the analogy between poetry and music, reaches a very different conclusion which marks him as one of the principal forerunners of the more liberal, 'romantic' theory of accent. In Milton, he finds, 'Pure *Iambics* are industriously avoided, and exchang'd for such other Movements, as steal along more Soft and Silent, as far as the Law of *Iambic* Measures will admit, and which may seem to resemble the Music of the Spheres . . .' ('An Essay on the Harmony, Variety, and Power of Numbers', in *Poems on Several Occasions: and Two Critical Essays* (1745), p. 126).

62. Fussell, p. 52.

63. *The Subtler Language*, ch. IV, esp. pp. 103–13.

64. Pope's *Iliad* (1715–20), xxi. 454 n.; *TE*, VIII. 439–40.

65. John Reynolds, *Death's Vision* (1709), pp. 33–4.

66. Consider Spitzer's account of *Timaeus* (31a, 32c): '. . . we find the Demiurgos, like a cup-bearer at a symposium, "harmoniously mixing" the body of the universe . . . which he created out of the four elements, "fitting them together by means of proportion" . . .: each of the two middle terms, water and air, located between fire and earth, has the same relationship with each other, as the two together have with the first and fourth elements; the *tetraktys* is a kind of double balance. Thus it had necessarily to become, along with the sphere, a symbol of perfection and equilibrium' (op. cit., p. 67).

67. Spitzer, op. cit., p. 46.

68. Shaftesbury, *Miscellaneous Reflections*, V. i, in *Characteristicks*, 5th ed., III. 263. See also *Soliloquy*, II. i, in ibid., I. 217; Francis Atterbury, Preface to *The Second Part of Mr. Waller's Poems* (1690), sigs. A7ᵛ–8ᵛ; John Dennis, 'Preface to *Britannia Triumphans*' (1704), in E. N. Hooker, ed. *Critical Works* (Baltimore, 1939), I. 376–9; and Charles Gildon, *The Laws of Poetry*, pp. 64–72.

69. *The Subtler Language*, pp. 111–12.

70. *Essay on Man*, i. 277–8, ii. 5–6; *Moral Essays*, II, ll. 63–4.

71. *Stichology*, p. 20.

72. 'Beauty and Music. An Ode', in *Poems on Several Occasions* (Oxford, 1757), p. 16.

73. Leon Battista Alberti, *Architecture*, IX. v; trans. G. Leoni (1755), p. 196.

74. *Correspondence*, IV. 274.

75. Wittkower, esp. Pt. IV.

76. Wittkower, 'Inigo Jones, Architect and Man of Letters', *JRIBA*, 3rd Ser., LX (January 1953), 83–8. Appended to the article is a transcript of the discussion which followed the reading of the original paper before the Royal Institute. Here, in answering G. E. Webb, Wittkower stressed that 'the Platonic position' was 'still alive' as late as the mid nineteenth century, though 'perhaps not in the sense in which it was alive to Inigo Jones' (p. 90).

77. Wittkower, *Architectural Principles*, pp. 144–5.

78. See, for example, Wolfgang Herrmann, *Laugier and Eighteenth Century French Theory*, Studies in Architecture, edd. A. Blunt and R. Wittkower, Vol. VI (1962), pp. 37–8; and Joseph Burke, 'The Grand Tour and the Rule of Taste', in R. F. Brissenden, ed., *Studies in the Eighteenth Century* (Canberra, 1968), pp. 239–40.

79. Wittkower, *Architectural Principles*, p. 142.

80. *The Garden and the City: Retirement and Politics in the Later Poetry of Pope, 1731–1743* (Toronto, 1969), p. 36.

81. See *Cours d'architecture*, V. xi–xii; 2nd ed. (Paris, 1698), II. 756–60. Like Alberti, Blondel believed that arithmetical and geometrical, as well as musical, proportions were useful to the architect.

82. Ibid., II. 785. See also V. xvi: 'Inductions pour prouver que les Proportions sont la cause de la beauté dans l'Architecture; Et que cette beauté n'a pas moins son fondement dans la Nature, que celle des accords dans la Musique.'

83. *A Treatise of the Five Orders of Columns in Architecture*, trans. J. James (1708), p. ix.

84. See Blondel, 2nd ed., V. xv.

85. See *Traité* (Paris, 1752), I. 14, 36. Newton's discovery that the colours of the spectrum are proportionately related to each other as the musical tones (see above, p. 6) seemed to the analogists convincing proof of the Pythagorean doctrine. To Briseux, the rainbow was a 'tableau naturel, que le Créateur présente à nos

yeux, pour nous initier au Sisteme des Arts' (I. 36). In this opinion he had been anticipated, in very nearly the same words, by Yves Marie de l'Isle André in ch. IV ('Le Beau Musical') of his *Essai sur le Beau* (Paris, 1741), pp. 207–8. See also 'Cosmetti', *The Polite Arts* (1767), pp. 32–3, and Francis Webb, *Panharmonicon* (1815), p. 2.

86. *The Analysis of Beauty*, ed. J. Burke (Oxford, 1955), p. 91. Ten Kate's discourse, dated 1724, was originally published in Amsterdam in 1728, prefixed to the French translation of Jonathan Richardson's *Account of Some of the Statues, Bas-Reliefs, Drawings, and Pictures in Italy* (1722). In 1732, J. C. Le Blon published an abridged version in English under the title, *The Beau Ideal*, with a Preface representing the work as '*the Product of the* ANALOGY *of the* ancient Greeks; *or the true Key for finding all harmonious Proportions in* Painting, Sculpture, Architecture, Musick, *&c. brought home to* Greece *by* PYTHAGORAS' (p. ii). Despite this fanfare, Le Blon omitted a long passage in which his author celebrates and explains the analogy; this oversight was corrected in a later edition (1769).

87. *Discours préliminaire sur le Beau Idéal des peintres, sculpteurs & poëtes*, prefixed to J. and J. Richardson, *Traité de la peinture, et de la sculpture* (Amsterdam, 1728), p. lxii.

88. See the Preface to *The Analysis of Beauty*; Burke ed., pp. 11–15.

89. For an interesting, if somewhat tendentious, discussion of Robert Morris (fl. 1728–61), see Emil Kaufmann, *Architecture in the Age of Reason: Baroque and Post-Baroque in England, Italy, and France* (New York, 1968), pp. 22–8. On strictly technical grounds, Professor Kaufmann, who is inclined to overpraise originality in architects, makes rather too much of Morris as a critic of Palladianism. Though Morris may have objected to certain features of the Palladian style, it is clear that the architects he most admired were Palladio and 'the *British Palladio*', Inigo Jones. (See *An Essay in Defence of Ancient Architecture* (1728), pp. 23, 25; and *Lectures on Architecture*, Pt. I (1734), p. 21). He has high praise, too, for the chief patrons of the movement, Burlington and Pembroke (*Essay*, pp. xii–xiii). Palladio's proportions please, he insists, because 'they are such which Nature herself dictates, Unison being always Harmony' (*Lectures*, p. 104).

90. *Lectures*, sig. a3ʳ.

91. *The Elements of Architecture* (1624), p. 53.

92. Introduction (dated 15 January 1732) to *Ancient Masonry, both in Theory and Practice* (1736), p. 7.

93. See James Lees-Milne, *Earls of Creation: Five Great Patrons of Eighteenth-Century Art* (1962), p. 87. The fact that Marble Hill was begun in 1724 makes it still less likely that the Burlington circle learned of the Pythagorean analogy through Ten Kate. As Lees-Milne puts it, 'Robert Morris's exegesis is the Pembroke Formula' (loc. cit.).

94. See 'Burlington and his Work in York', in W. A. Singleton, *Studies in Architectural History* (London and York, 1954), pp. 48–50.

95. Lecture VII (11 March 1733/4), in *Lectures on Architecture. Consisting of Rules Founded upon Harmonick and Arithmetical Proportions in Building*, Pt. I (1734), esp. pp. 101–3. Pt. II was published in 1736.

96. In the 'Preliminary Discourse' to his *General History of the Science and Practice of Music*, Hawkins writes: 'If we investigate the principles of harmony, we learn that they are general and universal; and of harmony itself, that the proportions in which it consists are to be found in those material forms, which are beheld with the greatest pleasure, the sphere, the cube, and the cone, for instance, and constitute what we call symmetry, beauty, and regularity . . .' (1853 ed., I. xiv). In the part deleted from the passage I quoted earlier (see above, p. 14), Hawkins cites the musical proportions discoverable in the buildings of the ancient architects as proof of the effectiveness of Pythagorean principles.

97. See Webb's curious monograph, *Panharmonicon . . . in which is attempted to be proved, that the Principles of Harmony more or less prevail throughout the whole System of Nature; but more especially in the human Frame: and that where these Principles can be applied to works of Art, they excite the pleasing and satisfying Ideas of Proportion and Beauty* [1815]. According to Webb, the Dorsetshire artist, Giles Hussey, applied the harmonic proportions in drawing portraits. Included in this work is an elaborate fold-out diagram illustrating how these proportions obtain in the works of Nature— in the planetary system, the human figure, horses, birds, butterflies, fish.

98. Wittkower, *Architectural Principles*, pp. 150–3, and P. H. Scholfield, *The Theory of Proportion in Architecture* (Cambridge, 1958), pp. 70–9.

99. Wittkower, ibid., p. 151.

100. Lecture VI, *Lectures*, p. 81.

101. *On Architecture*, III. i; trans. F. Granger (Loeb Classical Library, 1931–4).

102. *Essai sur l'architecture* (Paris, 1753); trans. (1755), pp. 9 ff.

103. See above, p. 19.

104. *Opticks*, 4th ed., Bk. III, Pt. i, Qu. 31.

105. See *Mountain Gloom and Mountain Glory: The Development of the Aesthetics of the Infinite* (Ithaca, N.Y., 1959).

106. *Life and Works of Sir Christopher Wren. From the Parentalia or Memoirs by his Son Christopher* [1903], Appendix: 'Of Architecture; and Observations on Antique Temples, &c.', p. 237.

107. *Traité du Beau* (Amsterdam, 1715), pp. 14, 16.

108. *Essai sur le Beau* (Paris, 1741), pp. 18–23.

109. *Les Beaux Arts reduits à un même principe* (Paris, 1746), pp. 86–7.

110. Sermon CXXXVII, 'The Wisdom of God in the Creation of the World', *Works* (1757), VIII. 136–8.

111. Ibid., VIII. 126.

112. Barrow, Sermon VI, 'The Being of God Proved from the Frame of the World', *Works* (1741), II. 69. See also Sermon XXXVI, 'Of the Goodness of God', ibid., III. 289.

113. South, Sermon XVIII, 'On the Mercy of God', *Sermons Preached upon Several Occasions* (1843), III. 362.

114. Clarke, 'A Discourse Concerning the Unchangeable Obligations of Natural Religion', *Works* (1738), II. 647. See also 'A Demonstration of the Being and Attributes of God', ibid., II. 546, 569–71; and Sermon I, 'Of Faith in God', ibid., I. 5–6.

115. Sermon VI, *Works* (1741), II. 68.

116. Sermon XCV, 'The Shortness and Vanity of Humane Life', *Works* (1738), I. 601.

117. *Creation. A Philosophical Poem, demonstrating the Existence and Providence of a God*, 2nd ed. (1712), Bk. VII, pp. 321–2.

118. See below, pp. 164 ff.

119. 'Epistle Dedicatory' to Evelyn's translation of Roland Fréart, *A Parallel of the Ancient Architecture with the Modern*, 4th ed. (1733), sig. (C)1^v.

120. *The Garden and the City*, esp. p. 36.

121. *Christianity as Old as the Creation* (1730), I. 67.

122. *The Polite Philosopher: or, An Essay on that Art which Makes a Man happy in Himself, and agreeable to Others* (Dublin, 1734), pp. 25–6. 'Behaviour', Forrester declares, 'is like Architecture, the Symmetry of the whole pleases us so much, that we examine not into its Parts, which if we did, we should find much Nicety required in forming such a Structure . . .' (p. 25).

123. 'Introduction' to Margaret Jourdain, *The Work of William Kent, Artist, Painter, Designer and Landscape Gardener* (1948), p. 15. See also Hussey's *English Gardens and Landscapes, 1700–1750* (1967), p. 11.

124. For a late statement of this paradox of Augustan aesthetics, see Henry James Pye's little-known poem, *Beauty* (1766). In architecture, Pye praises 'the discerning sons of Greece and Rome' for imitating 'sacred NATURE . . . E'er gothic structures idly pleas'd the heart, / With all the nice perplexities of art'; yet in gardening, he scorns those equally geometrical 'Gallic artists', such as Le Nôtre, for perversely forcing nature into 'a new creation of their own' (pp. 2–4).

125. *The Garden and the City*, p. 112.

126. *Imitations of Horace*, Epistles II. ii. 202–5 (1737).

127. See Miles Hadfield, *Gardening in Britain* (1960), chs. IV–V. Le Nôtre's theories were widely known through A. J. D. d'Argenville's *La Théorie et la practique du jardinage* (Paris, 1709), which saw five editions in Paris and three in The Hague; the English translation by John James (1712) went through three editions by 1743. As Hadfield points out, the currency of this mode was assured when Philip Miller, the most distinguished horticulturist of the period, used James's translation to instruct his readers in 'the designing or manner of laying out a fine garden or pleasure garden' (in *The Gardener and Florist's Dictionary* (1724) and *The Gardener's Dictionary* (1731)). Though the principles of the 'natural' landscape garden were followed in 'smart quarters', the French style continued to be popular until the end of the century. (See Hadfield, pp. 158 ff., 199.) Certainly, as Hussey observes, throughout the period 1700 to 1750, 'the majority of gardens remained of 17th-century types' (*English Gardens and Landscapes*, p. 18).

128. See 'On St. James's Park, as lately improved by His Majesty' (1661).

129. *Works*, 2nd ed. (1720), I. 186.

130. *The Theory of the Earth*, 2nd ed. (1691), Bk. II, chs. v–vi; see Figure 3, p. 231.

131. Ibid., Bk. I, ch. x; pp. 128–9.

132. *Mountain Gloom and Mountain Glory* (Norton Library paperback, New York, 1963), ch. VI, esp. 225–8, 235, n. 24.

133. Sermon VIII of *The Folly and Unreasonableness of Atheism* (1693), p. 12.

134. Derek Clifford, *A History of Garden Design* (1962), p. 123.

135. See ch. IV 'The Genesis of the Picturesque', in *Studies in Art, Architecture and Design. Volume One: From Mannerism to Romanticism* (New York, 1968), p. 100. Pevsner explains: 'The free growth of the tree is obviously taken to symbolize the free growth of the individual, the serpentine path and rivulet the Englishman's freedom of thought, creed and action, and the adherence to nature in the grounds, the adherence to nature in ethics and politics' (pp. 100–1).

136. *Epistle IV. To Richard Boyle, Earl of Burlington* (1731), ll. 113–20.

137. Professor Mack's theory (to which I subscribe) of what might be called the 'emblematic' impulse behind Pope's gardening has been disputed recently by John Dixon Hunt in an interesting but inconclusive essay which argues that Pope looks forward to the 'expressionism' of a later period rather than backward to an earlier iconographic tradition. (See 'Emblem and Expressionism in the Eighteenth-Century Landscape Garden', *ECS*, IV (1971), 294–317.

138. See below, ch. III, sec. i, esp. pp. 84–7.

139. From the prospectus of Pemberton's *View of Sir Isaac Newton's Philosophy* (1728), in *The London Journal* (16 April 1726).

140. *Physico-Theology*, 4th ed. (1716), pp. 36–7.

141. I am indebted to Louis Landa for first calling my attention to the Fairchild lectures, a treasury of what might be called hortico-theology apparently unknown to historians of gardening. For details and a list of the speakers, see the *Register of Benefactions, to the Parish of St. Leonard, Shoreditch*, compiled by John Denne, the vicar, in 1745 and printed in 1777 (pp. 26–7). The copy in the British Museum contains annotations by Henry Ellis adding information up to 1795. See also Ellis's *History and Antiquities of the Parish of Saint Leonard Shoreditch, and Liberty of Norton Folgate, in the Suburbs of London* (1798), pp. 31–5, 283–8. A pamphlet published in 1856 gives a further 'Short Account' of Fairchild and the lectures (B.M. call number: 4476.de.5.).

142. *The Wisdom of God in the Vegetable Creation* (1730), p. 24.

143. *The Wisdom and Goodness of God in the Vegetable Creation further consider'd* (1733), p. 22.

144. *Spectator*, No. 477 (6 September 1712).

145. Discourse III on 'The *glorys* of the vegetable kingdom display'd', in *Palæographia Sacra: or, Discourses on Sacred Subjects* (1763), p. 37.

146. *Elements of Architecture*, p. 109.

147. *Spectator*, No. 414 (25 June 1712).

148. *Characteristicks*, 5th ed. (1732), II. 393–4.

149. Lecture XII (25 November 1734), in *Lectures on Architecture*, Pt. II (1736), pp. 189, 199.

150. *English Gardens and Landscapes*, p. 29. See also Pevsner, p. 83, for an almost identical explanation.

151. Herrmann, ch. VIII, esp. pp. 140–6 and Plates 38–9.

152. *Spectator*, No. 414.

153. A. J. Sambrook has persuasively argued that Searle's plan (see Plate 10) is in some respects inaccurate, but for our present purposes it will serve. (See 'The Shape and Size of Pope's Garden', *ECS*, V (1972), 450–5.)

154. See Mack, *The Garden and the City*, pp. 53–6.

155. Ibid., p. 56.

156. *Ichnographia Rustica*, 3 vols. (1718), I. xviii–xix, xxxv–xxxvi; III. 9.

157. *The Villas of the Ancients Illustrated* (1728), p. 121; emphasis added.

158. That Pope saw the well-made garden as a reflection of the world's *concordia discors* may perhaps be inferred from the similar ways in which he describes the harmony of Windsor Forest and that of Villario's estate in the *Epistle to Burlington*, where 'The Wood supports the Plain, the parts unite, / And strength of Shade contends with strength of Light' (ll. 81–2). Cf. *Windsor Forest*, ll. 11 ff.:

> Here Hills and Vales, the Woodland and the Plain,
> Here Earth and Water seem to strive again,
> Not *Chaos*-like together crush'd and bruis'd,
> But as the World, harmoniously confus'd:
> Where Order in Variety we see,
> And where, tho' all things differ, all agree.
> Here waving Groves a checquer'd Scene display,
> And part admit and part exclude the Day . . .

159. *Divine Dialogues* (1668), II. 287.

160. Sidney's *Apologie for Poetrie* (1595), ed. E. S. Shuckburgh (Cambridge, 1891), p. 8.

161. *Essays of John Dryden*, ed. W. P. Ker (Oxford, 1900), II. 117–18.

162. J. Richardson (the elder), 'Essay on the Theory of Painting', in *Works*, ed. J. Richardson (his son), 2nd ed. (1773), p. 100. Cf. also Roland Fréart, *An Idea of the Perfection of Painting*, trans. J. Evelyn (1668), p. 21; Roger de Piles, *The Art of Painting* (1706), pp. 1, 15–16; Hildebrand Jacob, 'Of the Sister Arts', in *Works* (1735), pp. 396–8.

163. *The Advancement and Reformation of Modern Poetry* (1701), in Hooker, ed., *Critical Works*, I. 264.

164. *The Complete Art of Poetry* (1718), I. 51.

165. *The True Intellectual System of the Universe*, 2nd ed. (1743), I. 157.

166. Ibid., I. 154.

167. Ibid., I. 156.

168. Ibid., I. 157. Cf. the review of an unpublished work on hermeticism, carried in Dodsley's *Museum: or, The Literary and Historical Register*, No. XXXIII (20 June 1747), III. 257. Book I of this work, entitled 'Of Nature and Art', is summarized by the reviewer: 'The Author observes, that what we stile Nature may with great Strictness and Propriety be consider'd as the Art or Wisdom of God; and that what we call Art, is no more than the Imitation of the Wisdom of God, so far as it can be reached or imitated by the limited Nature of Man.'

169. *The Advancement and Reformation of Modern Poetry*, in Hooker, ed., *Critical Works*, I. 202.

170. *The Laws of Poetry*, p. 168. See also *The Complete Art of Poetry*, I. 95, where Gildon draws an analogy between the well-made poem and the creation, which was 'by *Art Divine* brought into order, and this *noble Poem* of the Universe compleated in *Number* and *Figures*, by the Almighty *Poet* or *Maker*'.

171. Only the first edition of this work (Edinburgh, 1739) should be consulted. (British Museum call number: 11632.cc.2.) The version published by the author's son in Browne's *Poems upon Various Subjects* (1768) is drastically abridged and revised. In its original form, the *Essay* was a collaboration, the first 200 lines—comprising all that will be of interest to the student of aesthetics—having been contributed 'by a Gentleman of a fine Genius and extensive Knowledge'. Whether Browne or his friend is meant by this attribution is not clear.

172. *The Power of Harmony*, pp. 10–11.

173. G. Leoni, trans., *The Architecture of A. Palladio; in Four Books*, 2nd ed. (1721), II. 41–2. See also Isaac Ware's translation, dedicated to Burlington (1738), p. 79.

174. *Epistle to Burlington*, l. 193. See William A. Gibson, 'Three Principles of Renaissance Architectural Theory in Pope's *Epistle to Burlington*', *SEL*, XI (1971), 487–505, esp. p. 502. The weakness of Gibson's argument is that it depends too exclusively on the theories of Robert Morris, whose views, though well known to Wittkower, Scholfield, and Kaufmann, are regarded by those authorities (I think mistakenly) as eccentric in the period. The evidence I have presented in this chapter should improve the cogency of Gibson's hypothesis.

175. *Journal to Stella*, Letter VII (26 October 1710); ed. H. Williams (Oxford, 1948), I. 72.

176. *De Finibus*, V. vi. 16.

177. *The Grounds of Criticism in Poetry* (1704), in Hooker, ed., *Critical Works*, I. 335–6.

178. *Soliloquy*, I. iii, in *Characteristicks*, 5th ed., I. 207.

179. *Lectures on Poetry*, pp. 4–5.

CHAPTER II

1. *The Dunciad*, iv. 16.

2. This motif in Pope's poetry is discussed at length in ch. III.

3. For the general background, see C. A. Patrides, *The Phoenix and the Ladder: The Rise and Decline of the Christian View of History* (Berkeley and Los Angeles, 1964) and Ernest Lee Tuveson, *Millenium and Utopia: A Study in the Background of the Idea of Progress* (Berkeley and Los Angeles, 1949), chs. I–II. From the tenor of the present study, however, it should be apparent that I do not concur with Professor Patrides's assertion that after Milton, 'no poet, either in England or on the Continent, was . . . concerned with the Christian view of history' (p. 66), or with Professor Tuveson's notion that after Godfrey Goodman traditional Christian teleology virtually disappeared (ch. III).

4. Cf. Sir Thomas Browne's observation that in Eden Nature was not at variance with Art, nor Art with Nature, 'they being both servants of [God's] Providence' (*Religio Medici*, Pt. I, sec. 16: *Works*, ed. Geoffrey Keynes (1928), I. 22).

5. See Kermode's introductions to *English Pastoral Poetry from the Beginnings to Marvell* (1952) and to the Arden Edition of *The Tempest*, 5th ed. (1954); and Tayler's *Nature and Art in Renaissance Literature*.

6. Northrop Frye offers a succinct account of the Christian humanist tradition defining the relationship of art to the 'two levels of nature': 'The traditional view of the relation of art to nature, as enunciated by Aristotle, broadened by the late Classical rhetoricians, and developed by Christianity, preserves a distinction that is much less clear in Pope. In this view there are two levels of nature. The lower one is the ordinary physical world, which is theologically "fallen"; the upper is a divinely sanctioned order, existing in Eden before the Fall, and mirrored in the Classical and Boethian myth of the Golden Age . . . The upper world is the world of "art" . . . and poetry, for all its Renaissance defenders, is one of the most important of the educational and regenerative agents that lead us up to the world of art' ('Nature and Homer', *TQ*, I (1958), 192–204). Though, as Frye believes, the distinction between the two levels of Nature may be blurred in Pope, it is none the less real and functional. We have seen, furthermore, that it continued to be an integral part of Augustan aesthetic theory, evident in Dryden, Jonathan Richardson, Dennis, Gildon, and others (see above, ch. I, sec. II, esp. pp. 50–1).

7. *TE*, I. 25, 27, 29.

8. See, in particular, J. E. Congleton, *Theories of Pastoral Poetry in England, 1684–1798* (Gainesville, Fla., 1952).

9. From 'Milton', *Lives of the English Poets*, ed. George Birkbeck Hill (Oxford, 1905), I. 163.

10. *An Epistle to Dr. Arbuthnot* (1734), l. 340.

11. *TE*, I. 32.

12. The metaphorical dimensions of Spenser's calendar structure have been explicated by S. K. Heninger, Jr., 'The Implications of Form for *The Shepeardes Calender*', *SRen*, IX

(1962), 309–21. Heninger shows that in the Renaissance the calendar was an emblematic device implying the 'Pythagorean tetrad', a theory of universal Order which saw the world as a synthesis of the four elements with correspondences in all spheres of life: the four humours, the four ages of man, the four seasons, etc. That Pope was widely read in Pythagorean theory at this stage of his career is doubtless questionable; certainly, however, he had sensed the significance of Spenser's form in relating 'the great and little worlds'.

13. *TE*, I. 33.

14. See *Paradise Lost* (1674), iv. 264–8, and *Paradise Regained* (1671), ii. 25–6.

15. *TE*, I. 59 n.

16. *Essay on the Writings and Genius of Pope* (1756), p. 10.

17. 'Pope', op. cit., III. 225.

18. 'Pope's *Ode for Musick*', *ELH*, XXVIII (1961), 163–86.

19. In this respect, Pope's view of the redemptive, idealizing function of poetry—or at least of pastoral and georgic—seems closer than we have supposed to that of the Renaissance. One recalls Sidney, for example, who in a famous passage in his *Apologie* (1595) had asserted: 'Onely the Poet, disdayning to be tied to any such subiection [to Nature], lifted up with the vigor of his owne invention, dooth growe in effect into another nature, in making things either better than Nature bringeth forth, or, quite anewe, formes such as never were in Nature . . .' 'Nature', he continued, 'never set forth the earth in so rich tapistry, as divers Poets have done, neither with so pleasant rivers, fruitful trees, sweet smelling flowers, nor whatsoever els may make the too much loved earth more lovely. Her world is brasen, the Poets only deliver a golden' (ed. Shuckburgh, p. 8).

20. See Theocritus, *Idyll I*; Virgil, *Eclogue III*; and Spenser's 'August'.

21. It is clear from his correspondence that Pope, at least when he thought of himself in a classical context, adopted the name of 'Alexis' as his own. On 10 November 1716 he wrote to Lady Mary Wortley Montagu, wishing that he could follow her abroad:

> But if my Fate be such, that this Body of mine (which is as ill-matched to my Mind as any wife to her husband) be left behind in the journey, let the Epitaph of Tibullus be set over it.
>
> > Hic jacet immiti consumptus morte Tibullus,
> > Messalam, terra, dum sequitarque, mari.
> >
> > Here stopt by hasty Death, Alexis lies,
> > Who crost half Europe, led by Wortley's eyes!

(George Sherburn, ed. *The Correspondence of Alexander Pope* (Oxford, 1956), I. 369).

22. In his note to line 39, Pope observed that Colin Clout was 'the name taken by *Spenser* in his Eclogues, where his mistress is celebrated under that of *Rosalinda*'.

23. 'Pope', op. cit., III. 224.

24. See Pope's note to l. 7.

25. Pope's decision thus to associate 'Winter' with the terrible hurricane of 1703 would have carried for his first readers a special significance, and one entirely apposite to his theme and emblematic strategy in the *Pastorals*. To divines and poets alike the storm seemed a sign of God's displeasure with a sinful world and a prefiguration of Nature's final dissolution. (See, for example, Benjamin Gravener (or Grosvenor), *A Discourse Occasion'd by the late Dreadful Storm* (1704); Defoe, ed., *The Storm: or, A Collection of the most Remarkable Casualties and Disasters which happen'd in the Late Dreadful Tempest, both by Sea and Land* (1704); and Anne, Countess of Winchilsea, 'A Pindarick Poem. Upon the Hurricane in November 1703, referring to this Text in Psalm 148. ver. 8. Winds and Storms fulfilling his Word'.

26. In *Paradise Lost* Milton's angels dwell in 'blissful Bowrs / Of *Amarantin* Shade' (xi. 77–8) wearing crowns of 'Amarant and Gold' (iii. 352). As Milton explains, the 'Immortal Amarant', which once bloomed 'In Paradise, fast by the Tree of Life', was at the Fall translated to heaven, 'where first it grew, there grows, / And flours aloft shading the Fount of Life' (iii. 353 ff.). References to Milton here and throughout are to H. C. Beeching, ed., *The Poetical Works of John Milton* (1938).

27. See, for instance, Reuben Arthur Brower, *Alexander Pope: The Poetry of Allusion* (Oxford, 1959), ch. I, and Giorgio Melchiori, 'Pope in Arcady: The Theme of *Et in Arcadia Ego* in his Pastorals', *EM*, XIV (1963), 83–93.

28. See Tayler, pp. 8, 176.

29. *Pope*. The Leslie Stephen Lecture for 1925 (Cambridge, 1925), p. 26.

CHAPTER III

1. *On the Sublime*, ix. 8–9; trans. W. H. Fyfe, Loeb Classical Library, 1965.

2. See above, pp. 19–22.

3. The earliest instance is probably the concluding couplet of the first of Pope's 'Verses in Imitation of Waller', written when he was thirteen: '*Jove* with a nod may bid the world to rest, / But *Serenissa* must becalm the breast' (*TE*, VI. 9). Composed in the same year as 'On Silence' (1703), the recently discovered manuscript verses 'on some flowers in silk wrought by a handsom young Lady' develop in a lighter vein a metaphor closely related to the *fiat* motif which Pope, as we shall see, later proposed more seriously—specifically, the analogy between divine and human art:

> Alike y^r owne, and natures products shine,
> since both alike are mad[e] by hands divine;
> Propitious Phœbus causes hers to rise,
> And these, ye aspect of y^r brighter eyes;
> your Scene, like that by gods and pencil wrought,
> starts from ye needle, and reflects ye Thought . . . (ll. 7–12)

The poem concludes: ''tis fitt that none / But Heavn's bright art should overcome y^r owne.' (See Howard Erskine-Hill, 'Alexander Pope at Fifteen: A New Manuscript', *RES*, N.S. XVII (1966), 268–77.)

4. *TE*, VI. 17.

5. *TE*, VI. 73. The Twickenham editors date the poem not later than 1710 (VI. 74).

6. 'The Universal Prayer', written *c.* 1715, l. 5 (*TE*, VI. 146).

7. *Imitations of Horace*, Epistles II. ii. 278 (1737).

8. *TE*, VI. 150.

9. See above, pp. 4 and 273, n. 13.

10. *Windsor Forest*, ll. 13–16.

11. *Essay on Man*, i. 169, 291.

12. *Cooper's Hill* (1642), ll. 205–6; in T. H. Banks, Jr., ed., *The Poetical Works of Sir John Denham* (New Haven, 1928).

13. Cf. *Essay on Man*, ii. 205: 'Extremes in Nature equal ends produce.'

14. Cf. *Paradise Lost*, vii. 242.

15. It is worth noting in this regard that when Pope wished to express the disorder that would result from the disruption of natural laws, which impose limits and fix bounds, his couplets, without of course becoming quite lawless themselves, are nevertheless no longer firmly closed, the usual full stop at the end of the distich giving way to commas:

> Let Earth unbalanc'd from her orbit fly,
> Planets and Suns run lawless thro' the sky,
> Let ruling Angels from their spheres be hurl'd,
> Being on being wreck'd, and world on world,
> Heav'n's whole foundations to their centre nod,
> And Nature tremble to the throne of God . . .
> 　　　　　　　　　　　(*Essay on Man*, i. 251–6)

16. *TE*, VI. 317.

17. *Essay on Man*, iii. 313–18.

18. Ibid., 293–6.

19. Cf. John Philips in *Cider* (1706), ii, who praises Queen Anne for her role in uniting the kingdoms of England and Scotland:

> . . . yet still some seeds remain'd
> Of discontent: two nations under one,
> In laws and interest diverse, still pursued
> Peculiar ends, on each side resolute
> To fly conjunction; neither fear, nor hope,
> Nor the sweet prospect of a mutual gain,
> Could aught avail, till prudent Anna said,
> Let there be union; strait with reverence due
> To her command, they willingly unite,
> One in affection, laws and government,
> Indissolubly firm; from Dubris south,
> to northern Orcades, her long domain.

(D. P. French, ed. *Minor English Poets, 1660–1780* (New York, 1967), vol. II.) Similarly, on the anniversary of Charles II's Restoration, John Garnett commemorates the act by which order was re-established after the chaos of civil war: 'May the same blessed spirit which pronounced the words, "let there be light and there was light"; which brought order at last, out of all this confusion; which on this day, manifested its-self, to men of every nation under heaven; and on this occasion, so remarkably distinguished our own; continue to bless both our church and our state, with its influence, and our governors with its direction . . .' ('A Sermon Preached before the University of Cambridge, on Whit-Sunday, 1748. Being the Anniversary of the Restoration of King Charles II', in *A Dissertation on the Book of Job*, 2nd ed. (1751), p. 342.)

20. *Paradise Lost*, vii. 216–17: 'Silence, ye troubl'd waves, and thou Deep peace, / Said then th'Omnific Word, your discord end.' Pope's allusions to the creation often owe as much to Milton as to the first chapter of Genesis.

In the 1712 manuscript, Pope's echo of the divine fiat is even clearer: '*Let there be Peace*—she said; and all was Peace.' For an interesting analysis of this passage, see Wasserman, *The Subtler Language*, p. 161.

21. Cf. the opening of Pope's paraphrase of Boethius, quoted above, p. 81. On the importance to Pope of Milton's image of the balanced world, see above, pp. 82–3.

22. See the 'Epistle Dedicatory' to Evelyn's translation of Fréart's *Parallel of the Ancient Architecture with the Modern*, 4th ed., sig. (b)1ᵛ.

23. Henry, *An Exposition of the Five Books of Moses* (1725), p. 4.

24. See the note to ll. 195–204 in *TE*, III. ii.

25. A further instance of this theme in Pope may be tentatively proposed. In *Moral Essay III* (1733), ll. 253–62, the description of the improvements to the countryside made by the Man of Ross was probably influenced by Milton's account of the Third Day of creation (*Paradise Lost*, vii. 276–338). In transforming an intractable natural setting into a kind of second paradise, the Man of Ross appears to imitate Milton's Deity, causing the waters to pour through the plain, crowning the mountains with woods (cf. *PL*, vii. 326), gracing the land with trees (cf. *PL*, vii. 323–5), and making the earth, as Milton puts it, 'a seat where Gods might dwell, / Or wander with delight, and love to haunt / Her sacred shades' (*PL*, vii. 329–31).

26. *Essay on Man*, ii. 57.

27. Reinforcing the allusion to Genesis here are the echoes of Dryden's christianized rendering of the account of creation in Ovid's *Metamorphoses* (i. 44–5): 'Then with a Breath, he gave the Winds to blow; / And bad the congregated Waters flow.'

28. *Essay on Man*, ii. 101.

29. *Imitations of Horace*, Sermons I. ii. 143 (1734).

30. *Essay on Man*, ii. 111–22.

31. Ibid., 197.

32. Ibid., 203–4. There is some doubt as to whether Pope's 'God within the mind' should be construed as the reason or the conscience. Maynard Mack holds the former interpretation (*TE*, III. i, p. xxxviii, and the note to the lines quoted above), Douglas H. White the latter (*Pope and the Context of Controversy: The Manipulation of Ideas in 'An Essay on Man'* (Chicago, 1970), pp. 103–6). Either reading seems tenable. Reason in the *Essay on Man* is not as passive a faculty as White believes (ibid., pp. 142–3), since, for example, in the passage immediately preceding the quoted lines it has the

power to turn 'the byass . . . to good from ill'; yet at ii. 215 it is clearly conscience, the 'heart', that knows Virtue from Vice.

33. *Rape of the Lock* (1714), iii. 46.

34. *Temple of Fame*, ll. 83–92.

35. See above, n. 3.

36. Pope to Oxford, from Twickenham, 3 March 1725/6; in Sherburn, ed., *Correspondence*, II. 369.

37. *Vertumnus and Pomona* (1712), ll. 2–3, 9–14.

38. *Imitations of Horace*, Epistles II. ii. 157–79.

39. See Fern Farnham, 'Achilles' Shield: Some Observations on Pope's *Iliad*', *PMLA*, LXXXIV (1969), 1571–81.

40. Sherburn, ed., *Correspondence*, I. 246.

41. These interpretations are conveniently reviewed in Felix Buffiere, *Les Mythes d'Homère et la pensée grecque* (Paris, 1956), pp. 155–65.

42. 'Epistle Dedicatorie', *Achilles Shield. Translated as the other seuen Bookes of Homer, out of his eighteenth booke of Iliades* (1598), sig. A2^{r-v}.

43. *L'Iliade d'Homere* (Paris, 1711), III. 485. The same point is made by André Dacier in his translation, *La Poétique d'Aristote* (Paris, 1692), p. 494. It is worth noting, since Pope also cites her in his note to l. 537, that both the Daciers commend the commentary of Damo, allegedly the daughter of Pythagoras, which, as recounted by Eustathius, became the basis for subsequent allegorizations of the episode.

44. See *TE*, VIII. 347–8, the note to l. 537.

45. See his letters to Bridges (5 April [1708]), Parnell (25 May or 1 June 1714), and Cromwell (21 August 1710), in Sherburn, ed., *Correspondence*, I. 43–5, 225–6, 96. Pope advised Cromwell against using the word *paradise* in translating Ovid, since 'in English it ever bears the Signification, & conveys the Idea of Eden, which alone is (I think) a reason against making Ovid use it, who will be thought to talk too like a Christian in your Version at least . . .'

46. See the letter of 29 November 1714, in Sherburn, ed. *Correspondence*, I. 270.

47. *TE*, II. 251–2.

48. *TE*, VIII. 363.

49. *TE*, VIII. 358.

50. A useful discussion of Vleughels's design and Pope's modification of it may be found in Farnham's article, p. 1575. The principal alteration is to Scene 11, which, presumably to complete the scheme of universal Nature, Pope represents as 'an entire Landscape without human Figures, an Image of Nature solitary and un-disturb'd' (*TE*, VIII. 370), removing two shepherds that Vleughels had included in the scene. Pope borrowed Vleughels's picture from Jean Boivin, *Apologie d'Homère et Bouclier d'Achille* (Paris, 1715), whose analysis of the shield provides the basis for his own.

51. As shown in the sketch included in the *Iliad* MS., Pope originally visualized the shield somewhat differently from Vleughels and Boivin, seeing eight instead of twelve scenes, but still arranging them as a series of balanced contrasts.

52. *The Iliad*, trans. A. T. Murray, Loeb Classical Library (1967); Bk. xviii, ll. 490–1.

53. *TE*, VIII. 364.

54. *TE*, VIII. 365.

55. *TE*, VIII. 439–40, note to *Iliad*, xxi. 454.

56. *TE*, VIII. 365.

57. In Book XVIII the formula occurs six times (Loeb trans., ll. 383, 393, 462, 587, 590, 614); in Pope's version, these have been reduced to a single reference to Vulcan's 'brawny Arms' (l. 484).

58. Loeb trans., ll. 410–13.

59. For an important discussion of the way allusion functions in Pope and other Augustan writers, see Earl R. Wasserman, 'The Limits of Allusion in *The Rape of the Lock*', *JEGP*, LXV (1966), 425–44.

60. *TE*, VIII. 342.

61. *Spectator*, No. 327 (15 March 1712).

62. Cf. the following gloss on Ezekiel 1: 20, in *Annotations upon all the Books of the Old and New Testament*, 3rd ed. (1657), vol. II: 'That one Spirit of God works all in all. The same Divine Inspiration which did drive the live wights, did also give a motion to the wheels . . . To signifie that Gods Spirit, the vigour, vertue, and instinct of it, gives motion to all things according to their several principles, and services: that God is present effectually in all the Instruments of his providence . . .' See also the similar comments of Samuel Clarke, *The Holy Bible . . . With Annotations and Parallel Scriptures* (1690), and Matthew Poole, *Annotations upon the Holy Bible*, 4th ed. (1700), vol. II.

63. Homer has simply, 'and therefrom made fast a silver baldric' (Loeb trans., l. 480).

64. The image is frequent in Milton. Cf. 'The pendulous round Earth with ballanc't Aire / In counterpoise' (*PL*, iv. 1000–1); 'And Earth self-ballanc't on her Center hung' (*PL*, vii. 242). With Pope's phrase, 'Heav'ns high Convex' (l. 560), cf. also Milton's 'uttermost convex' (*PL*, vii. 266). And with the image of Vulcan completing the shield by pouring 'the Ocean round' (l. 702), cf. Milton: 'for as Earth, so hee the World / Built on circumfluous Waters calme, in wide / Crystallin Ocean' (*PL*, vii. 269–71).

65. *TE*, VIII. 348.

66. See above, pp. 66–7.

67. We have remarked that Pope saw this dance as a synthesis of the previous two, being performed both in a circle and in a row (see above, pp. 95–6). In a note to the

present passage (*TE*, VIII. 356) he supplied other details which show that he believed the dance to be a scheme of reconciled opposites devised by Daedalus:

> There were two sorts of Dances, the Pyrrhick, and the common Dance: *Homer* has joyn'd both in this Description. We see the Pyrrhick, or Military, is perform'd by the Youths who have Swords on, the other by the Virgins crown'd with Garlands.
>
> Here the ancient Scholiasts say, that whereas before it was the Custom for Men and Women to dance separately, the contrary Practice was afterwards brought in, by seven Youths, and as many Virgins, who were sav'd by *Theseus* from the Labyrinth; and that this Dance was taught them by *Dædalus*: To which *Homer* here alludes.

68. Art as at least a partial consolation for mortality is a favourite theme in Pope's poetry of this period. To his friend, the painter Charles Jervas, he concludes, 'Alas! how little from the grave we claim? / Thou but preserv'st a Face and I a Name' (*Epistle to Mr. Jervas* (1716)). Cf. also *To Mr. Addison, Occasioned by his Dialogues on Medals* (1720).

69. Sherburn, ed., *Correspondence*, I. 67 (Pope to Cromwell, 11 July 1709). Sad or ironic references to his wretched physique—'this scurvy tenement of my body', as he wrote Steele (15 July 1712)—are frequent in Pope's letters of this period. (See *Correspondence*, I. 148; also I. 73, 89–90, 114, 138, 364–5, 369.) At one point early in his translation of the *Iliad*, Pope seems openly to empathize with Vulcan, whose 'awkward Grace' (i. 770) amuses the gods. In a footnote to the passage he writes:

> *Vulcan* design'd to move Laughter by taking upon him the Office of *Hebe* and *Ganymede*, with his aukward limping Carriage. But tho' he prevail'd and *Homer* tells you the Gods did laugh, yet he takes care not to mention a word of his Lameness. It would have been cruel in him and Wit out of Season, to have enlarg'd with Derision upon an Imperfection which is out of one's Power to remedy.   (*TE*, VII. 124)

70. See *Pope's 'Dunciad': A Study of its Meaning* (1955), esp. ch. VI. In what follows my general agreement with Williams's interpretation, the seminal reading of Pope's masterpiece, will be apparent.

71. *The Guardian*, No. 40 (27 April 1713); in *TE*, V. 224.

72. 'Verses to be placed under the Picture of England's Arch-Poet: Containing a compleat Catalogue of his Works' (1727?), l. 11. The reasons for attributing this poem to Pope are rehearsed by Norman Ault (*TE*, VI. 291–3).

73. The satiric function of Pope's parodies, 'either from profane or sacred writers', was well understood by Warburton, who, in a note to ii. 405 of the 1743 edition, admonished the reader not to mistake the object of the satire:

> It is a common and foolish mistake, that a ludicrous parody of a grave and celebrated passage is a ridicule of that passage . . . A ridicule indeed there is in every parody; but when the image is transferred from one subject to another, and the subject is not a *poem burlesqued* (which Scriblerus hopes the reader will distinguish from a *burlesque poem*) there the ridicule falls not on the thing *imitated*, but *imitating*. Thus, for instance, when
>
> > Old Edward's armour beams on Cibber's breast
>
> [*Ep.* II. i. 319], it is, without doubt, an object ridiculous enough. But I think it falls

neither on old king Edward, nor his armour, but on his *armour-bearer* only. Let this be said to explain our Author's Parodies (a figure that has always a good effect in a mock epic poem) either from profane or sacred writers.   (*TE*, V. 316–17)

74. *Essay on Man*, i. 129–30.

75. Cf. *Paradise Lost*, i. 19–22:

> Thou from the first
> Wast present, and with mighty wings outspread
> Dove-like satst brooding on the vast Abyss
> And mad'st it pregnant . . .

Pope may also wish us to recall *PL*, vii. 233–9, where at the moment of creation the Spirit of God, 'His brooding wings . . . outspred', produced not a leaden egg, but rather 'downward purg'd / The black tartareous cold infernal dregs / Adverse to life . . .'

76. See Williams, *Pope's 'Dunciad'*, p. 145. By noticing the relationship between Dulness and the Logos, Professor Williams has made the essential point about this passage, as indeed he has done about most other aspects of Pope's meaning and art in *The Dunciad*. But (with the exception of l. 53, which the Twickenham editor has traced to *PL*, iii. 11) no one has yet remarked Pope's debt to Milton in the passage, particularly to the accounts of the third, fifth, and sixth days of creation in *Paradise Lost*, Book VII. As I hope to show by focusing on the theme of creation in *The Dunciad*, Professor Williams's statement that Pope drew 'most of his Miltonic materials from satanic contexts' (ibid., p. 131) needs qualification: though Dulness and her 'Son' frequently resemble Satan, they also, as Deity and Messiah of the dunces' world, recall Milton's Father and Son. In order to emphasize this connection, I shall avoid rehearsing those other parodies—of Garth, Cowley, Parnell, etc.—already identified in the notes to the Twickenham edition.

77. So Pope, as Scriblerus, interprets the passage (*TE*, V. 50).

78. Matthew Henry, op. cit., p. 3.

79. *Ars Poetica*, ll. 1–13, 29–30.

80. See Williams, op. cit., ch. IV.

81. The notes to the Twickenham edition make clear that the spectacular stage effects detailed in the passage were, for the most part, actually conceived in Theobald's irrepressible imagination and dexterously accomplished by Rich.

82. Cf. also 2 Peter 3: 10–13.

83. With Pope's l. 242, compare *Ars Poetica*, ll. 29–30: 'The man who tries to vary a single subject in monstrous fashion, is like a painter adding a dolphin to the woods, a bear to the waves' (trans. H. R. Fairclough, Loeb Classical Library, 1970). Pope may also have had in mind Dryden's translation of Du Fresnoy's *Art of Painting*: 'In all Things you are to follow the Order of Nature; for which Reason you must beware of drawing or painting Clouds, Winds and Thunder towards the Bottom of your Piece, and Hell and Waters in the uppermost Parts of it: You are not to place a Stone Column on a Foundation of Reeds; but let every Thing be set in its proper Place' (1769 ed., p. 25).

84. Each day of creation is alluded to in the passage: the first and second days in l. 238; the fourth day in ll. 239–40; the third day in l. 241; the fifth day in l. 242; the sixth day in ll. 243–4.

85. See Warburton's note, *TE*, V. 399.

86. If, as Professor Wasserman suggests (*Subtler Language*, pp. 69–70), an Augustan reader would have seen Denham's famous description of the Thames as an expression of Nature's *concordia discors*, it is worth remarking in the present context what Pope later does with Denham's lines:

> Flow Welsted, flow! like thine inspirer, Beer,
> Tho' stale, not ripe; tho' thin, yet never clear;
> So sweetly mawkish, and so smoothly dull;
> Heady, not strong, and foaming tho' not full.   (*A*, iii. 163–6)

For the tide of eloquence implying Nature's harmony, Welsted substitutes a mug of small beer and flat music. Pope draws attention to the parody in a note to the passage.

87. As Pope here uses the contemporary vogue for Italian opera to parody the traditional idea of *musica mundana*, of music as a metaphor for world harmony, so he later extends the travesty to include *musica humana*, the notion, which underlies his *Ode for Musick*, that the 'real Essence' of the soul is 'Harmony'. Accordingly, the youth who returns from the Grand Tour infatuated with Italian opera is shown to have undergone a more than Ovidian metamorphosis: instead of a soul, his spiritual essence, there is now only an '*Air*, the Echo of a Sound'; with pun doubtless intended (soul–solo), there is now 'nothing but a Solo in his head' (iv. 322–4 and n.).

88. Pope's note explains: '*Noῦs* was the Platonic term for *Mind*, or the *first Cause*, and that system of Divinity is here hinted at which terminates in blind Nature without a *Noῦs*.' He had Shaftesbury, 'one of these later Platonists', principally in mind.

89. Cudworth, op. cit., p. 114.

90. See *A*, iii. 18; i. 56; i. 149, 178, ii. 351; ii. 336, 355, 359, *B*, iii. 295.

91. See *A*, i. 148–50, 177–80; *B*, iii. 293–6.

92. Among the literary sources for the passage, the activity of the dunces recalls two very different contexts in *Paradise Lost*: the first presents the angels, who have been summoned 'before th'Almighties Throne', wheeling 'Orb within Orb' about the Deity (v. 583 ff.); the second depicts Sin after the Fall pulled by an irresistible sympathy toward earth, 'so strongly drawn / By this new felt attraction and instinct' (x. 262–3). One may also be reminded of the attitude of 'the righteous' toward God in Pope's paraphrase of Boethius: 'Thee they regard alone; to thee they tend; / At once our great original and end . . .' (*TE*, VI. 73).

93. *TE*, V. 264. The passage was added to the preface in 1751.

94. For a useful discussion of Pope's intentions in the passage, see Arthur Friedman, 'Pope and Deism (*The Dunciad*, iv. 459–92)', in J. L. Clifford and L. A. Landa, edd., *Pope and His Contemporaries: Essays Presented to George Sherburn* (Oxford, 1949), pp. 89–95.

95. *TE*, V. 387.

CHAPTER IV

1. James R. Sutherland, 'John Gay', in Clifford and Landa, edd. *Pope and His Contemporaries*, pp. 201–14. This excellent essay is of fundamental importance to a critical appreciation of Gay's poetry.

2. See 'Gay', *Lives of the English Poets*; G. B. Hill, ed., II. 282.

3. Maynard Mack, 'Gay Augustan', *YULG*, XXI (1946), 6–10.

4. Sven M. Armens, *John Gay: Social Critic* (New York, 1954). Only recently has Gay begun to receive the serious critical attention he deserves. Three studies are especially noteworthy: Adina Forsgren, *John Gay, Poet 'of a Lower Order': Comments on His Rural Poems and Other Early Writings* (Stockholm, 1964); Patricia Meyer Spacks, *John Gay*, Twayne's English Authors Series (New York, 1965); and John Chalker, *The English Georgic: A Study in the Development of a Form* (1969), ch. V.

5. *Guardian*, No. 40; *TE*, V. 222. For Pope's view of pastoral, see above, ch. II.

6. *Trivia*, iii. 263. My quotations from Gay are from *The Poetical Works of John Gay*, ed. G. C. Faber (1926).

7. *The Tea-Table: A Town Eclogue* (1720), l. 38.

8. *Trivia*, ii. 45.

9. *The Short Stories of Ernest Hemingway* (New York, 1953), pp. 210, 215.

10. Bonamy Dobrée, *English Literature in the Early Eighteenth Century, 1700–1740* (Oxford, 1959), p. 141.

11. See Hoyt Trowbridge, 'Pope, Gay, and *The Shepherd's Week*', *MLQ*, V (1944), 79–88.

12. Pope in *The Guardian*, No. 40; *TE*, V. 229.

13. Gay's opening clearly burlesques Pope's in 'Messiah'. Where Pope had begun—

> YE Nymphs of *Solyma!* begin the Song:
> To heav'nly Themes sublimer Strains belong.
> The Mossie Fountains and the Sylvan Shades,
> The Dreams of *Pindus* and th'*Aonian* Maids,
> Delight no more—O Thou my Voice inspire
> Who touch'd *Isaiah*'s hallow'd Lips with Fire!

—Gay follows:

> SUBLIMER strains, O rustick Muse, prepare;
> Forget a-while the barn and dairy's care;
> Thy homely voice to loftier numbers raise,
> The drunkard's flights require sonorous lays,
> With *Bowzybeus*' songs exalt thy verse . . .

As John Robert Moore has suggested, if Gay in the figure of Bowzybeus is alluding to a specific contemporary bard, he may have in mind Sir Richard Blackmore—whose *Creation*, one might add, treats the same theme as that Silenus sings in Virgil's *Sixth Eclogue*. (See 'Gay's Burlesque of Sir Richard Blackmore's Poetry', *JEGP*, L (1951), 83–9.)

14. See 'Friday; or, The Dirge', ll. 58, 76, 125, 126.

15. *An Epistle to Her Grace, Henrietta, Dutchess of Marlborough* (1722), l. 3.

16. Mack, *YULG*, XXI (1946), 8.

17. Joseph Addison, 'An Essay on Virgil's Georgics', *Works* (1761), I. 244.

18. Clifford and Landa, edd., *Pope and His Contemporaries*, p. 205.

19. See, for example, Armens, pp. 4–5, 9–10, 74; and George Sherburn, 'The Restoration and Eighteenth Century (1660–1789)', in Albert C. Baugh, ed., *A Literary History of England* (New York, 1948), p. 919.

20. *Poetical Works*, ed. Herbert Davis (1967), p. 93, ll. 53–63.

21. See below, chs. VI–VII, where I discuss the meanings of prudence in some detail and suggest the importance of the concept in *Tom Jones* and *The Vicar of Wakefield*.

22. The view has recently been advanced that the walker-narrator of *Trivia* is to be regarded as a kind of Swiftian persona, the butt of Gay's irony. (See Alvin B. Kernan, *The Plot of Satire* (New Haven, Conn., 1965), pp. 36–50.) There is so little evidence in the poem itself to support such a reading that it scarcely needs discrediting; Arthur Sherbo, however, has been at some pains to do so. (See 'Virgil, Dryden, Gay, and Matters Trivial', *PMLA*, LXXXV (1970), 1063–71.) It seems clear enough that the walker and the author of *Trivia* are meant to be indistinguishable.

23. *Theory of the Earth* (1690), Bk. III, chs. VII, X. In Burnet's view Vesuvius and Ætna would 'stand till the last fire, as a type and prefiguration of it, throughout all generations'. He takes 'these two Volcano's as a pattern for the rest; seeing they are well known, and stand in the heart of the Christian World, where, 'tis likely, the last fire will make its first assault' (p. 58). He predicts that Vesuvius and Ætna will erupt as Christ appears, and that Rome and Naples will 'be absorpt or swallowed up in a Lake of fire and brimstone, after the manner of *Sodom* and *Gomorrha*' (pp. 84–5). Though published too late to have had any bearing on Gay's description, works such as Samuel Catherall's *An Essay on the Conflagration* (Oxford, 1720) and Joseph Trapp's *Thoughts upon the Four Last Things* (1734), Pt. II, reveal how the details of Burnet's account were used by the poets of the religious sublime.

24. Addison, *Works*, I. 238–9.

CHAPTER V

1. 'Towards Defining an Age of Sensibility', *ELH*, XXIII (1956), 144–52.

2. From Fielding's Preface to his own and William Young's translation of Aristophanes' *Plutus, the God of Riches* (1742), p. x.

3. References to *Tom Jones* are to the fourth edition, 1749 (title-page reads 1750), 4 vols.

4. See below, p. 300, n. 2.

5. See Wayne C. Booth, *The Rhetoric of Fiction* (Chicago, 1961), pp. 71 ff.

6. Review of Roscoe's edition of Fielding's *Works*, in *The Times*, 2 September 1840; quoted in F. Homes Dudden, *Henry Fielding: His Life, Works, and Times* (Oxford, 1952), II. 616.

7. Booth, p. 217.

8. *A Portrait of the Artist as a Young Man* (New York, 1957), p. 215.

9. *Joseph Andrews* (1742), III. i. Quotations from this novel are from the Wesleyan Edition, ed. Battestin (Oxford, 1967).

10. The metaphor of the universe as a vast and intricate machine implying the existence of God, the supreme Artificer, was a commonplace in the period. With the passage in *Tom Jones*, for example, compare John Spencer, *A Discourse Concerning Prodigies* (1665), sig. (A): '*To shew how many wheels in some great Engine, move in subordination to the production of some great work, were [not] to obscure and eclypse the art of the Artificer.*' See also Henry More, *Divine Dialogues* (2nd ed., 1713), Dialogue II, p. 117; Thomas Burnet, *Theory of the Earth*, 2nd ed. (1691), p. 107; John Ray, *The Wisdom of God Manifested in the Works of the Creation* (5th ed., 1709), pp. 3?–3; Isaac Barrow, *Sermon VI,* 'The Being of God Proved from the Frame of the World', *Works* (5th ed., 1741), II. 75; John Tillotson, Sermon CXXXVII, 'The Wisdom of God in the Creation of the World', *Works* (1757), VIII. 138; Samuel Clarke, Sermon I, 'Of Faith in God', *Works* (1738), I. 6, and 'A Discourse Concerning the Unchangeable Obligations of Natural Religion', ibid., II. 647–8; Richard Kingston, *A Discourse on Divine Providence* (1702), pp. 48–50; and William Sherlock, *A Discourse Concerning the Divine Providence* (9th ed., 1747), pp. 10–11.

11. In *Critical Observations on Shakespeare* (1746) Upton advised literary critics that the best artists understand the principles of subordination and relationship, keeping in mind the whole design and not just the part. He then anticipates Fielding's analogy between the two artists, human and divine:

> And were it not a degree of prophanation, I might here mention the great Designer, who has flung some things into such strong shades, that 'tis no wonder so much gloominess and melancholy is raised in rude and undisciplined minds, the sublime Maker, who has set this universe before us as a book; yet what superficial readers are we in this volume of nature? Here I am certain we must become good men, before we become good critics, and the first step to wisdom is humility. (2nd ed., 1748, pp. 134–5)

12. For an excellent analysis of the way in which Fielding's rhetoric and syntax attest a world of order see Henry Knight Miller, 'Some Functions of Rhetoric in *Tom Jones*', *PQ*, XLV (1966), esp. pp. 227–35.

13. *The True Intellectual System of the Universe* (2nd ed., 1743), II. 879–80. A copy of the 1678 edition of this work was in Fielding's library. On Fielding's probable use of Cudworth in *Amelia* see Ralph W. Rader, *MLN*, LXXI (1956), 336–8.

14. 'Preface to the Reader', *Theory of the Earth*, 2nd ed. (1691), sig. a2ᵛ.

15. See Battestin, *The Moral Basis of Fielding's Art* (Middletown, Conn., 1959; 2nd printing, 1964), esp. ch. VI.

16. See 'The Concept of Plot and the Plot of *Tom Jones*', in Crane, ed., *Critics and Criticism Ancient and Modern* (Chicago, 1952), pp. 616–47. The essay is reprinted in

Battestin, ed., '*Tom Jones*': *A Collection of Critical Essays*, Twentieth-Century Interpretations (Englewood Cliffs, N.J., 1968).

17. See, for example, Sheldon Sacks, *Fiction and the Shape of Belief* (Berkeley and Los Angeles, 1964).

18. See Battestin, 'Tom Jones and "His *Egyptian* Majesty"': Fielding's Parable of Government', *PMLA*, LXXXII (1967), 68–77.

19. Dorothy Van Ghent seems to have been the first critic to compare the structural design of *Tom Jones* to that of a 'Palladian palace': see *The English Novel: Form and Function* (New York, 1953), p. 80. See also Frederick W. Hilles, 'Art and Artifice in *Tom Jones*', in Maynard Mack and Ian Gregor, edd., *Imagined Worlds: Essays on Some English Novels and Novelists in Honour of John Butt* (1968), pp. 91–110. To demonstrate the 'Palladian' structure of *Tom Jones*, Professor Hilles offers a 'ground plan' of the novel based on John Wood's original design for Prior Park (p. 95).

20. The phrase describing Allen's mansion is Joseph Andrews's (III. vi); earlier in that novel Fielding himself had referred to it as a 'Palace' (III. i), and he praised it again in *A Journey from This World to the Next* (I. v). Both Prior Park and Wilton are among the estates complimented in *Tom Jones* (XI. ix).

21. Sermon XVIII, *Sermons* (1843), III. 363.

22. Rapin, *Whole Critical Works* (3rd ed., 1731), II. 150; see also II. 151–3, 195–7.

23. See Aubrey Williams's important essays, 'Poetical Justice, the Contrivances of Providence, and the Works of William Congreve', *ELH*, XXXV (1968), 540–65, and 'Congreve's *Incognita* and the Contrivances of Providence', in Mack and Gregor, edd., *Imagined Worlds*, pp. 3–18. In an article which serves admirably to complement my own approach to *Tom Jones*, Professor Williams has recently turned his attention to Fielding: see 'Interpositions of Providence and the Design of Fielding's Novels', *SAQ*, LXX (1971), 265–86. It is a happy coincidence that Professor Williams and I independently reached many of the same conclusions concerning the influence of the doctrine of Providence upon narrative (or dramatic) structures in the period. The present essay was originally presented as a lecture at The Johns Hopkins University in October 1966.

24. Dobson, *Fielding* (1907), p. 126. Cf. Dudden, II. 621–2.

25. See *Critics and Criticism*, p. 624.

26. See Van Ghent, *The English Novel*, pp. 78–80.

27. See Morris Golden, *Fielding's Moral Psychology* (n.p., 1966), ch. VI.

28. See Ian Watt, *The Rise of the Novel* (Berkeley and Los Angeles, 1957).

29. Sermon CXXXVIII, 'The Wisdom of God in his Providence', *Works* (1757), VIII. 145.

30. See Battestin, *The Moral Basis of Fielding's Art*, pp. 159, n. 1, and 161, n. 28.

31. Turner, *A Compleat History of the Most Remarkable Providences, both of Judgment and Mercy, Which have Hapned in this Present Age* (1697).

32. Sermon XXXVI, *Works* (1757), III. 40.

33. Ibid., III. 27.

34. Ibid., III. 29.

35. Sermon XCVIII, *Works* (1738), I. 620.

36. See the *Covent-Garden Journal*, No. 18 (3 March 1752).

37. Sermon XVIII, *Sermons* (1843), III. 365–6.

38. Sermon VIII, ibid., I. 121–36.

39. See above, Ch. III, sec. iii, esp. pp. 114–15.

40. Sermon I, 'Of Faith in God', *Works* (1738), I. 6.

41. Sermon XCVIII, ibid., I. 619.

42. Sherlock, *A Discourse Concerning the Divine Providence* (9th ed., 1747), pp. 40–2.

43. Ibid., p. 43.

44. Clarke, 'A Discourse Concerning the Unchangeable Obligations of Natural Religion', *Works* (1738), II. 602.

45. Sermon XCVIII, 'The Event of Things not always answerable to Second Causes', ibid., I. 619–20.

46. *The Champion* (8 January 1739/40). Quotations from this journal are from the 1743 reprint.

47. *The Champion* (4 March 1739/40).

48. *The True Patriot* (24 December 1745).

49. *The Champion* (22 January 1739/40).

50. *The Champion* (4 March 1739/40).

51. With Adams's remarks compare, especially, Tillotson's Sermon CXXXVIII, 'The Wisdom of God in His Providence', *Works* (1757), VIII. 140–60.

52. For an excellent discussion of the theme of Fortune and Providence in *Amelia* see D. S. Thomas, 'Fortune and the Passions in Fielding's *Amelia*', *MLR*, LX (1965), 176–87.

53. *Joseph Andrews* (III. i). For Imlac's 'Dissertation upon Poetry' see Johnson's *Rasselas* (1759), ch. X.

54. Clarke, 'A Discourse Concerning the Unchangeable Obligations of Natural Religion', *Works* (1738), II. 597–8.

55. See Richard H. Tyre, 'Versions of Poetic Justice in the Early Eighteenth Century', *SP*, LIV (1957), 34.

56. Dennis, *The Usefulness of the Stage* (1698), in Hooker, ed., *Critical Works*, I. 183.

57. See, especially, chs. LXVI–LXVII.

58. See Battestin, 'Osborne's *Tom Jones*: Adapting a Classic', *VQR*, XLII (1966), 383.

59. Sermon XCV, 'The Shortness and Vanity of Humane Life', *Works* (1738), I. 602.

CHAPTER VI

1. See above, pp. 87–8.

2. For the derivation of *prudentia* from *providentia*, see the *O.E.D.* under 'prudence'. Cf. Joseph Spence in *Polymetis* (1747), p. 138: 'The Romans seem to have called this [prudence] indifferently by the name of Prudentia, or Providentia; the reason of which may be gathered from Cicero's derivation of the word Prudentia.' In a note, Spence quotes from *De Oratore* as follows: 'Sapientis est providere; ex quo sapientia est appellata prudentia.'

3. See Bossu's influential discussion of the epic fable in *Traité du poème épique* (1675): 'THE first Thing we are to begin with for Composing a *Fable*, is to chuse the Instruction, and the point of Morality, which is to serve as its Foundation, according to the Design and End we propose to our selves.' Once the moral has been settled upon, the poet invents an action which will allegorically embody it. ('W.J.', trans., *Treatise of the Epick Poem*, 2nd ed. [1719], Bk. I, ch. vii; I. 28–9).

4. See *Fiction and the Shape of Belief*.

5. Walter Miller, trans. (Loeb Classical Library, 1913).

6. Critics recently have begun to direct serious attention to this theme in the novel: see Eleanor N. Hutchens, *Irony in 'Tom Jones'* (University, Ala., 1965), ch. V; Glenn W. Hatfield, *Henry Fielding and the Language of Irony* (Chicago, 1968), ch. V. The original version of the present chapter appeared in *ELH* in 1968.

7. See Cicero, *De Inventione*, II. liii. 160: 'Prudentia est rerum bonarum et malarum neutrarumque scientia. Partes eius: memoria, intelligentia, providentia. Memoria est per quam animus repetit illa quae fuerunt; intelligentia, per quam ea perspicit quae sunt; providentia, per quam futurum aliquid videtur ante quam factum est.'

8. Cf. Cicero, *De Natura Deorum*, III. xv. 38, and *De Finibus*, V. vi. 16.

9. Dominicus Mancinus's influential work on the cardinal virtues, *Libellus de quattuor virtutibus et omnibus officiis ad bene beateque vivendum*, was originally published at Paris in 1488. In the sixteenth century at least three English translations appeared: an anonymous prose version, *c.* 1520; Barclay's *The myrrour of good maners*, *c.* 1523; and Turberville's *A plaine Path to perfect Vertue*, 1568.

10. See Denham's 'Of Prudence'.

11. Smart, *The Student's Companion* (1748), s.v. 'Prudence'.

12. Harris, 'Concerning Happiness, A Dialogue', in *Three Treatises* (1744), p. 171.

13. *The British Magazine*, IV (March 1749), 77.

14. Ibid., IV. 78.

15. Ibid., IV. 78–9.

16. Ibid., IV. 79.

17. See above, pp. 153, 158–9.

18. 'An Essay on the Knowledge of the Characters of Men', in *Miscellanies* (1743), I. 183.

19. Cicero, *De Officiis*, II. iii, III. xvii.

20. Ibid., III. xxv.

21. Barrow, Sermon II, *Works*, 5th ed. (1741), II. 26.

22. *The Covent-Garden Journal*, No. 29 (11 April 1752).

23. Ibid., No. 69 (4 November 1752).

24. South, Sermon IX, 'The Wisdom of This World', *Sermons Preached upon Several Occasions* (1843), I. 140.

25. Tillotson, Sermon CXXXVI, 'The wisdom, glory, and sovereignty of God', *Works* (1757), VIII. 109.

26. Benjamin Hoadly, Letter XXX, *The London Journal* (20 April 1723), in John Hoadly, ed., *Works* (1773), III. 105. See also Letter XC, *The London Journal* (25 July 1724), where Hoadly further analyses 'this *Cunning*' as being 'but the Ape of Wisdom', a 'Bastard Species' (ibid., III. 328–9).

27. 'The Moralist', No. XXXII ('Some Thoughts on Cunning'), op. cit., III (July 1748), 281.

28. See *The True Patriot*, 14 January 1746.

29. First translated into English in 1685 under the title, *The Courtiers Manual Oracle: or, The Art of Prudence*. My references are to *The Art of Prudence* (1702).

30. De Britaine, *Humane Prudence*, 12th ed. (1729), p. 61.

31. See, for example, Nathaniel Lardner, *Counsels of Prudence for the Use of Young People* (1735). Another work, which I have been unable to locate, is *The Young Gentleman and Lady Instructed in Principles of Politeness, Prudence, and Virtue*, 2 vols.; it was advertised as printed for Edward Wicksteed and published in October 1747.

32. Burgh, *The Dignity of Human Nature* (1754), p. 3.

33. Ibid., p. 4.

34. Quoted from the 1st ed. (1752).

35. Quoted from the 1741 reprint (I. 23).

36. Cf. *Phaedrus*, 250D: 'wisdom would arouse terrible love, if such a clear image of it were granted as would come through sight' (trans. H. N. Fowler, Loeb Classical Library, 1914). See also Cicero, *De Finibus*, II. xvi, and *De Officiis*, I. v; and Seneca, *Epistulae Morales*, CXV. 6. The specific notion of the naked charms of Virtue, imaged as a beautiful woman, is only implicit in Plato. Fielding was especially fond of this commonplace: see, for example, *The Champion* (24, 26 January 1739/40), and 'An Essay on Conversation' and 'An Essay on the Knowledge of the Characters of Men'—

both published in the *Miscellanies* (1743), I. 159, 217. For a discussion of this image and its relation to the moral theme of Fielding's last novel, see Alan Wendt, 'The Naked Virtue of Amelia', *ELH*, XXVII (1960), 131–48.

37. See Hunter, *The Reluctant Pilgrim: Defoe's Emblematic Method and Quest for Form in 'Robinson Crusoe'* (Baltimore, 1966).

38. Fielding, *The Author's Farce*, ed. Charles B. Woods (Lincoln, Neb., 1966), p. xvi.

39. Spence, *Polymetis*, p. 66.

40. The quotation is from Jacob Boehme, *The Way to Christ* (Bath, 1775), p. 56, as given in Frank Manley, ed., *John Donne: The Anniversaries* (Baltimore, 1963), p. 38. On the identification of 'the noble Virgin Sophia' with the biblical figure of Wisdom, see Manley's Introduction, pp. 37–8.

41. The definition of *idea* given in George Richardson's *Iconology: or, A Collection of Emblematical Figures, Moral and Instructive* (1778–9), is as follows: 'In general, [Idea] is the image of any thing, which, though not seen, is conceived in the mind. Plato defines it, the essence sent forth by the divine spirit, which is entirely separated from the matter of created things' (I. 82).

42. *Phaedo*, 99D–E.

43. See Isaac Fuller and Peirce Tempest, *Iconologia: or, Moral Emblems, by Caesar Ripa* (1709), Figures 229 and 269, folios 57 and 67.

44. For a discussion of the relationship between poetry and painting in the eighteenth century, see Jean H. Hagstrum, *The Sister Arts: The Tradition of Literary Pictorialism and English Poetry from Dryden to Gray* (Chicago, 1958).

45. For Fielding's compliments to Hogarth, see, among many other references, the Preface to *Joseph Andrews* and *Tom Jones* (I. xi, II. iii, III. vi, VI. iii, X. viii), where Fielding refers the reader to particular Hogarth prints to clarify the description of Bridget Allworthy, Mrs. Partridge, and Thwackum.

46. Done at the command of Louis XIV, Le Brun's series depicting the victories of Alexander now hangs in the Louvre. Copies of the official engravings by the Audrans were commissioned in England and published by Carington Bowles. The series was much admired: see, for example, Farquhar's *Beaux' Stratagem* (1707), IV, and Charles Gildon, *The Complete Art of Poetry* (1718), I. 230. When Louis Laguerre was commissioned to commemorate Marlborough's victories over the French, he looked to Le Brun's *tableaux* for a model (see Margaret Whinney and Oliver Millar, *English Art, 1625–1744* (Oxford, 1957), pp. 305–6).

47. In describing Allworthy's seat, Fielding's intentions are as much allusive and symbolic as they are chorographical. The description is based upon elements associated primarily with Sharpham Park and secondarily with Hagley Park and Prior Park, the estates of Lyttelton and Allen respectively. From the doorway at Sharpham Park Fielding would have looked daily across the moors at Glastonbury and Tor Hill. The prospect from Allworthy's Paradise Hall corresponds in general with the view westward from Tor Hill (see Wilbur L. Cross, *The History of Henry Fielding* (New Haven, 1918), II. 165). The 'Style' of Paradise Hall itself is doubtless in honour of a mutual friend of Fielding's and Lyttelton's, Sanderson Miller (1717–80), amateur architect and pioneer of the Gothic revival. In 1747–8 and 1749–50 Lyttelton erected

a ruined castle and a rotunda of Miller's design at Hagley Park; indeed, until his second wife disapproved, he had wanted Miller to build him a Gothic house. Like Allworthy's mansion, furthermore, Hagley Hall is situated on the south side of a hill, nearer the bottom than the top, yet high enough to command a pleasant view of the valley. And many of the details in Fielding's description echo Thomson's celebration of Hagley Park in 'Spring', ll. 900–58 (*Seasons*, 1744 ed.). At the same time, in the third paragraph of the chapter, Fielding does not forget Ralph Allen, whose house, an example of 'the best *Grecian* Architecture', he had praised earlier in *Joseph Andrews* (III. i, vi) and *A Journey from This World to the Next* (I. v): Allen's Palladian mansion stands on the summit of a hill down which a stream falls into a lake which is visible 'from every Room in the Front'.

48. For an elaborate gloss on the sun as '*A fit Emblem, or rather Adumbration of God*', see William Turner's *Compleat History of the Most Remarkable Providences* (1697), pp. 14–19. The sun, according to Turner (and many others), is 'the *Eye of Heaven*' (p. 14) and a symbol of God's 'Benignity and Beneficence' (p. 18). It is with this latter attribute of the Deity that both Barrow and Fielding particularly associated the sun. Wrote Barrow: 'Such is a charitable man; the sun is not more liberal of his light and warmth, than he is of beneficial influence' (Sermon XXVII, 'The Nature, Properties and Acts of Charity', op. cit., I. 261). In the verse epistle 'Of Good-Nature', Fielding, recalling Matthew 5: 45, exclaims: 'Oh! great Humanity, whose beams benign, / Like the sun's rays, on just and unjust shine.'

49. Erwin Panofsky, *Meaning in the Visual Arts*, Doubleday Anchor Books (Garden City, N.Y., 1955), pp. 146–68.

50. Because she regards past, present, and future, Prudence is represented in Dante's *Purgatorio*, XXIX, as a figure with three eyes. See also Francisco degli Allegri, *Tractato Nobilissimo della Prudentia et Iustitia* (Venice, 1508): British Museum, Prints and Drawings, 163*.a.23.

51. Richardson, op. cit., II. 23–4. For earlier emblems of Prudence, based on Ripa and representing a figure with two faces, see the following: Jacques de Bie and J. Baudoin, *Iconologie* (Paris, 1644), pp. 160, 164, and Fuller and Tempest, op. cit., Figure 251 and folio 63.

52. See Aristotle, *Rhetoric*, II. xii–xiv.

CHAPTER VII

1. Introduction to the Century Classics edition (New York, 1900).

2. The opinions, respectively, of Boswell, Horace Walpole, and Thomas Davies. (See Ralph M. Wardle, *Oliver Goldsmith* (Lawrence, Kan., 1957), p. 1.)

3. Boswell's *Life of Johnson*, ed. G. B. Hill, rev. L. F. Powell (Oxford, 1934), II. 236.

4. The most conspicuous instance of this sort of criticism is Robert H. Hopkins, *The True Genius of Oliver Goldsmith* (Baltimore, 1969), ch. 5, 'Fortune and the Heavenly Bank: *The Vicar of Wakefield* as Sustained Satire'. Others who, in one way or another, find the vicar and his religion the butt of Goldsmith's satire are W. O. S. Sutherland, Jr., *The Art of the Satirist: Essays on the Satire of Augustan England* (Austin, Tex.,

1965), pp. 84–91; Clara M. Kirk, *Oliver Goldsmith* (Twayne's English Authors Series (New York, 1967)), ch. 3; and Richard J. Jaarsma, 'Satiric Intent in *The Vicar of Wakefield*', *SSF*, V (1968), 331–41, for whom 'the character of Primrose stands as one of the most savage indictments of *bourgeois* values in eighteenth-century literature' (p. 339). Poor Dr. Primrose! In the pages of the critics his trials, it would appear, continue.

5. See Wardle, p. 75.

6. See Hopkins, ch. 5, esp. p. 208, where 'the surface level' of the *Vicar* is said to be 'best understood as a trap for the naive reader who responds only to literature that appears to reflect his own sentimental attitudes'.

7. See 'Patterns of Disguise in *The Vicar of Wakefield*', *ELH*, XXV (1958), 90–104.

8. See 'Observations on *The Vicar of Wakefield*', *CamJ*, III (July 1950), 621–8. For an equally astute and much more exhaustive discussion of comparable rhetorical features in Fielding, see Henry Knight Miller, *PQ*, XLV (1966), 209–35; and 'The Voices of Henry Fielding: Style in *Tom Jones*', in Miller, E. Rothstein, and G. S. Rousseau, edd., *The Augustan Milieu: Essays Presented to Louis A. Landa* (Oxford, 1970), pp. 262–88.

9. Jefferson, pp. 624, 626. 'Art of this kind', he remarks, 'is refreshing in an age like ours when actuality exerts so great a pressure on literature and the problem of transforming it is one of such difficulty.'

10. See Battestin, *The Moral Basis of Fielding's Art*, ch. III.

11. See, for example, Oswald Doughty, ed., *The Vicar of Wakefield* (1928), p. xxxix; Jefferson, p. 621; Kirk, p. 101; Ronald Paulson, *Satire and the Novel in Eighteenth-Century England* (New Haven, 1967), pp. 270, 274; and Hopkins, p. 207.

12. See, for example, Morris Golden, 'Image Frequency and the Split in the *Vicar of Wakefield*', *BNYPL*, LXIII (September 1959), 473–7; and Michael E. Adelstein, 'Duality of Theme in *The Vicar of Wakefield*', *CE*, XXII (February 1961), 315–21.

13. Quotations from Goldsmith are from *The Collected Works*, ed. Arthur Friedman, 5 vols. (Oxford, 1966). The above quotations from *The Vicar of Wakefield* may be found in IV. 14, 33.

14. See, for example, Simon Patrick, *The Book of Job Paraphras'd* (1697), 'Appendix', pp. 213–18; and Matthew Henry, *An Exposition of the Five Poetical Books of the Old Testament* (1725), pp. 14–16.

15. Cf. Isaac Barrow, Sermon X, 'Of Patience': When adversity strikes, we must find solace in 'A thorough persuasion, that nothing befalleth us by fate, or by chance, or by the meer agency of inferior causes, but that all proceedeth from the dispensation, or with the allowance of God, that *Affliction doth not come forth of the dust, nor doth trouble spring out of the ground*; but that all, both *good and evil, proceedeth out of the mouth of the most High* . . . as *Job*, when he was spoiled of all his goods, acknowledged, *The Lord gave, and the Lord hath taken away*' (*Works*, 5th ed. (1741), III. 82). In his influential discussion of Job, Thomas Sherlock, Bishop of London at the time Goldsmith was writing his tale, makes the same point more forcibly: 'The patience of Job is much talked of, and we seldom look farther for any use of this book; but in truth the book was written in opposition to the very ancient opinion, which intro-

duced two independent principles, one of good, the other of evil. For this reason Satan, the author of Job's misfortunes, is brought in with a permission from God to afflict Job; and the moral of the history lies in Job's reflexion: "the Lord gave, and the Lord hath taken away" . . .' (*Dissertation II: The Sense of the Ancients before Christ on the Circumstances and Consequences of the Fall* (1725), in *Works*, ed. T. S. Hughes (1830), IV. 157.)

16. Matthew Henry may be allowed to summarize the orthodox interpretation of God's rebuking the false comforters for not having 'spoken of me *the thing that is right*, as my servant Job *hath*' (Job 42: 7–8):

They had wrong'd God by making Prosperity a Mark of the true Church, and Affliction a certain Indication of God's Wrath: But *Job* had done him right, by maintaining that God's Love and Hatred is to be judg'd of by what is *in Men*, not by what is *before them*, Eccles. 9. 1. Observe, (1.) Those do the most Justice to God and his Providence, who have an Eye to the Rewards and Punishments of another World, more than to those of this; and with the Prospect to those, salve the Difficulties of the present Administration. *Job* had refer'd things to the future Judgment and the future State, more than his Friends had done, and therefore he spoke of God *that which was right*, better than his Friends had done. (pp. 133–4)

The same construction of the passage is to be found in William Warburton, *The Divine Legation of Moses Demonstrated*, 2nd ed. (1742), Vol. II, Pt. ii, p. 530; in Charles Peters, *A Critical Dissertation on the Book of Job* (1751), p. 7; and in William Hawkins, *Works* (Oxford, 1758), I. 343–4, 349. Goldsmith apparently reviewed Hawkins's *Works* for *The Critical Review*; see above, p. 199, and below, n. 20.

17. Citing this text, William Hawkins makes clear that what Job is seeking is not merely oblivion, but peace and happiness beyond the grave (I. 337).

18. Peters, p. 427. See also Daniel Bellamy, *A Paraphrase on the Sacred History, or Book of Job, with Observations from Various Authors* (1748), where the quotation from Seneca concludes the 'General Application to the History of Job' (p. 128, n. (b)). In his edition of Goldsmith's *Collected Works*, Friedman cites *The Spectator*, No. 375 (10 May 1712).

19. *The Anatomy of Melancholy*, intro. Holbrook Jackson, Everyman's Library (1964), III. 425–6.

20. See Friedman's note, Goldsmith's *Collected Works*, I. 198, n. 4. The evidence suggests that Goldsmith probably began to compose the *Vicar* some time in 1760 or 1761, though a slightly earlier date is possible (see Friedman's discussion, IV. 3 ff.).

21. With the general position of the reviewer, compare Goldsmith's essay, 'Some Remarks on the Modern Manner of Preaching', *The Lady's Magazine* (December 1760). Though he objects to the hauteur and coldness of English preachers, who prefer wasting time on 'speculative trifles' to moving their congregations in matters of importance to their salvation, Goldsmith yet reveals his allegiance to the Church of England and acknowledges that her divines have effectually vanquished their enemies the deists, who 'have been driven into a confession of the necessity of revelation or an open avowal of atheism' (Friedman, ed., III. 154–5).

22. Sherlock, esp. IV. 166–77.

23. Warburton, II. ii. 484–555, esp. p. 545.

24. See the Preface to Grey's edition of Job, in Hebrew and Latin (1742), and his *Answer to Mr. Warburton's Remarks on Several Occasional Reflections, so far as they concern the Preface to a late Edition of the Book of Job* (1744); Brown's *Job's Expectations of a Resurrection considered* (Oxford, 1747); Peters's *Critical Dissertation on the Book of Job* (1751); Hawkins's *Review of a Book* [by John Towne], entitled, *A Free, and Candid Examination of the Principles advanced in the Right Rev. the Lord Bishop of London's very elegant Sermons*, ch. III, in *Works* (Oxford, 1758), Vol. I; and Parry, *A Defense of the Lord Bishop of London's Interpretation of the famous Text in the Book of Job, I know that my Redeemer liveth, &c.* (Northampton, 1760). See also the anonymous *Impartial Examination of the Bishop of London's late Appendix to A Dissertation on the Sense of the Ancients before Christ upon the Circumstances and Consequences of the Fall* (1750).

25. See Costard's *Some Observations tending to Illustrate the Book of Job, and in Particular the Words, I know that my Redeemer liveth, &c.* (Oxford, 1747); Garnett's *Dissertation on the Book of Job, Its Nature, Argument, Age, and Author*, 2nd ed. (1751); and Towne's *Free and Candid Examination of the Principles advanced in the Right Rev. the Lord Bishop of London's very elegant Sermons* (1756).

26. See Bellamy's *Paraphrase* on Job (1748); Worthington's 'Dissertation on the Design and Argumentation of the Book of Job', in *An Essay on the Scheme and Conduct, Procedure and Extent of Man's Redemption*, 2nd ed. (1748); Hodges's *Elihu: or, An Enquiry into the Principal Scope and Design of the Book of Job*, 2nd ed. (1751); Chappelow's *Commentary on the Book of Job*, 2 vols. (Cambridge, 1752); and Heath's *Essay towards a New English Version of the Book of Job* (1756). Originally delivered and published in Latin at Oxford in 1753, Bishop Lowth's important lectures on Job as a poem are Nos. 32–4 of his *Lectures on the Sacred Poetry of the Hebrews*, trans. G. Gregory, 2 vols. (1787); a second Latin edition appeared in 1763.

27. Though the question was much debated, the notion that Job was the author of the book enjoyed the weighty authority of Albert Schultens (see Grey, *An Answer to Warburton*, p. 27), and was accepted or favourably considered by Brown (p. 51), Peters (p. 4), and Lowth (*Lectures* (1787), II. 353–4).

28. See Costard, p. 25, and Heath, p. v.

29. For a full and perceptive discussion of the subject through the seventeenth century, see Barbara K. Lewalski, *Milton's Brief Epic: The Genre, Meaning, and Art of 'Paradise Regained'* (Providence, R.I., 1966), ch. II ('Job as Epic: The Exegetical and Literary Tradition'). Though, as Miss Lewalski shows, most seventeenth-century critics considered Job an example of epic poetry, the emphasis in the following century is on its dramatic qualities: see, for example, Sherlock, IV. 174; Warburton, II. ii. 486; Edward Young, *A Paraphrase on Part of the Book of Job*, in *Poetical Works* (1741), I. 120 n.; Grey, *Answer to Warburton*, p. 21; Costard, pp. 25–6; Bellamy, p. iii; Garnett, pp. 18–19, 300; Heath, p. vii; Lowth, II. 386 ff.; Parry, p. 6. In the first quarter of the century Richard Blackmore (*A Paraphrase on the Book of Job*, 2nd ed. (1716), Preface) and Matthew Henry (pp. vi, 10) may be mentioned as continuing the view of the poem as an epic.

30. Moses Maimonides was the chief authority for the view that Job is a parable, '*setting forth the opinions of men about providence*' with its hero standing as a figure for '*every virtuous man*' (Chappelow, II. ii). Worthington read the poem as an allegory of the fall and redemption of man (pp. 414 ff.). See also Blackmore, p. xxiii.

31. Garnett, especially, stresses the pastoral aspect of Job:

> . . . there is a pleasure in going back to the primitive simplicity of those early ages of the world, and compareing them with the luxury of later times, in surveying princes feeding their flocks when their dominions consisted of but little more than the neighbouring vales, and their subjects were sheep and oxen . . . princes were then what nature form'd them for, the guardians of both the lives and the liberties of their people: their business was the preservation and well being of their flock, they lived in ease and affluence, and the tranquillity of the rural life, unattended with ambition, and undebauched by luxury, was accompanied with innocence and contentment . . . Consistent therefore with the manners of the old world is the picture we are here presented with of Job: the images under which the economy of his family, the affluence of his fortunes, the piety of his conduct, the calamities that befall him, and his emerging at length out of them are convey'd, are all of this cast plain and pastoral . . .   (pp. 37–8)

32. See above, pp. 164–5.

33. On this point, see especially Blackmore (pp. xxix–xxxiii), Henry (p. 10), Bellamy (p. i), and Worthington (p. 443).

34. Blackmore, pp. xxxiv–xxxv.

35. Lowth, II. 416–17.

36. Hodges, pp. 74, 146–50, and *passim*.

37. See Grey, *Answer to Warburton*, pp. 37–40; Garnett, p. 294.

38. Adelstein, p. 317.

39. Dahl, p. 99, n. 3.

40. See above, p. 171.

41. Worthington, p. 442. Since Job, like all men, has only a 'partial view', it was 'rash and presumptuous' of him 'to judge of the ways of providence by outward appearances' (pp. 387–8).

42. Heath comments as follows on Job 42: 1 ('I know that thou [God] art able to do everything, and that wisdom cannot be attained without thee'): 'The word סִכְפָה, I am apt to believe, is here used in a good sense, and means *prudence, wisdom, knowledge* . . . The root ڪ in the Arabic hath the idea of *vision*, from whence, by metaphor, it comes to signify *knowing, understanding*; and, as a verb, signifies, *rem percepit, novit*; it implies an intuitive knowledge of any thing . . .' (p. 171, n.).

43. Garnett, pp. 179, 180–1.

44. Henry, p. [110], misnumbered 102.

45. *Vicar*, IV. 44. The reading is that of the first edition; in the second edition, the second sentence is omitted.

46. *The Babler*, II (1767), 56.

47. *An Impartial Examination of the Bishop of London's late Appendix to A Dissertation on the Sense of the Ancients before Christ upon the Circumstances and Consequences of the Fall* (1750), p. 61.

48. Paulson, p. 270.

49. Macaulay's impatience with Goldsmith's plot has been shared by most critics of the *Vicar*: 'The fable is indeed one of the worst that ever was constructed. It wants, not merely that probability which ought to be found in a tale of common English life, but that consistency which ought to be found even in the wildest fiction about witches, giants and fairies.' 'Goldsmith', *Encyclopaedia Britannica*, 11th ed., XII. 216). The second half of the tale, according to James, 'becomes almost infantine in its awkwardness, its funny coincidences, and big stitches of white thread' (op. cit., p. xvi).

50. Blackmore, p. xxiii.

51. Peters, p. 110.

52. Consider Matthew Henry's discussion of the suddenness of Job's afflictions:

> They all come upon him *at once*; while one Messenger of evil Tidings was speaking another came, and before he had told his Story a third, and a fourth follow'd immediately. Thus *Satan* by the divine Permission order'd it, (1.) That there might appear a more than ordinary Displeasure of God against him in his Troubles, and by that he might be *exasperated* against the divine Providence, as if it were resolv'd right or wrong to ruin him, and not give him Time to speak for himself. (2.) That he might not have leisure to consider and recollect himself, and reason himself into a gracious Submission, but might be overwhelm'd and over-power'd by a Complication of Calamities ... (3.) They took from him *all that he had*, and made a *full End* of his Enjoyments.   (p. 14)

53. Blackmore, p. xxv.

54. Hodges's *Elihu* (1750) is a notable example of this interpretation. See also Hawkins, I. 340. In Elihu, according to Hodges, the author of Job 'intended to exhibit the Humanity of our Lord, as it was to be united to the second Person of the Essence, and so One with Him who speaks out of the Whirlwind ...' (2nd ed. (1751), p. 99). A young man despised and contemned, he represents the double nature of Christ, the God who, to redeem mankind, condescended to suffer in the flesh: in Elihu is shown 'How he was to be a King, and a very poor Subject; to be universal Monarch, and yet pay Tribute; to be the mighty God, and a most oppressed Man ...' (p. 102). When he appears at last, he does so 'in the Capacity of a Moderator and Judge ... and just when the Knot required and deserved a divine Person to untie it, He seems to challenge an Authority more than Human' (p. 144 n.).

Garnett, though he stops short of identifying Elihu and Christ, nevertheless emphasizes that he is God's 'inspired prophet' and 'representative' disguised as a mere man. With Job and his false friends he is 'one more personated character', but unlike them he does not assume a role out of 'meer vanity'; he 'speaks the language of God himself' and prepares the way for the 'catastrophe' (pp. 243–4).

Elihu, indeed, may have influenced Goldsmith's choice of a name and age for Sir William in his impersonated character. He is 'Elihu the son of Barachel' (of which, phonetically, 'Burchell' is a reasonable English approximation) and, like Christ, he is a 'young' man (Burchell being represented as 'about thirty' years old (IV. 28)—a circumstance that has led some readers to accuse Goldsmith of an inconsistency in making Sir William so close in age to his nephew).

55. Such is Warburton's explanation of the conclusion of Job (II. ii. 490–1), citing Horace's famous rule: '*Nec Deus intersit, nisi dignus Vindice nodus*' (*Ars Poetica*, 191). See also Costard (p. 26), Worthington (p. 443), and Hodges (p. 144 n.; quoted above, n. 54).

56. Garnett, pp. 179, 249. See also his sermon on Job 42: 10 (1748), in ibid., pp. 338–9.

57. Hawkins, I. 349.

58. See above, p. 198 and n. 16.

59. Sherlock's Discourse XXXIX is designed to teach 'that God does not ordinarily dispense the rewards and punishments due to virtue and vice in this life; but that he has appointed another time and place, how far distant we know not, in which all accounts shall be set right, and every man receive according to his works' (*Works* (1830), II. 275). Citing Psalm 37: 25 as an apparent contradiction of this doctrine, he proceeds as follows to explain its true significance:

> There are some passages of holy writ, which at first hearing, and before they are duly weighed, may seem to promise more to the righteous in this life than we have been able to find either reason or experience to justify . . . The truth is, that this passage in the Psalms relates not to our present purpose; it describes a general case of providence over good men in providing them the necessaries of life, whilst they endeavor to serve God, but of a just reward for them in this world it says nothing: 'The seed of the righteous', says the Psalmist, 'shall not beg their bread.' Take it literally, and make the most of it, it will bear no resemblance to a just reward for their goodness: for if the righteous and the wicked were to be distinguished in this life by temporal prosperity and adversity, we might expect to hear of much better promises to the good than this, 'That their seed should not beg their bread;' we might expect to hear of crowns and sceptres to be given them: but of this we hear nothing. (II. 283)

The passage, instead, signifies no more than 'the providential care of God over the righteous in supplying their natural wants' (II. 283).

60. Garnett, Sermon on Jas. 5: 11 ('Behold we count them happy, which endure. Ye have heard of the patience of Job . . .'); op. cit., p. 368.

61. Burton, III. 425.

62. See above, pp. 150 ff.

63. Goldsmith's letter to his brother, the Revd. Henry Goldsmith, from London, *c.* 13 January 1759. (Katherine C. Balderston, ed., *The Collected Letters of Oliver Goldsmith* (Cambridge, 1928), p. 60.)

64. See Goldsmith's review in *The Monthly Review*, XVII (July 1757), Article 5; Friedman, ed., I. 82.

65. Henry, p. [112], misnumbered p. 104.

CHAPTER VIII

1. Canto vi; 4th ed. (1700), p. 83.

2. 'Strephon and Chloe' (1731), ll. 233–4. Quotations from Swift's poetry are from *Poems*, ed. Harold Williams, 2nd ed. (Oxford, 1958), 3 vols.

3. This in essence is Herbert Davis's observation, for whom Swift was 'the most extreme example that we have ever had in England of reaction against the heroic or romantic view of the poet's function and art'. (See 'Swift's View of Poetry', in M. W. Wallace, ed., *Studies in English by Members of University College, Toronto* (Toronto, 1931), pp. 9–58.) See also Maurice Johnson's 'Introduction' to *The Sin of Wit: Jonathan Swift as a Poet* (Syracuse, N.Y., 1950).

4. See above, p. 292, n. 73.

5. See *Life against Death: The Psychoanalytical Meaning of History* (Middletown, Conn., and London, 1959), pp. 179–201. Brown borrowed the phrase from Middleton Murry. For perceptive discussions of the scatological element in Swift's verse, see also Maurice Johnson (pp. 110–21) and Donald Greene, 'On Swift's "Scatological" Poems', *SR*, LXXV (1967), 672–89.

6. 'Strephon and Chloe', l. 20.

7. See above, p. 51.

8. 'A Beautiful Young Nymph Going to Bed' (1731 ?), ll. 25, 67.

9. Cf. Ralph Cohen's observation that 'dismemberment' is 'the specifically Swiftian version of Augustan harmony'; Swift, Cohen continues, 'sees a competitive world in which the parts remain separate and inharmonious, even grotesque' ('The Augustan Mode in English Poetry', *ECS*, I (1967), 3–32, esp. p. 9). See also the illuminating essay by A. B. England, 'World without Order: Some Thoughts on the Poetry of Swift', *EIC*, XVI (1966), 32–43. England, however, hints that Swift's 'satiric apprehension of disunity' (p. 32) in the human sphere reflects his lack of confidence in the Augustan ideal of Order itself. But Swift was no nihilist. His Augustinian awareness that discord is the condition of fallen man should not be construed as a denial of the harmony of the world at large. That he subscribed to the ideal of universal Order while deploring 'the Vice of Pride' which prompted men to violate that ideal is perfectly clear, for example, in his sermon on 'Mutual Subjection'. Similarly, as Roger Savage suggests in discussing Swift's parodies of Homer and Virgil in the 'Description' poems, the contrast between the realities of the human condition and the classical ideal of '*la belle Nature*' may serve a 'double function', enabling Swift to deal directly 'with life as it is lived', yet at the same time implying 'that somewhere, however far away, order, decorum and nobility do really exist'. (See 'Swift's Fallen City: *A Description of the Morning*', in Brian Vickers, ed., *The World of Jonathan Swift: Essays for the Tercentenary* (Oxford, 1968), p. 190.)

10. See *ECS*, I (1967), 9–13, and *The Unfolding of 'The Seasons'* (1970), esp. pp. 63–4, 72–3, 100–1.

11. *The Rape of the Lock*, i. 130. See Cohen's discussions of this point, *ECS*, I (1967), 11–12; and 'Transformation in *The Rape of the Lock*', *ECS*, II (1969), 213–14.

12. To suggest that Swift not only reviles and castigates the victims of his satire but is capable of pitying them to a degree will seem sentimental to some readers—to Geoffrey Hill, for instance, for whom, if there is 'compassion' at all in 'A Beautiful Young Nymph Going to Bed', 'it exists principally for the eye of the beholder'. (See 'Jonathan Swift: The Poetry of "Reaction"', in Vickers, ed., op. cit., p. 208.) Such a response is not far removed from the chilling aestheticism of the narrator in *A Tale of a Tub*, who, forgetting that even whores can be wretched, is revolted by the spectacle of the 'Woman *flay'd*' only because 'it altered her Person for the worse'. It is precisely the 'beholder' of Corinna's 'mangled Plight', or of the 'Woman *flay'd*', whose sensibilities Swift is least interested in soothing.

13. On Swift's religion and his career as a divine, see the following authoritative studies by Louis Landa: 'Swift, the Mysteries and Deism', *University of Texas Studies in English, 1944* (Austin, 1945), pp. 239–56; 'Introduction' to the sermons in Landa's edition of Swift's *Irish Tracts (1720–1723) and Sermons* (Oxford, 1948); and *Swift and the Church of Ireland* (Oxford, 1954).

14. Donald Greene would deny that Swift's Augustinianism was unfashionable, but his arguments to disprove the generally optimistic tenor of late-seventeenth- and early-eighteenth-century theology with respect to human nature are idiosyncratic and strangely oblivious of both the history and homiletic literature of the period. Robert South, the only prominent divine he cites who actually wrote during the period in question, was, like Swift, a High Churchman opposed to the Latitudinarian emphasis on works—which emphasis, stressing St. James rather than St. Paul in matters of salvation, both South and Swift criticized, with some justification, as 'Pelagian' or 'Socinian'. In doing so, however, they were opposing the main current of divinity moving from the Cambridge Platonists through Barrow and Tillotson to Clarke and Hoadly. All of this is well known from the studies of R. S. Crane, R. N. Stromberg, Professor Cragg, and others whom Greene ignores. It was, of course, precisely the vogue of this rational theology, deplored by Wesley and Whitefield, which gave rise to the Methodist movement in the 1730s: to Whitefield, for example, Archbishop Tillotson, the most influential of the Latitudinarians, was not so much a Christian as a moral philosopher scarcely distinguishable from the deists and stoics. To generalize about the literature of the period, if Swift and Johnson and Cowper may be classified as Augustinian in their views of human nature, Addison and Steele, Fielding and Sterne—even Richardson, as recent scholarship has disclosed—were, despite apparent differences, all in the camp of the Latitudinarians. For Greene's views, see 'Augustinianism and Empiricism: A Note on Eighteenth-Century English Intellectual History', *ECS*, I (1967), 33–68, esp. pp. 39–51; he is answered in the same journal by Vivian de Sola Pinto (II (1969)) and Paul C. Davies (V (1972)).

15. Landa, ed., *Irish Tracts (1720–1723) and Sermons*, p. 188.

16. *A Tale of a Tub*, edd. A. C. Guthkelch and D. Nichol Smith, 2nd ed. (Oxford, 1958), p. 176. Quotations from the *Tale* are from this edition.

17. *A Satyr against Reason and Mankind* (1679), l. 29.

18. In 1948 Ricardo Quintana first proposed that the 'author' of the *Tale* should be taken as a dramatic character distinct from Swift himself, and in fact as the embodiment of the follies Swift meant to satirize. Most critics have adopted this basic approach to the work, though opinions differ concerning both the identity of the persona and the extent and consistency of his role. He has been called, variously, an

Ingénu (Elliott), the Tale-Teller (Price), a Gnostic (Paulson), a Bentleyan-Critic (Levine); but most often he is characterized as a Modern Grub-Street Hack (e.g. Ewald, Starkman, Clark). The question of consistency is more vexed: it is said that there is a single persona operating throughout (e.g. Paulson and Clark); that there are six personae (Quintana); that there is one who functions only in the digressions and preliminaries (Harth); that, though there is a persona, he is too protean to be characterized at all (Rosenheim). Finally, there are those who reject the hypothesis of a persona altogether (Ehrenpreis and Stout).

See the following, in the order given above: Quintana, 'Situational Satire: A Commentary on the Method of Swift', *UTQ*, XVII (1948), 130–6; Robert C. Elliott, 'Swift's *Tale of a Tub*: An Essay in Problems of Structure', *PMLA*, LXVI (1951), 441–55; Martin Price, *Swift's Rhetorical Art: A Study in Structure and Meaning*, Yale Studies in English, Vol. 123 (New Haven, 1953), pp. 86–95; Ronald Paulson, *Theme and Structure in Swift's 'Tale of a Tub'* (New Haven, 1960); Jay Arnold Levine, 'The Design of *A Tale of a Tub* (With a Digression on a Mad Modern Critic)', *ELH*, XXXIII (1966), 198–227; William Bragg Ewald, Jr., *The Masks of Jonathan Swift* (Oxford, 1954), chs. II–III; Miriam Kosh Starkman, *Swift's Satire on Learning in 'A Tale of a Tub'* (Princeton, 1950); John R. Clark, *Form and Frenzy in Swift's 'Tale of a Tub'* (Ithaca, N.Y., 1970); Quintana, *Swift: An Introduction* (Oxford, 1955), pp. 53–5; Phillip Harth, *Swift and Anglican Rationalism: The Religious Background of 'A Tale of a Tub'* (Chicago, 1961), pp. 5–6; Edward W. Rosenheim, Jr., *Swift and the Satirist's Art* (Chicago, 1963), pp. 138 ff.; Irvin Ehrenpreis, 'Personae', in Carroll Camden, ed., *Restoration and Eighteenth-Century Literature: Essays in Honor of Alan Dugald McKillop* (Chicago, 1963), pp. 25–37, and *Swift: The Man, His Works, and the Age*, Vol. I (1962), esp. p. 197; and Gardner D. Stout, Jr., 'Speaker and Satiric Vision in Swift's *Tale of a Tub*', *ECS*, III (1969), 175–99.

My own view, which will be apparent from the discussion to follow, is that the 'author' of the *Tale* is indeed a persona, rather more than less clearly defined, whose voice from his first appearance in the 'Epistle Dedicatory' may be heard throughout the work, most obviously in the digressions, but plainly enough in the narrative itself, which, though ostensibly the 'objective' history he is writing, he interrupts frequently to address the reader with comments and self-congratulation. I suggest that it is the persona's mind and character—his megalomania, his materialism, his devotion to all things Modern: ultimately, in Swift's terms, his madness—that determines the peculiar form and rhetorical texture of the work he is supposedly writing.

19. Cf. the passage quoted above (p. 224), in which Swift refers to '*Parodies, where the Author personates the Style and Manner of other Writers, whom he has a mind to expose*'.

20. *Leviathan*, I. viii; ed. Michael Oakeshott (Oxford, 1946), p. 44. The relevance of this passage to the *Tale* was first suggested by Robert H. Hopkins, 'The Personation of Hobbism in Swift's *Tale of a Tub* and *Mechanical Operation of the Spirit*', *PQ*, XLV (1966), 372–8.

21. H. Davis and L. Landa, edd., *A Proposal for Correcting the English Tongue, Polite Conversation, Etc.* (Oxford, 1957), p. 49.

22. See above, p. 55.

23. Since Miss Starkman first made the observation, most critics agree that important targets of Swift's satire in the *Tale* are the materialism of Hobbes and the mechanism of Descartes: see, for example, Starkman, ch. II; Ewald, p. 22 and n. 58; Harth,

pp. 76–85; Ehrenpreis, *Swift*, I. 220–1; Philip Pinkus, 'The Upside-Down World of *A Tale of a Tub*', *ES*, XLIV (1963), 167–9; Hopkins, *PQ*, XLV (1966), 375; Clark, pp. 44–8.

24. Several critics have noticed this peculiarity of the Teller's mind: see, for example, John M. Bullitt, *Jonathan Swift and the Anatomy of Satire* (Cambridge, Mass., 1953), p. 136; Hopkins, *PQ*, XLV (1966), 374–5; Clark, p. 76; and esp. Maurice J. Quinlan, 'Swift's Use of Literalization as a Rhetorical Device', *PMLA*, LXXXII (1967), 517–18. Quinlan remarks that though the device is a favourite one with Swift, it is particularly prominent in the *Tale*. By disregarding the presence of the persona, Stout reaches the extraordinary conclusion that Swift himself, not the Teller, is a corporealist! (*ECS*, III (1969), 188).

25. On this point, see Starkman (pp. 56–63) and esp. Harth (pp. 76–85).

26. H. Davis, ed., *Gulliver's Travels* (Oxford, 1959), pp. 182–5.

27. *The Life and Opinions of Tristram Shandy, Gentleman*, ed. Ian Watt (Boston, Mass., 1965), p. 469. Quotations from *Tristram Shandy* will be from this edition

28. Boswell records Johnson's remark: 'Nothing odd will do long. "Tristram Shandy" did not last.' (*Life of Johnson*, edd. G. B. Hill and L. F. Powell (Oxford, 1934), II. 449.)

29. See above, p. 7.

30. *The Subtler Language*, pp. 169–72.

31. *An Enquiry Concerning Human Understanding* (1748), in *Essays and Treatises on Several Subjects* (1758), p. 293.

32. The question of Sterne's attitude toward Locke continues, not without reason, to vex his readers. Traditionally, critics have attributed the distinctive formal features of *Tristram Shandy* to Sterne's sense of the implications of the *Essay Concerning Human Understanding*, a work that he greatly admired. (See MacLean, Work, Watt, and Tuveson.) Opposition to this view has been gaining steadily since 1954, when John Traugott argued that throughout the novel Sterne strove deliberately to subvert Locke's rationalism. Traugott (pp. 44–9) and Cash, for example, rightly point out that the principle of the 'association of ideas', which had been thought to account for the erratic structure of the novel, has no prominence in Locke, who discusses it in a chapter added as an afterthought to the 4th edn. of the *Essay* (II. xxxiii), where it is treated as a species of madness interfering with the rational processes of thought. These critics insist that, though Sterne used this principle as a comic device, principally in the famous opening scene and in the characterization of Uncle Toby, it did not otherwise influence his conduct of the narrative. Associationism as a basis of epistemology was the later development of Hartley and Hume, who elaborated Locke's view—a circumstance that has prompted one critic to propose Sterne's indebtedness to Hume (Doherty). Still more damaging to the traditional view is the fact that Sterne, unlike Locke, seems profoundly to have distrusted the reason as a means to knowledge and communication. *Tristram Shandy*, indeed, has been characterized as a 'devastating' practical criticism, 'among the most effective before the recent developments of phenomenology', of the rationalist-empiricist philosophy extending from Hobbes through Locke to Hume (Theobald).

But if the traditional notion of Locke's influence upon *Tristram Shandy* needs serious qualification, it still has much to recommend it. For one thing, it is hardly likely that Sterne, who by his own admission valued the *Essay* next to the Bible, would have meant to deal quite so irreverently with Locke as Traugott supposes. For another, *Tristram Shandy* is obviously constructed on an associational principle, and it is as probable that in this Sterne, like Hartley and Hume, was elaborating an idea implicit in Locke (Tuveson and Watt), as that he was following some other source, Montaigne for example (Anderson). Even Cash, while rejecting the association principle as a possibility, explains the novel's narrative method in terms of Locke's 'psychology of the train of ideas', the view that the mind is a constant flux of ideas which cannot be arrested. Other aspects of the form and meaning of *Tristram Shandy* are clearly *implicit*, at least, in the *Essay*: for example, Locke's views on duration and the imprecision of language, his emphasis on sensation, and, perhaps most fundamentally, the subjectivism to which his premisses logically lead. Sterne departs from Locke chiefly in three respects, all of them related to his positive attitude toward the passions and the imagination: (1) he openly criticizes Locke's disparagement of wit as a faculty of the mind inferior to judgement; (2) he regards the passions, as Theobald has pointed out, not as 'peripheral aberrations' but as 'integral' to human activity, sensing that 'the world is apprehended not rationally and empirically, but emotively'; and (3) he finds at least a partial solution to the problem of solipsism in the human capacity for sympathy—a characteristic of his 'sentimentalism' which Traugott associates with Hume (pp. 73–4), but which may more cogently be traced to the influence of Shaftesbury and the Latitudinarian divines. These are all crucial differences between Locke and Sterne, and all affect the novel in important ways. But if Sterne was aware of the limitations of Locke's rigid rationalism, it seems equally clear that he was profoundly influenced by Locke's epistemology. Without the *Essay*, *Tristram Shandy* would not be the book it is.

References above are to the following critics, taken in order: Kenneth MacLean, *John Locke and English Literature of the Eighteenth Century* (New Haven, 1936); James A. Work, ed., *The Life and Opinions of Tristram Shandy, Gentleman* (New York, 1940), esp. pp. xvi, xlix–l, lxx; Ian Watt, ed., ibid., esp. pp. xiii–xiv, and 'The Comic Syntax of *Tristram Shandy*', in H. Anderson and J. S. Shea, edd., *Studies in Criticism and Aesthetics, 1660–1800: Essays in Honor of Samuel Holt Monk* (Minneapolis, 1967), pp. 315–31, esp. p. 328; Ernest Tuveson, 'Locke and Sterne', in J. A. Mazzeo, ed., *Reason and the Imagination: Studies in the History of Ideas, 1600–1800* (New York and London, 1962), pp. 255–77; John Traugott, *Tristram Shandy's World: Sterne's Philosophical Rhetoric* (Berkeley and Los Angeles, 1954), esp. Pt. I; Arthur H. Cash, 'The Lockean Psychology of *Tristram Shandy*', ELH, XXII (1955), 125–35; Francis Doherty, 'Sterne and Hume: A Bicentenary Essay', *Essays and Studies, 1969* (1969), pp. 71–87; D. W. Theobald, 'Philosophy and Imagination: An Eighteenth Century Example', *The Personalist*, XLVII (1966), 315–27; Howard Anderson, 'Associationism and Wit in *Tristram Shandy*', PQ, XLVIII (1969), 27–41.

33. See *An Essay on Criticism*, ll. 68–71.

34. Cf. Theobald's remark that by emphasizing the difficulties of effective communication through language, Sterne implies the inability of the individual to attain any clear sense of his own identity: 'For "I" only has meaning in a society of at least two people' (op. cit., p. 324). Tristram's doubts about his identity occur in Volume VII, as he races across France fleeing from Death as his author had done before him. With the single exception of ch. xxvii, Sterne makes no attempt to relate this volume to the story of the Shandys; the fictional distance between Tristram and himself is no longer operative. Twice described as 'a man with pale face, and clad in black'

(pp. 380, 402), Tristram here *is* Sterne, the consumptive priest, as Sterne at other times is Yorick. Sterne seems intuitively to have understood the notion of modern psychologists that we are not one person but many. In this respect, the difference between Sterne and Swift, who adopts various masks for satiric purposes, is that Swift remains distinct from his *personae*, assuming the face of the Enemy so as to expose his true character. The failure to observe this distinction vitiates Gardner Stout's recent essay on *A Tale of a Tub* (see *ECS*, III (1969), 175–99).

35. See Sterne's statement to Jean-Baptiste Suard, the text of which is given in Traugott, pp. 153–4, n. 2.

36. These ambivalent aspects of the Hobby-horse have been remarked by Joan Joffe Hall, for whom it implies 'a solipsistic view of the universe' ('The Hobbyhorsical World of *Tristram Shandy*', *MLQ*, XXIV (1963), 139); and D. W. Theobald, who observes that in the world of *Tristram Shandy* the 'only anchor individuals seem to have upon existence lies in their obsessions of varying degrees of absurdity' (op. cit., p. 322).

37. *Epistle to Cobham*, l. 174.

38. Cf. Tuveson on the importance of Bacon to Locke's subjectivism, citing *Novum Organum*, I. xli–xlii (in Mazzeo, ed., op. cit., pp. 257–9).

39. See the perceptive articles by A. R. Towers, 'Sterne's Cock and Bull Story', *ELH*, XXIV (1957), 12–29; and Robert Alter, '*Tristram Shandy* and the Game of Love', *ASch*, XXXVII (1968), 316–23.

40. Cf. above, pp. 233–4.

41. See Locke's *Essay*, II. xi. 2.

42. See above, n. 39.

43. For a clear, succinct, and judicious exposition of Sterne's view of human nature as a mixture of self-love and social, see Sec. iv of Gardner Stout's introduction to his edition of *A Sentimental Journey* (Berkeley and Los Angeles, 1967).

44. See above, p. 3.

45. In treating these implications of Sterne's form, my discussion will be seen to agree in general with the interesting interpretation recently advanced by William V. Holtz in *Image and Immortality: A Study of 'Tristram Shandy'* (Providence, R.I., 1970). Holtz's study came to my attention after the present chapter had been written.

46. See 'Did Sterne Complete *Tristram Shandy*?', *MP*, XLVIII (1951), 172–83.

47. On this point, see the perceptive essays by A. A. Mendilow, 'The Revolt of Sterne', in his *Time and the Novel* (London and New York, 1952), pp. 165–99; and B. H. Lehman, 'Of Time, Personality, and the Author: A Study of *Tristram Shandy*', University of California *Publications in English*, VIII (1941), 223–50.

48. In the unlikely event that any reader should have forgotten it, the sentence reads: 'So that when I stretch'd out my hand, I caught hold of the Fille de Chambre's   .'

49. 'Essay on the Theory of Painting', in *Works*, ed. J. Richardson the younger (1773), p. 2.

Index

(Italic figures indicate sections wherein topic is treated at length.)

DATE DUE			